A STern

D1607657

— DISCOVERING THE SOUTH —

DISCOVERING
─ THE SOUTH ─

ONE MAN'S TRAVELS THROUGH

A CHANGING AMERICA

IN THE 1930S

✦

Jennifer Ritterhouse

THE UNIVERSITY OF NORTH CAROLINA PRESS

CHAPEL HILL

This book was published with the
assistance of the Fred W. Morrison Fund
of the University of North Carolina Press.

Manufactured in the United States of America
Designed by April Leidig
Set in Baskerville by Copperline Book Services

The University of North Carolina Press has been a
member of the Green Press Initiative since 2003.

Cover illustrations courtesy of the Southern Historical Collection,
University of North Carolina at Chapel Hill; map, © 1938 The Macmillan Co.

Library of Congress Cataloging-in-Publication Data
Names: Ritterhouse, Jennifer Lynn, author.
Title: Discovering the South : one man's travels through
a changing America in the 1930s / Jennifer Ritterhouse.
Description: Chapel Hill : University of North Carolina
Press, [2017] | Includes bibliographical references and index.
Identifiers: LCCN 2016039784| ISBN 9781469630946 (cloth : alk. paper) |
ISBN 9781469630953 (ebook)
Subjects: LCSH: Southern States—History—1865–1951. |
Daniels, Jonathan, 1902–1981—Travel. | Newspaper editors—Travel.
Classification: LCC F215 .R58 2017 | DDC 975/.04—dc23 LC record
available at https://lccn.loc.gov/2016039784

Portions of this work appeared earlier in somewhat different form in
"Woman Flogged: Willie Sue Blagden, the Southern Tenant Farmers
Union, and How an Impulse for Story Led to a Historiographical
Corrective," *Rethinking History: The Journal of Theory and
Practice* 18, no. 1 (January 2014): 97–121.

FRONTISPIECE
Jonathan Daniels. Photo by Alfred Eisenstaedt/
Pix Inc./The LIFE Picture Collection/Getty Images.

To Stephen, Sophie, and Paul

✦ ✦ ✦

A traveler comes to destinations.
Or hopes to.

———————

JONATHAN DANIELS,
A Southerner Discovers the South

✦

CONTENTS

Acknowledgments xiii

INTRODUCTION
The Same Journey, Writ Small,
That the United States Was On
I

CHAPTER ONE
We So-Called Free Moderns
Raleigh, North Carolina
20

CHAPTER TWO
This Division between Faith in Democracy
and Power Descending from Authority
From Raleigh to Lookout Mountain, Tennessee
50

CHAPTER THREE
The Demand for Justice Will Not Be a
Cause Furthered Only by Radicals
Scottsboro, Alabama
71

CHAPTER FOUR
A Quaint and Quixotic Group of Gentlemen
Nashville, Tennessee
100

CHAPTER FIVE
Tenants Are Able to Hold Their Heads a Little Higher
Memphis, Tennessee
128

CHAPTER SIX

Naked and Hot as If She Were Stripped in the Sun
Marked Tree, Arkansas
160

CHAPTER SEVEN

The Most Interesting Man I Met
From Hot Springs, Arkansas, to Tuskegee, Alabama
175

CHAPTER EIGHT

As Furious as the Last Horseman
of a Legion of the Bitter-End
Birmingham, Alabama
203

CHAPTER NINE

A Red-Headed Woman Immaculate and
Immediate from the Beauty Parlor
Atlanta, Georgia
222

CHAPTER TEN

The Newly Exciting Question of
the Possibility of Democracy
From Atlanta to Raleigh, North Carolina
241

CONCLUSION

Only All Together Shall Any of Us Overcome
270

Notes 295

Bibliography 333

Index 351

ILLUSTRATIONS

Josephus and Adelaide Bagley Daniels
with their four sons 22

Jonathan and Elizabeth Bridgers Daniels
with their daughter 27

Howard W. Odum on the University of
North Carolina campus 44

Route of Jonathan Daniels's tour 49

TVA workers with bucket and dipper 63

TVA commissioner David E. Lilienthal 66

NAACP representatives visiting the Scottsboro Boys 74

Senators Robert F. Wagner and Edward P. Costigan 86

Nashville Agrarian Donald Davidson 103

Sharecropper cabin 115

Southern Tenant Farmers Union secretary-treasurer
H. L. Mitchell 133

Evicted sharecroppers 140

Day laborers in Memphis being hired to pick cotton 140

House at Delta Cooperative Farm 151

Flogging victim Willie Sue Blagden 164

Main Street, Marked Tree, Arkansas 170

People on the street in Marked Tree, Arkansas 170

Victor C. Turner Sr. 182

Dicksonia 187

Mary Chappell 199

Iron ore mine and company houses in Birmingham 209

Barbershop window with CIO sign 214

Margaret Mitchell 227

A woman and her daughter walking to Sunday school 244

Ernest D. LeMay testifying before a Senate
civil liberties committee 266

Jonathan and Lucy Cathcart Daniels with
President Franklin Roosevelt 289

ACKNOWLEDGMENTS

IT HAS TAKEN ME A LOT LONGER to "discover the South" than it took Jonathan Daniels. Fortunately, I have received a lot of help and support along the way, for which I am very grateful. First, there are the many family members, friends, colleagues, students, and even unsuspecting acquaintances who have indulged or at least endured the kind of obsessiveness it takes to complete a work of scholarship while also teaching and meeting the other obligations of a college faculty member as well as raising a family. Some of these good people read all or part of the book in manuscript, including Paul Labys, Jacquelyn Hall, Robert Korstad, Carrie Grabo, Zach Schrag, Lindsey Bestebreurtje, Emily Bingham, Rob Ferguson, Kathleen Clark, Charles Eagles, Sam Lebovic, Michael Goldfein, Celeste Sharpe, Linda Simon, Sally Brett, Pamela Grundy, Martha Bewick, and the students in my Fall 2015 section of History 352. I want to thank all of them for their time and comments.

Long before there was any manuscript to read, Jane Dailey and Glenda Gilmore kindly read grant proposals and wrote letters of recommendation. Jacquelyn Hall and William E. Leuchtenburg also offered early encouragement, and friends in Utah, including Dan McInerney, Susan Matt, and Sue Wurtzburg, formed working groups that helped me get the project started. Throughout those early days, I was blessed with both supportive colleagues in the history department at Utah State University and a terrific circle of friends in Salt Lake City and Ogden—too many to name, but including Marjukka Ollilainen, David Ferro, Lisa Campbell, Lisa Gabbert, and many others whose friendship I appreciate.

When I moved to Virginia in 2010, I gained a wonderful new set of colleagues and friends. I feel fortunate to have settled into a vibrant community in Fairfax and Falls Church. The Department of History and Art History at George Mason University fosters a culture of collegiality and provides the daily warmth that allows the intellect to spark. I particularly appreciate the mentorship of my colleagues Cindy Kierner, Jane Censer, and Rosie Zagarri, as well as the all-in-it-together friendship of Joan Bristol, Randolph Scully, and Zach Schrag. Brian Platt is supportive and generous with his time despite his long list of duties as department chair. Sam Lebovic not only suggested valuable readings but took time to read chapters and provide very helpful comments. Working with my M.A. and Ph.D. students, especially those with whom I have done readings courses and independent studies, has also been energizing.

The Department of History and Art History has supported my work financially as well as intellectually, as have other institutions. A sabbatical from Utah State University in 2007 allowed me to do preliminary research, and subsequent travel grants from the College of Humanities, Arts, and Social Sciences and the Women and Gender Research Institute at USU helped as well. I also benefited from a research stipend during my first two years at George Mason University, which made it possible for me to take my research significantly further. Most crucial of all, a faculty fellowship from the National Endowment for the Humanities gave me the focused time I needed to draft the majority of the manuscript. I am grateful to the NEH and, having also served on NEH review panels, deeply admire its work.

As the book's final shape became clearer and the possibilities of a companion website emerged, I was thankful to receive a Nelson Research Grant from the Department of History and Art History and to be able to participate in a digital history workshop at the Roy Rosenzweig Center for History and New Media. The Discovering the South website (www.discovering thesouth.org) is the result, and the Nelson funds enabled me to complete a couple of final research trips as well.

Archival research for this project has taken me to a number of places, even as I have also benefited from several repositories' willingness to look up collections and scan or photocopy materials. Librarians and archivists who have been especially helpful include Matt Turi and Laura C. B. Hart at the Southern Historical Collection at the University of North Carolina at Chapel Hill, Jim Baggett at the Department of Archives and Manuscripts at the Birmingham Public Library, Chuck Barber at the Hargrett Rare Book and Manuscript Library at the University of Georgia, Howard Robinson and Jason Trawick at the Alabama State University Archives, Dwayne Cox at Special Collections and Archives at Auburn University, Dana Chandler at Tuskegee University Archives, Michael Kates at the Fort Des Moines Museum and Education Center, and Teresa Gray at the Special Collections and University Archives at Vanderbilt. I also appreciate help with illustrations and understanding copyright from the friendly pros at the Library of Congress Prints and Photographs Reading Room.

My first publication based on this research was "Dixie Destinations: Re-reading Jonathan Daniels's *A Southerner Discovers the South*," which appeared in the online journal *Southern Spaces*. I developed a better understanding of the project from working with editor Allen Tullos and receiving the anonymous peer reviewers' comments. I am grateful to them and to James Goodman, Elizabeth Payne, and Jason Manthorne, who were the editor and peer reviewers for another article I published along the way. Thanks also to Cindy Kierner for the opportunity to share my research on Blagden with Mason's History Ph.D. colloquium, where I appreciated the participants' excellent questions and thoughtful responses.

In addition to these articles, conference papers helped me work out ideas and receive feedback. I am thankful for comments from Robert Korstad, Randal Jelks, and Daniel Letwin, as well as audience members at the International Society for Travel Writing's "Traveling South" conference in 2010 and the annual meetings of the Southern Labor Studies Association and the Southern Historical Association in 2015. Participating in and presenting my work for the Southern Intellectual History Circle in recent years has been especially valuable. I have treasured Michael O'Brien's insights, in particular, and it is wrenching to remember that he's gone.

As I moved toward publication, Geri Thoma and Chuck Grench read proposals and rough drafts and helped me decide to submit my manuscript to UNC Press. Brandon Proia has been a great reader and hard-working editor, and it has been a pleasure to work with Mary Carley Caviness again. I also want to thank Mark Simpson-Vos and John Sherer for their support and Joanna Ruth Marsland for putting me in touch with Lucy Daniels. During the UNC Press peer review process, Glenn Eskew gave me an extraordinarily helpful reading of the manuscript, while another, anonymous reader also asked excellent questions, provided valuable suggestions, and encouraged me to make much-needed cuts. I am deeply indebted to both.

I want to thank Lucy Daniels and Mary Lee for help with photographs, and William C. Barclift for both a photograph and sharing his memories of his mother, Mary Chappell. Victor C. Turner Jr. allowed me to interview him by phone, which was both helpful and quite meaningful to me, and I was sad to learn of his passing. Thank you to Vic Turner for letting me know and for the work of the community service organization he and his family started, Hannah's Socks.

So many people have contributed to this project in so many ways that I know these acknowledgments can never be complete. I think of Erin Kellen driving me around Lowndes County, Alabama, or Spencer Roberts helping me with StoryMap. I think of the many conversations with Megan Brett, Erin Bush, George Oberle, and others, as well as the long, deep, sustaining conversations with Molly Rozum, Carric Grabo, Joan Bristol, and my mentor of mentors, Jacquelyn Hall. My final words of thanks must be to my parents, Pat and Charles Ritterhouse, and above all to my husband, Paul Labys, who has carried me through an even longer journey than this attempt to discover the South. Now we have Sophie and Stephen journeying alongside, and that fact is what makes me happiest of all and most thankful that, with everyone's help, this book is finally finished.

— DISCOVERING THE SOUTH —

The Same Journey, Writ Small,
That the United States Was On

✦

THIS BOOK IS about three overlapping journeys: one man's actual travels and both his and the United States' metaphorical journeys from Jim Crow toward a greater commitment to democracy. On May 5, 1937, Jonathan Worth Daniels, a brilliant, young, white newspaper editor from Raleigh, North Carolina, set out on a ten-state driving tour of his native South with the goal of writing a book. Like other Depression-era writers, Daniels was moved by the plight of the "forgotten man," particularly the desperately poor sharecropper. But his interests were also broader and his aspirations greater than those of others who documented southern rural poverty in the 1930s. He hoped to change Americans' very perceptions of a region that had been both caricatured and romanticized and was widely misunderstood. The South "has been wanting discovery for a long time," Daniels explained. "Natives and foreigners, first depended upon to present the South, broke it instead into fragments"—fragments that he now intended to put back together for his readers. One thing he knew for sure was that "the South is two races. Uncle Tom is as essential as the Colonel; burrhead is as indispensable as redneck."[1]

Daniels's language was satirical, but his purpose was democratic. "There are as many Souths, perhaps, as there are people in it," he wrote. "Maybe the only certain South is the addition of all the Southerners."[2] While he arranged to interview well-known writers and political figures, he also promised to look for as many different southerners as he could, people of all classes and colors whose perspectives, along with his own, would add up to a truer picture of the region.

Jonathan Daniels's intentions for his trip were democratic politically as well as culturally. He not only insisted that blacks and poor whites had as much claim to a southern identity as the "Colonel" of the moonlight-and-magnolias myth but also made sure to visit a number of the most important people and places associated with ongoing efforts to transform the South into a more egalitarian and racially inclusive society. Spurred by the economic crisis and the New Deal, a variety of individuals and organizations were working to change the southern social and political order. Some were liberals who wanted to work gradually within the system. Others were more radical and wanted quicker and farther-reaching change. This was especially true of those who had been drawn to the newly influential Communist Party, which had tripled in size in the past few years and now claimed about 75,000 members.[3] Daniels was suspicious of Communists but sympathetic to socialists, while he himself was a liberal. He was a strong supporter of President Franklin Roosevelt, as was his father, Josephus Daniels, who had been Roosevelt's political mentor and boss as Secretary of the Navy during the Woodrow Wilson years. Given the personal connection, Jonathan Daniels embodied Roosevelt's hopes for a "new generation" of liberal-minded leaders in the South in the most direct and intimate sense.[4]

By the summer of 1938, when Daniels published an account of his trip, Roosevelt had begun to take steps to hurry this new generation along. Daniels's travels took place within a national political scene that was becoming increasingly complex and contentious. After many brief statements, the president first spelled out a vision for the South in a March 1938 speech in Gainesville, Georgia. "Today, national progress and national prosperity are being held back chiefly because of selfishness on the part of a few," he said. Describing Georgia (home of his Warm Springs polio treatment center) as his second home state, Roosevelt lamented that "the purchasing power of the millions of Americans in this whole area is far too low." Low wages were the reason why. Higher wages and increased buying power would mean "many other kinds of better things—better schools, better health, better hospitals, better highways." But, Roosevelt warned, "These things will not come to us in the South if we oppose progress—if we believe in our hearts that the feudal system is still the best system. When you come down to it," he insisted, "there is little difference between the feudal system and the Fascist system. If you believe in the one, you lean to the other."[5]

Roosevelt's speech infuriated many white southerners. They resented the comparison to Hitler's Germany and Mussolini's Italy and denounced the president as an arrogant outsider who had no right to criticize. Many argued that the region's low wages for both blacks and whites were the result not of selfishness on the part of elites but of necessity as employers in the South's post–Civil War "colonial" economy had long struggled to compete with more established and politically favored industries in the North. Not only southern industrialists but also most politicians insisted that only the promise of cheap, nonunion labor could bring jobs to the desperately poor region. Democratic National Committee chairman James Farley reported that southern members of Congress were "seething" at "the inference that those who had opposed [Roosevelt] had been purchased by the vested interests."[6] And yet southern congressmen, virtually all of whom were members of the president's own party, had repeatedly blocked or substantially weakened proposed New Deal reforms.

Decades of one-party rule in the South had given conservative southern Democrats enormous power in Congress, where they had used it both to pass New Deal initiatives and to prevent them from fundamentally challenging the southern status quo of racial and class hierarchy. Initially, this had meant insisting on lower minimum-wage standards for the South under the National Industrial Recovery Act and tailoring other new laws such as the Agricultural Adjustment Act of 1933 and the Social Security Act of 1935 to southern landowners' and employers' advantage at the expense of farm workers and domestic servants, including the majority of black southerners.[7] By 1936, however, it was clear that the New Deal was unleashing political forces both nationally and within the South that were beyond conservative southern Democrats' control. In early 1937, a political blunder on Roosevelt's part gave southern Democrats an opportunity to oppose the popular president. That blunder was the infamous "court-packing" plan: Roosevelt's proposed legislation to increase the size of the U.S. Supreme Court, which had struck down several key pieces of New Deal legislation in its previous two sessions. Southern Democrats led the fight in Congress against the court reform bill and became more openly defiant of the president and New Deal liberalism in general. Some even joined northern Republicans and business leaders from around the country in endorsing a "Conservative Manifesto" drafted primarily by a North Carolina Democrat, Senator Josiah W. Bailey, long a Daniels family nemesis.[8]

It was largely this political problem of southern recalcitrance within his own party that motivated Roosevelt to declare the South "the nation's No. 1 economic problem" in July 1938. Less than a week later, Jonathan Daniels's book about his trip, with its promise to "discover the South" in all of its political and cultural complexity, appeared.[9] The coincidence of Daniels's timing was, in a larger, atmospheric sense, really no coincidence. Rather, it was a case of a man's personal journey and the nation's historical journey simultaneously converging on a single but still distant and only dimly seen destination: a South that would be truly new because it would be more racially and socially just.

Discovering the South narrates this convergence. It seeks to explain not only Daniels's gradual transformation as a liberal and the significance of his car trip to it, but also the significance of the South and southerners in the transformation of American democracy. It was in the late 1930s that the United States began to transition from the Jim Crow era into what is best understood as the long civil rights era: a thirty-year period when the question of whether or not African Americans would be able to exercise full and equal citizenship rights became as central and defining a question for U.S. politics and culture as the question of whether or not slavery would be allowed to expand or continue had once been. Just as one might explain the coming of the Civil War by pointing to the political and cultural developments of earlier decades, I examine the time when this "irrepressible conflict" of the twentieth century emerged—the time when the battle lines between the civil rights activists of the 1950s and 1960s and some of their fiercest opponents began to be drawn.

What was the true nature of the South and its problems, and who was trying to address them—in what ways, against what opposition, and with what results—during the Roosevelt years? More provocatively, why, in the late 1930s when Jonathan Daniels, Franklin and Eleanor Roosevelt, and a great many other Americans were "traveling," did the destination of a more just and egalitarian South prove so impossible to reach? My answers to these questions highlight the ambivalent influence of a range of liberal and progressive white southerners, all of whom shared a commitment to improving the South as a region but who differed in their readiness to accept racial change, leading many to abandon a movement to expand democracy that they had helped get started. Keeping the focus on what is visible from Jonathan Daniels's perspective, I also emphasize the power of conservative and reactionary white southerners to forestall political and social change. Meanwhile, I try to keep black activism in view and make it clear that the battles in the South were taking place within the context of a national turn toward democratic ideals that made future changes in southern social relations possible but still far from easy. Ultimately, it would take a black-led, grassroots movement to bring the country forward in a drive for racial equality that, by the 1950s, had unfortunately lost some of the emphasis on economic justice for both blacks and poor and working-class whites that had characterized earlier activism.

The slight left turn that put the United States on the road to a Second Reconstruction came in the 1930s, though there was much navigating to be done over the subsequent three decades. Jonathan Daniels's trip lasted a scant six weeks, and my account digs into only its ten richest days in May and June 1937. Nevertheless, it is a central contention of this book that Jonathan's roomy black Plymouth can carry any willing passenger deep into an understanding of civil rights, southern, and U.S. history because his moral and political journey was the same journey, writ small, that the United States in the mid-twentieth century was on.

How Civil Rights Became the Question That Defined a New Era

The New Deal turned out to be a mixed bag for blacks and other racial minorities. Relief and employment programs brought material benefits, and decades of neglect gave way to new ideas about the federal government's responsibility to its citizens, including people of color.[10] But New Deal policies also discriminated. Labor laws allowed for regional wage differentials that mapped onto racial disparities. Welfare-state provisions in the landmark Social Security Act excluded the majority of nonwhite workers from coverage by exempting employers in agriculture and domestic service from participating and paying taxes. Federal housing policies did more, especially in the long run, to foster the growth of middle-class white suburbs than to provide low-income housing in cities. Farm programs benefited white southern landowners while displacing their disproportionately black tenants.

The list of discriminatory policies is so long and their impact has been so deep and long-lasting that some historians describe the New Deal as a "raw deal" that not only failed to address racial inequalities but actually widened the gaps between first-class/white and second-class citizens.[11] Yet it is also true that the New Deal facilitated change and helped make civil rights a significant subject for political debate for the first time in decades.

There were many reasons for this complicated outcome, some of which were political, some economic, some demographic. Although millions of white southerners also migrated, the singular importance of black migration from the South to the North and West cannot be overstated. Pushed by the horrors of life under Jim Crow and pulled by job opportunities in industry as the flow of European immigrants was cut off by World War I and postwar legal restrictions, black migrants not only shaped new lives for themselves but also reshaped the nation's political and economic landscape. By the 1930s, four northern, industrial states with large black populations

(New York, Pennsylvania, Illinois, and Ohio) added up to more electoral votes than the eleven, predominantly agricultural states of the former Confederacy.[12] As a coalition of blacks, liberals, and organized labor emerged outside the South, white southerners lost their pride of place as the dominant faction within the Democratic Party, even though seniority rules gave their senators and representatives outsized power in Congress. Some liberal Democrats were ready to write off the South, and for a brief period in 1937–38, Franklin Roosevelt himself became willing to risk alienating conservative southern voters because he could not accomplish New Deal goals against the opposition of conservative southern congressmen. Indeed, publications like the *Saturday Evening Post* were starting to ask "Whose Party Is It?" by February 1937, three months before Jonathan Daniels departed on his tour.[13]

Hundreds of historians have written about Roosevelt and the New Deal, but governance, even in its many and various forms, was only part of the equation. The emergence of civil rights as a definitive national issue depended less on what the New Deal did and more on what it made possible. As historian Thomas Sugrue neatly summarizes, the "New Deal unleashed great expectations about government and a rhetoric of rights that became increasingly powerful. By pushing national politics leftward, the New Deal made room for dissenters on moral, religious, and economic issues to organize."[14]

Dissenters who organized have been the subjects of much historical scholarship. One large body of work examines blacks' struggles for full and equal citizenship, particularly the efforts of the National Association for the Advancement of Colored People (NAACP) and other advocacy and civil rights organizations.[15] The history of black activism prior to the *Brown v. Board of Education* decision in 1954 is now well documented, and historians have begun to ask hard questions about the strategies black leaders and their white allies pursued over the years. Many have noted middle-class biases, and an increasing number emphasize the ideological and practical limitations of racial liberalism, especially in the post–World War II period when the chill of the Cold War affected decision making.[16] The great success of the NAACP's legal strategy in *Brown* and the cases that led up to it actually narrowed the definition of what "civil rights" might mean, argues legal historian Risa L. Goluboff. Prior to *Brown*, "legal professionals disagreed about what civil rights were, where in the Constitution courts could find authority to protect them, who exactly should provide that protection, and how they should do so," she writes. By pursuing a legal strategy that highlighted "the stigma of governmental classifications, not the material inequality black workers experienced as a result of the interdependent public and private Jim Crow complex," NAACP lawyers helped enshrine a definition of civil rights that was more limited than black workers and their allies wanted and needed.[17] It was a strategy that won, and the benefits of the *Brown* decision in overturning the "separate but equal" doctrine and validating blacks' ongoing struggles deserve to be celebrated. But the victory was partial; in contrast, workers' rights advocates in the 1930s and 1940s tried to challenge racial inequality more fully, but with limited success.

Historians have studied the workers' rights advocates of the 1930s and 1940s mostly in the context of studying organized labor, especially the centrally important Congress of Industrial Organizations (CIO). The CIO was first founded in 1935 as the Committee for Industrial Organization within the decades-old American Federation of Labor (AFL). Committed to unionizing workers across entire industries rather than more narrowly according to their trades, the CIO promoted racial inclusivity as well as dramatic action and, by August 1937, claimed over 3.4 million members. More than one historian has echoed the sentiments of an enthusiastic contemporary observer who proclaimed that "the working class of America came of age in 1937"—again, the same year that Daniels traveled.[18]

This "age of the CIO" was also a time when other organizations on the political left were thriving. Scholars have written detailed histories of the Communist Party-USA, the Socialist Party of America, and many other left-leaning religious, pacifist, and civil liberties groups. The Popular Front period from 1935 to 1939 has attracted particular interest. Meeting in Moscow in the summer of 1935, the Seventh World Congress of the Communist International, or Comintern, called for cooperation among liberals, socialists, and Communists in the fight against fascism in Europe. In the United States, Popular Front ideology encouraged leftists and left-leaning liberals to forge alliances and attempt to set aside their differences on such questions as revolution versus reform and the other personal and organizational rivalries that had often divided them.

Though it was never without internal conflicts, this left-liberal cooperation had a significant impact on American politics and culture. The Popular Front "was the insurgent social movement forged from the labor militancy of the fledgling CIO, the anti-fascist solidarity with Spain, Ethiopia, China, and the refugees from Hitler, and the political struggles on the left wing of the New Deal," explains scholar Michael Denning, in a definition that captures the cultural ramifications of political developments. He argues that "the heart of the Popular Front as a social movement lay among those who were non-Communist socialists and independent leftists, working with Communists and with liberals, but marking out a culture that was neither a Party nor a liberal New Deal culture." Any historical account of the Popular Front "must give the Communist Party its due" because "it was without doubt the most influential left organization in the period and its members were central activists in a range of formations and institutions." But "the Popular Front was more a historical bloc . . . than a party," writes Denning. It was "a broad and tenuous left-wing alliance" in which the fellow travelers were not only the most numerous but ultimately the most widely influential participants.[19]

The German-Soviet nonaggression pact signed in August 1939 and the subsequent devastation of Poland by both German and Russian forces ended the Popular Front in a political, organizational sense, and to many it was a disillusioning, bitter betrayal. But the new class consciousness and "working-class ethnic Americanism" that characterized the literature, music, and movies of what Denning calls the "Cultural Front" were more lasting. "Indeed, Popular Front attitudes so impressed themselves on the American people that a 1942 *Fortune* poll found that 25 percent of Americans favored socialism and another 35 percent had an open mind about it," Denning observes.[20] Though not "fellow travelers" by the usual definition, Americans who held such views had, like Jonathan Daniels, been "traveling." Driven by the economic turmoil, New Deal responses to it, and the steering of black, left, and labor dissenters-who-organized in a newly conducive climate, these politically "middle" Americans rode along, allowing the nation to complete its slight left turn into a new era — the long civil rights era — that was defined by efforts to expand democracy and guarantee the rights of citizenship to a broader segment of the American people, including people of color.

Connected to historians' accounts of black, left, and labor activism in the 1930s and 1940s is another substantial body of scholarship that focuses on the political and cultural influence of dissenters from the South, both black and white. Published in 1981, Anthony P. Dunbar's *Against the Grain* is an important early work that emphasizes the religious roots of white southern leftists' socialism and pacifism. The 1970s and 1980s also saw the publication of a number of biographies and other studies of white southern liberals and moderates, two of which have been particularly valuable to my research on Jonathan Daniels: Charles W. Eagles's excellent 1982 biography, *Jonathan Daniels and Race Relations: The Evolution of a Southern Liberal*, and John T. Kneebone's impressive *Southern Liberal Journalists and the Issue of Race, 1920–1944*, published in 1985.

By the mid-1990s, historians were able to take stock of white southern dissenters and do a better job of including black leaders and intellectuals in broader overviews. John Egerton's 1994 book, *Speak Now against the Day: The Generation before the Civil Rights Movement in the South*, is a wide-ranging survey of those who challenged the southern social and political order in large ways and small, with varying results. Published just two years later in 1996, Patricia Sullivan's crucial *Days of Hope: Race and Democracy in the New Deal Era* focuses more closely on blacks and dissenting southern whites who worked in the New Deal and in the "Washington-centered phase of what had become a loosely jointed movement to expand political democracy in the South." Sullivan's final chapters shift the scene from Washington to places southern as she argues that "the energy for expanding voting rights shifted to the South during the war years and was carried forward by locally and regionally based organizations." Her account ends in 1948 with the "closing circle of Democratic Party politics," when the "bipartisan embrace of the cold war hastened the breakup of the CIO and contributed to a weakening of popular confidence in the democratic process and in the federal government." Former vice president Henry Wallace's third-party campaign for the presidency in 1948 "employed strategies that anticipated the civil rights movement of the 1960s."[21] But, like Egerton, Sullivan considers her generation of radicals and progressives (the name Wallace supporters chose for themselves as the Progressive Party) to be a generation "before" the civil rights movement rather than the ones who started it.

A great deal of new scholarship published in the 2000s challenges this view. Most notably, Glenda Elizabeth Gilmore's *Defying Dixie: The Radical Roots of Civil Rights, 1919–1950*, published in 2008, focuses on many of the same black and white southern dissenters as Sullivan and Egerton but also finds a larger and more influential left in and around the Communist Party. Gilmore argues that it was initially "Communists who promoted and practiced racial equality and considered the South crucial to their success in elevating labor and overthrowing the capitalist system. They were joined in the late 1930s by a radical Left to form a southern Popular Front that sought to overturn Jim Crow, elevate the working class, and promote civil rights and civil liberties." Anticommunism constrained but did not kill off this left-led movement. "During and after World War II," Gilmore writes, "a growing number of grassroots activists protested directly against white supremacy and imagined it poised to fall of its own weight. They gave it a shove."[22]

Gilmore's book is one of many recent studies that find the first push of

the civil rights movement taking place in a period that has often been depicted as, at most, a preview. In an incisive 2005 essay titled "The Long Civil
Rights Movement and the Political Uses of the Past," Jacquelyn Dowd Hall
put a name to this emerging trend in historical scholarship and called for a
more self-conscious and significant reinterpretation. Attuned to the ways in
which the architects of the New Right had begun in the 1970s to reinvent
themselves as "color-blind" conservatives and simultaneously to advance a
short, ideologically narrow, and shallow version of civil rights history, Hall
outlined a Long Civil Rights Movement (LCRM) framework that is longer,
broader, and deeper. Her essay defined six key interpretive points, and a
growing body of scholarship that fleshes out this interpretation has made
it possible for her to sum up the LCRM thesis all the more succinctly. She
argues that "the civil rights movement took root in the structural changes
and political possibilities of the late 1930s, accelerated during World War
II, stretched far beyond the South, was reshaped by the Cold War, and was
continuously and ferociously contested. Indeed, from the New Deal onward,
it has faced a 'long conservative movement,' and neither of these movements
can be understood without the other."[23]

Discovering the South reflects the influence of LCRM scholarship but shifts
the analytical emphasis from the "movement" to an "era" because of what is
visible from Jonathan Daniels's perspective.[24] To trace Daniels's actual and
metaphorical journeys is to write history in a different way than it is usually
written. Like a biographer, I follow my main character and try to show how
he acted in and reacted to the world around him. But, having set out to write
history rather than biography, I have been equally as interested in the world
as in Daniels. My intention has always been to make Jonathan's Plymouth
my vehicle and Jonathan himself my proxy traveler. Unable to time-travel
to the 1930s South myself, I looked for someone I could follow through the
southern landscape to see what I could see. Daniels's extremely well-chosen
route, as well as his excellent timing and credentials and connections, made
him appealing as a guide even before I got to know him as well as I now do.
In the 1930s South, who but a prominent journalist (and, almost as inevitably,
a white male one) could have managed to interview both Margaret Mitchell and black educators at Tuskegee Institute, both a Mississippi aristocrat
like William Alexander Percy and the socialist organizers of the Southern
Tenant Farmers Union, all within a few weeks? Although Daniels's journey
has taken me to far fewer black and female southerners than I would like, his
personal story has turned out to be compelling, and accompanying him on

his travels has allowed me to write about places and put human faces to abstract topics like the debate between the Nashville Agrarians and the Chapel Hill Regionalists over New Deal land reform policies and the deep anxieties that even liberal southerners like Daniels felt about federal intervention in the region. In my view, places and faces are important: academically trained historians need to do as much as we can to bring the past to life.

Even more significant in an analytical sense is the fact that following Daniels has required me to reckon with a very wide range of southerners. Though he set out to visit people and places he associated with efforts to bring social justice and democratic change to the South, Daniels also intentionally and unintentionally met people who opposed such changes. He interviewed conservatives, reactionaries, even a possible fascist. Thus, while Hall and other LCRM scholars have emphasized that the longer, broader, deeper civil rights movement was always contested, *Discovering the South* concentrates on this contest between the developing movement and the developing opposition. In contrast to both LCRM scholarship and the smaller number of works that have focused on what historian Jason Morgan Ward calls the "long segregationist movement" and others have called the "long backlash," this book offers a vantage point for seeing both sides.[25] I explore the political and cultural moment in which both long movements began — haltingly began, in the case of the civil rights movement, because of the effectiveness of the opposition and the debilitating ambivalence of potential white allies. Many white southern liberals of the 1930s envisioned a reform movement in the South that focused on problems of poverty and cultural and economic development and only incidentally addressed racial issues and blacks' political and economic needs. Caught in the middle between blacks' rising expectations and the race-baiting and red-baiting of white opponents, these "regionalist" liberals found the center could not hold — or at least they were not the troops to hold it — as the 1940s dawned.[26] This book thus argues for both an opening and a narrowing of political possibilities. The broad coalition in favor of expanding the New Deal in the South that came together by the end of 1938 quickly shrank because many otherwise liberal white southerners blanched at the prospect of racial change and were especially unwilling to challenge segregation. Yet it was these and other black and white liberals' as well as leftists' confrontation with the South's myriad problems that made the late 1930s the start of a new era — the long civil rights era — when the question of whether or not American democracy would be expanded to include people of color as equal citizens became central and defining.

Daniels's Book about His Journey, and Mine

Jonathan Daniels took to the road in 1937 because, like other writers, journalists, filmmakers, and photographers of the period, he felt he needed to. That the South *needed to be seen* was a widespread sentiment in Depression America. No part of the country had been harder hit by the economic crisis, and none would produce more haunting images of poverty and hardship. As a journalist and would-be author, Daniels shared the documentary impulse that motivated now-famous observers like John Steinbeck and Dorothea Lange and that took Erskine Caldwell and photographer Margaret Bourke-White, as well as James Agee and Walker Evans, into the Deep South in the summer of 1936, resulting in two of the best-known photo-documentary books of all time, *You Have Seen Their Faces* and *Let Us Now Praise Famous Men*.

Although he did not have the foresight to take along a camera or a photographer in the summer of 1937, Daniels did take a sort of make-up trip with photographer Alfred Eisenstaedt a year later, right at the moment when his *A Southerner Discovers the South* was about to be released. He and Eisenstaedt retraced much of his earlier journey and collaborated on a *Life* magazine photo-essay that was unfortunately never published. Buried for decades in *Life*'s archives but now visible through the Discovering the South website (www.discoveringthesouth.org), Eisenstaedt's stunning images make it all the more clear that it is, first, as a documentary endeavor that Daniels's travels need to be understood.

A Southerner Discovers the South was the product of Daniels's 1937 trip and, along with his unpublished daily journal, it is one of the two most important of the many sources on which my account of his actual and metaphorical journeys is based. It is also a very enigmatic book. While it included scenery and local color and centered on interviews with both well-known people and hitchhikers, waitresses, and other ordinary folk, *A Southerner Discovers the South* was a decidedly intellectual take on the documentary, "I've seen America" genre.[27] Heralded in its day as "the best book on the modern South," it offered an extended meditation on the problems and possibilities of the region, especially if aided by favorable federal policies and an expanded New Deal.[28] Daniels embraced New Deal social planning with the strong caution that the people at the grass roots must be allowed to maintain their independence; they must be given opportunities, not told how to live their lives. His book was about competing visions for the South and about race and class divisions and conflicts. Historian George Brown Tindall described it "the most informative panorama of the South" in the Great Depression.[29]

Above all, the book was a challenge to simplistic renderings of a vast and complicated region. Presented from the point of view of a liberal-yet-loyal white southerner, Daniels's narrative traced the intellectual and emotional journey of his generation of white southern liberals and delivered their pained critiques. As black intellectual and critic Sterling Brown observed, though Daniels knew "how to disarm Southern prejudices," the South was nonetheless "taken severely to task." "Tabooed subjects," including the brutality of racial oppression and the similarities between the Ku Klux Klan and "the Brown Shirts of Germany and the Black Shirts of Italy," were "brought out in the open."[30]

Daniels was an astute observer with a wide-ranging eye and plenty of reading under his belt to help him understand what he was seeing. Equally important, he was no dogmatist and not one to reduce ambiguities and complexities to simple formulas, nor did his documentary format require him to. Unlike another white newspaper editor from North Carolina who would write of *the* mind of *the* South just a few years later, Daniels produced a less categorical and more elastic book that offers at least as much open-ended reportage as wrapped-up analysis. Much of the appeal of *A Southerner Discovers the South* for its contemporary audience lay in readers' sense of getting to see for themselves. Because of Daniels's relaxed, informative but never insistent authorial voice, the reader felt, as distinguished historian William E. Leuchtenburg has observed, like "an unseen passenger in the car, invited to tag along." People, places, and issues became real, if also harder to reduce and stereotype. As Leuchtenburg remembered of his own first encounter with the book as a teenager growing up in Queens during the Great Depression, *A Southerner Discovers the South* encouraged readers "to think that the South was no simple place, that one needed to study its past to comprehend its present, that there were mysteries to explore."[31]

Unfortunately, for twenty-first-century readers, the mysteries in *A Southerner Discovers the South* are surface level as well as deep. Daniels wrote journalistically for an audience already familiar with then-current issues and events. Determined to keep his tone light and his pressure on white readers' racial and regional prejudices gentle, he also shaped his book in ways that did not always do justice even to his own point of view.

Part of the "generation of 1900" that included William Faulkner, Thomas Wolfe, Robert Penn Warren, Allen Tate, and many other well-known white southern intellectuals and writers, Jonathan Daniels was a classic example of the conflicted white southerner.[32] He was a white southern liberal caught in the contradictions between the Jim Crow culture into which he was born and the principles of democracy and simple decency in which he believed. In his case, he had learned an especially progressive, reform-minded politics from a father who, in a quintessentially southern paradox, had also led his state's bitter and violent campaign to disfranchise black voters. Josephus Daniels was a towering figure in his son's life, and he has also loomed large in histories of the racist extremism that inflamed the South in the 1890s— a decade that saw hundreds of lynchings of black men and women, as well as the hardening of segregation and the decimation of black voting rights that had supposedly been guaranteed a quarter-century earlier under the Fourteenth and Fifteenth Amendments.[33]

Taking hold in every southern state in the 1890s and early 1900s, disfranchisement eliminated not only blacks but also many whites from the voting pool, particularly poor, uneducated whites who could not afford or saw no reason to pay poll taxes or meet other cumbersome requirements. The result was a shrunken electorate—a withered body politic—and an elite control over government that was as "feudal" as Franklin Roosevelt charged in the extent to which it benefited wealthy planters and industrialists. Their ability to maintain low wages and a segregated labor market resulted in a perpetuation of blacks' and poor whites' economic dependency. Discrimination against blacks thus "served as the linchpin," explains historian Robert Korstad, in a system of racial capitalism that many whites proudly called "white supremacy" but that really meant white-elite supremacy and that benefited rich and powerful white men more than women of any race or class.[34]

Tragically, this system of racial capitalism was one that Josephus Daniels helped create even as he aimed for something better—better for a larger number of white people, that is. A well-meaning and even admirable man in many respects, Josephus failed to understand that it was precisely the drag of his own racism that made him and other southern Progressive Era reformers miss the mark of democracy and fairness, even as they advocated for such actually progressive reforms as education and woman suffrage. Indeed, the elder Daniels was largely a populist (and a William Jennings Bryan Populist) at heart, except when it came to empowering black people.

Predicated on the belief that eliminating black voters was the key to eliminating corruption in politics, Josephus Daniels's "whites-only progressivism" was a heavy inheritance for his son Jonathan—who was prone to racist and sexist thinking of his own, as my intimate portrait will show.[35] But Jonathan's mind and career were also enriched by the ties to the national Democratic Party and particularly to Roosevelt that his father afforded him. The changing political context of the 1930s had an impact on him, as did his southern tour, the significance of which this book will show. The story of Daniels's longer, moral and political journey is that of his evolution from an economically progressive but racially reluctant "white southern liberal" to a still-cautious version of a "racial liberal." Like many who worked in the New Deal, Daniels gradually came to realize that a blanket economic approach to problems perceived in terms of class and poverty was insufficient because racial minorities also faced particular problems of discrimination, exclusion, and violence that had to be particularly addressed. He never became a radical (far from it), and he always worried a great deal about losing a political center that he hoped could include white southerners. Nevertheless, from the 1940s on, Daniels supported most civil rights initiatives and, in this respect, traveled further than most of his white southern liberal contemporaries—albeit at a slow pace, like that of the nation as a whole.

Daniels's transformation illuminates the transformation of twentieth-century American politics and culture precisely because it was slow and difficult. To understand how hard it was for even a liberal-minded man like Jonathan to break through ingrained patterns of thinking and being in a society structured around racial and class divisions and antagonisms—to understand how hard it was for him to travel as far as he did—is to begin to understand why the United States got only as far as *it did* on the basis of the liberalism that emerged from the New Deal. The road beyond the nation's midcentury left turn would be long, narrow, and frequently obstructed, and the main drivers who took the United States down that road would include black and white radicals as well as liberals, especially black liberals in the NAACP and other organizations. Jonathan Daniels went along but was never a driver in this activist sense, either before or after 1938. Instead, his slow personal journey shows what it took for the United States even to get started down the road to the Second Reconstruction. The black-led mass *movement* that wrested change from a reluctant nation and a defiant white South in the 1950s and 1960s could not have taken off and gained as much ground as it did if the United States had not already entered the long civil rights *era*—if it had not emerged into new political and human rights territory through New Deal–inspired journeys like that of Jonathan Daniels.

It is by identifying the overlap and narrating the convergence between Daniels's actual and metaphorical journeys and the nation's journey that *Discovering the South* turns *A Southerner Discovers the South* and the many other sources on which it is based into a work of historical scholarship. Daniels's book offers a window—specifically, the windows and windshield of his big, comfortable Plymouth—and there is much to be gained by sitting in the passenger seat next to Jonathan, listening to him and looking out. Physically languid but intellectually dynamic, Daniels was a witty, charismatic man and a vibrant talker and storyteller. Nothing in this book is fiction, but I have tried to make my central character—smart, cheerful, hard-drinking, and rather bawdy thirty-five-year-old Jonathan—into a protagonist. It is he who takes us from place to place, and he who will get us back home again. If he seems to disappear at any point, perhaps the reader can imagine that he has merely pulled over for a cigarette and is standing just outside the driver's side door, his arm draped casually along the roof of the Plymouth, while I, the mildly asthmatic historian, lean forward from the backseat to offer some context or fill in information that Daniels has not provided and, in many cases, would not have been able to provide.

Just as a film director might cut between interior shots within the Plymouth and exterior and even aerial shots that show it on the road, I try throughout the book to present both intimate and historically removed perspectives. I take advantage of hindsight and a huge amount of historical scholarship, acknowledging my many debts to other scholars mostly in the notes. My method is to read *A Southerner Discovers the South* and other sources closely and make connections between them. I have also selected which parts of Daniels's life and trip to discuss in depth and which to abridge in favor of a streamlined account that more clearly advances both my main argument about how and why a new civil rights era began in the late 1930s and the other, related arguments I make along the way. Much like Daniels himself, I am particularly interested in showing that there was *variety* among southerners, whose positions within race, class, and gender hierarchies shaped their individual experiences and points of view. But whereas he could claim, with false reserve, to be depicting "only one man's South," I acknowledge the larger interpretive mission that he, too, was on.[36] I always accompany but also step beyond my guide. As a historian, I share his goal of "discovering the South" for readers, uncovering, introducing, and exploring a region and a history that are too often oversimplified but lay at the heart of American politics and culture, even in the twenty-first century.

A Map

Chapter 1 begins with biography, explaining who Jonathan Daniels was and why he traveled. I emphasize his lifelong effort to get some distance on the powerful father whose racist extremism he disagreed with but whom he dearly loved. I also discuss Daniels's reputation and views as a white southern liberal, laying groundwork for one of this book's most important themes: how political and cultural influences from the left, the left wing of the New Deal, and African Americans working primarily through the NAACP compelled white southern liberals of the 1930s to debate new ideas and, in some cases like Daniels's, gradually evolve into racial liberals and civil rights advocates. Critics of post–World War II racial liberalism are correct to lament that integration was a limited and primarily middle-class goal and that describing racism as a problem of "hearts and minds" obscured the deep economic inequalities on which American apartheid was based. But such critiques must not lose sight of the realm of the politically possible, a realm whose shifting borders white southern liberals' nervous responses to proposals for racial change help to illuminate. Meanwhile, the economic emphasis of "regionalist liberals" like Daniels—especially their often-ambivalent and impeding, yet nonetheless wise concern for the problems of poor and working-class whites in tandem with those of African Americans—deserves renewed attention that this book can only begin to provide.

After the biographical background in Chapter 1, each of the next eight chapters traces Daniels's route and opens up from one or more stopping points on his southern tour. I use his encounters to explore various factors that made the late 1930s the start of a new national journey away from racial capitalism and toward an expansion of democracy, not just for blacks but for poor and working-class Americans of all colors. I ask what developments taking place in the South in the 1930s helped put the United States on the road to the Second Reconstruction, and when and how southern opponents of social and political change tried to block that path.

Some chapters address the first of these two questions more fully than the second, and others vice versa, but all show controversy and contestation. Chapter 2 gets Daniels started on his trip and highlights the transformative potential of New Deal initiatives such as the Tennessee Valley Authority, which, though discriminatory in practice, reiterated the principle of democratic rather than oligarchic rule. Chapter 3 looks through Daniels's eyes to assess the legal and political impact of the Communist-led crusade against racial injustice in the Scottsboro case and the concurrent NAACP-led fight for federal antilynching legislation. Though no such law was ever passed, both the Scottsboro mobilization and the NAACP's legal efforts were crucial for bringing together the coalition of blacks, leftists, and left-leaning liberals that did the most to steer the nation into the long civil rights era.

While these two early chapters show at least as much turmoil as social change, Chapter 4 moves fully into an oppositional viewpoint as seen in

Daniels's interview with the most reactionary of the Nashville Agrarians, Donald Davidson. Because Daniels drove immediately from Nashville to Memphis, Chapter 5 then shifts to the opposite end of the political spectrum to see what the socialist leadership of the Southern Tenant Farmers Union advocated on many of the same questions that animated Davidson and his circle of traditionalist intellectuals. I also draw on recent, revisionist scholarship to explain the internal as well as external challenges that beset and ultimately broke up this interracial but not fully integrated union. Chapter 6, set in the Arkansas-Mississippi Delta around Memphis, where Daniels lingered longer than in any other place he visited, investigates the breakdown of planter paternalism and southern "chivalry," as seen in the dramatic and long-misinterpreted story of a middle-class white woman who was beaten for her union sympathies.

Chapter 7 is the start of *Discovering the South*'s second half and follows Daniels swiftly from Arkansas to Tuskegee, Alabama. There we see the quiet but tenacious character of one well-educated black man's efforts to advance in the Jim Crow South, poised against the brutality of debt peonage ("slavery by another name") in the Alabama Black Belt.[37] From this black informant, Daniels learned the chilling tale of the Dickson brothers, who were twice investigated for holding black farm workers against their will in violation of federal laws, including the Thirteenth Amendment. Even a federal prosecutor thought one of the socially prominent Dickson brothers had killed at least "six negroes and three white men." Yet neither a 1903 nor a 1946 investigation resulted in a trial, and Daniels himself felt compelled to tell their story only obliquely for fear that one of the brothers might "drive to Raleigh in his car and shoot" him.[38] Together with Daniels's interview with irate Birmingham coal baron Charles F. DeBardeleben, recounted in Chapter 8, the story of the Dickson brothers illustrates the extent to which white violence in defense of racial capitalism was an accepted element of white southern society. The politically connected DeBardeleben's anticommunist rhetoric and shifting party affiliations also provide an early glimpse of some of the tactics recalcitrant white southerners would employ, especially after World War II, to prevent social change.

Yet there were, in fact, changes taking place in the South in the 1930s. Though centered on DeBardeleben, Chapter 8 is simultaneously a history of the CIO's successful effort to achieve interracial unionism and win the right of collective bargaining against the spitting anger of the kind of industrialists he represented—those who fomented and financed the "long backlash." The so-called agitators like CIO organizer William Mitch "seemed far less agitated about the present situation than Mr. DeBardeleben did," Daniels noted.[39] Bitter as the fight was, Birmingham in 1937 was a place where those who hoped to expand democracy, including democracy in the workplace, were winning.

More subtly than Chapter 8, Chapter 9 is also a story of contrasts, specifically the contrasting elements of old and new that both Margaret Mitchell and her home city of Atlanta embodied. Like DeBardeleben's rant, Mitchell's reactionary politics and incredible cultural influence make it all the more clear that the late 1930s was a time when the long segregationist movement coalesced just as much as it was a time of progressive ferment—"very basic, vital ferment," in the words of contemporary sociologist Arthur F. Raper.[40] The ferment was there, but so was the fist that would repeatedly punch the rising dough of the early movement for an expanded democracy back down again. Chapter 10 examines the critical and popular responses to Jonathan Daniels's *A Southerner Discovers the South* and its contributions to this yeasty political environment. It and my conclusion also contemplate whether Daniels was "the same man at the end of his journey," as he suggested was usually the case for travel writers.[41] The advantage of hindsight allows me to see that he was not. Having completed his tour of the South, Daniels had also traveled a considerable distance on his metaphorical journey away from the separate-but-equal liberalism of his younger years and toward a truer conception of democracy. He would soon embark on another, equally important adventure as Franklin Roosevelt's "chief advisor on domestic race relations" from 1943 to 1945.[42] Writing more than thirty years after Daniels's death in 1981, I can see that his personal moral and political journey was no more finished when he published *A Southerner Discovers the South* in 1938 than was the nation's journey toward the Second Reconstruction, which was just getting started.

CHAPTER ONE

We So-Called Free Moderns

✦

RALEIGH, NORTH CAROLINA

O N A CLOUDY DAY in February 1937, Jonathan Daniels received a letter from Harold Strauss, a New York editor, who hoped to interest him in writing a book about the history of Tennessee. It would begin, stereotypically, "up in the hills with the old-time mountaineers completely cut off from civilization." It would end with "the entrance of the New Deal" and the dawning of a new era of hope for the South.[1]

Daniels was flattered and thought the project might "pull me out of the rut of non-accomplishment," as he wrote to his father. He had published his first novel seven years earlier but felt his failure to sell a second one he had written "makes me look like a complete dud."[2] This usually latent sense of inadequacy had recently been aroused by a visit from his old college friend Thomas Wolfe, who by 1937 was already the author of *Look Homeward, Angel* and several other books. But a letter from his famous father — former Secretary of the Navy Josephus Daniels, then serving as ambassador to Mexico — was even more of a goad. "The interviews with Tom in the News and Observer were very interesting," Josephus had written. "I wondered how he could say: 'Hell, I have no time to read Gone With the Wind or any other long book,' when he himself offends more than anybody else along that line. . . . People are interested in southern stories and you have a good one," he added, bringing up the sore subject of Jonathan's rejected manuscript. "Why don't you publish it now? I think it would be a good time."[3]

Instead, Jonathan Daniels took the trip and wrote the book that became *A Southerner Discovers the South*. To suggest that he did so because he wanted to impress his father would be an oversimplification. But he did dedicate the book to Josephus (as "A Better Southerner"), and neither it nor Daniels's personal journey and its relationship to the national journey away from Jim Crow racial capitalism can be understood without examining their father-son relationship. It was there and in Jonathan's frustrated ambitions as a novelist and full-fledged participant in the South's literary renaissance that his 1937 journey began.

✦ ✦ ✦

TO HAROLD STRAUSS, the important thing was that Daniels, the intelligent and well-read young editor of the *Raleigh News and Observer*, had ever felt inclined to write a novel at all. The book Strauss proposed was to be a nonfiction "prose epic" that blended research with poetic license. "It may be necessary to invent typical characters, such as mountaineers, industrial workers and farm workers," he explained, "and at other times it may be necessary to rely pretty much on factual exposition." This "combination of fact and fiction" was what made Strauss think Daniels was "one of the few men in the country who could do the book the way it should be done."[4]

Daniels's novel, *Clash of Angels*, had certainly been imaginative. The angels of the title were Jehovah and Lucifer (the hero), and the setting was Heaven, although God (the "Contriver") was nowhere to be found. Published in 1930, the book was a product of the twenties, both Daniels's twenties and the 1920s, a time when "the problem was not communism and capitalism," as he later reflected, "but religion and atheism, the monkey bill and so forth."[5] Like other southern intellectuals who came of age in the 1920s, Daniels chafed against his region's Victorian culture and religious fundamentalism. He found a strong ointment for his irritation in Baltimore journalist H. L. Mencken's acerbic essays about the South (and America) as anti-intellectual and backward, along with a great deal of other reading. By the time he wrote *Clash of Angels*, he had embraced a modernism that accepted uncertainty and conflict and perhaps even Lucifer's fate of plunging into the infinite abyss that, in his novel, lay beyond Heaven's clifflike "Edge."[6] Daniels also reveled in, rather than trying to repress, the less "civilized" aspects of human existence, including sexuality. His youthful philosophy, in Lucifer's words, was "Do what your heart says do, and afterwards let it be as it may be."[7]

As freeing as it felt, however, Daniels also found his modernist intellectual rebellion difficult because he loved his home and family and was more than a little intimidated by his father, who had "a great, great patriarchal sense."[8] His older brother Worth, a doctor, diagnosed his case perceptively when he read *Clash of Angels* in manuscript. "I see in it [an] obvious basis for your functional trouble in the neck," he wrote, "and I believe the very writing of it—that is getting down in black and white your conflict with father's god—has been the therapy you needed."[9] Another brotherly letter

Josephus and Adelaide Bagley Daniels with their sons (l to r) Worth, Jonathan,
Josephus Jr., and Frank in Washington, D.C., in the 1910s. Jonathan Daniels
Papers, #3466, Southern Historical Collection, Wilson Library,
University of North Carolina at Chapel Hill.

warned Jonathan against telling Josephus about the novel's contents until
it was accepted for publication. "If you showed it now pressure might be
brought to bear to get you not to publish it. I don't mean physical or financial pressure but filial duty and consideration pressure which is much more
powerful and much more unpleasant." None of the four Daniels boys wanted
to see Josephus hurt, "but he must learn to look upon you with a little more
detachment . . . as another distinct individual and not as a part of himself."[10]

As Daniels's brothers saw, writing *Clash of Angels* was largely an act of
youthful self-assertion rather than a true expression of his spiritual beliefs.
But it did mark Jonathan as a budding modernist with aspirations to join
the other young writers who were bringing about the Southern Renaissance.
"The year 1929," when Wolfe's *Look Homeward, Angel,* William Faulkner's
Sartoris and *The Sound and the Fury,* and Robert Penn Warren's first book,
a biography of abolitionist John Brown, were all published, was "specially
significant," as eminent southern historian C. Vann Woodward once pointed
out.[11] Even before *Clash of Angels* appeared in early 1930, Daniels had begun

to envision a southern story that would more closely resemble the fiction of his contemporaries, "a satirical novel with its scene in the low country of the South where even today the virtues of modern American civilization are not held ultimately good."[12]

But whether or not he could pull off such a satire depended on more than just his talents as a novelist. He would have to challenge a "New South creed" that his father had often, if not uncritically, espoused. Josephus Daniels's fame and political influence were enough to make him an overbearing parent, no matter how gentle his demeanor with his sons. None felt the pressure more keenly than Jonathan, the son whom Josephus had chosen, seemingly at birth, to be his "partner" and heir apparent as editor of the *News and Observer*, which he had owned since 1894. Jonathan's first major conflict with his father was over Prohibition, for he was an enthusiastic drinker while Josephus was a devout, old-school Methodist and totally committed "dry." His single most famous act as Secretary of the Navy had been to eliminate the officers' wine mess, banning alcohol from all ships and bases in 1914. For decades, many Americans would believe, incorrectly, that this was how a cup of coffee became a "cup of Joe."[13]

In good ways and bad, Jonathan's cup of Joe ranneth over. Even his midthirties, when he wrote *A Southerner Discovers the South*, were marked by his efforts to establish an identity apart from Josephus—yet close to Josephus, for he not only loved and admired his father but also believed in many of the same ideals. For Jonathan in his twenties, the father-son issue was paramount. Thus, where one fellow journalist saw him trying in *Clash of Angels* "to clear the cobwebs of a dead theology out of your own brain," Daniels himself would later see little more than a "cobweb blasphemy" and "a nice little part of your juvenilia."[14] Even as he wrote the novel, he wondered at his own audacity, assuring one correspondent that he knew "enough to know that it's either going to be a magnificent and universal satire or else the very worst adolescent rot ever poured on paper."[15] Although the novel did get some nice reviews, critic Heywood Broun, whom Daniels particularly admired, was unkind enough to highlight its intellectual immaturity. "Here is a truly remarkable book for a youngster to have written," Broun's blurb for the Book-of-the-Month Club newsletter began, "and its chief flaw is that he is still too young to have written it."[16]

The truth was that Jonathan always had been young—precocious, but therefore almost always younger than everyone else around him. When he started at Centennial School, the public school he attended in Raleigh, his first-grade teacher fretted because he already knew the Greek mythology she was reading to her students. "What am I going to read to Jonathan?"[17] He ended up skipping a grade after the family moved to Washington, D.C., in 1913, when he was not quite eleven. Life in Washington during the Wilson years was an education in itself for "a boy staring with bird-steady eyes," but it was one that Daniels moved through quickly.[18] By the fall of 1918 he had left his private school, St. Albans, without graduating and enrolled as a sixteen-year-old freshman at the University of North Carolina.

At UNC Daniels joined a fraternity, Delta Kappa Epsilon, even though he knew his father, a man of the people, maintained a strict policy of not joining any organization that was not open to all (white) comers. Characteristically, Jonathan wrote to Josephus for advice about joining and then alleged that his father's delay in responding had compelled him to make his own decision. (His older brother Worth had simply joined without asking.)[19] As a "Deke," Jonathan felt like "the cream of the earth," but he was not enough of a "professional fraternity man" to seek admission to the Order of Gimghoul or the Order of the Gorgon's Head, secret societies at UNC. The biggest part of him wanted to be a serious intellectual. He remembered "doing more reading outside of classes than in classes" and putting "a terrible strain on the library. . . . I belonged to the group that read *Vanity Fair* and *The Smart Set*, which were [for] the new sophisticated young man. The F. Scott Fitzgerald generation, the Mencken period."[20]

Daniels's literary interests led him to join the fledgling Carolina Playmakers theater group, where he worked with Wolfe and playwright Paul Green. He also began "fooling with" the student newspaper, the *Tar Heel*, only to be elected managing editor his senior year. It was his desire to become editor-in-chief that led him to stay on for a master's degree in English—still only his fourth year at UNC, and he was still only nineteen.

The big campus issue that year, 1921–22, was the arrest of some prostitutes at the Alpha Tau Omega house. Joseph Ervin, a student politician who was in ATΩ (and whose brother Sam would become famous as a North Carolina senator), pleaded with Jonathan not to print a story about the episode because it "would be a great injury to the University." "We finally agreed to go to see President Chase about it," Daniels remembered. "Ervin stated his case and I stated mine. And Chase said, 'It happened, didn't it? . . . 'Well, I think Jonathan should print it.'"[21]

Though vindicated, Jonathan could not feel too superior because, a year earlier, he had been compelled to print the news that he himself had been put on probation after getting so drunk at a dance that he slid unceremoniously to the floor. One more violation and he could have been expelled, and so he sobered up. Before that, though, he had definitely drunk his share of bootleg liquor, sometimes making his own by boiling down a common diuretic of the day called sweet spirit of niter. "Gosh, the stuff we drank. How we lived through it!" he would marvel. He was also an accomplished gambler, nicknamed "Dice" Daniels for his talent at craps. Although his temperance was short-lived, he would eventually give up gambling for good when, a dozen years later in the midst of the Great Depression, he inadvertently got hundreds of dollars ahead of some impecunious companions, including Ogden Nash. To leave them in so much debt would have been ungentlemanly, but trying and failing to lose for hours on end was excruciating.[22]

Jonathan's probation during his senior year proved fortunate. He was completely sober at a subsequent dance where he met Elizabeth Bridgers—"Bab" or, less often, "Babs." She was a student at Smith College at home for a visit in Raleigh. Her grandfather, Colonel Robert Rufus Bridgers, had been a Confederate politician, a railroad president, and an old political enemy of Josephus. Her father, Robert Rufus Bridgers Jr., had died young, and her mother, Annie Cain Bridgers, a Christian Scientist, had moved the family to Boston while she studied spiritual healing. Thus, Jonathan had not known Bab in childhood, nor did he ever know who brought her to the dance. Instantly attracted to one another, they sat up all night talking. "We were the young enchanted," the elderly Daniels would remember, "and I fell very much in love."[23]

But love and marriage would have to wait because Josephus had plans for Jonathan. After he finished his master's degree, he would spend the summer of 1922 apprenticing at the *Louisville Times*, his mother's cousin's newspaper in Kentucky. Then Josephus wanted him to go to law school. "Graduation is a step," he advised, but now it was time "to study something you do not love—to drudge through practical things" that would prepare him for the future they both anticipated, when he would "be editor of the paper."[24] Jonathan was not interested in law school, but he was interested in Bab, who by the summer of 1922 had dropped out of Smith and was going to New York to study art. So he enrolled at Columbia University and spent a year depleting the bank account his father had set up for him. He also failed all his classes. But it was a wonderful time, and if he "could change it for all A's," he "wouldn't have changed it."[25] Back in Chapel Hill in the summer of 1923, he took a twelve-week review course and passed the North Carolina bar. Then he and Bab got married.

At twenty-one, Jonathan went to work for the *News and Observer*. He spent much of his first few months covering sports—a "young Adonis" of the sports page, in the words of columnist Nell Battle Lewis. But in those days at the *News and Observer*, nobody could do any one thing. They "had to write obituaries and personals and every sort of thing." He did his share and felt that no one could say he was given special privileges simply because he was the boss's son. Yet it *was* because he was the boss's son that he was chosen to become the newspaper's Washington correspondent in 1926, when he was only twenty-four years old.[26]

Those were happy days in Washington for Jonathan and Bab, who had great faith in her ambitious young husband's talents. In addition to her love of art, she shared his literary interests, writing book reviews for the *News and Observer* and trying her hand at stories and plays like her older sister, Ann Preston Bridgers, a successful actress and playwright. Inclined to exuberance, Bab frequently signed letters to family members with the words "Love, love, love," and when she became pregnant, her eager anticipation was palpable. "I'm tickled to death about this event," Jonathan wrote to his mother, Adelaide Worth Bagley Daniels, known as "Addie." But Bab was "so happy about it" that he sometimes felt "like I'm not taking half the interest in it that I ought." He was sure she would be fine but knew he would "be a nervous boy when the time comes." When the time did come, the fact that the birth of their daughter, Adelaide Ann, was by caesarean section proved especially worrying.[27]

The addition of Adelaide Ann made Jonathan impatient to leave Washington and move back to Raleigh. Josephus also wanted help researching and writing his autobiography, which would eventually fill six volumes. And so, in 1927, Jonathan and his young family moved home. Settling down in an apartment not far from Wakestone, the colonial revival mansion that Josephus and Addie Daniels had built in 1920, he and Bab lived a literary life as he helped with the memoirs, wrote a weekly column for the paper, and dug into the biography of his most prominent Confederate ancestor, Major William Henry Bagley, for a speech that another relative would give. (Bagley's widow, Jonathan's redoubtable "Granny," had died the year before, taking along her well-known "pianistic feat" of playing "Dixie" and "The Star-Spangled Banner" simultaneously—the sectional-reconciliation accompaniment to the more sober and symbolic fact that the Confederate Bagleys had given a son, Worth, to die in 1898 as the only American naval officer killed in the Spanish-Cuban-American War.)[28]

Other than his family obligations, Jonathan's main focus in the late 1920s was the novel that became *Clash of Angels*. He labored over it, discussing it in letters to his sisters-in-law, Ann and Emily Bridgers, while keeping its con-

Jonathan and Elizabeth Bridgers Daniels with their daughter,
Adelaide Ann, ca. 1926. Courtesy of Lucy Daniels.

tents secret from Josephus. Ann had made a small fortune on *Coquette*, a play
she had coauthored with George Abbott that became a hit on Broadway in
1927, with Helen Hayes in the starring role. She offered to take Jonathan and
Bab to Europe for an extended writer's sojourn, and she was also eager to
help Jonathan sell his book. As it happened, it was another Raleigh connection, Dr. Hubert Royster's daughter Virginia, who helped him the most by
introducing him to her friend Noble Cathcart, one of the founders of the *Saturday Review of Literature*. Cathcart, in turn, introduced him to Amy Loveman,
his "good angel," another founder of the *Saturday Review* who was becoming
even more influential as one of the readers for the new Book-of-the-Month
Club. Loveman liked his manuscript and agreed to help him find a publisher.
He and Bab had an exciting few months in the fall of 1929 as they waited
for Jonathan's first novel to be published and their second child to be born.[29]

There was some uncertainty about the due date because Bab had been
menstruating irregularly.[30] She was also sick more often and more seriously
than she had been with Adelaide Ann. Still, everything seemed fine until
Friday the 13th of December, when her doctor decided to induce labor before
the baby got any bigger. At fifty-seven, Dr. Elizabeth Delia Dixon Carroll
was less of a novelty as Raleigh's first female physician than she had been

when she started her practice thirty years earlier. Back at the turn of the century, people never knew whether to be more surprised to learn that she was a doctor or that she was the sister of novelist Thomas Dixon Jr., author of several bitterly racist and reactionary books, including *The Clansman* in 1905, which was made into the film *Birth of a Nation* in 1915. In stark contrast to his depictions of the ideal of southern ladyhood in his novels, brother Tom had been the only member of their prominent western North Carolina family to support Delia's professional ambitions, which by definition made her something of a "New Woman" for the urbanizing and industrializing "New South." Tom had even helped pay for her schooling at the Woman's Medical College of the New York Infirmary, the only school in the country where she could earn her degree. She graduated with honors in 1895 and was fortunate, upon moving to Raleigh, to become the staff physician for all-female Meredith College, a new institution that was another sign of social change. By the mid-1920s, when Bab chose her as an obstetrician, Carroll was a highly respected figure in the community—one who would be deeply mourned when she was killed in a car accident just a few years later in 1934.[31]

On Friday the 13th of December, 1929, Dr. Carroll decided it was time to induce labor. She instructed Bab to take a dose of quinine, followed the next morning by a dose of castor oil. When Jonathan took her to the hospital at noon on the 14th, she was "as bright and pretty as could be and happy over the thought that it would soon be over." A little after one o'clock, Dr. Carroll had a nurse call Jonathan, who had gone home for lunch, to tell him to bring back some lunch for Bab. That afternoon, a nurse told Addie Daniels that she "just didn't see where Bab put away everything she ate" and so for supper, with Dr. Carroll's permission, Addie sent her "a bird and some spoon bread."

"Somewhere between six and seven o'clock," Addie Daniels would remember, "the nurse called Dr. Carroll because she did not like the color of the show, which was a very bright red. Dr. Carroll came down, made an examination and said everything was progressing all right." Yet Addie soon learned that the baby had been breach all along and "there was so little fluid in the uterus that it could not be turned." The doctors "were very much afraid that this show indicated that there was a separation of the after-birth from the walls of the uterus, and under those conditions the danger to the mother was not so great but it was very great for the child." By ten o'clock, Dr. Carroll had consulted two colleagues and decided to try to advance the labor, "which had never been anything but slight," by inserting fluid-filled dilating bags into Bab's cervix. "They gave her ethylene gas for this and because of the full stomach she reacted very badly," Addie reported. By midnight, the doctors decided to do a caesarean section.[32]

When they made the incision, "they found the uterus had ruptured entirely at the place of the old incision"—the caesarian section by which Adelaide Ann had been born. The baby boy never breathed, and Bab's breathing had become labored. They gave her morphine, and she seemed to improve greatly by Sunday afternoon, so much so that Jonathan left the hospital for a short time. When he returned, he found that her condition had deteriorated. She was given oxygen, but by Tuesday afternoon she had become so weak that she could inhale but not exhale. Jonathan and his brothers "gave her artificial respiration as long as they could hold out." Then they solicited the help of some men from the American Telephone Company who had been trained in CPR. "Bab realized what they were doing and would tell them when it was right and when it was wrong," Addie wrote. "One man hesitated to see if she had improved and could take a breath, but she told him, 'I have done all I can for myself. You will have to keep it up.'" She told another man about her cousin who worked for the phone company and was "doing very well."

"I am telling you all these little things just to show you how completely in control of her faculties she was," Addie Daniels observed in a long letter, presumably to a relative. "I don't want to make it harder for you or for myself," Addie wrote, "but those days of fighting were almost beyond description." Bab's fight ended at 10:30 on the night of Tuesday, December 17, about three and a half hours after the telephone company crew had been called in. "The men kept up the artificial respiration until she died. She was only unconscious a few moments."

The next day, her son's body was placed with her in a casket, and both were buried in a cemetery over 100 miles away in Wilmington. Bab "had always laughingly said that she wanted to be buried with her own people when she died," Addie explained, "and she wanted Jonathan to marry again, but she didn't want to be by herself when she arose from the dead." Jonathan drove down to Wilmington to visit the grave a week after the funeral and "came back, I think, in a better frame of mind," Addie concluded. But she knew her son well enough to know that he was "heart-broken."[33]

✦ ✦ ✦

WITHIN DAYS OF Bab's death, Josephus learned what *Clash of Angels* was about. He asked Jonathan to join him for an evening carriage ride, and they had what Jonathan would remember as "a right tragic little time" about it.

"The boy was going to write a book that would—you know." Jonathan stopped himself from saying more in a 1972 interview, even though by that time his father had been dead for more than twenty years.[34] After the carriage ride, Josephus wrote Jonathan a letter. It was Christmas eve, just seven days after Bab's death. "I have been groping these days and it helps me to know that you understood me," he began. "I would no sooner strangle a child of your brain than your child of flesh and blood"—surely a terrible metaphor to use with a man who had just buried a baby, no matter how Josephus intended his words. "I love you so much that I fain would shield you now as when you were a little boy," he continued. "If I have been fearful . . . that in your early writings you might use your talent of satire unwisely, . . . it is because I feared your true faith would be misunderstood." There were other "wrongs that need to be pilloried for the good of mankind" that Jonathan could write about instead of religion. "Beliefs that Christian people hold sacred should be treated with respect for those to whom they are verities."

Josephus wrote more—two more pages in his cramped cursive—about his beliefs and his prayers that he might "be worthy of your mother and our sons whose love crowns my life." Then he got back to his main point of asking Jonathan to "postpone publication" of his novel. He assured his son that they were "partners forevermore," yet when he finally encouraged him to make his own decision, he put it in terms of taking "whatever course your sense of duty prompts."[35]

Jonathan published the book. He also hit the road. His mother-in-law and two unmarried sisters-in-law were leaving for New York and eventually for Europe and wanted to take three-year-old Adelaide Ann. "This is not a very gallant thing to say," he later explained, "but the Bridgers women wanted my child, you see, just a very natural loyalty. And so I moved in as the male appendage in a group of single women."[36] Within weeks, Adelaide Ann would have a new name, Elizabeth, just like Bab.

Jonathan's first few letters back to Raleigh in January 1930 suggest a man working to hold himself and everyone around him together. "Mrs. Bridgers went all to pieces nervously on the train coming up and I decided to get off here," he wrote to his mother from Washington. He and Adelaide Ann stayed with his brother Worth's family for several days while his mother-in-law recovered at the Powhatan Hotel. "It is very nice being here with Worth and Jo," Jonathan reflected, "but I don't have as much to occupy my mind here as I will in New York and I think that's the best thing for me to do."[37]

In New York, Daniels occupied himself briefly by working for Henry Luce's new magazine, *Fortune*, which published its first issue in February.

Then he won a Guggenheim fellowship for creative writing, and so off he went with his daughter and the three "Bridgers women" to Europe. (Josephus would have to send his gift for Jonathan's twenty-eighth birthday on April 26—a pocket-sized edition of the New Testament—to Paris.)[38]

The novel Daniels proposed in his Guggenheim application would have been quite different from *Clash of Angels*, although similar in its rejection of orthodoxy—in this case, the orthodoxy that historian Paul M. Gaston later named the "New South creed." That synthesis of economic and social philosophies had emerged from the post-Reconstruction South as a wedding of the region's desperate need for industrial development with whites' fealty to the antebellum social order and the Confederacy's "Lost Cause." Henry W. Grady, editor of the *Atlanta Constitution* in the 1880s, and other proponents of this first "New South" had vowed to lure Yankee capital southward and "northernize their region's economy while doing their best," in historian James C. Cobb's words, "to restore and then to uphold the most definitively 'southern' ideals of the Old South, especially its racial, political, and class hierarchies." Though a seemingly contradictory mix of plantation romance and hard-headed willingness to see the South's vast pool of cheap labor and abundant natural resources mercilessly exploited, the New South creed succeeded as a unifying faith. "Defeated and embittered, southern whites drew determination and hope from the New South's promises of an affluent golden age just ahead," Cobb explains. "They also found pride and reassurance in its celebration of a carefully constructed golden age" of past nobility and heroism.[39] As a result, "good children" of the South "grow up with an almost filial love for General Lee and 'Stonewall' Jackson," Daniels's letter to the Guggenheim Foundation affirmed. "Bad children grow up bored and irritated at the reiteration of the virtues of the days 'before the war.'"[40]

"Bad child" that he was, Jonathan wanted to take aim at the New South creed just as other Southern Renaissance writers were starting to do. Set on a South Carolina plantation, his proposed novel would focus on "a group of wealthy young Southerners, dissatisfied with the bright and shining South of today, who wish to recreate after their own ideas the perfect civilization of the traditional Old South." They would come into conflict with a present-day southern society that, "while quite willing to join in the erection of monuments to the heroic defenders of a noble order," is actually "glad enough that the noble order and all its heroes are dead forever." Meanwhile, the Old South vision of the young "reactionary revolutionists" had been a romantic fiction all along.[41] Daniels wanted to write about aristocrats because he considered them "decorous and comic." His goal was "to satirize the old notion

that the South was superior and should rebel from America." His protag-
onists were "seeking the recreation of a South that never existed."[42] Thus,
the novel would critique the Old and New South simultaneously, the former
for not living up to the plantation myth and the latter for being unromantic,
venal, and hypocritical.

Daniels's chosen themes were like those of Southern Renaissance writers
such as Wolfe, Faulkner, and Warren, but his talents as a fiction writer were
simply not comparable. Or perhaps his despair at Bab's death made writing
a comic novel an insurmountable challenge. For a year and a half, he wrote
and rewrote and completed drafts and submitted them to publishers. But
"the novel fell on its face," as he put it, "and I came back, of course very much
crushed by this—although I was having a big time in New York City."[43]

Back from Europe by the end of 1931, Daniels returned to *Fortune* magazine. He was making $100 a week "and that was damn good money, and I
was drinking a hell of a lot and playing around." He thought he "probably
would have gone to hell in a hack" if he had not met Lucy Cathcart, the
sister of his friend Noble Cathcart of the *Saturday Review*. A diary entry for
January 30, 1932, indicates that he and the Cathcarts met for dinner and
saw *The Animal Kingdom*, a "light play" by Philip Barry. After that, he and
Lucy sat up talking. "She told me about herself. She has long fits of unhap-
piness over apparently unimportant matters. One is just over that has lasted
a month. . . . After she left college without finishing her father did not speak
to her for a year. Now they only speak to each other when there is a third
person in the room."[44]

Perhaps it was their parallel struggles with grief and depression and their
fathers that drew Jonathan and Lucy together. One early love letter sur-
vives among Daniels's papers. "Oh, Lucy darling," he wrote, "I feel so damn
young. So damn and grand and young. I thought I was well on the way to
dry and stiff old age and now I've turned about-face and gone young. I wish
you were here now so I could tell you how lovely you are and that you don't
look human and I don't think you are and I'm glad you're not."[45] It was an
odd form of praise—"you don't look human"—almost reminiscent of a line
from Philip Barry's more famous (but later) play-cum-movie *The Philadelphia
Story*, in which a stiff and conventional character tells his fiancée, played by
Katharine Hepburn, that she is "like some marvelous, distant . . . queen, . . .
so cool and fine . . . like a statue." Unlike Hepburn's character, who decides
to call off the wedding, Lucy apparently welcomed Jonathan's worshipful
wooing. They were married in April and would go on to raise three daughters in addition to Jonathan and Bab's daughter Elizabeth.[46]

In the fall of 1932, Jonathan, Lucy, and six-year-old Elizabeth moved to Raleigh, where they would soon occupy a new house built in the corner of a Daniels family compound centered around Josephus and Addie Daniels's Wakestone. Josephus had been in a serious car accident and needed help with the *News and Observer*. Plus, with a new wife, Jonathan "wanted to escape [the] feminine hierarchy" of his Bridgers in-laws. In short, his destiny as a son, a husband, a father, and a newspaper editor—rather than a novelist— seemed to be calling. He definitely had misgivings, realizing "that I was coming back to a paper under a very dominant father." But he had "always counted on being editor," regardless of his literary ambitions, and national politics were about to give him the chance.[47] Franklin Roosevelt would soon be elected president. Although Josephus rather hoped his former assistant would make him Secretary of the Navy again for old times' sake, he was to become ambassador to Mexico from 1933 to 1941—a comfortable posting for a man in his seventies.

✦ ✦ ✦

THE ELDER DANIELS had had a long and, as even his admiring son Jonathan had to admit, not always noble career. His commitment to the Democratic Party had been absolute since at least 1880, when he quit school at the age of eighteen to edit the Wilson, North Carolina, *Advance*. Being a young Democrat in those days in North Carolina meant getting out from under the "Redeemer" generation of Democrats, those white men who had fought the Civil War and then fought to regain political control of the state and end Reconstruction. Such men had to be venerated for their wartime heroics and resistance to federal occupation. Yet what had they done lately to move the South forward? By the 1880s, eager young men like Josephus wanted PROGRESS. They could hardly say so directly, but it had occurred to them that their fathers' failure to win the war had left them with a host of problems. The South was poor and would grow poorer still as the profitability of agriculture declined in the 1880s and 1890s. Yet the older generation of Democrats had done far too little to promote industry and public education, which the younger generation saw as the South's only hope. Gathering with other like-minded men, all under thirty, who founded the Watauga Club in Raleigh in 1884, Josephus Daniels embraced a vision of a modern, industrialized South that, in his case, went beyond New South boosterism to advocate a host of progressive reforms. But, when an even more reform-minded alliance between Populists and Republicans threatened their party's rule, Daniels and his fellow North Carolina Democrats determined that one "reform" mattered to them more than any other: eliminating blacks from the electorate.[48]

In the distinctive case of North Carolina, the discontent among farmers that gave birth to the new People's Party or "Populists" throughout the South and Midwest also led to a "fusion" government. Recognizing from the 1892 election results that, together, the Populist and Republican candidates had achieved a majority, leaders of the two parties hashed out an agreement to cooperate in selecting candidates for state offices in 1894. These fusion candidates stunned the state's Democratic leadership by gaining control of both houses of the General Assembly. Then they stunned the Democrats still further by enacting numerous reforms, raising taxes on corporations and railroads, lowering interest rates for individual borrowers, and increasing state spending on schools and public services. Fusionist electoral reforms, including simplified ballots and fairer registration procedures, ensured that eligible black men would be able to vote in the next election in 1896, as a startling 85 percent of the state's black electorate did, securing the governor's seat for white Republican Daniel Russell. In the General Assembly, Democrats won only 45 of 169 seats in 1896, with eleven seats going to black Republicans. On the local level, black men were elected to dozens of offices, particularly in black-majority counties in the eastern part of the state.[49]

Although he agreed in principle with many fusion policies and energetically supported Populist-Democrat William Jennings Bryan on the national stage in 1896, Josephus Daniels considered North Carolina's new political alliance unnatural. Affiliated with the party of the elite, white Republicans who made common cause with Populists must surely be hypocrites, while blacks, in his view, simply did not belong in politics. In the *News and Observer*, he reduced the 1896 election to a single question: "Whether North Carolina is to be governed during the coming years by the white man or the black man and his tools."[50] Then, when voters gave the wrong answer, Josephus stepped up his rhetoric, becoming a central figure in North Carolina's infamous white supremacy campaign of 1898.

For months prior to the 1898 election, the *News and Observer* attacked fusion policies and politicians in an effort to help the Democrats regain control. Crude cartoons aggravated the assault and were one of Daniels's cleverest innovations. Democratic governor Elias Carr had discovered young cartoonist Norman E. Jennett back in 1895, when he was scratching images into woodblocks with a pocket knife to print in the tiny *Sampson Democrat*. Josephus promptly hired him in time to use his cartoons to some effect in the

1896 campaign. Then, pausing only long enough to allow Addie Daniels to stuff the boy's pockets with biscuits, he put Jennett on a train for New York, where he had been accepted at art school. In 1898, Josephus called him back and resumed his political tutelage. "He devoured the editorial page to see what I was writing about." Then he would draw a sketch and "we would decide together what particular Republican or Populist deserved to be hit over the head that day," Josephus recalled.[51]

As the 1898 campaign progressed, Daniels and Jennett hit not only at politicians but also at the heart of white fears and prejudices. On the front page of a late September issue, "The Vampire That Hovers over North Carolina" was a bat-winged black caricature, four column-widths wide, with claws reaching for a half dozen helpless white citizens. Across its wings were emblazoned the words "Negro rule." An October cartoon was subtler, though not by much. It showed a demurely dressed white woman being manhandled by apelike black men gathered at the window of a black postmaster—the same patronage job Josephus Daniels's widowed mother had once held, now given to a black man at the expense of white women's security, both physical and economic.[52]

The need to "protect white womanhood" was the clarion call of the North Carolina white supremacy campaign, just as it had become the rationale for racist extremism throughout the region by the 1890s. Lynching had a long history in the pre–Civil War South, as in the frontier West, involving more white than black victims and attributable at least in part to the limited reach of the criminal justice system, as well as an overall culture of violence. After emancipation, however, as vigilante justice became less common elsewhere in the country, lynching in the South took on a distinctly racial character and purpose. And it became more horrific. Mobs grew larger and invented new forms of torture for their now almost exclusively black victims. They also made lynching a spectacle, bleeding and burning their human prey slowly to prolong the excitement and displaying their victims' charred and mutilated bodies for all to see. To justify the violence, lynchers and their apologists turned to the age-old argument that men had to be able to protect their wives and daughters. It was the threat of the black beast rapist that had called down such cleansing fires, white southerners argued. Yet, analyzing whites' own newspaper coverage, contemporary black critic Ida B. Wells showed that rape or attempted rape or the vague charge of "assault" on a white woman was even *alleged* in less than a third of cases—a figure that more than a century of subsequent scholarship has lowered still further. White men lynched black men more often on charges of murder (of a white person) than on charges of actual or attempted sexual assault. They also lynched for a variety of other reasons, including disputes over money, black participation in politics, and breaches of everyday racial etiquette—that is, when blacks got "uppity" instead of acting poor (but happy and carefree), meek, and deferential. In short, by the late nineteenth century, lynching had less and less to do with any form of justice, even vigilante, and became instead a form of terrorism, intended to keep all black southerners fearful and submissive.[53]

No matter what the reality, whites' rhetorical justification for lynching was *always* the need to protect white womanhood. It was a powerful lie that had the added advantage of keeping white women frightened enough to want to defer to white men. Made to feel vulnerable, they understood, in historian Jacquelyn Dowd Hall's words, that their "right to protection presupposed their obligation to obey."[54]

It would take decades for a small minority of white southern women who saw through the lie to find an effective means to revolt against such "chivalry," founding the Association of Southern Women for the Prevention of Lynching in 1930. Meanwhile, one of the most prominent woman's rights advocates in the late nineteenth-century South not only embraced the rape-lynch mythology but infamously helped to advance it by insisting that the circle of white men's protection should extend to all white women, regardless of class. Rebecca Latimer Felton was a prominent speaker for the Woman's Christian Temperance Union. In addition to her warnings about the dangers of alcohol, one of her stock speeches was "Woman on the Farm," in which she extolled white women's material as well as moral contributions to the family and lamented white men's failure to understand that they would "never raise a more important crop than their children." In August 1897, Felton added two new points to this standard speech. One, a call for improved access to educational facilities for white women, including admission to the University of Georgia, went virtually unnoticed. The other struck the South's opinion makers like lightning. Having scolded southern white men for failing to "put a sheltering arm about innocence and virtue," Felton concluded hyperbolically that if "it needs lynching to protect woman's dearest possession from the ravening human beasts—then I say lynch, a thousand times a week, if necessary."[55]

"'Lynch,' Says Mrs. Felton," was the *Atlanta Constitution*'s headline the next day.[56] Felton's bombast, which she explained as a reaction to news coverage of several lynchings of black men accused of raping white women, became news in itself, resounding in the white South's echo chamber of racial and sexual fears. Her most incendiary lines were repeated so often that it took hardly any effort for a Wilmington, North Carolina, editor to remember and reprint her speech a year later in the midst of the 1898 white supremacy campaign. Alongside Jennett's cartoons, the repetition of Felton's words was the crudest but also one of the most potent elements of a well-orchestrated political effort.

Meeting in March 1898, Josephus Daniels, future North Carolina senator Furnifold McLendel Simmons, and future governor Charles B. Aycock had determined to make "home protection" their theme. Simmons organized a speakers bureau, and Democratic Party rallies were scenes of impassioned pleading for white men to do their duty to their womenfolk by voting for the party of "White Government." Any white man who had defected to the Populists in 1894 or 1896 was assured that his disloyalty and pandering to black aspirations had "opened the gates of hell for some distant white woman" who had been raped or threatened.[57] Her supposed assailant, in this elaborate political fantasy, was a black man who had grown drunk on talk of political equality and thought he deserved social and sexual equality too and tried by force to take it. "Protect Us," the Democrats' parade floats demanded, speaking for the women who rode on them—young, attractive, white women dressed in flowing white gowns to emphasize their purity. White women and girls were active participants as well as symbols in the 1898 campaign, and Simmons made sure their presence was felt in rallies across the state.

And then there were the newspapers. For months, Josephus Daniels's *News and Observer* and other Democratic papers published false accounts of "Negro atrocities" on a near-daily basis, manufacturing a rape scare although a later historian's analysis of the state's own crime statistics confirms that there was certainly no rape epidemic—indeed, there was "no appreciable increase in either rapes or 'assaults with intent to rape' in either 1897 or 1898."[58] Because Daniels was the state's most prominent editor, the accumulation of his attacks made an enormous impact. Ultimately, though, it was the white *Wilmington Messenger*'s revival of Felton's speech that proved most incendiary. The repetition of Felton's words called forth a bold rebuttal from black Wilmington editor Alexander Manly, the effect of which was to throw gasoline on the fire that the white supremacy campaign had started.

On August 18, 1898, Manly, the handsome, "black" (actually mixed-race) owner of the Wilmington-based *Daily Record*, published an unsigned editorial that countered Felton largely by agreeing with her, up to a point. "Mrs. Felton begins well for she admits that education will better protect the girls on the farm from the assaulter," the editorial averred. "This we admit and it should not be confined to the white any more than to the colored girls." Respectable African Americans were just as committed to home protection as respectable whites, and "if the papers and speakers of the other race would condemn the commission of the crime because it is crime and not try to make it appear that the Negroes were the only criminals, they would find their strongest allies in the intelligent Negroes themselves." But not all whites were respectable. "We suggest that the whites guard their women more closely, as Mrs. Felton says," the editorial went on, chiding white men. "You leave your goods out of doors and then complain because they are taken away." White men's neglect encouraged white women to look elsewhere. Manly's most provocative assertion was that white women "are not any more particular in the matter of clandestine meetings with colored men than are the white men with colored women. Meetings of this kind go on for some time until the woman's infatuation, or the man's boldness, bring attention to them, and the man is lynched for rape." Manly, who was himself the acknowledged son of an antebellum North Carolina governor and his slave, took this dangerous argument still further. "Every Negro lynched is called a 'big burly, black brute,'" he wrote, "when in fact many of those who have thus been dealt with had white men for their fathers, and were not only not 'black' and 'burly' but were sufficiently attractive for white girls of culture and refinement to fall in love with them as is very well known to all."[59]

That lynching covered up consensual relationships between black men and white women was something Ida B. Wells had suggested before. She had called out "the old thread bare lie that Negro men rape white women" in an editorial in 1892—only to be banished from her Memphis home, her press destroyed while she was luckily away, and her life threatened.[60] The same would be true for Manly after his editorial was quickly picked up and reprinted in white North Carolina newspapers. The *Wilmington Messenger* printed it virtually every day until the election on November 8, in which the Democrats regained the majority in the legislature.

The explosion came two days later, on November 10. First, white men under the leadership of Alfred Moore Waddell, a Democrat and aging former congressman, burned down the building that housed Manly's *Daily Record* offices. Then, having failed to catch Manly himself, Waddell's men marched on a prosperous black neighborhood, killing an unknown number of residents. They also forced some of the city's elected leaders—including a white Republican mayor and a number of aldermen—to resign, and Waddell himself became mayor. Within a month, 1,400 black citizens had fled, many banished at gunpoint. Although often described as the Wilmington "riot," it was actually a massacre, a pogrom, a coup d'etat. "We have taken a city," one white minister boasted from the pulpit. "To God be the praise."[61]

Josephus Daniels certainly accepted no blame. "If any reader is inclined to condemn the people of Wilmington for resolving to expel Manly from the city," the *News and Observer* chastised, "let him reread the libel upon the white women of the state that appeared in the *Daily Record*."[62] Over the next few years, Josephus worked alongside the victorious Democrats to amend the state constitution to disfranchise black voters. Since 1870 the Fifteenth Amendment had made it impossible to deny citizens the right to vote on the basis of "race, color, or previous condition of servitude." But, like those in other southern states, North Carolina's Democrats found other means, including poll taxes and literacy tests. Josephus himself traveled to Louisiana to learn about the efficacy of that state's "grandfather clause." Under such a law, illiterate white voters could be exempted from the literacy requirement if one of their ancestors had voted before January 1, 1867 — the year black men had first gained the right to vote under Congressional Reconstruction. With a large population of poorly educated white farmers and mill hands, North Carolina was the kind of southern state where white support for the disfranchisement of black voters depended on this crucial exemption. North Carolinians got it, along with other discriminatory provisions, in an amendment to the state constitution that took effect in 1902. George Henry White, who represented the state's Second Congressional District from 1897 to 1901 (and who was also a frequent target of Josephus Daniels's poison pen), would be not only North Carolina's but also the South's last black congressman for almost seventy years.[63]

Late in life, Josephus Daniels would admit that the *News and Observer* had been "cruel in its flagellations" during the white supremacy campaign, "too cruel" given "the perspective of time."[64] But he never doubted that the elimination of black voters had been necessary. To his way of thinking, the "race question" stood in the way of badly needed reforms. Never mind that some of the reforms he wanted had actually been attempted when the fusionists were in charge. And never mind that the disfranchisement of black voters and solidification of one-party rule had paved the way for elite control and the perpetuation of the "feudal," bordering on "fascist," system of racial capitalism that Franklin Roosevelt would denounce in 1938. (It is noteworthy, in light of his long association with Daniels, that Roosevelt said specifically that southerners needed representatives "whose minds are cast in the 1938 mold and not in the 1898 mold.")[65]

Whatever the platform, a black-white coalition was, to Josephus Daniels's mind, simply unnatural. And, in truth, it was shaky: how could it be otherwise in such an overwhelmingly racist and class-stratified society, where a truly interracial and egalitarian political culture could hardly be expected to spring to life fully formed?[66]

White elites' worldview, on the other hand, was rooted in centuries-old practices of mastery over the workforce—practices that were commonplace in a region that was just one generation removed from slavery when business leaders and politicians began their "New South" race to industrialize. "Textile mill owners were key supporters of the Democratic Party in North Carolina," explains historian Robert Korstad, "and their attitudes and policies toward their workers manifested white supremacy's deep-seated class assumptions most starkly." Especially in textiles but also in tobacco and other industries, bosses reserved all skilled and semiskilled jobs for white people, relegating blacks to the lowest-paid and least desirable positions. But white southern industrial workers could count on "few other spoils of the new order." Their wages were low, requiring women and children to work alongside their men ("and mill owners adamantly opposed child labor laws," Korstad points out).[67] Yet organizing to demand higher wages and better working conditions was almost unthinkable, not only because industrialists and their political allies suppressed union sentiment in every possible way but also because the vast numbers of poor farm people who could be brought in to take over striking workers' jobs meant that mill hands had very little bargaining power. Black workers were in an even more powerless position both on farms and in factories. Yet the option to replace white workers with black ones was industrialists' ultimate ace in the hole.

This was the social order that Josephus Daniels's commitment to white supremacy and Democratic Party rule resulted in, one that became entrenched by the turn of the twentieth century and was only weakly and fitfully challenged until the New Deal. Josephus frequently railed against plutocrats but not against the divide-and-conquer strategies of racial capitalism. After disfranchisement, he, like many leading white southerners, saw the "race question" as settled, something he "never discussed."[68]

HOW SURPRISING, THEN, that his son Jonathan should denounce the "shocking verdict" of death to alleged black rapists in the Scottsboro case in one of his first editorials after taking the helm of the *News and Observer* in the spring of 1933. Over the next few weeks, Jonathan also praised sociologist Arthur F. Raper's unflinching new study, *The Tragedy of Lynching*, and lamented black poverty and the injustices blacks faced in southern courts. "I hope that I am not making your paper too much of a colored boy's friend," he wrote to his father in July, less than three months after Josephus and Addie Daniels departed for Mexico in grand style on April 11.[69] Josephus did not object to Jonathan's editorials, but he did feel some concern as he watched his son make a name for himself as a liberal. Indeed, it was primarily as a (white) "Southern liberal" (the S was always capitalized, and one's self-consciousness as a southerner was key, while the whiteness was taken for granted) that Jonathan Daniels would come to be known from the early 1930s on, and this is also how he has been remembered by historians.

White southern liberals have long attracted historians' attention because they seem so anomalous. How were a handful of white men and women able to overcome prejudice and societal pressures to advocate egalitarian views on race and class issues? And to what extent did they, really? Prior to World War II, to be a white southern liberal was to suggest that the South (and the nation) ought to do a better job of upholding the "equal" side of the "separate but equal" principle. The "liberal" viewpoint among whites was that blacks ought to get justice in the courts and more educational and economic opportunities on their own side of the color line. Liberals opposed lynching but struggled with the question of whether Congress ought to pass a law to make it a federal offense.[70] It was true that state officials almost never prosecuted anyone for lynching. In Georgia, for example, 441 blacks and 19 whites were lynched between 1880 and 1930, yet the state's first successful prosecution of lynchers came only in 1926—in a case where the victim was white.[71] It was also true that proponents, working mainly on behalf of the NAACP, had put some real teeth into the legislation proposed in the 1920s and again in the 1930s by including the possibility of a fine or prison time for any law enforcement official found to have been negligent in protecting those who were already in custody from mob violence.

But how would white southerners react to the presence of federal investigators in their communities? Even as their own ideas about states' rights changed over time in defense of the New Deal, most white southern liberals believed that a significant number, if not the majority, of their fellow white southerners were unreconstructed rebels who would simply prove defiant. "Outside" pressures such as a federal antilynching law would be ineffective at best, they argued. Better to be patient and allow educated white southerners like themselves to promote gradual changes in the "folkways" of their people.

Only in 1935 would white southern liberals' most important organization, the sixteen-year-old Commission on Interracial Cooperation, first support a federal antilynching bill, which failed to survive a Senate filibuster. And only during and after World War II would any but the most "radical" white southerners—mostly labor activists, especially Communist Party members—publicly insist that segregation had to be eliminated. By the early 1940s, white southern liberals would feel increasing pressure to respond to the moral challenges of leftists and of blacks themselves, whose protests against job discrimination and other injustices were becoming more persistent. In this changing political environment, support for integration would become the new litmus test for white southerners' "liberalism," and the difficult new questions would have to do with how much and how fast.

Before World War II, white southern liberals were less publicly conflicted. They were also more *economic* in focus—an aspect of white southern liberalism that deserves careful analysis. As David L. Carlton and Peter A. Coclanis argue in an insightful essay, the historical scholarship on white southern liberals has been somewhat distorted by the projection of post-1960s thinking onto the past. "The major literature . . . generally takes commitment to an integrated society as the basic criterion for assessing liberal credentials," they write. But southern liberalism initially "organized itself not around *race* but around *region*." What mattered most was not individuals' racial views, which varied, but their deep-seated identification with and commitment to solving the problems of the *South*.[72]

Influenced by Chapel Hill "Regionalist" social scientists such as Howard W. Odum and Rupert B. Vance, Depression-era "regionalist liberals" understood that the problems of the South were many but pointed to a single main source: region-wide economic underdevelopment that had grown steadily worse, at least compared with the North, since the Civil War. Vance argued persuasively in *Human Geography of the South* (1932) that the eleven states of the former Confederacy plus Oklahoma and Kentucky suffered from a disadvantaged "colonial" economy comparable to those of other peripheral regions that produced goods for a metropolitan core. He and especially Odum endorsed regional planning and a scientific approach to designing public policies that could address the South's economic, educational, and public health needs. As historian Bruce J. Schulman writes, "It was Odum who established the portrait of the South as a land rich in resources, yet impoverished in its economic and institutional development." His sociological analysis, worked out over more than a decade and culminating in *Southern Regions of the United States* (1936), made him the "intellectual mentor" of a generation of young southern liberals who shared his faith in planned regional development, as well as his desire to see the South fully reintegrated into the national mainstream.[73]

Scientifically planned development would benefit both blacks and whites, regionalist liberals argued, and some black intellectuals, most notably Fisk University sociologist Charles S. Johnson, endorsed regionalist liberalism because of this potential. Still, whites who emphasized region over race could have both valid and less-than-admirable reasons for lumping black and white southerners' problems together rather than splitting them along race lines. On the one hand, liberals had a better chance of avoiding other white southerners' prejudices if they wrote in even-handed terms that tried to incorporate African Americans without drawing attention to the fact that, as a group, blacks most needed the rising tide that was supposed to lift all boats. On the other hand, there was the underdiscussed reality that blacks consistently occupied the least seaworthy craft. Regionalist liberals' almost reflexive even-handedness—their tendency to write as if black and white southerners were all in the same boat—could hide their ignorance of or lack of commitment to blacks' true needs and goals.

Even beyond this suspect tendency to obscure black and white southern-ers' distinctive problems by focusing on their collective problems, regionalist liberalism "harbored some striking tensions," as Carlton and Coclanis show. On the left were Popular Front liberals "with roots in rural insurgency, orga-nized labor, and radical ideological perspectives [that] stressed a class-based community of interest among the black and white poor." On the right, "a whiggish, old-progressive strain saw insurgency as the enemy of progress." They placed their hopes in the leadership of an elite, educated class.[74]

Jonathan Daniels stood somewhere in the middle of the regionalist liberal pack. He was an elite and felt most comfortable with fellow intellectuals like *Richmond Times-Dispatch* editor Virginius Dabney—who proved a prime example of an erstwhile liberal who failed the litmus test of integrationism and became a self-styled "conservative" by the late 1940s.[75] But Daniels also had left-leaning impulses, much like his Populist-leaning father. Biographer Charles W. Eagles attributes much of the liberal character of Jonathan's thought to the influence of Josephus, arguing that the son "inherited much of his democratic philosophy but with one major difference: for the younger man democracy increasingly involved blacks, whereas for his father it had usually been limited to whites only."[76]

Eagles's assessment is correct but understates the impact of witnessing blacks' own efforts to advance, as well as the leftward pull of the Popular

Regionalist sociologist Howard W. Odum on the University of North Carolina campus in 1925. Portrait Collection #P0002, North Carolina Collection Photographic Archives, Wilson Library, University of North Carolina at Chapel Hill.

Front. Even more heavily influenced by the Regionalist social scientists from his beloved UNC, Daniels would maintain his emphasis on the need for economic development in the South into the 1960s and beyond.

Born in 1902, the same year North Carolina's new disfranchisement amendment took effect, Jonathan had the advantage of growing up in a very different political and interpersonal environment than his father. Rather than struggling to make ends meet and participating in the heated political battles of the post-Reconstruction decades, he saw Addie Daniels's back-porch charity to black supplicants and Josephus Daniels's cordial relationship with their Raleigh next-door neighbor, Wesley Hoover. Hoover was a mixed-race saloonkeeper whom Josephus "respected," despite their differing views on alcohol, and whom he would give "every courtesy in the world," Jonathan recalled, "except, of course, he could never call him 'Mr.'"[77] Jonathan also got more formal education and a wider experience of the world than Josephus did as a boy, including a front-row seat at a 1919 race riot in Washington, D.C.

By 1926, when Jonathan (again in Washington as a correspondent for the *News and Observer*) witnessed a major Ku Klux Klan rally, he could remark with dispassionate cynicism on the same class and gender dynamics among white southerners that Josephus and his cronies had exploited in the 1898 white supremacy campaign. "The poor Kluckers are a sad looking lot," he wrote in a letter to Bab. "The big boys are all pretty bright looking men, the exploiters, but the poor devils in the plain white uniforms with no gold, red and green trimmings are about as dumb looking and pathetic as you would see anywhere in the world. They are the suckers." Jonathan recognized that the "poor privates" were not actually the poorest of white southerners but instead "looked like small storekeepers and their wives. Plain, honest, poor people" for whom the Klan gave "the illusion . . . that they really are God's chosen, Christian people." Never one to question his prerogative to evaluate and comment on female beauty, Jonathan assured Bab that "the women were the worst." Most "were great breasted, fat women who looked like sour faced hippopotami in nurses' uniforms. They were all serious faced, not a sense of humor in the lot."[78]

Bab was, of course, a very different kind of southern woman—a New Woman who was much more in tune with the female obstetrician she had chosen and the cosmopolitan crowd of her playwright sister than with the traditionally minded women of the Klan. In fact, she had just been to see a movie, that still-questionable medium of "flaming youth" in the 1920s. "I'm sorry that the movie menu was not the best," Jonathan consoled in the very next line of his letter. "But you aren't really country yet" (she was away in the western North Carolina mountains, convalescing from Adelaide Ann's birth) "or you wouldn't be so particular about what you see."[79]

As Jonathan's smooth segue from the Klan to the movies from women who were "country" to one who was not—indicates, his moderate racial views fit into his larger package of "modern" sensibilities. But the fit was far from obvious or automatic. It would take him a lot longer to consistently apply his "naturally . . . underdog-supporting" and often iconoclastic ways of think-ing to the problems that blacks and other minorities faced than to problems that he himself felt more directly: Prohibition, restrictive moral standards, religious orthodoxy, the political power wielded by the "exploiters" who mo-bilized the "suckers" among whites.[80]

By the late 1930s, Daniels's perspective would have broadened consider-ably, thanks mostly to the influence of more open-minded white southern liberals like his friend W. T. Couch, the director of the University of North Carolina Press. One expanding episode that also shows the ripple effect of a growing left took place in 1936. Communist Party vice presidential candi-date James W. Ford was in Durham on a campaign stop, and Chapel Hill literature professor Eston Everett Ericson not only attended the rally but also joined Ford for dinner. The next day, the *News and Observer*'s managing editor Frank Smethurst lambasted Ericson for violating southern racial etiquette. Segregation at the dinner table was sacrosanct, and James W. Ford was black. Although he need not have said anything, a few days later Jonathan made a point of agreeing with Smethurst. White southerners, he wrote, "believe, quite apart from prejudice, that the public welfare will best be served by preserving racial integrity and that the best way to preserve racial integrity is to keep the races wholly apart in their social relationships." Ericson should have known that his action "would subject the University to unpleasant criticism"—as indeed it did, after the *News and Observer* complained about it.[81]

In the view of his friend Couch, Jonathan had "gone haywire." "If you really believe it hurts anybody for a white man to eat with a Negro, why not establish an inquisition and fire all the members of the faculty who have eaten with Negroes, or who have condoned any association other than a menial one?" Couch demanded in a "Personal and Confidential" letter. "And why not extend this inquisition to Duke? And to the rest of North Carolina and the South?"[82] Couch's reference to Duke may have carried particular meaning for Jonathan. It certainly would have for Josephus, who reminded his son of how he himself had unwisely "let an incident grow into an issue" thirty years earlier when he excoriated John Spencer Bassett, a professor at Duke (then called Trinity College), for praising Booker T. Washington too highly.[83]

Jonathan did not back down in public, although he did concede in a second editorial that "one man's foolishness, even one professor's foolishness in a delicate matter, is hardly worth prolonged discussion" (much less the dismissal from the university that some who had read his first editorial were advocating).[84] To private critics like Oswald Garrison Villard, a northern civil rights advocate and the editor of the *Nation*, Daniels was somewhat more apologetic.[85] To Couch, he bared his white southern liberal soul—if, in fact, a "liberal" was what he was. "Dear Couch," he wrote, "Of course, it is no fun being in disagreement with people, yourself included, with whom in general I see eye to eye. It would be much simpler and much more comfortable to find the pattern of thinking under this word 'liberal' and wear it always like a cloak or a chain. But I'm not a liberal. I hope you're not. You're W. T. Couch and I'm Jonathan Daniels and while our philosophies in general may conform to one general pattern or another, it would be a pity if our convictions were always prints from the same plate."

His individuality asserted, Daniels proceeded to sketch the pattern on the "plate" of white southern liberalism that his words and deeds and those of others like him had by this time etched rather clearly. "I hold to the faith that the happiness of the South, white and black, will best be preserved by a stern insistence upon the separation of the races," he wrote. "I am as angry as you are at the unjust treatment of the Negro. While I approve of separate schools, I hate the discrimination that has been made in distinction's name. I believe I have shown that I am anxious to improve the condition of the Negro in every particular. But I honestly believe . . . that the color line should be sternly drawn." Daniels explained that he set down his philosophy "in order that if it be considered treason to liberalism, my confession may be entered." But it was far from treason to white southern liberalism as it existed even in the middle to late 1930s. The question was whether Jonathan would be among those like Couch who were beginning to etch a new pattern and a new "plate"—the liberalism of the 1940s and beyond.

This is where Daniels's modernism in other respects—in fact, his very desire to *be* modern—mattered a great deal. "Eating with a man of whatever color is so little a thing," he mused in his letter to Couch. "But you know as well as I do that throughout the history of the illogical creature called man eating has been invested with a symbolical quality which even we so-called free moderns do not wholly escape."[86] This was the sticking point: how was a "so-called free modern"—a self-conscious modern who had once gone so far as to publish a book like *Clash of Angels*—to navigate between old and new ideas about race? The Ericson affair in 1936 was one spur to Daniels's thinking on that question. His 1937 travels would be another.[87]

Of course, the very inspiration for Daniels's trip depended on the national reputation as a liberal that he had been cultivating. This reputation had as much to do with his regionalist thinking and his support for labor unions and Franklin Roosevelt as it did with his racial views, although highly visible statements of his belief in equal justice, such as a letter to the *Nation* that he wrote in January 1934, did not hurt. This was the Jonathan Daniels whom New York editor Harold Strauss knew, the one who, by early 1937, had been writing liberal-minded editorials, essays, and book reviews about the South for years.

The only problem was that, once Jonathan started thinking about writing a book, he could draw on much closer contacts in the publishing world than Strauss. In the spring of 1937, he and Lucy made a trip to New York to talk business. Over lunch with his old friend Amy Loveman, George Stevens of the *Saturday Review of Literature*, and James Putnam, an editor at Macmillan, the book that Daniels had started to contemplate got quite a bit bigger. No longer a history of Tennessee, this was to be a contemporary story of the entire region. Jonathan left the job of working out a contract to his literary agent and returned to Raleigh—only to be invited to lunch with Edward Aswell, a Harper's editor who was barnstorming the South in hopes of finding another *Gone with the Wind*. "Of course all this is confidential," he wrote to his father, detailing the terms of his Macmillan contract, which included a $1,000 advance. But "it made me feel good to have both [Harper's and Macmillan] wanting me."[88] Lucy could see it, too. "The very idea" of writing another book had "been like a tonic" for Jonathan, she wrote to her in-laws. "I wish you could see him with his books and maps planning his tour." He was as excited as "a little boy with his first set of trains."[89]

In his excitement, Jonathan wrote to Josephus for suggestions about "the interesting things . . . you think I ought to see" and "the names of people . . . who would help me to see what I ought." He also laid out his itinerary for his father: "I am planning to leave here shortly after the first of May and follow the main street of the new industrial South from Greensboro to Charlotte, Spartanburg and Greenville; then turn to the right and cut through the Great Smoky Mountains National Park to Knoxville; then . . . Chattanooga and from Chattanooga by Scottsboro, Alabama, through the Tennessee Valley to Memphis; from Memphis through the Marked Tree area where the tenant farmers union was active and on to Little Rock and Hot Springs."[90] In Hot Springs, Arkansas, the westernmost point of his journey, Daniels would spend a few days at a Southern Newspaper Publishers Association meeting before heading south through Mississippi to New Orleans. Then he would race along the Gulf Coast to Mobile and up through Montgomery and Birmingham to Atlanta. Finally, he would swing through central Georgia and down the west coast of Florida, then back up the East Coast by way of Savannah and Charleston and on home to Raleigh. Altogether, he thought the trip would take six or eight weeks, and he had been unable to persuade Lucy, who was busy with family and other obligations, to come along.

Perhaps it was anticipating the solitude of so much time on the road that put Jonathan in a philosophical mood. "I grow more and more excited as the day of my departure on my journey approaches," he wrote to his parents on April 28. "Maybe I'll catch my lost youth," he joked, having turned thirty-five two days before. "At any rate I expect to see for the first time [a] South that I've been talking about very cockily for a long time. And the more I plan, the more I discover that must be seen."[91]

Later, Daniels would explain his trip as part of his very job as a journalist. "There has grown up a cynicism among newspapermen that the man who writes editorials is generally a fellow grown too fat or too old, too slow or too dull to go out and get the news," he wrote in 1940. But he had become an

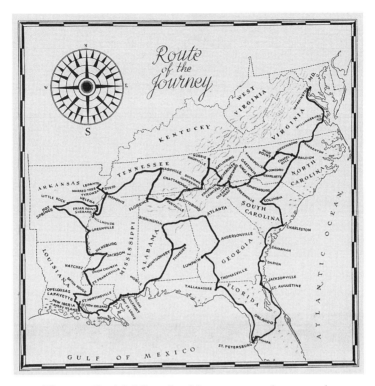

The route Daniels followed on his tour appeared on a map in
A Southerner Discovers the South. Jonathan Daniels Papers,
#3466, Southern Historical Collection, Wilson Library,
University of North Carolina at Chapel Hill.

editor when he was "young enough to be damned if I was going to sit behind a desk and grow sonorous and stout. . . . I had big feet and I let them take me places. . . . I put my hat on my head, and went out." He "was editor still," but doing "what I think is the most important work an editor can do, trying hard—and it is hard—to understand the things and the people he is paid to explain to his readers. It may be a trade secret," Daniels confided, "but it is easier for an editor to explain things to you in high moral certainty than it is for him to understand those things himself." A deeper understanding made it "a good deal harder" to write with "certainty, neatly and clearly." But traveling and talking to people enabled him "to write about the South with more satisfaction to myself and maybe more sense for my readers."[92] And so, on Wednesday, May 5, 1937, Jonathan Daniels put his hat on his head and went out.

CHAPTER TWO

This Division between Faith in Democracy and Power Descending from Authority

✦

FROM RALEIGH TO

LOOKOUT MOUNTAIN, TENNESSEE

LEAVING HOME AT 9:37 in the morning, Jonathan Daniels drove through the familiar streets of Raleigh, only to see on Johnson Street the unfamiliar sight—an "omen, good or ill"—of a black man with a wooden leg mowing a lawn. He followed his well-beaten path to Chapel Hill, where he discovered he had lost the key to his Plymouth's spare tire. He drove on to Burlington, twenty-eight miles farther along N.C. State Highway 54, and then stopped to find a mechanic to cut him a new one. As he waited, Daniels noticed some irises growing in a field across the street from a textile mill. The flowers were almost as blue as the red-brick mill's blue-painted windows—painted, he thought ironically, "to keep out the shadow-making sun and protect the quality of the superior synthetic light within." Red brick and blue paint were the colors of the mill country, he mused, especially during the night shifts when "the lighted blue windows make one of the too few additions to beauty in the South which industry can claim."[1]

Although he would squeeze both a book chapter and a *Virginia Quarterly Review* article out of the "Gold Avenue" of the textile industry in the Piedmont, Daniels allotted only a single day of his trip for the mill towns of North and South Carolina. As a newspaperman and North Carolina native, he already knew what he would see in Burlington and along U.S. Route 29 south from Greensboro. He had expressed his sympathies for white southern industrial workers before, notably during the General Textile Strike of 1934 when his calls for "reason and reasonableness" earned him bitter criticism from "the propertied people of the State."[2] He would write sympathetically of mill workers again in *A Southerner Discovers the South*. But the first part of his travels had a different emphasis. From Raleigh to Little Rock, he would devote most of his attention to examining what he came to think of as "the dark problem of the little man on the land."[3]

Even from the highway, Daniels could see evidence of the hunger and hopelessness on southern farms. Farming had been a mostly losing proposition in the South for decades, but the hard times of the Great Depression were especially, stunningly cruel. When Franklin Roosevelt spoke, in his second inaugural address, of "one-third of a nation ill-housed, ill-clad, ill-nourished," he would have had to adjust his percentage significantly upward if he had been referring to the South alone. Although most Americans lived in urban areas by the 1930s, two-thirds of the South's population was rural, and most of that rural population was poor. "Even in 'prosperous' 1929 southern farm people received an average gross income of only $186 a year compared with $528 for farmers elsewhere," a 1938 government report lamented. "Out of that $186 southern farmers had to pay all their operating expenses—tools, fertilizer, seed, taxes and interest on debt—so that only a fraction of that sum was left for the purchase of food, clothes, and the decencies of life. It is hardly surprising, therefore, that such ordinary items as automobiles, radios, and books are relatively rare."

This was the rural South's appallingly low *average*. Conditions were worse for the 53 percent of the region's farm families who were tenants or sharecroppers. Many thousands of them were "living in poverty comparable to that of the poorest peasants in Europe." The 1938 report found that "the average tenant family received an income of only $73 per person for a year's work. Earnings of sharecroppers ranged from $38 to $87 per person, and an income of $38 annually means only a little more than 10 cents a day."[4]

Jonathan Daniels was well aware of the poverty of southern farmers. He had read studies like Arthur Raper's *Preface to Peasantry* and Howard Odum's *Southern Regions of the United States*, both of which had been published in 1936 by his friend W. T. Couch at the University of North Carolina Press.[5] He had also read newspaper accounts of the mass evictions of sharecroppers taking place in the Arkansas-Mississippi Delta and other plantation areas. Thousands of cotton farmers had been thrown off their rented or sharecropped land as a result of fundamental economic and technological changes and the disruptive effects of New Deal policies.[6] Small farms were being consolidated into large-scale and, increasingly, mechanized operations. The question was, what should be done to ease the pain of this transition?

The very nature and impact of New Deal programs were also in question. What would the New Deal mean for the South? One look at the landscape, especially in the vast area where the Tennessee Valley Authority (TVA) was active, made it clear that the New Deal was going to be transformative. But in what ways and to whose benefit? The more Daniels thought about and planned for his trip, the more he realized how complicated it all was. The best he could do was to bear witness. He could try to render accurately the people and issues he was being paid (paid more than ten times a sharecroppers' annual earnings, just in his advance from Macmillan) to explain to his readers.

✦ ✦ ✦

ON HIS FIRST-DAY DRIVE down "Gold Avenue," Daniels did make a few small efforts to "discover" the South's textile mills. He stopped for the night at the Poinsett Hotel in Greenville, South Carolina. From there he called on some acquaintances in the newspaper business, as he would in virtually every city and town he visited. Two men named Cantwell and Smith took him out for dinner and drinks "and then out to try to show me a mill in operation at night," he noted in his journal. "Only one running but it [was] a monster—surrounded by the familiar ferocious fence." Though several flood lights illuminated the gate, there was no one around to let them in. "Finally a man came out, some petty foreman on his way home to eat or screw," Jonathan wrote crudely, apparently untroubled by the fact that his wife, Lucy, at the very least, would eventually see everything he wrote because he relied on her to type up his notes.[7]

This Greenville anecdote was one of many little stories from his journal that Daniels would clean up for publication. When he wrote about the departing foreman in *A Southerner Discovers the South*, it would be the newspaperman named Cantwell who speculated that he was sneaking "home to a hot meal or a new wife." Daniels portrayed himself as having been interested only in the man's palpable fear: "He saw us and was afraid. The gate swayed behind him as he backed against it. Smith asked him if we could get in. 'No,' he said, as if he were pleading with us. 'No.'"[8]

This was melodrama, to be sure, but Daniels did sense fear that early May night. "I never saw such huge mills nor such fences and fortifications," he wrote in his journal. "Such fences indicate a sense of fear and such fear obviously indicates some sense of guilt."[9]

Against mill owners' fear Daniels contrasted mill workers' passion for cars. Automobiles had "multiplied in the mill villages." In front of "houses that need to be painted, men rubbed new cars with chamois to bring out the last gleam or tried to fix clattering old engines with pieces of wire." Clearly,

these men and their families wanted to be going places. "Their secret concern is with wheel, not shuttle" or loom. "They mean to move," and their
restlessness "indicates a faith that there is still somewhere to go. And maybe
a determination to go there." At the very least, it indicated that there was
"no dependable docility" among the white industrial workers of the South.[10]

The restlessness of the masses and the fear it produced among the upper
classes explained a great deal, in Daniels's view. He looked for evidence of
class conflict everywhere he went. He began the second day of his trip with
a visit to Conestee, south of Greenville, because Cantwell and Smith had
assured him it was the most degraded of mill villages. Everyone was working, but the wages were low and "if good times should crack," he noted in
his journal, "this old mill which even now has broken window panes would
be one of the first to shut down and here would be a stranded population."
Though less than ten miles from the center of Greenville, Conestee was isolated, with one employer, one company-owned store, a church, and plenty
of broken-down cars. Its small, company-owned houses were "spread over a
wide area with room enough . . . for each family to have very large gardens
but [I] saw none." Multitudes of reformers had recommended such gardens
for mill workers' self-improvement. But Conestee's workers seemed unaware
of "how short the distance was between eating and owning . . . a Ford" and
"not eating and burning up the porch railings for fuel."[11]

In noting the absence of gardens at Conestee, Daniels was implicitly com-
paring poor whites with poor blacks. "Undoubtedly Charlotte's Negro housing [is] worse" than that in most textile mill villages, he had observed in his
journal the day before, "but somehow the Negro has developed a genius in
making the most of less—a little grows less in a little white man's hands—a
Negro can give to little comfort, snugness, light and security—Poor whites
are rootless. Negroes wherever they are put down roots and harvest bright
flowers."[12]

Daniels's observations mirrored the conventional wisdom of his class of
elite white southerners. Together with his suggestion that unemployed mill
workers might become desperate enough to burn up their own porch railings
for firewood, his words reveal his deep ambivalence about poor and working-
class whites. Were they restless or shiftless? Were they simply poor and white
or were they poor white trash?

The record-breaking popularity of Erskine Caldwell's darkly comic novel
and play *Tobacco Road* certainly had many Americans thinking the latter.
Caldwell's irritating caricatures would be on Daniels's mind throughout his
journey. At first, he had admired *Tobacco Road* for its emotionally detached,

modernist, "hard style." He had even gone so far as to describe Caldwell's subsequent novel, *God's Little Acre*, as "one of the finest studies of the Southern poor white which has ever come into our literature."[13] But, once the Broadway adaptation of *Tobacco Road* began to reach an audience of millions in a remarkable seven-year run, Daniels quickly came to realize that too many people insisted on seeing Caldwell's fictional stories as social commentaries that either agreed or disagreed with their regional prejudices. "Put a slut in a book about the South and there are patriots who will regard it as a slander on the whole region and every female in it," he wrote, just as "there are non-Southerners who will accept it as a panoramic photograph of Dixie." Such readers "on each side of the Mason-Dixon line should be disregarded as unimportant to life and letters, living and dying, but in the aggregate these two masses of literate humanity provide bulk to obscure vision even when they talk loud and long of seeing the truth." The problem was "not so much that literature confuses as that the easily confused are able to read."[14]

In *A Southerner Discovers the South*, Daniels would try to show both southern "patriots" and "non-Southerners" a more accurate picture. The South "as portrayed with big mansions fronted with huge columns, as in [Stark Young's novel] 'So Red the Rose,' is not the true South," he would explain in author interviews. "Neither is it the true South as presented in the squalor of 'Tobacco Road.' I believe the honest-to-goodness South lies somewhere between these two ideas, and it was my purpose to find it on my tour."[15]

Even as he sought this in-between, Daniels struggled to decide what he really thought about poor and working-class white southerners. Were they sound material upon which to base an extension of democracy, as President Roosevelt and others argued? Daniels believed in democracy in principle, yet he considered many white southerners "rootless" and degraded. Looking at a mill village like Conestee—which he disguised in his book as "Cotswold"—he had to stretch to reach a sympathetic note. "In the company commissary a pretty blonde girl, almost incredibly pregnant, went heavily past me," he wrote. "My hat was already off but figuratively it came off again in my heart. I recognized her as omen. I never saw a dying cotton mill village that was not heavy with child."[16]

He never saw this particular woman, either. Nor, as his journal reveals, did he stop at the company-owned commissary, though he did drink a Coca-Cola in a store a few miles down the road. "It may be necessary to invent typical characters," Harold Strauss had suggested in the letter that inspired Daniels's book.[17] Though he went with a different editor, a different publisher, and a different project, he seems to have taken the possibility of invention to heart. Daniels dreamed up symbolic women even more freely (and leeringly) than symbolic men. In his view, if there was no pregnant young blonde in evidence near the dying textile mill at Conestee, there should have been.

After the decrepit mill village, Daniels's second day on the road was beautiful and serene. He drove northwest from Conestee through Greenville and into the southern Appalachian mountains, soon crossing back into North Carolina. Parts of his route along U.S. Route 276 and U.S. Route 64 were lovely with a "magnificence of dogwood" and "the earth bright with tiny wild flowers." For lunch, he stopped at West's Café in Highlands, where for forty cents he got eggplant, spinach, potatoes, rib stew, and custard pie, along with two cups of coffee. For a bed, he chose the little town of Franklin and the Tremont Inn, run by one of the few female newspaper editors he had ever known, a Mrs. Johnston of the *Franklin Press*.[18]

In two days, Daniels had traveled 429 miles.[19] His third day would begin with fewer small towns as he approached Great Smoky Mountains National Park. Along the way, he noticed a large black man plowing with a team of oxen in a river valley—one of the many black southerners he would remark upon but not stop to talk to. Like most whites of his era, Daniels looked at black people much more often than he listened to them, even though he claimed in *A Southerner Discovers the South* that he had spoken "everywhere to Negroes."[20] His claim was false but telling. Throughout his trip, Daniels would have encountered black people constantly but superficially, as bartenders and bellboys in the South's finest hotels and as maids and cooks in private homes. To meet educated, middle-class blacks who could offer informed analyses of the South's problems would have required advance planning that he did not do, other than planning a side trip to Tuskegee Institute (which did prove more upsettingly informative than he anticipated).

Meanwhile, Daniels justifiably assumed that approaching any of the black farm families he saw from the road would be pointless. It would probably only worry and perhaps even frighten them (or make them angry, a reaction that a well-meaning white liberal like Daniels may not have considered). Whatever the emotions, his intrusion would likely yield nothing more on the surface than the lowered gaze and nodding agreement that, for any black person who did not want trouble, were the obligatory responses to an unfamiliar white man's questions. Even though some white southerners—labor organizers, left-leaning writers like Caldwell—were able to engage black people and win their confidence, Daniels was not among them and did not even try. "I did not stir the stupid ignorance or the cackling laughter[,] one of which I knew would be lifted to meet a strange man's prying," he explained, noting that, if he had approached, "the stupidest seeming clod, black as the buckshot earth, would send word about me by the grapevine telegraph that would run ahead of my car." His words were insulting, but his point was astute. Daniels clearly knew that ignorance and laughter were part of blacks' protective mask against white supremacy and that even "the stupidest *seeming* clod" was not so stupid at all.[21]

Still, neither Daniels nor his white readers questioned whether one could truly "discover the South" without actually talking to black southerners. He and other whites simply took his authority for granted, one of the many unexamined privileges of their whiteness.

In Cherokee, North Carolina, Daniels did speak to an Indian postmistress. She responded to his request for a postcard with a genial "All righty" that he thought typically American — as culturally hybrid as the complaint of a Native American man at a neighboring cafe that the slot machine he was playing was "a gyp."[22]

A few miles beyond Cherokee, Great Smoky Mountains National Park turned out to be "beautiful," with "whole mountainsides of laurel and rhododendron" that had been planted by the Civilian Conservation Corps (CCC), one of the first and most popular programs created under the New Deal. By 1937 when Daniels traveled, the CCC had already put roughly half of the more than 3 million young men it would eventually employ to work, planting trees, fighting soil erosion, and developing state and national parks. Required to be single and between eighteen and twenty-five years old, these young recruits promised to send $25 of the $30 they earned each month home to their families. They also agreed to live under military-style discipline in rustic camps in the wilderness — camps that were typically all-white or all-black. Because of racism, blacks "had a more difficult time than whites getting into the Corps, found their segregated camps situated even farther away from nearby communities because of local protests in every region of the country, . . . and were rarely allowed to take on administrative responsibilities," explains CCC historian Neil M. Maher. This was despite an antidiscrimination clause in the 1933 law that created the CCC.[23]

Jonathan Daniels did not see the CCC men who had planted the laurel and rhododendron trees he admired. By 1937, they would have been devoting less time to planting and more time to building roads, campgrounds, and visitors' centers to increase tourism to the national park. This work proved controversial among preservationists, who favored less intrusion upon the natural environment, but it was very popular with local residents and dramatically increased the number of out-of-town visitors.[24] On the far side of the park, Daniels found Gatlinburg, Tennessee, ugly and disappointing—nothing but a "town for tin can tourists," he jotted in his journal. ("Maybe one day, if properly advertised, even Gatlinburg will be world renowned for its beauty," he wrote out of the other side of his mouth in his book.)[25]

From Gatlinburg, it was on to Sevierville and then Knoxville, where Daniels noticed a big truck carrying the Ethiopian Clowns baseball team from Miami, Florida. The Depression had been hard on black baseball, so the barnstorming Clowns used comedy and cartoonishly "African" war paint and grass skirts to attract audiences. They made money (especially for white owner Syd Pollock), but many blacks considered them an embarrassment, and the team would not be admitted to the Negro American League until 1943—and then only after promising to drop the "Ethiopian" and at least some of the antics.[26]

Although his curiosity may have been piqued, Jonathan had not gone to Knoxville to watch baseball. He was there to inspect and write about the TVA, the massive New Deal project that was transforming the region. That he would take time to visit the dams and hydroelectric power plants of the four-year-old TVA was a foregone conclusion. Nothing was bigger news in the 1930s South. "Never before in the Tennessee Country, and probably never anywhere else in the world, had so great an enterprise gone so rapidly into action," marveled Nashville intellectual Donald Davidson, who objected to this intrusion of the federal "Leviathan." Yet even he had to admit that the TVA's first thrust into regional planning and development "seemed to be governed by a genius, zeal, and experience of a high order."[27]

Planning was, indeed, a passion for Franklin Roosevelt and his advisers, particularly the members of his "Brains Trust." Economist Rexford Tugwell explained in June 1933 that "the cat is out of the bag. There is no invisible hand. There never was." Instead, it was up to the government to provide economic and social planning and regulation—"to supply a real and visible guiding hand to the task which that mythical, nonexistent, invisible agency was supposed to perform, but never did."[28]

Roosevelt, too, considered planning to be "the way of the future." Influenced by urban planners and Progressive Era reformers, he suggested in early 1932 that "something new" had emerged: "Not a science, but a new understanding of problems that affect not merely bricks and mortar, subways and streets." Planning on a broader scale could improve "the economic and social life of a community, then of a county, then of a state; perhaps the day is not far distant when planning will become part of the national policy of this country," he hoped.[29]

The TVA was the most ambitious and farthest reaching of all New Deal planning efforts. It embodied the notion that planning worked best at the regional level—a notion that had many proponents but was especially popular with Howard Odum and other Regionalist social scientists in the South.[30]

The promise of federal funds also made the TVA an easy sell in a desperately poor region that was dominated politically by members of Roosevelt's own party. The Tennessee Valley stretched across Virginia, North Carolina, Kentucky, Mississippi, Alabama, and Georgia, as well as Tennessee, covering an area about the same size as the state of Ohio. Some 2 million people lived in the flood-prone Tennessee River's watershed, most of them small farmers living in houses with no electricity or plumbing and working the land with tools that "Moses and Hammurabi would have been at home with" (as one Depression-era observer wrote of the South's small farmers in general). More than 80 percent of this poor and uneducated population was white—indeed, white, Anglo-Saxon Protestants of English and Scots-Irish heritage—which factored into the case for government largesse. Even in his initial request to Congress, Roosevelt described the TVA as "a return to the spirit and vision of the pioneer." Five years and millions of federal dollars later, the *New York Times* assured its readers that "TVA's Domain" remained a "land of individualists"—a far cry from commonplace descriptions of the supposedly lazy or greedy nonwhites who benefited from government jobs and other programs.[31] Meanwhile, the congressmen who created the TVA—especially the southern senators and representatives, all but three of whom voted for the expensive federal project—spoke of those who would be helped by it in archetypal terms as "the farmers" and "the people."

Although flood control was often listed first among the TVA's goals, the agency's true mission was to address a host of interrelated economic and social problems. Deforestation had compounded the effects of the Tennessee River's annual spring floods, resulting in widespread erosion and depletion of the soil. By the start of the Great Depression, "85 percent of the valley's 13 million acres of cultivated land suffered from soil erosion, with 2 million of those acres so deeply gullied that agronomists doubted that the land could be restored."[32] Fighting erosion and planting trees would be important work for the TVA and was often done in cooperation with the CCC, the Soil Conservation Service, and other federal agencies. Between 1933 and 1942, approximately 5,000 young, white men would be stationed in segregated camps in the Tennessee Valley each year.[33]

Eroded soil required fertilizer, and producing fertilizer would be another part of the TVA's mandate. Indeed, the first dam in what became the TVA system had been started during World War I to supply hydroelectric power to two nitrate plants at Muscle Shoals, Alabama. At the time, the nitrates were needed for explosives, but the end of the war ended the munitions program and Wilson Dam remained incomplete. Complaining of waste and the possibility of mismanagement, the Republican administrations of the 1920s hoped to sell off the dam and other properties to private investors, including Henry Ford. But progressives in Congress were determined to keep Muscle Shoals in the public interest. Throughout the 1920s, Republican senator George Norris of Nebraska was the leading champion of a federal flood control and development project, and he would introduce Roosevelt's TVA plan in the Senate in April 1933.

Roosevelt asked for "a corporation clothed with the power of government, but possessed of the flexibility and initiative of private enterprise." Congress gave the TVA remarkable autonomy to acquire real estate for and build dams, reservoirs, power plants, transmission lines, and other structures and to pursue navigation, flood control, and reforestation projects. However, the question of how much electrical power the TVA should generate remained hotly contested.[34]

The fact that the TVA produced any electricity at all put it in competition with privately owned power companies, which were organized into a trust. The Commonwealth and Southern (C&S) holding company owned all of the common stock in the Tennessee Electric Power Company, Alabama Power, Georgia Power, and Mississippi Power. C&S wanted the TVA to sell electricity only onsite at its power plants—and thus, effectively, only to C&S—rather than building transmission lines and competing for municipal and private customers. But public power advocates within the TVA and beyond had a different vision. "People wanted cheap power, and towns and rural districts throughout the region were clamoring for their own public systems," writes a biographer of TVA commissioner David E. Lilienthal. Because of their poverty, southerners needed inexpensive electricity to be able to participate in the modern world. In addition, Lilienthal and other public power advocates hoped to provide a "yardstick" that would allow consumers and their governments to know how much it really cost to produce and transmit electricity in the absence of profit motives and monopoly control.[35]

Jonathan Daniels yearned for that yardstick. Hostile to monopolies in general and power companies in particular (especially Duke Power in North Carolina), both Jonathan and his father had long been champions of cheap electricity as both a social good and a necessity for regional development. Jonathan thus approached Knoxville and Norris Dam on the third and fourth days of his journey feeling very self-conscious as a journalist about his own bias in favor of the TVA because "of the lower and lower power rates in the Southeast which had clearly resulted from its policies." He claimed, disingenuously, to have been "only vaguely aware" at first of the private power companies' "extravagance in the use of public resources for power and profit alone." More likely, he hoped to persuade readers of *A Southerner Discovers the South* to support the TVA, which was facing new political obstacles in 1937–38, by suggesting that he, too, had required proof of its benefits.[36]

Still, the visible reality and magnitude of federal intervention in the South unexpectedly shook Daniels and roused what he understood as the bristling SOUTHERNER within him. He looked upon the electrically lit and carefully laid-out model town of Norris, Tennessee, as "a town without a cemetery, a town created without pain," as he wrote in his journal, and he scorned it as a falsehood.[37] The inexpensive, healthy, but uninteresting food at the Norris community center was emblematic, in his view, for whenever experts were in charge, those experts were nearly always scientists, while he knew for certain that "food and living were among the arts."[38] He thought the blandness of Norris might turn more people into enemies of New Deal government planning than the fulminations of any conservative critic. One analogy for the TVA was federal invasion: "The last earlier and significant representative of the USA" in the Tennessee Valley had been William Tecumseh Sherman, while the TVA's "movement in occupation in 1933 was perhaps no less invasion (listen to the power companies) but a strange new blessed one for a South which is nearly always late in being lucky."[39]

Yet the question of *how* the TVA promised to bring the blessings of civilization to the South prompted another analogy that Daniels had to ponder. Perhaps these government engineers—and geologists, chemists, agronomists, malaria specialists, and who knew what else—were latter-day carpetbaggers. Or worse, they might be like the Yankee schoolmarms and other nagging moralists who had come to the South after the Civil War to improve it. "I think at this moment that I'll make the theme of my book a preference for Southern good-natured but cruel carelessness [over] the imposition from above of Yankee good intentions," Daniels scribbled in his journal. "I would much prefer a sloppy South to a South planned by Yankees."[40]

It was a reaction that Daniels found hard to shake off even after he learned that Norris did have a cemetery and did know pain, at the very least the pain of the cemetery's first burial, a fourteen-year-old boy who had killed himself rather than endure his religious-fanatic father's attempts to beat the devil out of him. The family was white, as all Norris residents were: the TVA excluded blacks from its "model community." But they were not from one of the Appalachian counties that had supplied so many of the Norris Dam workers. In fact, the mountaineer-workers had driven the father out after the boy's suicide, leaving the rest of the family "happier after he was gone."[41] And so, Daniels thought, Norris was not merely modern, model houses and curving streets but *people*. He need not fear that social planning had "succeeded an individualism which once made every mountaineer an underfed king on his side of the creek."[42]

A conversation with David Lilienthal, the youngest and most politically prominent of the three TVA commissioners, was also reassuring. Over breakfast with Daniels on May 9, Lilienthal flatly rejected the notion that only government authorities had the wisdom to make a new civilization for their constituents. Not a southerner but (as Daniels thought of such things) a Yankee and a Jew, Lilienthal spoke hearteningly of "damn social workers" and of another man who was "not an economist, thank God." Just thirty-eight years old and dapper in a gray suit and maroon sweater vest, his balding head close-cropped, Lilienthal asserted his belief that the people of eastern Tennessee were as "capable of taking care of themselves as any on earth."[43]

These were sentiments Lilienthal had expressed countless times, especially in speeches to local and regional business groups. Social planning in America *had* to be seen as compatible with American individualism. Indeed, the challenge for Depression-era visionaries was to reap the benefits that planning seemed to bring to increasingly ordered societies like the Soviet Union and fascist Italy without importing the repressive characteristics of those regimes. In the United States, *democratic* social planning that preserved "the principles of persuasion, consent, and participation" would protect the rights and ensure the well-being of a liberty-loving people—or at least the dominant majority.[44] Like the congressmen who created the TVA, social planners often defined "the people" in implicitly racial terms or accepted the narrow and exclusionary definitions of the locals whose participation and consent they needed. "Grassroots democracy" was a potent ideology employed throughout the New Deal, but the cooperation it required allowed for co-optation as well because of local control over the implementation of policies and allocation of resources.[45] The true grass roots were further down than many New Deal programs ever reached.

Lilienthal was a good example of a New Deal social planner who sincerely believed in grassroots democracy but accepted racial discrimination and exclusion. "We must . . . get down to legume roots," he told Daniels, joking that "mere grass" was not "definite enough" for the TVA's agricultural experts.[46] Yet, "the best that can be said" of Lilienthal's racial views in the 1930s, according to biographer Steven M. Neuse, is that he "was a typical New Deal liberal on race. He felt uneasy about bias and bigotry and was glad when African Americans got an opportunity," but he "failed to use institutional means to right wrongs. He never addressed the segregated situation at Norris, and once when [his] daughter Nancy was disturbed by a 'White Only' sign at Norris Lake, Lilienthal could do no better than counsel that segregation 'should be approached as a fact,' and that 'there was no use pretending that there would be anything but social distinctions and with them segregation, perhaps for generations to come.'"[47]

Questions about how the TVA could help black southerners were not even on the table during Lilienthal's breakfast with Daniels. But Jonathan— still more of a segregationist than even a "typical New Deal liberal on race"—remained skeptical about the potential impact of federal intervention and planning. Perhaps this was why he became so fascinated, early the next afternoon on May 10 at Chickamauga Dam, by the workers' paper cups.

Watching the big diesel Caterpillars bulldoze the earth, Daniels was most impressed by the heft and sweat and working conditions of the brawny black laborers. Black men working at "old time physical labor"? That was a familiar sight in the Depression-era South. But "dainty" paper cups handed one by one to solemn black workers by water boys who were no longer using the old bucket-and-dipper system that had always been good enough for field hands? That was the kind of innovation that made an observant white southerner like Daniels stop and think about the changes that were bound to come along with the dams of the TVA and other federal projects.[48] Such by-the-book solicitude for blacks threatened to undermine the psychological wage of racial superiority that the South had long paid to its working-class whites, regardless of the fact that the TVA was following local custom by employing blacks almost exclusively in menial and manual labor jobs. In an impoverished region where nonelite whites wielded little political or social power, cultural displays of white superiority and black inferiority were sacred. For, as C. Vann Woodward once explained it, it "took a lot of ritual and Jim Crow to bolster the creed of white supremacy in the bosom of a white man working for a black man's wages."[49] Even if the TVA made sure that white men were *not* working for black men's wages by segregating its workforce, the lesson still applied, and a new kind of ritual of "one man, one cup" might seem to confuse the racial hierarchy.

Lewis Hine captured this image of a water boy and two workers on the road to the Norris Dam construction site in 1933, when the TVA was still using the old bucket-and-dipper system that had long served the South. Lewis Hine Photographs for the Tennessee Valley Authority, RG 142, National Archives and Records Administration, College Park, Md.

Still, at least the TVA's cups were individual and sanitized. Daniels would think back on them favorably a few days later during a visit to the Delta Cooperative Farm at Hillhouse, Mississippi. Delta Cooperative was an effort by Christian socialists to resettle evicted sharecroppers, both black and white. "Interesting in comparison with the paper cup sanitation among Negro TVA workers on Chickamauga dam is the common towel Christianity in the kitchen of the staff house and office at Delta," Daniels noted in his journal. "I used it when Miss Rex, who poured water into a pan for me with a dipper, said, 'Will you share our towel?'—but I shared with little Christianity."[50] He explained his aversion more fully, though not completely, in *A Southerner Discovers the South*. "God, I am sure, will remember me as He remembered the one good deed of the man who once in his life gave a starving man an onion," he wrote. "I am a hypochondriac who is afraid of germs."[51] What he neglected to add was that the germ he was most conscious of was the "germ" of blackness. In this, he was like most white southerners of his era, for even those who were deeply committed to racial equality often had to overcome a visceral racism instilled in them from childhood, despite the supreme contradiction of whites' reliance on black cooks, nurses, and other household workers to perform the most intimate labor in their homes.[52]

Whither the South?—the central question that Daniels promised his readers to ask, if not programmatically to answer—came down to such things as individual paper cups and common towels shared across race lines. The Depression had opened the door to many possibilities, from socialist cooperatives to scientific planning and a much expanded role for the federal government. There were also traditionalists who advocated a shoring up of individual ownership and even a return to subsistence farms. Meanwhile, the Communist Party had gained the most members and greatest influence it had ever had in American life as a result of the economic crisis. Because the party was in the vanguard of the fight for racial equality, as well as workers' empowerment, thousands of Americans believed the Communists were doing more than anyone else to maintain and extend democracy within the United States.

Many more Americans eyed Communists with great suspicion. This was true on the political left as well as the right and center. Even during the late 1930s Popular Front period of left-wing alliances, liberals and socialists frequently accused Communists of insincerity and a preference for rule-or-ruin tactics when it came to organizing. "I know that the talk of these people about the Bill of Rights is the sheerest hypocrisy and the moment they secured control the rights which I want for them would be instantly denied me," explained one aggrieved liberal, who could not "imagine any greater disservice [one] could render the liberal cause in the South than to become a smoke-screen behind which sinister forces were attempting to operate."[53] The readiness of those on the right to suspect that "sinister forces" were indeed at work vastly complicated the issue. Although most often remembered as part of the red scare that followed World War II, the House Un-American Activities Committee was created in 1938 and chaired by a southern Democrat, Texas congressman Martin Dies. The Dies Committee, too, would loudly claim to be protecting democracy, even when its tactics violated individuals' freedom of speech and other rights.

The question of how to preserve and strengthen America's democratic system had become increasingly urgent with the rise of fascism in Europe. As Roosevelt put it in a message to Congress, "Unhappy events abroad have retaught us two simple truths about the liberty of a democratic people. The first truth is that the liberty of a democracy is not safe if the people tolerate the growth of private power to a point where it becomes stronger than their democratic state itself. That, in its essence, is fascism. . . . The second truth is that the liberty of a democracy is not safe if its business system does not provide employment and produce and distribute goods in such a way as to sustain an acceptable standard of living." For Daniels as for any thoughtful American who feared fascism, Roosevelt was right when he added that "both lessons hit home."[54]

It was hard for Jonathan Daniels to imagine a racially inclusive democracy or even a nonsegregated South in 1937 or 1938, but he was sympathetic to those who were racially subjugated and those who were economically dispossessed. Like many in the New Deal era, he lumped together a variety of left-of-center sentiments under the general heading of "liberalism" while avowing himself a liberal—at least on most issues. He was also conscious of the fact that, in the Roosevelt years, the American political system was in the process of working out what "liberalism" was going to mean. The classical liberalism of the nineteenth century had, after all, defined the role of government as laissez-faire. As Roosevelt and his allies devised a new kind of liberalism that strengthened the federal government to meet the needs of a modern, industrialized, pluralistic society, many southern Democrats clung to states' rights and resisted social change to an extent that made them profoundly "conservative" by the emerging new definitions.[55]

Because he wanted his book to sell, Daniels tried to keep the tone of *A Southerner Discovers the South* light and its content acceptable even to conservative white southern readers. "We Southerners" were the first two words of a first chapter that split the difference between claims of innocence and claims of expertise. He was a native, right down to his black Mammy (his childhood nurse Harriet entered on page two). He was a highly educated commentator ("for nearly ten years now I have been reading books about the South for *The Saturday Review of Literature*"). And yet he was somehow also a naive "discoverer" ("until this trip I had hardly been south of my own state of North Carolina which is regarded as far north by some who live deep in Alabama. I think, therefore, that I can look at the South with some detachment.")[56]

For all his authorial subterfuge, Daniels did make arguments and draw out themes as opportunities arose, notably in an early chapter about his conversation with David Lilienthal that he titled "Breakfast with a Democrat." His admiration for Lilienthal ("a pleasant, round-faced man, spectacled" with "none of the wide-eyed staring of the Utopian in his eyes") became his judgment about the TVA and federal planning more generally: "The South can be helped—is being helped—by young men like Lilienthal. He may be

TVA commissioner David E. Lilienthal testifying before a Senate committee
in June 1937. Harris and Ewing Collection, Library of Congress, Prints
and Photographs Division, Washington, D.C. [LC-DIG-hec-22951].

a carpetbagger. If so, he is one who comes neither to steal our money nor
reform our manners and morals but in the best sense of leadership to share
our destiny."[57] Daniels would think back on his "Breakfast with a Democrat"
often as he looked around the South for the new generation of leaders that
he, along with Roosevelt, hoped to see taking charge.

Even more fundamental than his favorable judgment on the TVA, Daniels
used his conversation with Lilienthal to frame some of the ideological debates he would highlight in his book. Lilienthal had provided the analytical
starting point, explaining his long-standing and widely publicized feud with
TVA chairman Arthur E. Morgan as more than a mere disagreement about
how much electricity the TVA should produce in competition with private
power companies. Nor was it simply that Lilienthal found the idealistic Morgan too preachy, on the one hand, and too trusting of profit-seeking businessmen and retrograde state and local politicians, on the other. It was instead a
"philosophic difference," as Daniels recorded in his journal, between those
like Morgan, "who would impose the good life ('the new civilization')," and
those like Lilienthal, "who believe the people, given the opportunity, can

provide it for themselves."[58] In *A Southerner Discovers the South*, Daniels would extrapolate broadly from Lilienthal's comments. This "division between faith in strength rising from the democracy and power descending from authority" was not rare, he observed, but instead "fundamental and at the same time bewildering in the South where the toughest Bourbons are often the noisiest Jeffersonians and all slaveholder-thinkers vote the straight Democratic ticket."[59]

Daniels's analysis was briefly stated but insightful. He knew from long experience that, in the South, it was not simply that democracy did not extend to black people, but also that the rhetoric of democracy had often been used for antidemocratic purposes among competing groups of whites. In the 1920s, the Ku Klan Klansmen whom Daniels despised had been among the "noisiest" Jeffersonians, modifying Thomas Jefferson's vision of a republic of small property owners "to suit a modern class structure," in the words of historian Nancy MacLean.[60] A decade later, it was also self-styled "Jeffersonian Democrats" who met and formed clubs in advance of the 1936 presidential election to complain that Roosevelt's New Deal policies were "anti-Democratic and anti-American." Some supported Republican candidate Alf Landon (and Daniels would be intrigued to see a leftover Landon campaign flyer on a certain desk when he got to Birmingham). But most "Democratic doubters" continued to vote the party ticket, adding to the confusion about what it really meant to be a Democrat and/or a democrat.[61]

Jonathan Daniels had always been a member of the Democratic Party, and he tried to be a genuine "small-d democrat" like, or perhaps even more faithfully than, his father. Josephus, too, was a noisy Jeffersonian—so much so that his wife, Addie, in a moment of exasperation, once insisted that, when he died, he would not "want to go to Abraham's bosom as do most of the faithful" but would "ask St. Peter to take you to Jefferson's wisdom" instead.[62] The wisdom that Josephus quoted most often was Jefferson's principle of "equal rights to all and special privileges to none," yet he was the same man who had played such a central role in eliminating not only black North Carolinians but also a good many whites ones from the electorate. Jonathan was by no means eager to see blacks vote in significant numbers, but neither did he like the kind of elite dominance and lack of widespread political participation he saw in North Carolina and other southern states. He did not consider his father an old-fashioned and elitist "Bourbon," much less a "slaveholder-thinker," and yet it was hard to distinguish their Jeffersonian rhetoric from his. It really came down to ideas about class and the rights of working-class people. Jonathan was prescient to sense that federal standard setting for workers—the very insistence on minimums and standardization that resulted in the requisitioning of paper cups for the black workers at Chickamauga Dam—had more potential to disrupt the southern status quo than any amount of Jeffersonian rhetoric or debate over "grassroots democracy" versus social engineering and "uplift." The "division between . . . faith in democracy and power descending from authority" was fundamental, but in an environment where "democracy" had too often gotten mixed up with "slaveholder-thinking," it would be the hard-won labor standards and, eventually, federal antidiscrimination efforts like the Fair Employment Practices Committee of the early 1940s and the Civil Rights Act of 1964, as well as the benefits working-class people and their allies could gain over time by demanding they be enforced, that brought the most social change.[63]

Norris, Tennessee, would not be the last place Jonathan Daniels saw a conflict between bottom-up and top-down approaches to reforming the South, "nor was David Lilienthal the last man I heard speak of it." Soon after meeting him, Daniels foreshadowed, "I was to pass the scene of similar conflict among Southerners on a mountain top at Chattanooga."[64]

To guide him to the top of majestic Lookout Mountain on Monday, May 10, Daniels picked up a twelve-year-old local boy named Joe Reams. Joe was undoubtedly white, given that Daniels did not identify him by race. (Meanwhile, an elevator operator he and Joe encountered at the Ruby Falls tourist attraction on Lookout Mountain was simply "a Negro," ageless and sexless, though undoubtedly male, given that Daniels did not identify him by gender.) A friendly and talkative boy, Joe was another sign of a changing South that was not lost on Jonathan in the impressionable early days of his journey. While he had promised Joe fifty cents, he quickly learned from the boy's honesty that he also made a kickback at every tourist stop they visited: forty cents on the dollar they paid to "See Rock City" and thirty-five cents on the dollar-and-a-half at Ruby Falls. Joe could also direct him to the cheapest and best souvenir stands and get a percentage back on his every purchase. Altogether it made a wage that was perhaps double what a boy his age could make picking cotton from dawn to dark in some farmer's field. Tourism and other service industries were creating a new economy for those who could find or cleverly carve out a niche in it. Joe was smart, and he was a nice kid. He would have shown Daniels to the cleanest and cheapest of the new tourist homes for free.[65]

It was too bad that Joe did not know where to find the one hotel that Daniels was curious about: the posh, if occasionally bankrupt, Lookout Mountain Hotel, where the Southern Policy Committee (SPC) had met a year before in May 1936.[66] Daniels was a founding member of the SPC, a group devoted to discussing and influencing regional and national politics. For him, this organization was as valuable a forum for developing and expanding on his liberal ideas as groups like the Commission on Interracial Cooperation and the Young Men's and Young Women's Christian Associations were for other budding white southern liberals and radicals.

Because he had not attended the Lookout Mountain meeting, however, Daniels had missed the shouting match that had become the subject of so much laughter among his Chapel Hill–based SPC friends.[67] He would get his chance to interview one of the combatants when he got to Memphis. Socialist William R. Amberson was a professor at the University of Tennessee Medical School and had been a key adviser for the Southern Tenant Farmers Union. The other antagonist, Agrarian Allen Tate, was unavailable for an interview, but he would see Tate's close friend Donald Davidson in Nashville. From where he stood on Lookout Mountain, Nashville and Memphis were just one and two days away, respectively. Daniels drove down the mountain without having seen the exact site of Tate and Amberson's war of words but thinking as he went that their argument about cooperatives versus individual ownership in southern agriculture had been important—perhaps as important to the future of the nation as the Civil War "Battle above the Clouds" that had taken place at Lookout Mountain in 1863 had been.

The South had always been a rural and agricultural society. Land and the labor to work it: these were the two key considerations that had set the terms for nearly all else, especially the fundamental relationship between blacks and whites. Now, slightly more than half of the region's farm population was landless: there were perhaps 5.5 million whites and 3 million blacks among the sharecropper and tenant farm families of the southern states.[68]

To make matters worse, thousands of these tenant farmers and sharecroppers had been evicted from their homes since the start of the New Deal. The creation of government subsidies under the Agricultural Adjustment Act had given landowners the ready cash they needed to replace year-round tenants with cheaper day laborers and invest in tractors and other labor-saving machines. Now, seven and a half years into the Great Depression (or more, if one remembered that the South's economic problems had started long before the stock market crash of 1929), both these displaced farm workers and unemployed and underemployed industrial workers in the South's hard-hit cities and mill villages were struggling to organize, sometimes across race lines. Planters and industrialists had responded to the labor unrest with little of their vaunted paternalism and often with terrible violence. As bad as they had been, traditional, supposedly paternalistic, economic and social arrangements had eroded along with the region's gullied landscape. What, if anything, the federal government was going to be able to do or even try to do about the so-called tenant problem and ongoing labor disputes was far from clear.

In short, anyone with any knowledge of the still unwinding path of Hitler's Germany or Mussolini's Italy had to be at least a little worried about the South, with its almost inconceivable poverty and its rogues' gallery of race-baiting demagogues and homegrown Blackshirts and Klansmen. Fascism could emerge in the South, Daniels thought, even though it seemed "absurd to use a foreign term for a condition that was American before Mussolini was born." He believed that "Southern lynchings represent not merely degrading cruelty but a wild outlet for despair." All too often, demagogues had led the white southern masses "against Negroes when what they wanted, as other men in other lands have wanted, was bread."[69]

Whether or not the New Deal, with its emphasis on "grassroots democracy" and social planning, could rehabilitate the whole South as effectively as the TVA and CCC were rehabilitating some of its natural resources was impossible to know. Wary of federal intervention, Daniels would find both the reactionary and radical alternatives of his day even more troubling. He feared homegrown fascists but had also watched with apprehension as the Communist Party grew. He had read about the Communists' rallies and marches and mass protests, most of which had taken place outside the South but the largest of which had focused on racial injustice in his own beloved land. The morning after his visit to Lookout Mountain, Daniels would see the place where many of those cries of injustice had originated. On May 11, 1937, he was driving to Scottsboro, Alabama.

— CHAPTER THREE —

The Demand for Justice Will Not Be a
Cause Furthered Only by Radicals

✦

UST PAST THE Alabama state line, Jonathan picked up a hitchhiker named Joe Poe. Joe was a sixty-seven-year-old white man from Georgia. He was an unemployed cotton mill hand ("nobody wants old ones") on his way to Birmingham to look for work.[1] "He knew as well as I did that there was not going to be any job for him in Birmingham," Daniels wrote in *A Southerner Discovers the South*.[2] His portrait of Joe Poe as an example of the southern poor white revealed both sympathy and cynicism, with a few brushstrokes borrowed, consciously or not, from Erskine Caldwell. Joe was "pitiful" and "looked a great deal like a chipmunk. . . . His skin was brown as old leaves and his eyes were dark like a small beast's eyes, bright and ready for fear." He smelled "like the earth" and had already spent a day and a night on the road that Daniels had covered since breakfast.[3]

If he had not been distracted by Joe, Jonathan might have commented on how closely that road paralleled the tracks of the Southern Railway running from Chattanooga. It was, after all, events that began on a Southern Railway freight train back in 1931 that had put the little town of Scottsboro, Alabama, on his itinerary. For six years, "Free the Scottsboro Boys" had been a rallying cry at marches and protests around the country and even abroad. The long, loud effort to fight the legal lynching of the Scottsboro defendants had helped forge alliances among Communists, socialists, and liberals that had since become stronger with the Communist Party's call for a Popular Front against fascism in 1935.

Yet Scottsboro itself was unremarkable and quiet by the time Jonathan and Joe arrived there on Tuesday, May 11. They found a place to park alongside the "huge, ill-kept but not unpleasant Courthouse Square," and Joe got out to look for another ride. Jonathan's reason for stopping was "to look at the little town that has grown so big in the world's vocabulary since March 25, 1931, when the arrest of nine young Negroes for the rape of two white women in a moving [freight] car began making little Scottsboro a prodigious, ugly name." The quiet of the courthouse square helped him find an apt simile for the effects of the Scottsboro case on the South and the nation. It was like "a rock flung into a pond," he wrote: "the water grows slick calm again at the center while the rings go on forever."[4]

Daniels had felt the ripples himself and had written several editorials on the Scottsboro injustice for the *News and Observer.* But his mental dam of opposition to outside "interference" in the South still held. Unlike a growing number of other white southern liberals, he opposed federal antilynching legislation that was hotly debated in Congress during the same years when the Scottsboro Boys' fates were decided in state and federal courts. The seeming contradiction between his outspokenness on Scottsboro and his reticence on lynching highlights the ideological transition taking place in the New Deal years, as even many southern liberals began to admit the failures of local leadership and acknowledge the need for national solutions to problems of racial injustice and mob murder. No federal antilynching bill would survive in Congress in this period, and Daniels would continue to oppose any such law for several years longer than many of his white southern liberal peers. Nevertheless, events in Alabama, as well as a particularly horrific lynching in Duck Hill, Mississippi, and the ongoing debate over a federal statute would shake his confidence in localism. As deep as his desire to see the South solve its own problems was, by 1937 the waters of Daniels's political consciousness were a lot more troubled than he depicted the glassy "pond" of Scottsboro, Alabama, to be.

THE "ROCK" HAD ACTUALLY plunged in at Paint Rock, a crossroads depot about twenty miles west of Scottsboro that was equally quiet when Daniels stopped there after walking a bit and drinking a Coca-Cola at a Scottsboro grocery store. "I found nobody in Paint Rock who would admit remembering that exciting afternoon in 1931," he wrote.[5] Yet excitement there had been when a posse stopped and searched a forty-two-car freight train after a stationmaster up the line reported that a gang of black hoboes had beaten up some white hoboes and thrown them off. No one expected to find two white women dressed in overalls in one of the freight cars, and there would be many conflicting accounts of how soon and under what circumstances the women began claiming they had been raped.

Nine black youths stood accused, only one of them as old as twenty, the two youngest only thirteen. Within minutes, these nine young men—Olen Montgomery, Clarence Norris, Haywood Patterson, Ozie Powell, Willie Roberson, Charlie Weems, Eugene Williams, and brothers Andy and Roy Wright—were tied up and shuffled onto the back of a flatbed truck for the twenty-mile ride to the Scottsboro jail. Within hours, a mob had gathered around the jail, in the same courthouse square that Daniels later found so quiet. "Give 'em to us," someone shouted as night fell. And: "If you don't we're coming in after them." Scottsboro's mayor pleaded with the mob to go home and "protect the good name of the city." Sheriff M. L. Wann telephoned the governor, who sent the National Guard.[6]

No one moved on the Scottsboro jail that night, but the crowds in the courthouse square only grew larger and more festive as the nine defendants were rapidly convicted and sentenced to death. The one exception was thirteen-year-old Roy Wright, whose jury hung because seven of the jurors insisted on the death penalty even though the prosecutor, knowing Wright ought to be tried in a juvenile court under Alabama state law, had sought only life imprisonment.

On the day the defendants were sentenced, the Communist Party–USA issued a statement condemning the Alabama courts. James Allen, a Chattanooga-based organizer, had heard about the case on the radio, and his wife, Isabelle, and another party representative had gone to Scottsboro to sit in on the trials. It is no exaggeration to say that Allen's "early and relentless coverage" of the case saved the Scottsboro Boys' lives. Allen was an avid supporter of the Communist Party's policy of self-determination for the Black Belt, a policy that encouraged efforts to organize blacks in the Deep South as not only the nation's most oppressed proletariat but also one with a strong separatist tradition. The party's legal arm, the International Labor Defense (ILD), found it relatively easy to persuade the Scottsboro Boys' families to let them represent the young men in an appeal. From there, the story became incredibly complex.

The ILD succeeded in making the case an international cause célèbre but clashed with the NAACP, which had belatedly offered help. By January 1932, the NAACP had withdrawn from the case and accused the Communists of caring more about publicity than the defendants' fates. But the NAACP capitalized on the Scottsboro case as well, positioning itself as a moderate, non-

Juanita Jackson (l), Laura Kellum, and Dr. Ernest W. Taggart of
the NAACP visiting eight of the nine Scottsboro Boys in January 1937.
Visual materials from the NAACP Records, Library of Congress, Prints
and Photographs Division, Washington, D.C. [LC-USZ62-116731].

communist alternative in the quest for social change. As historian Glenda
Gilmore writes, Scottsboro was "a kaleidoscope through which the images
of the South's 'race problem' reshuffled themselves as they passed from hand
to hand. The NAACP, the Communist Party, white liberals, and dedicated
white supremacists all read different narratives in its shards."[7]

In November 1932, the U.S. Supreme Court overturned the Scottsboro
convictions in *Powell v. Alabama*, setting an important precedent for defendants' right to counsel, including effective, and not merely pro forma, representation.[8] The 7–2 decision meant the Scottsboro Boys would be granted
new trials, which would take place in a changed venue, Decatur, Alabama,
beginning with the prosecution of Haywood Patterson in March 1933.

Patterson had been eighteen or nineteen years old when he was arrested in
1931. Like all of the Scottsboro Boys, he had grown up in crushing poverty
and was desperate for work. A rumor that government jobs hauling logs on
Mississippi river barges were available in Memphis led him to hop a Southern Railway freight train, something he had done many times before. This
time, three friends from Chattanooga, Andy and Roy Wright and Eugene
Williams, had decided to come along.[9]

The trouble had started when a white boy stepped on Patterson's hand.
He was clinging to the side of a tank car when several white youths walked
across the top of it and then turned around and walked back. The second

time the white boy stepped on his hand, Patterson complained. The boy called him a "nigger bastard" and ordered him off this "white man's train." Patterson said he had as much right to be there as "you white sonsofbitches," who were, after all, only hoboes like himself. The words were enough to make a fight inevitable. Patterson and the other black youths got the best of it, throwing or chasing all but one of the white riders off the slow-moving freight. The last of the white boys, Orville Gilley, tried to jump off but was left hanging from the side of a car, in danger of falling beneath the wheels as the train picked up speed. Patterson helped pull Gilley back on, saving his life. And then it was over. Charlie Weems and Clarence Norris had taken part in the fight along with Patterson, the Wright brothers, and Williams. Ozie Powell had watched it from a neighboring car. Willie Roberson and Olen Montgomery had each been alone at the other end of the train and had no idea there had even been a fight. A few other black youths who had participated got off before Paint Rock, just in time to save themselves from more trouble than they could possibly imagine.[10]

By the time Patterson's second trial started, the nine Scottsboro defendants had spent two full years in jails and prisons, including many months on death row. They had taken beatings at the hands of police officers and prison guards and had often fought among themselves or with other prisoners. They had seen lynch fires in the eyes of courtroom spectators and crumpled under the questioning of angry prosecutors. They had also been bewildered when white Communist Party members and black NAACP representatives and a host of other visitors had come to see them and when letters, telegrams, and packages from strangers started pouring in.

Perhaps most bewildering of all was the dynamic new defense lawyer the ILD had recruited for the second set of trials, Samuel Leibowitz of New York City. Tall, vigorous, and brilliant at the age of thirty-seven, Leibowitz was widely regarded as the best criminal lawyer in the country, a man who "had defended seventy-eight individuals charged with first-degree murder" and seen seventy-seven of them acquitted (the other case ended in a hung jury). Despite his reluctance to work with Communists, Leibowitz was eager to take on a more noble cause than his usual defense of big-city gangsters. Reading the transcripts from the initial trials convinced him of the Scottsboro Boys' innocence. He took on their defense pro bono, with the one stipulation that he planned to distance himself, at least rhetorically, from the Communists. Knowing the South only from romanticized histories of the old plantation that saturated American popular culture, he was naively confident that the Alabama courts would go his way once he demonstrated the many reasons to doubt the Scottsboro Boys' guilt, regardless of the color of their skin.[11]

In Decatur, Leibowitz mounted a thorough and energetic defense, challenging the prosecution's witnesses, particularly accuser Victoria Price, whom he cross-examined for four hours. He found her canny and unshakeable, no matter how inconsistent and improbable her testimony. She fumed as Leibowitz introduced evidence about her criminal record over prosecutors' objections, and she denied his accusations about her sexual history, including his suggestion that she had spent the two nights prior to the alleged rape sleeping in hobo jungles with white men.[12]

Throughout the cross-examination, Price dodged each of Leibowitz's hardest questions with a stubborn "No" or a petulant "I won't say" while sticking to one simple storyline: "Those Negroes and this Haywood Patterson raped me." Yet the testimony of Scottsboro physician R. R. Bridges, who had examined Price and the other accuser, Ruby Bates, within two hours of the alleged crime, seemed to show that no rape had taken place. Neither young woman had been particularly agitated, neither showed cuts and bruises or other signs of violence, and the only sperm the doctor and his assistant could find in either woman's vagina was dead, indicating that intercourse had taken place at least twelve hours earlier, not on the train. "In other words," Leibowitz asked Dr. Bridges, "the best you can say about the whole case is that both of these women showed they had sexual intercourse?" "Yes, Sir," he replied.[13]

What should have been the most compelling part of Leibowitz's defense came at the very end. Ruby Bates had disappeared from her home in Huntsville, Alabama, just weeks before the scheduled start of the new trials. Now she was back—as a witness for the defense. She testified that she and Price *had* slept in the hobo jungles and *had* engaged in consensual sex with white men on the nights prior to the Scottsboro Boys' arrest. On that fateful morning, they had been traveling with two white men, Orville Gilley and Lester Carter, who had fought with Patterson and the other black youths. Carter (who also testified for the defense) had been forced off the train, while Gilley had been pulled back on. After the fight, which had taken place in a neighboring car, none of the black boys had touched or even spoken to Bates and Price. She had cried rape because Price told her to, because Price said they "might have to stay in jail" unless they could distract attention from the fact that they were traveling, in violation of the well-known federal Mann Act, illegally and across state lines in the company of men.[14]

Ruby Bates's testimony on Thursday, April 6, 1933, made Jonathan Daniels burn with shame for his native region. He had just taken over as editor of the *News and Observer*. In fact, Josephus and Addie Daniels had not yet left for the ambassador's residence in Mexico City. But even with Josephus looking over his shoulder, Jonathan would not entertain the theory that prosecutors had instantly put forth to discredit Bates: the idea that she had been bought off, as prosecutor Wade Wright put it in his closing statement, "with Jew money from New York."[15] Instead, Jonathan penned a sober editorial titled "Southern Honor on Trial." "Unless the pattern of lying in the Scottsboro case is more complex than now appears," he wrote, Bates's testimony "makes it apparent that a terrible crime was committed in Alabama but it was done not by the Negroes but by those who posed as their victims." He decried the "cold-blooded ruthlessness" with which Price and other witnesses would have "lied [the Scottsboro Boys] to death." Justice and honor in the South were "as much on trial in Decatur, Alabama," as the young black men at the bar.[16]

Although Jonathan Daniels was by no means the only white southerner to advocate for justice for the Scottsboro Boys in the early 1930s, he was more forceful and single-minded on the subject than other white southern journalists. In part, this is because he was lucky in his timing: he had been in Europe on his Guggenheim fellowship when the case broke. He had missed the confusing early months when the controversy over the role of the Communist Party was at its most explosive. His absence early on made it considerably easier for him to become, in historian James Goodman's words, "one of the few white editors below the Mason-Dixon line to credit the ILD and Leibowitz with saving the lives of the Boys and awakening the nation and the South to the 'danger of injustice in Alabama.'"[17]

Daniels's outspokenness on the Scottsboro case also reflected his own sensitivities. Like other white southern liberals, he objected to northern critics' tendency to ignore distinctions of class and conscience among white southerners. Too often, the lynch mob was taken to represent the white South while those who risked social ostracism and even their own personal safety and economic security to stand up to the mob got relatively little recognition for their efforts. Still in his early thirties, Daniels also hoped for generational change, which northerners' blanket condemnations could only discourage. He seized an opportunity to challenge outsiders'—and an insider's— monolithic view in January 1934 after the *Nation* ran a reactionary letter about the case from Agrarian and poet John Gould Fletcher. "Is this the voice of the South?" the magazine's editors asked.

Daniels replied emphatically that it was not. "I have read with considerable interest and some little resentment the letter of John Gould Fletcher in which he undertakes to express the view of the South . . . as one of resentment against the North and of determination, as a result, to do what we please with the damn niggers," he protested. "I am perhaps guilty of sass to my elders in expressing the opinion that Mr. Fletcher's views are those of an educated Southerner of twenty-five years ago but not of today." Much had changed in the South, Daniels insisted. "White men and Negroes have learned slowly that they are not master and slave but men, black and white, who share a common destiny." The white southerner was starting to understand "what he so long refused to see: that the ignorance of the Negro, the exploitation of the Negro, injustice to the Negro result only in ignorance, poverty, and injustice for all," white as well as black.[18]

When Haywood Patterson's second trial resulted in a verdict of guilty despite Bates's testimony, Daniels considered it "shocking." He acknowledged that Patterson had been convicted "in the name of Southern honor" of a different sort than the honor he had said was on trial. Rather than the "common tradition of justice" that Leibowitz had counted on, here was the "Southern honor" that defended white womanhood at all costs. Yet Daniels still held out hope that honorable people including southerners might rally to the cause of truth and fairness. The case would surely go to appeal and "in this appeal the demand for justice in Alabama will not be a cause furthered only by radicals. Upon the facts brought out at the present trial, upon the facts in the judge's charge alone, men and women everywhere whose interest is only to see justice done can rally."[19]

Daniels emphasized Judge James E. Horton's charge to the jury because of the fine balance it had struck between southern patriotism and high principle. Horton had foregrounded his regional credentials, which traced back to some of Alabama's earliest settlers as well as a Confederate father and grandfather. But "you are not trying state lines," he had insisted. The only question for jury members was whether or not they believed that Haywood Patterson had raped Victoria Price. Both Price and Bates were "women of the underworld," women "of easy virtue," and both had perjured themselves at some point: Bates had told two completely different stories under oath, and Price had at the very least given "false testimony about her movements and activities in Chattanooga" before getting on the train. If the jury wanted to convict Patterson on the basis of Price's testimony and yet felt she had lied about any material point, they must acquit instead. And they must not be biased because of Patterson's race. "We are a white race and a Negro race here together—we are here to live together—our interests are together,"

Judge Horton had stressed. Intolerance and hate were prevalent but would not abide. "The great things in life, God's great principles, matters of eternal right, alone live."[20]

In Daniels's eyes, this was an "excellent" statement showing that "in Alabama as elsewhere just men wish only justice."[21] It also showed that Horton considered Price and Bates to be liars and tramps. Whether or not a woman's moral character or sexual history ought to matter in a rape case would become a fraught legal question by the 1970s and 1980s, when advocates for rape victims challenged a criminal justice system and media that often subjected accusers to public humiliation and added emotional trauma. Leibowitz's attack on the women's morals and Horton's reiteration of it in his charge might seem unfair in this respect—if consent had been an issue in the Scottsboro case or, indeed, if a rape had taken place. As Horton recognized (and a later judge denied), Leibowitz wanted to introduce evidence about Price's and Bates's sexual activities to explain where the semen in their vaginas had come from, as well as to show they had lied under oath. Such evidence would be admissible even under twenty-first-century rape shield laws, which provide an exception for evidence about a woman's sexual experiences that "is offered to prove that a person other than the accused was the source of semen, injury, or other physical evidence." Sometimes called the "Scottsboro rebuttal provision," this exception was not part of the law in 1933, nor were there legal protections in place for rape victims.[22] Instead, both misogyny and notions of "chivalry" came into play as all parties—and especially the white men who were in charge of prosecution, defense, punishment, and the shaping of public opinion—tried to evaluate Price's and Bates's accusations and Bates's reversal, all of which were complicated by elements of racism, anti-Semitism, antiradicalism, and sectional pride.

Jonathan Daniels was one public opinion maker who was ready to believe in the perfidy of women, particularly women of Price's and Bates's social class. It was Daniels's "refus[al] to accept Victoria Price as an emblem of Southern womanhood" that most allowed him to reconcile his defense of the Scottsboro Boys with his own loyalties to the white South. For, "if the womanhood of the South is sacred," he vowed, "it is too sacred to reduce it to the level of an Alabama prostitute who has tangled herself repeatedly in a maze of falsehood."[23] Despite regional paeans to white southern women's pious and pure nature, Daniels had long known that unchaste white women existed. Indeed, one of his very first controversial decisions as an editor had been to publicize the arrest of prostitutes (he called them "whores") at the Alpha Tau Omega house back at the University of North Carolina.[24]

The social world that Price and Bates inhabited was beyond Daniels's firsthand experience. Both lived in Huntsville, Alabama, and both were cotton mill workers—when the mills were running. Price, who was twenty-one years old when she charged the Scottsboro Boys with rape, had started in the mills at age ten and was the sole support of a widowed, disabled mother. She made $1.20 a day but, in the hard times of 1931, could get work only five or six days a month. She supplemented her income by charging men for sex, and she had also been arrested and convicted for bootlegging, as well as vagrancy, adultery, and fornication.[25] She had good reason to be afraid when deputies stopped the train at Paint Rock. She knew how authorities treated women whose lives made a mockery of the South's pious and pure gender ideal. Crying rape in Paint Rock was not only a way to save herself some jail time but also made white men treat her like a lady, at least for a while.

Ruby Bates was also an underemployed textile mill worker and occasional prostitute. She lived with her mother and siblings in a rented shack in a poor neighborhood where they were the only white family on the block. Her mother had fled an abusive husband and reportedly drank and "took men for money whenever she got the chance." But Ruby had "been quiet and well-behaved—until she started running around with Price."[26] She had been a reluctant accuser from the start, unwilling to identify any of the defendants in a lineup or on the witness stand in Scottsboro. But she did claim that she and Price had been raped, and the result had been death sentences for nine boys hardly any older—and some of them younger—than her own seventeen years. By March 1933, as the second set of trials neared, Bates was feeling considerable regret. She ran away to New York City and found a job in a nearby tourist camp. Desperate to talk to someone about what she had done, she seized on a newspaper photograph of the Reverend Harry Emerson Fosdick, pastor of the Riverside Church, and called him at his office. Fosdick encouraged her to recant, leading to her dramatic appearance in court on April 6.[27]

In his charge, Judge Horton encouraged jurors to consider Bates's contrition alongside her admitted lack of virtue. Yet the jury voted unanimously to convict Patterson on the very first ballot. The twice-condemned man was stoic, but Samuel Leibowitz was stricken. He had not only been confident in his case but also thought the laughter he had heard coming from the jury room and the smiles on the jurors' faces must be good omens. How could anyone smile as he prepared to send another human being to the electric chair?[28]

The next day, Leibowitz arrived in New York seething with anger. When a reporter asked him about the verdict, he let loose. "If you ever saw those creatures, those bigots whose mouths are slits in their faces, whose eyes popped out at you like frogs, whose chins dripped tobacco juice, bewhiskered and filthy, you would not ask how they could do it," he spat.[29] It was a profoundly damaging statement that worsened his clients' predicament. Newspapers around the South reprinted his words with bitter condemnation, and even Daniels would quote him verbatim five years later in *A Southerner Discovers the South*. "I failed to find in the Scottsboro country any white folk who would meet the specification," he added. "Unless we count Joe Poe—and I for one refuse to count him."[30]

Daniels's dig at Joe Poe was not only gratuitous but also illogical. It was precisely people like Joe—some of the poorest of white southerners, transient in search of work—who had set the Scottsboro case in motion. On what grounds could he or Victoria Price and Ruby Bates be denied to "count" in an honest look at the southern social structure?

If Daniels objected to Leibowitz's aspersions on the Decatur jury, he still believed its verdict was wrong, as an editorial he published in the *News and Observer* reiterated. The article, titled "A Suggestion to the South," was Daniels at his most even-handed and pragmatic. He praised Judge Horton and acknowledged that the Scottsboro case inevitably raised "the emotionally overcharged question of the relations of whites and blacks." He also conceded that the defense attorneys had contributed to an impasse. This was because they were "not Southerners. They were city men from far away. They were—there is no use caviling—Jews. They represented radical labor. In fact, they represented all the things of which the simple men and women of Alabama are suspicious and distrustful." The only way forward was for Leibowitz and the ILD to withdraw and allow southern lawyers to take over the defense. Daniels pledged the *News and Observer*'s support for such a plan and asked for help from "other southern people and organizations interested in the vindication of southern justice."[31]

Daniels's idea was ahead of its time in April 1933, when few people on either side of the case were willing or able to be so coolly rational. First, Judge Horton would surprise everyone by setting aside Patterson's conviction. Those attending court in Horton's hometown of Athens, Alabama, on June 22, 1933, thought they were going to hear the defense's motion for a new trial—a technicality that Leibowitz had left to others. Instead, Horton read a seventeen-page document of his own composition in which he reviewed the evidence from Patterson's trial in careful detail—up until the very end, when he offered a bit of speculation. "History, sacred and profane," he wrote, teaches us "that women of the character shown in this case

are prone for selfish reasons to make false accusations both of rape and insult upon the slightest provocation, or even without provocation for ulterior
purposes." Clearly, this was what he believed had happened in Scottsboro.
Noting that Price's testimony "bears on its face indications of improbability
and is contradicted by other evidence," he invalidated Patterson's guilty verdict and ordered a new trial.

In addition to Price's lies, it was the medical evidence that had convinced
Horton of the Scottsboro Boys' innocence. Dr. Bridges's testimony had cast
doubt on the question of whether or not Price and Bates had been raped,
but that was only part of it. Years later, Horton revealed to historian Dan
Carter something he had never before made public: that Bridges's assistant,
a young doctor named Marvin Lynch who was just getting established in
Scottsboro, had approached him during the trial requesting a private conversation. Alone in a men's restroom with a bailiff standing guard, Lynch
told Horton that he had thought all along that Price and Bates were lying
about the rape, and he had accused them of lying when he examined them in
Scottsboro. They had not even become indignant; instead, they had laughed
at him.[32]

Unable to persuade Lynch to tell his story on the stand, Horton allowed
the case to go to the jury. But he refused to let Patterson go to the electric
chair or even to another appeal without acting on his conscience. He would
lose his electoral bid for a sixth term as judge of Alabama's Eighth Circuit
Court as a result.

Forced into a new trial, Alabama attorney general Thomas E. Knight Jr.
made sure Patterson faced a new judge. Elderly William Callahan of Decatur was by no means the "wise judge" who "points the way" that Daniels
had seen in Horton.[33] Instead, with his narrow and prejudicial rulings, it was
no surprise in the fall of 1933 when all-white juries convicted Patterson for a
third time and Clarence Norris for a second time, sentencing both to death.

Leibowitz appealed these verdicts. On April 1, 1935, the U.S. Supreme
Court ruled in *Norris v. Alabama* that, because state officials had systemat-
ically excluded blacks from jury rolls in clear violation of the Fourteenth
Amendment, Norris's and Patterson's convictions were invalid. Daniels's
editorial response focused not on the jury question but on the obstinacy of
Knight and other Alabama officials, who responded to the decision with an
immediate promise to "prosecute to the end." Angrier and less optimistic
than he had been in 1933, Daniels charged that, if the state of Alabama
were to execute any of the Scottsboro Boys after all that had taken place,
"their execution would be [a] lynching . . . Horrid as lynching is," he went

on, "it would have been in this case less horrible than the long, cold-blooded determination to bring these men to death" on the basis of a falsehood. The "justice of Alabama is on trial," he concluded yet again. This time, however, he had to admit that "Alabama does not care."[34]

DANIELS COULD HAVE TAKEN the political implications of his own editorial further than he was willing to in 1935. Just three weeks after the Supreme Court announced its decision in *Norris v. Alabama*, the Atlanta-based Commission on Interracial Cooperation (CIC) endorsed a proposed federal antilynching law for the first time. The endorsement reflected an important ideological shift as even *southern* liberals, who had largely shared their compatriots' commitment to states' rights, conceded the limitations of moral suasion techniques like Daniels's repeated appeals to "Southern honor" in the Scottsboro case and admitted the need for a federal law. After arguing for years that white southerners could solve their region's race problems themselves through education and advocacy, in 1935 the liberals of the CIC set off on a new course. They did so because, like the mobilization around Scottsboro, the fight for federal antilynching legislation was helping to forge a coalition among blacks, leftists, and left-leaning liberals that forced the issue repeatedly in Congress and before a wider public. This was the coalition that did the most to steer the United States slightly leftward into the long civil rights era. By the late 1930s, the question for Daniels and other Americans, including southerners, was whether they would help with the steering or at least ride along. Or would they fight for the wheel to try to keep the South and the nation on a more conservative course?

Founded in 1919 in the midst of a post–World War I surge in racial violence, the CIC was "*the* organization of Southern liberalism" in the 1920s and 1930s. It loosely connected several thousand white liberals and moderates to denounce violence and promote "better understanding" between blacks and whites. A small number of African Americans, most of them ministers or educators, also participated, although they had limited influence, and their most important roles were usually behind the scenes. W. E. B. Du Bois and other contemporary black leaders criticized the CIC for its inattention to black voices, particularly the rising voices of protest emanating from the NAACP and the Harlem Renaissance.[35] Yet CIC chairman Will Alexander argued that the group's moderation and resistance to "agitation" was its greatest strength. Though he personally opposed segregation and was a deeply committed reformer, Alexander felt that, in the South, only those perceived as moderate could serve as "the leaven which, if kept alive and working, will permeate the mass of white and Negro citizens with a new race attitude."[36]

When the NAACP first succeeded in getting an antilynching bill introduced in Congress in the early 1920s, some CIC members supported it. Others, including influential CIC research director T. J. Woofter Jr., dismissed it as "partisan and sectional"[37]—a reminder that, prior to the late 1930s, white southern liberals identified foremost with region while expressing a range of opinions even on matters of racial justice, let alone integration, which was not yet part of the definition of liberalism. The antilynching bill's chief sponsor was a Republican, Leonidas C. Dyer, who represented a heavily black district in St. Louis. His position reflected in part the growing political strength of African Americans, who were moving north by the thousands in the Great Migration. Proponents of the bill also pointed to another recent political change: Prohibition. The NAACP's legal experts argued that the ratification of the Eighteenth Amendment had altered the constitutional equation, upending the long-standing argument that only states and not the federal government had jurisdiction over criminal matters, including mob murder.

In addition, recent investigations by the NAACP and other groups showed that many lynchings involved victims who were taken from the custody of law enforcement officials. In 1920, this was true in more than half of recorded cases.[38] How, then, could opponents of a federal law argue that local authorities could handle the problem themselves?

The Dyer bill defined a lynch mob as "five or more persons acting in concert for the purpose of depriving any person of his life without authority of law as a punishment for or to prevent the commission of some actual or supposed public offense." It made participation in a lynch mob a felony punishable by a minimum of five years in prison. It also held any county in which a lynching occurred liable for compensation of the victim's family and included a prison term of up to five years and a fine of up to $5,000 for any state or municipal officer who was found to have been negligent in protecting a prisoner.[39] Endorsed by President Warren G. Harding, the bill survived the House Judiciary Committee and made it to the floor in early 1922. Two days of rancorous debate ended in the Dyer bill's passage by a vote of 230 to 119, although only eight Democrats, all from northern or border states, supported it.

In the Senate, the Dyer bill barely made it out of committee before it fell victim to a southern Democratic filibuster. According to the *Washington Post,* it was the first time "that filibusterers frankly avowed that they were filibustering."[40] Southern opposition rested on "ancient states' rights dogma," as well as vitriol, such as a Tennessee representative's charge that it was a "bill to encourage rape." Reintroduced in 1923 and 1924, the Dyer bill again faced filibusters and never came to a vote.[41]

In the fall of 1933, the NAACP decided it was time to try again. The number of reported lynchings had been declining since the turn of the twentieth century but suddenly jumped from a low of ten in 1929 to twenty-one the next year. The year 1933 was also proving deadly, with a final tally of twenty-eight victims. Meanwhile, the arrival of Franklin Roosevelt in the White House seemed to offer new hope. NAACP leaders such as James Weldon Johnson and Walter White were well aware that the New Deal was generating new answers to decades-old questions about federal authority versus states' rights. And, though they did not emphasize the connection, they were not unaware of how much the Communist Party and ILD had upstaged their organization by making Scottsboro an international rallying cry for racial justice. Under White's leadership as executive secretary, the NAACP Legal Committee drafted a bill similar to the Dyer bill, and Senators Edward P. Costigan of Colorado and Robert F. Wagner of New York agreed to support it.[42] The Costigan-Wagner bill passed the Senate Judiciary Committee with minor amendments. Then, in the midst of a major NAACP lobbying and publicity campaign, it got a gruesome boost in public opinion from the October 1934 lynching of Claude Neal.

Arrested and charged with the brutal murder of a white farmwoman in Marianna, Florida, Neal had been moved across state lines to a jail in Brewton, Alabama, for his own safety. A week after his arrest, a mob of white men entered the jail, seized him, and drove him back to Marianna, where they held him for hours before torturing and killing him. Afterward, they displayed his body before a crowd of more than 4,000 men, women, and children. Fifteen newspapers had time to print stories about the anticipated lynching before it took place, yet neither local authorities nor the governor had been able or willing to prevent it. Their inaction, plus the fact that Neal had been transported across state lines, added considerable weight to the argument that lynching ought to be a federal offense.[43]

Southerners in Congress disagreed. The Costigan-Wagner bill arrived on the Senate floor in early 1935, at roughly the same time the Supreme Court was considering *Norris v. Alabama*. Like their predecessors in the 1920s, southern Democrats determined to filibuster. "We will fight it out . . . if it takes all summer," Senator Josiah Bailey of North Carolina vowed. Conservatives

Senators Robert F. Wagner of New York and Edward P. Costigan of Colorado, Democrats and authors of an antilynching bill that failed to survive a southern Democratic filibuster in 1935. Harris and Ewing Collection, Library of Congress, Prints and Photographs Division, Washington, D.C. [LC-DIG-hec-38351].

like Bailey and Walter F. George of Georgia delivered familiar arguments about state sovereignty and the founding fathers' vision of a limited federal government. Ellison D. "Cotton Ed" Smith of South Carolina and even Alabama liberal Hugo Black invoked visions of Reconstruction and federal troops occupying private homes. South Carolinian James F. Byrnes acted on the principle that the best sectional defense was a good offense. Insisting that race relations in the South were generally harmonious, he reminded Senator Costigan of deadly labor disputes that had killed miners in his home state of Colorado and encouraged Senator Wagner to focus on gangland murders in New York.[44]

The fact that both Costigan and Wagner were Democrats made the 1935 debate more complicated than the 1920s debates over the Dyer bill had been. Roosevelt's popularity had inhibited most southern Democrats from challenging the president and the more liberal elements within their party. Nevertheless, southern politicians recognized that New Deal reforms, particularly in agriculture and labor relations, could threaten their long-established dominance at the local and state levels. They were the beneficiaries of the South's one-party politics and disfranchisement-shrunken electorate; for them, stasis meant reelection and seniority. Not since the Populists had they seen such threats to the status quo as were emerging within national Democratic Party circles. Yet how could they take on Roosevelt or do more than ensure that local, loyal functionaries were the ones signing off on federal farm subsidies and handing out relief? Touching on the sacred ground of race relations, the Costigan-Wagner bill was one liberal Democratic measure that southern congressmen could vehemently reject without the least fear of upsetting their white constituents. Like the Dyer bill before it and similar bills after it, the Costigan-Wagner bill died against a wall of Solid South opposition.[45]

Jonathan Daniels loathed hidebound southern conservatives like Bailey, but he was nevertheless a holdout from the liberal position on a federal antilynching law — as, indeed, was Roosevelt, who privately supported the measure but refused to spend any political capital on an effort he considered futile and divisive.[46] Daniels's opposition partook of both Roosevelt's political calculation and the states' rights doctrines of southern congressmen, although he differed significantly from the latter in that he advocated state-level action not as a constitutional prerogative but as an achingly necessary reform.

Most of all, Daniels reiterated the traditional arguments of white southern liberals, making the same points the CIC had been making for years prior to its endorsement of Costigan-Wagner. His editorials in the *News and Observer* show that he understood why his contemporaries' views were changing, even if he did not fully agree with them. More subtly, his editorials and *A Southerner Discovers the South* reveal how current events shook his thinking and contributed to the slow process by which he eventually changed his mind and became a racial liberal.

One of the first editorials Daniels wrote after taking over the *News and Observer* focused on Arthur F. Raper's *The Tragedy of Lynching*, a vitally important 1933 book that laid the groundwork for the CIC's 1935 endorsement. Raper was a North Carolina–born sociologist who had studied under

Howard Odum at Chapel Hill. In 1926, he succeeded Woofter as the CIC's research director, and in 1930 he took the lead when a new CIC committee, the Southern Commission on the Study of Lynching, decided to investigate every lynching that took place in the South that year.

With the help of a black sociology student from Atlanta University named Walter R. Chivers, Raper produced a comprehensive and chilling study. Like Ida B. Wells decades earlier, he showed that the vast majority of lynchings resulted from causes other than rape or attempted rape of a white woman. His research also revealed a correlation between lynching and white rural poverty, finding that most of the cases in 1930 took place in counties with high rates of farm tenancy, below-average per capita wealth, few educational facilities, and weak community structures and practices of law enforcement. Thus, his primary explanation for lynching was economic competition between blacks and poor whites. He also cited cultural isolation, noting that lynchers were usually poorly educated, unemployed and unattached white men in their late teens and early twenties. They exercised the "least public responsibility" and were "farthest removed from the institutions and agencies determining accepted standards of conduct."[47] Nevertheless, Raper did not excuse white southern elites or local authorities. Instead, he highlighted the threat to democratic principles inherent in communities' conspiracies of silence and "showed that townspeople of power and position were accomplices to the crimes, in one way or another."[48]

In addition to exploring the causes of mob violence, Raper's book described case after case in awful detail, deliberately unsettling readers like Daniels. "No sane man could read this book without being revolted by the record of cruelty and brutality," he wrote in the *News and Observer*—one of hundreds of newspapers and magazines, including dozens of white newspapers in the South, that described Raper's book for an audience of millions who would never read his academic study.[49] In Daniels's view, *The Tragedy of Lynching*, though "written in a day of supposed enlightenment, is a record of still existing barbarism. If any argument were needed against the savagery of lynching, this book provides it."[50]

The question was, where would Daniels and other white southern liberals take Raper's argument? Raper himself became an advocate for a federal antilynching law, not least because it would have allowed the black and white dissenters he found in the communities he studied to testify in federal court.[51] His position challenged that of the CIC's other lead figure on lynching, Jessie Daniel Ames, who had founded the Association of Southern Women for the Prevention of Lynching in late 1930. Like Raper, Ames believed there were white as well as black southerners in every community who opposed lynching. As a veteran of the woman suffrage movement, she particularly hoped to see organized white womanhood bring its influence to bear. But she considered the push for a federal law to be, at best, a distraction. Only education and cultural change could eliminate the problem. She thought the threat of federal prosecution would merely antagonize white southerners and drive community demands for vengeance into the courts, promoting legal lynchings (like the one that had happened at Scottsboro) to replace the mob murders that were already on the wane.

Throughout the 1930s, Daniels tended to agree with Ames rather than Raper, even as the "southern liberal mainstream," not to mention northern liberals and radicals, flowed Raper's way.[52] Daniels wanted action, but like Ames, he wanted it to take place at the local and state levels, which meant the main priority had to be on education and building respect for the rule of law. He explained his point of view at length in a December 1933 editorial, written soon after the Costigan-Wagner bill was drafted. "Important as lynching is as a national phenomenonon," he wrote, "it is essentially a crime against State laws and its cure lies in creating an understanding throughout the most backward localities of America of the importance of upholding the law." The fact that 1933 was "with one exception, the worst year for lynchings in the last decade" certainly made the push for federal legislation understandable. "The proposal to put the eradication of lynching in the hands of the Federal government" was also "a proposal in the spirit of the times which have turned over to the Federal government most of the difficult problems of the States." But strengthening the federal government seemed to mean weakening state and local authority. "Such a transfer of power and responsibility might result in immediate gains," Daniels conceded. "But in lynching more than in any other crime the State responsibility ought to be maintained." He admitted that "the greatest obstacle to convictions in lynchings has been the condoning of the crime" by local communities. "Under Federal authority that difficulty would remain and be deepened by local antagonism against unknown Federal agents." Like other white southern liberals, Daniels wanted *southern* authorities to do their duty. "Arm the states," he urged. "Most Governors, given the power, could be relied upon to uphold the sacredness of the laws and the Courts."[53]

It was an approach that had seemed to work in North Carolina and elsewhere in the 1920s, and Daniels and others would repeatedly cite the overall decline in the number of lynchings as a sign that state-level efforts could be effective.[54] But state officials' inaction in the Claude Neal case was a devastating rebuttal. Daniels wrote about the Neal lynching but dodged the question of whether the mob's long delay meant that state authorities should have been able to prevent it. Instead, he focused on the cold cruelty of the mob itself. "It is possible to understand, if not excuse, a lynching which grows from a swift frenzy," he argued, "but Florida has added something new to the history of brutality in America by indulging in acts commonly associated only with frenzy and perversion after long deliberation and after sending out invitations to the neighbors." His bitterly ironic title for this editorial was "R.S.V.P."[55]

If Daniels had accepted evidence of southern authorities' unconcern—evidence such as Arthur Raper's finding that, "in a survey of 100 lynchings, at least half were carried out with police officers participating, and in nine-tenths of the others the officers condoned the mob action"—then his position might have been different.[56] "If there were any real basis for the assumption that States do not strongly condemn lynching," he wrote in a *News and Observer* editorial in early April 1937, "then it might plausibly . . . be argued that a Federal anti-lynching statute be adopted." But, he protested, "the contrary is true."

And so, states did not need to be punished by the federal government, which is how Daniels, not to mention southern congressmen, persisted in seeing antilynching bills. Daniels's chief objection to a 1937 bill introduced by Harlem representative Joseph A. Gavagan was "its basis upon the principle that the power of the Federal government should be used to punish states." He did not oppose the growth of the federal government in and of itself, and he made a point of educating *News and Observer* readers about why. "Because of the development of huge economic units of wealth and power," he wrote, "there are fields of legislation into which the Federal government must enter in order to provide effective regulation." But "the basic principle behind all such legislation is that of co-operation, not intimidation. There has never been a time when force bills ought to have been adopted. . . . At this late day when admittedly lynching is being practically obliterated, there is even less excuse than formerly."[57]

Two weeks after Daniels wrote these words, an especially brutal lynching in Duck Hill, Mississippi, exposed the tragic flaw in his optimistic argument. Roosevelt Townes and Robert "Bootjack" McDaniels had been arrested for the murder of a white Duck Hill merchant. After their arraignment at the Montgomery County courthouse in Winona, a mob of 100 or more white men seized them, pushed them into a school bus that had been stationed near the courthouse, and drove them back to Duck Hill, with another busload and several carloads of white men following. There the mob chained Townes and McDaniels to trees and tortured them with a blowtorch until they confessed. After Townes admitted to having pulled the trigger, the mob burned him to death in a brushfire. McDaniels died from a single bullet to the head.[58]

Daniels's editorial on April 15, 1937, was one of the most anguished he ever wrote. Titled simply "Southern Scene," it began by noting that William Faulkner, "the novelist who has disturbed the South by depicting the degenerate and horrid aspects of Southern life," was from Oxford, Mississippi. "The latest Mississippi lynching took place on Tuesday at Duck Hill." Daniels quoted, in italics for emphasis, from national news coverage about how Roosevelt Townes had been "*tied to a stake . . . and tortured slowly to death by flames from a blow torch.*" Nothing Faulkner had ever written was more terrible. "No horror ever attributed to the South could be more ghastly than that white hand holding a blow torch to that Negro's body. No people anywhere could be more dreadful than the white men whose eyes watched that and permitted that." Was it any wonder that northern congressmen were urging the passage of a federal law against such brutality? "God help the South for it contains men like these!," he exclaimed. White southerners might "fear the Gavagan anti-lynching bill, but even more we should fear ourselves or our fellows who hold the blow torch against flesh. At a distance they are indistinguishable from other Southerners who are as sick over sadism and lynching as any decent law-abiding men anywhere."[59]

The events at Duck Hill occurred just three weeks before Daniels set off on his southern tour. He would discuss the lynching at least once during his journey, on the night of May 19 when he was in Greenville, Mississippi. He had gone there to meet William Alexander Percy, the aristocratic white poet, son of a senator, uncle and adoptive father of novelist Walker Percy, and, in recent scholarship, window onto the world of southern gay men.[60] Daniels knew Percy as a man of letters and wrote about him in *A Southerner Discovers the South* as someone who needed little introduction, even though his most famous work, his best-selling memoir *Lanterns on the Levee: Recollections of a Planter's Son*, would not be published until 1941. On the night of Daniels's visit, Percy—"a diminutive man, neat and clean to perfection," who himself quoted a neighbor who said he looked like "a combination of Lord Byron and Helen of Troy"—went to bed early, leaving Daniels to sit up talking with two other white Mississippi writers, Roark Bradford and David Cohn. They were good company, especially because they were both inclined to "talk the vernacular: 'the poor bastard'—'the simple son-of-a-bitch'—etc."[61]

On no subject were Cohn and Bradford more plainspoken than that of poor whites. Daniels embellished on his notes from their conversation in *A Southerner Discovers the South*, quoting himself as saying, "I can't understand . . . such people as those who lynched a Negro up at Duck Hill with a blow torch." Cohn responds, "That's only a hundred miles from here. . . . There are plenty of people who could do it. You don't know how they hate the Negro. They feel vastly superior but they have to compete on the same economic level. That's the basis for a stinking bitterness—the killing kind."[62] Cohn then goes on to tell a story, which he actually did tell that night. In his journal Daniels wrote: "Cohn says he went up into hill country around time of lynching and heard them discussing what they were going to do—They suggested getting the women to pick the Negro's eye balls out with needles—Would they do that? I asked. You're damn right they would, he said."[63]

Unintentionally, Daniels had recreated the same kind of question-and-answer dialogue that had gotten Samuel Leibowitz into trouble back in 1933. How could the jury do it? the reporter had asked Leibowitz. Would they do that? Daniels asked Cohn. The two men's answers were very much the same: "They're terrible people," as Daniels has Cohn reply in his book. Despite his patriotic defense of Scottsboro residents, Daniels was not just reporting Cohn's sentiments but revealing his own anxieties about the penchant for violence and brutality among southern whites. He ended the chapter about his visit with Percy, Cohn, and Bradford on an unusually pessimistic note. "I felt suddenly that I was glad I would be gone from the Delta before at last the barbarians came down. With blow torches or needles or ballots. They would rise about the stone knight in the cemetery"—Percy's monument to his father and, by extension, to an aristocratic and paternalistic ethos—"like the waters of the flood."[64]

Seeing the Deep South for the first time and hearing the reports of men like Cohn and Bradford affected Daniels profoundly. In June 1937, just days after he returned from his tour, an Alabama Supreme Court decision pushed him close to the "Alabama does not care" moment he had reached in 1935 in relation to Scottsboro. The case had to do with a sheriff who admitted to having felt "forced," because of "popular excitement," to arrest an innocent man who was subsequently lynched. The sheriff was accused of negligence, but the Alabama Supreme Court ruled that "the 'wrong man' issue was not before it" and acquitted him of any wrongdoing. Daniels was disgusted. It was the "sinister aspects" of lynching, including "the possible mobbing of innocent men," that gave rise "to the repeated attempts to bring the Federal power to bear on lynching cases," he wrote. "It is not enough to raise opposition" to federal bills, he added. "Some means must be found for erasing the cause of lynchings. It will then be simpler to deal with the effects."[65]

Before his trip, Daniels probably would have written more confidently about education as the "means" by which lynching could be eradicated. Afterward, he began to take a different tack. He continued to doubt the efficacy of a federal law and argued, with the same attention to political expediency that Roosevelt had long shown, that the inevitable Senate filibuster was enough of a reason to give up the fight. In January 1938, Daniels dismissed the whole antilynching debate as not just a red herring but a "red whale" that was "big enough for a whole company of politicians to hide behind." The Gavagan bill was "by no means the most important bill before the Congress for southern white men or black ones but it provides a roost for Southern politicians, and also Northern ones, who know that it is safer to be a patriot than to take a position on contested questions." Much like Roosevelt, Daniels wanted congressmen to "turn their energies to important legislation designed to lift the earnings of the farmer and the wages of the worker." He still believed that "only education and government by an educated people will put a final end to lynching." But now he also argued that "the best way to reduce lynchings in the South is to improve the economic condition of the people."[66] This was a different solution but a federal one nevertheless. Like other white southern liberals, Daniels was losing his faith in localism and accepting the fact that the South needed federal help, perhaps even on racial matters, although he much preferred that help to come in the form of jobs programs and labor laws rather than criminal justice.

Still, his doubts about the white southern masses and the ability or willingness of state and local authorities to restrain their potential for violence would contribute to his growing support for civil rights initiatives. The Gavagan antilynching bill died in February 1938 in a Senate filibuster that turned out to be the last major congressional fight over the issue for the next decade. Ten years later, when a federal antilynching law was again on the table as part of President Harry Truman's civil rights agenda, Daniels would finally endorse it.

✦ ✦ ✦

GIVEN HIS SUSTAINED commitment to state and local rather than federal action on lynching, it is a little surprising that Daniels failed to mention some white Alabamans' efforts to free the Scottsboro Boys in *A Southerner Discovers the South.* He visited two of their most prominent local advocates, Grover C. Hall and James E. Chappell, when he passed through Montgomery and Birmingham in June 1937. Their work in support, albeit at arm's length, of the Scottsboro Defense Committee (SDC) was the kind of local effort he had asked for back in 1933. Yet, in his travelogue Daniels left this aspect of the Scottsboro case—and even recent developments in its resolution—unexplored.

The SDC had formed at the end of 1935 as a Popular Front collaboration of five groups: the ILD, the NAACP, the American Civil Liberties Union, the Methodist Federation for Social Service, and the League for Industrial Democracy (a socialist advocacy group headed by Norman Thomas). By the time it came together, the state of Alabama had reindicted all of the Scottsboro defendants in the wake of the Supreme Court's decision in *Norris v. Alabama*, and a new round of trials was about to begin, starting as before with the prosecution of Haywood Patterson.

Opening in Decatur on January 20, 1936, Patterson's trial—his fourth since his arrest in March 1931—went very much like his third trial had, with Judge William Callahan again in charge. The jury deliberated for eight hours and found Patterson guilty of rape but, because of one juror's preference for leniency, sentenced him to seventy-five years in prison rather than the electric chair.[67]

Prosecutor Thomas Knight was flabbergasted and decided to postpone the remaining trials. The Scottsboro Boys were handcuffed together in groups of three and put into the back seats of three police cars for the ninety-mile ride back to the Birmingham jail. On the way, Ozie Powell got into an argument with one of his guards. When the officer reached back from the front seat and hit him in the head, Powell hushed but went to work fishing a small knife out of a hiding place in his pants. Then he reached forward with his free hand and slashed the officer in the throat. Swerving the car to a stop, the other officer leapt out, turned back, and shot Powell in the head. It would be called an escape attempt. Powell survived but mentally was never quite the same. The injured officer's throat required ten stitches. As much as their supporters tried to downplay the incident, it hurt the Scottsboro Boys' public image. The fact that Patterson had been given time rather than the death penalty also contributed to a slackening of interest—as if the nine young men were not dying already from their long imprisonment. When Powell's mother asked him why he had attacked the officer, he said there was no need for him "to express any further cause." He had "done give up."[68]

It was under these circumstances that the chair of the SDC, a white, Yale-trained minister from the Midwest named Allan Knight Chalmers, decided to try to recruit some white Alabamans into his organization. "My task was not going to be an easy one," he later reflected. His own committee was divided on the question of whether it was even worth trying, and he had very few leads. Respected Socialist Party leader Norman Thomas had written to George Fort Milton, editor of the *Chattanooga News*, but Milton's reply had been irritated and noncommittal: "If he could be in Birmingham on the day of [Chalmers's] arrival he would." Luckily, Milton showed up. He had, after all, been the head of the Southern Commission on the Study of Lynching and was one the South's leading white liberals. After Patterson's first Decatur trial he, like Daniels, had publicly expressed his belief in the Scottsboro Boys' innocence. Still, it took Milton "an hour and a half to satisfy himself that my attitude toward the case was a suitable one," Chalmers remembered. "It was only then that he called a Mr. Chappell of the Birmingham *News* and *Age-Herald*."[69]

James E. Chappell would play a key role in the protracted resolution of the Scottsboro case as Chalmers's first white Alabama contact. The "five minutes" that he reluctantly agreed to give Chalmers turned into two hours and culminated in a promise to assemble some of his friends for a meeting. Those friends included prominent journalists, lawyers, and clergymen, several of whom would go on to become members of a new (and pointedly independent) local group, the Alabama Scottsboro Fair Trial Committee. In the summer and fall of 1936, the Alabama committee quietly negotiated with state officials for a change of venue and a different prosecutor. They also tried to come to an agreement with a local lawyer who could replace Leibowitz. In short, they started doing the kinds of things Daniels had long before said would be necessary to preserve "the honor of Alabama" while achieving some kind of justice for the defendants.

Daniels spent several hours with Chappell when he visited Birmingham on his tour. In addition to being the editor and general manager of two Birmingham newspapers (the *Age-Herald* and the *News*, which published in the morning and evening, respectively), Chappell was the president of the Southern Newspaper Publishers Association, which is how Daniels knew him. They chatted about the Scottsboro case, among other topics, in Chappell's office on June 2, 1937. During the previous two days, Daniels had also seen Grover C. Hall.[70]

Hall was the editor of the *Montgomery Advertiser* and had been one of the fieriest defenders of his home state against external criticism. He assumed the Scottsboro "gorillas" were guilty as charged and thought various white Alabamans—the crowds in Scottsboro and Decatur, the officer who shot but did not kill Ozie Powell—had shown remarkable restraint. He had been invited to join the Alabama Scottsboro Fair Trial Committee in 1936 but had declined, saying he preferred to "remain aloof from all organized propaganda agencies." In June 1937, however (less than two weeks after Daniels's visit, although this may have been a mere coincidence), Hall suddenly agreed to meet with Chalmers. Afterward, he wrote an influential editorial urging state officials to seek a compromise because "nothing could be gained by demanding the final pound of flesh." It was the first of many efforts Hall would make on the Scottsboro Boys' behalf.[71]

Even before Hall changed course, Alabama officials had begun to look for a way out. The Scottsboro case had already cost the state a comparative fortune, and Knight, who was still leading the prosecution even though he had been elected lieutenant governor in 1935, was sick of it.[72] First, he buttonholed Chalmers during one of his visits to Birmingham: "Plead the Boys guilty and I'll see to it that they get only seven years . . . and that will let them out almost at once." Chalmers felt obligated to take the offer to the defendants, who preferred, in Andy Wright's words, to "rot here till I die before I'll say I did something I didn't do."[73]

Then, in December 1936, Knight showed up in New York unannounced to try to strike a deal with Leibowitz. After several meetings, they worked out a plan. The state would drop all charges against Olen Montgomery, Willie Roberson, Eugene Williams, and Roy Wright. Three others, Clarence Norris, Charlie Weems, and Andy Wright, would be guaranteed short sentences if they pled guilty to simple assault for the fight on the train. Haywood Patterson would continue to serve his seventy-five-year sentence but would be paroled when Norris, Weems, and Wright were. Ozie Powell would be tried for assaulting the deputy but not for rape. Knight and Leibowitz parted with promises to get the necessary approvals from the people they represented. Chalmers and the SDC reluctantly agreed to the compromise, and Leibowitz made arrangements to go to Alabama to speak to the Scottsboro Boys themselves.[74] "Then," as Chalmers put it, "came the double cross."[75]

Knight and attorney general Albert A. Carmichael broke off communications as abruptly as Knight had started them. For weeks, no one on the defense side could figure out what was happening. Then, on May 17, 1937, Knight suddenly dropped dead at the age of thirty-nine from a liver and kidney disease.[76] It was not clear whether the compromise had died with him. A week later, Judge Callahan set a date, July 12, to begin the trials that had been postponed back in January 1936.

Despite calls for compromise from Hall, Chappell, and other leading white Alabamans, the trials did, in fact, begin on July 12. By the time the first four concluded, all of the efforts of the SDC and the Alabama Scottsboro Fair Trial Committee had been shown to be almost meaningless (which may be the most important reason Daniels did not write about them). Clarence Norris was convicted of rape and sentenced to death. Andy Wright and Charlie Weems were convicted of rape and sentenced to ninety-nine years and seventy-five years, respectively. Ozie Powell pled guilty to assaulting the deputy and, with Leibowitz fighting hard for leniency, he was sentenced to the maximum: twenty years. Only then did prosecutors announce that the state was dropping all charges against Olen Montgomery, Willie Roberson, Eugene Williams, and Roy Wright. They, unlike the others, were free to go.

Leibowitz pointed out how illogical it all was, and the SDC drove home the point with a pamphlet titled *Four Free, Five More in Jail — on the Same Evidence*. It would largely be up to Chalmers and the Alabama committee to continue the fight for pardons or paroles, and it was here that Grover Hall proved most helpful — until he, too, died suddenly in 1941. Sadly, no pardons would be forthcoming and no paroles would be granted for more than six years, when Weems was released in November 1943. Norris and Andy Wright were paroled in 1944 but soon ended up back inside on parole violations, Norris until 1946 and Wright until 1950. Powell was paroled in 1946 and returned to his home state of Georgia. Patterson escaped from Kilby Prison in 1948. He died, at the age of 39, in 1952.

None of the Scottsboro Boys found life after prison easy, but one did at least eventually gain a measure of justice. By the early 1970s, Clarence Norris had settled into a quiet life in Brooklyn but was technically still a fugitive because he had violated his 1946 parole by leaving Alabama. His fugitive status gnawed at him, plus he wanted to clear his name. With the help of the NAACP, he finally got the attention of Alabama attorney general William Baxley. Baxley read Judge Horton's 1933 opinion setting aside the verdict in Haywood Patterson's second trial and became convinced that Norris was innocent. He recommended a pardon, and in October 1976, Alabama governor George Wallace (then in the midst of his own rehabilitation campaign) granted it. Norris's pardon amounted, in the words of one legal scholar, "to an official recognition of his innocence and, by necessary implication, the innocence of the eight young men accused with him."[77]

That was something Victoria Price would never concede. When the National Broadcasting Company (NBC) aired a made-for-television movie called "Judge Horton and the Scottsboro Boys" in April 1976, both Price and Ruby Bates sued. The film's producers had thought both women were dead, and Bates did die shortly after her suit for invasion of privacy, defamation, and libel was filed. As in the 1930s, Victoria Price held out to the end, seeking $6 million in damages. The hearings took place in Winchester, Tennessee, about 45 miles north of Scottsboro. After listening to the testimony, the judge dismissed the case on the grounds of insufficient evidence and the filmmakers' First Amendment rights. An appeals court upheld the dismissal, but when the U.S. Supreme Court agreed to hear the case, NBC decided to settle. The terms of the 1981 settlement were never disclosed. Price died in 1982.[78]

Long before the deaths of Price, Bates, and all of the others who were directly involved (Clarence Norris was the last survivor, passing in 1989), some of the broader ramifications of Scottsboro—the case and the controversies surrounding it—were starting to become clear. For one thing, the Supreme Court's decisions in *Powell* and *Norris* established important legal precedents for defendants' right to counsel and for eliminating racial discrimination in the selection of juries. The "due process revolution" in criminal cases would not arrive until the 1960s, but it would depend upon such precedents.[79]

Equally important, the ILD's highly publicized defense of the Scottsboro Boys helped the Communist Party and the left more generally achieve in the 1930s the greatest influence it has ever had in American politics and culture. Particularly during the Popular Front period from 1935 to 1939, the party and its newfound allies pushed both New Deal policies and the American people leftward and helped put racial justice on the nation's political and social agenda. Thus, Scottsboro had "far-reaching ripples," as historian Glenda Gilmore has observed, sounding a lot like Jonathan Daniels. Like a rock thrown into the still waters of a pond, the Communist Party's "political campaign to free [the Scottsboro Boys] caused a few white Southerners and many white Northerners to question the southern legal system. It also focused world opinion on antidemocratic practices in the South" at a time when the threat of fascism in Europe was encouraging many Americans to rededicate themselves to the preservation of democracy.[80]

Daniels shared his contemporaries' concerns about democracy's survival in a world of dictatorships. As much as he distrusted the Communist Party, he was willing to admit that Communists had fought on the side of justice in the Scottsboro case. Although the little town was quiet, visiting Scottsboro on May 11, 1937, was nonetheless unsettling. Daniels knew the Scottsboro Boys' imprisonment was a travesty, and he wanted white Alabamans to do something honorable to correct it. He was not sure whether they would or could, and if he was apprised of how little the local Alabama Scottsboro Fair Trial Committee was able to accomplish, he would have surely found that fact almost as discouraging as the Senate filibusters and the horrifying events in Marianna, Florida, and Duck Hill, Mississippi. Still, Daniels wondered whether outside intervention in the South could be effective. It was much easier to approve of the federal government sponsoring economic development projects like the TVA than it was to imagine federal prosecutors trying to punish lynch mobs, much less complicit sheriffs. Surely any attempt to enforce a federal law would only make recalcitrant white southerners all the more defiant.

In fact, there were those in the South who opposed even the TVA. Daniels intended to interview one such New Deal critic in the evening of the very same day he visited Scottsboro. If ripples from the left and from the NAACP's antilynching campaign were starting to wear away at the dam of his own commitment to southern home rule, there were other white southerners, including intellectuals, who were intent on building thicker walls. His night in Nashville would uncover a citadel of sectional resistance to social and economic change.

CHAPTER FOUR

A Quaint and Quixotic Group of Gentlemen

✦

AFTER HIS STOPS in Scottsboro and Paint Rock, Jonathan got back in his car and back into the mind-set of a Depression-era documentarian. He made some notes about the "Alabama roadside—[a] quarry or gravel pit—and big Negroes all in white . . . pick axing—swinging strong—convicts I think." He also picked up another hitchhiker, recording some facts about his life: "Mr. Freeman . . . about 55—born near Greenville, S.C.—went west as a cowboy—been in 30 states and lived in 10." In Florence, Alabama, about a hundred miles west of Scottsboro, Jonathan happened upon "an unexpectedly literate filling station attendant." He asked him about the book he was reading and then quizzed him about local reactions to other books, including Carl Carmer's *Stars Fell on Alabama* (1934). He was not surprised to learn that "Alabama did not like" it.[1] A northerner who had taught at the University of Alabama in the 1920s, Carmer had written a colorful account of the state's people and folkways interspersed with his own adventures, including his attendance at a Klan rally in Tuscaloosa. Many white Alabamans considered it an unkind exposé, as well as an abuse of their hospitality—"just what an interloping damn Yankee professor would do, the common opinion seemed to run."[2]

Jonathan may have taken the gas station attendant's words as a warning not to analyze too deeply. While not a direct inspiration for his book, *Stars Fell on Alabama* was the kind of first-person narrative that, in the 1930s, was developing into the new genre of documentary expression.[3] When he took to the road in 1937, Daniels was consciously following the lead of other writers, including a number from the left who set out to describe the economic hardships of the Great Depression. Their exposés appeared in newspapers and magazines and in books like John L. Spivak's *America Faces the Barricades* (1935) and James Rorty's *Where Life Is Better: An Unsentimental Journey* (1936). Decades later, the most famous of these writers would be those who had also published fiction (John Steinbeck, for one) and those who had collaborated with photographers. Erskine Caldwell's collaboration with photographer Margaret Bourke-White, *You Have Seen Their Faces* (1937), was the first of several important photo-documentary books that combined images and text in a stunning depiction of poverty in the South.

As more and more writers took up the genre, its political perspective broadened from left to center, and many, including Daniels, tempered their documentary claims to suggest they were writing about just one observer's America or, as Daniels put it, "only one man's South."[4] These late-thirties writers would "look *for*" and document the country "and not just economic conditions," writes William Stott. Their "reportorial method was Sherwood Anderson's: a compilation of extraneous firsthand impressions, with repeated disclaimers to any general truth. Each writer insisted he spoke only for himself and from his particular experience; each admitted cheerfully that other people not only might but inevitably would disagree."[5]

It was a cheery sort of relativism that was temperamentally the opposite of the orthodoxy of the man Daniels was going to Nashville to interview: "the poet-voice of the Southern Agrarian," Donald Davidson. A forty-three-year-old English professor at Vanderbilt, Davidson was one of the "Twelve Southerners" who had contributed to the 1930 manifesto *I'll Take My Stand*, a widely debated collection of essays defending white southerners' supposedly age-old values and traditional, agrarian way of life. As a staunch defender of *the* South, Davidson could hardly be expected to appreciate Daniels's sensibility—his suggestion that "there are as many Souths, perhaps, as there are people living in it."[6] Davidson would avoid reviewing and even delay reading *A Southerner Discovers the South* "out of a certain cordial impulse," but he knew the genre. He had recognized a similarly "realistic" eye and lack of "doctrine" in Sherwood Anderson's *Puzzled America* (1935) and suggested these traits proved Anderson's affinity with the pragmatic Roosevelt administration. Indeed, they made Anderson "the unofficial Poet Laureate of the New Deal"—which meant he was on the opposite side of a deepening political divide from Davidson himself.[7]

For Davidson was a conservative.[8] He would fight for decades for the preservation of what he called a "provincial" way of life. He loathed the forces of modernity that created a world beyond individual men's comprehension and control, and he particularly resisted racial change, which chipped away at the bedrock of his understanding of human civilization. "His conception of the South as the enduring source of identity, order, meaning, and being in the world depended on the subordination of blacks and the maintenance of racial purity among whites," explains one sympathetic historian. David-son "believed that the South was the last incarnation of that ancient, ho-mogenous, independent, and moral community of Anglo-Saxon farmers in which Thomas Jefferson had so eloquently placed his hopes for the future of mankind."[9] Grounded in this belief, Davidson opposed even minimal, New Deal challenges to the southern social order, and he experienced the long civil rights era as nothing less than a long siege.

Only after the pitched battles of the 1950s and 1960s would intellectuals reexamine Davidson's work and that of the other Nashville Agrarians and find in their Depression-era essays the roots of a twentieth-century southern conservative tradition. As interest in conservative thought rose along with the late-twentieth-century rise of the right and the regional shift in the Re-publican Party's center of gravity, Davidson and his friends became newly relevant and divisive figures whose ideas about economics and government were inseparable from a legacy of racism and romanticism for the South's "Lost Cause." Even those who genuinely hoped to cultivate the Agrarians' legacy for some other reason—because they valued organic farming or de-tested Sunbelt suburban sprawl—discovered that the thorny overgrowth of neo-Confederatism (a crop the Agrarians' themselves had undeniably planted) made it difficult to clear the ground.[10] By the end of the twentieth century, the Nashville Agrarians had found their way posthumously to the front lines of the culture wars amidst Confederate flag controversies and other issues.[11] They might have been happy to serve because, no matter how "sensitive" or "soft-spoken" Daniels found Davidson to be, he and his fel-low Agrarians had always been cultural warriors. They fought what Da-vidson himself in a 1935 essay called the "war of cultures in our time": "a war between urban civilization—which is industrial, progressive, scientific, anti-traditional—and rural or provincial civilization—which is on the whole agrarian, conservative, anti-scientific, and traditional."[12] In this war, Jonathan Daniels was an embedded journalist on the modernist side, while the mild-mannered Davidson was the diehard of his conservative platoon.

WHEN HE GOT TO NASHVILLE on the evening of May 11, Daniels went straight to the Andrew Jackson Hotel on the corner of Sixth Avenue and Deaderick Street, just across the square from the state capitol (and later to be torn down to make way for the Tennessee Performing Arts Center). Opened in 1925, the hotel was a twelve-story brick building with 400 guest rooms. It

Nashville Agrarian Donald Davidson in 1947.
Vanderbilt Photographic Archives, Special Collections
and University Archives, Jean and Alexander Heard
Library, Vanderbilt University, Nashville, Tenn.

boasted modern air conditioning and two restaurants, the Surf Rider and the Golden Horn.[13] The place was so crowded when Daniels arrived that the clerk had to find him a bathroom where he could wash up because it was going to take a while to find him a bed. The state legislature was in session, there was some sort of bankers' conference going on, and the lady gardeners of Tennessee had apparently all turned out to see the city's iris gardens in bloom.[14]

Daniels must have taken a taxi from his hotel to the Vanderbilt University campus, where he was to meet Davidson. After their conversation, first in Davidson's "book-lined study at Vanderbilt" and then in his living room, the somber poet—tall, lanky, his light-colored hair already noticeably thin—would have to drive him back to his hotel.[15] Daniels's notes give no indication of how much time they spent together. "The talk with Donald Davidson," he jotted, "sensitive—disturbed about making a living—says all of his group come from agricultural origins—living room decorated without personality." Daniels wrote a few more lines indicating that he and Davidson had discussed a local bank fraud scandal (which Davidson's friend Robert Penn Warren would later turn into the novel *At Heaven's Gate*). But that was all.[16] The half-dozen pages Daniels would devote to the Nashville Agrarians in *A Southerner Discovers the South* were based far less on the interview than on his prior reading and opinions.

Like virtually every commentator then and since, Daniels began his discussion with a nod to the *Fugitive*. This was the literary magazine that four of the "Twelve Southerners" who later contributed to *I'll Take My Stand* had published from 1922 to 1925. The four—Davidson, Warren, John Crowe Ransom, and Allen Tate—were all poets and all affiliated with Vanderbilt University. They were also all southerners, although not particularly writing as such in this period. Later accounts would often suggest they had discovered the South and their own southern identities only in 1925 in response to the humiliations of the Scopes trial. Attacks on the region by H. L. Mencken and others undoubtedly did stiffen their resolve to defend it but, as a number of scholars have explained, their transition from Fugitives to Agrarians was not so simple and took a slightly different course for each man. Ransom's and Tate's defense of what they saw as southern tradition, although thoroughly devout, was always more philosophical or intellectual than Davidson's, which absorbed both mind and heart.[17]

Donald Davidson was a deeply loyal man: loyal to home, in Campbellsville, Tennessee, where he was born in 1893 and grew up the son of a schoolteacher; loyal to family, including the Confederate grandparents whose stories he drank in as a boy; loyal to friends, especially his *Fugitive* intellectual circle, which he struggled to hold together as long as he could. Davidson committed himself to the Agrarian cause with the fervor of one defending home and family. It was not that he was blind to the South's diversity or its flaws, but from the mid-1920s on, manning the citadel of his own vision of the South was his first, all-consuming priority.

Robert Penn Warren, by contrast, gave the impression that he was much less serious about Agrarianism—an impression that is supported by contemporary sources but that he would strategically reinforce in later years, as his political views shifted. Twenty-five years on, he would remember that his friends' Agrarian cause attracted him "because he was young, away from home, and sentimentally attached to a familiar way of life. He was willing to affirm his roots, not as a thought-out philosophy but as an intuitive response."[18]

It was Tate who, in March 1927, first specifically suggested that he, Davidson, and Ransom ought to assemble a book of essays about the South.[19]

It took them three years to get free of other obligations and recruit Warren and the other eight contributors, six of whom had past or present ties to Vanderbilt. *I'll Take My Stand* appeared in November 1930. Unlike Ransom and Davidson, Tate and Warren hated the sensationalist title, borrowed from the song "Dixie." But no one could deny that it did its job of getting people's attention. Although the deepening economic crisis hurt sales, *I'll Take My Stand* was a great success insofar as it sparked controversy and debate.[20] Jonathan Daniels made no effort to summarize the book's contents in *A Southerner Discovers the South* because he expected his readers to know about it already. Plus, with twelve different essays on different topics by different authors, *I'll Take My Stand* was difficult to summarize.

Davidson offered one of the clearest summations of his, Ransom's, and Tate's overlapping goals for the book in a letter recruiting an essay on the southern economy from historian and political scientist Herman Clarence Nixon. "What we wish," he wrote in January 1930, "is a group of closely associated articles and essays that will center on the South as the best historical and contemporary example in American society of a section that has continuously guarded its local and provincial ways of life against a too rapid modernization." They did not "advocate a restoration of the 'Old South' scheme," and they were "not going to give ourselves up to a purely sentimental and romantic recession to the past." But they were "firmly convinced that the South needs to be redefined, understood, and, so far as possible, placed in a favorable and appealing light—and for two reasons: (1) to save the South, so far as it can be saved, from the 'New South' people who are ready to sacrifice local integrity for 'prosperity' and the vague sort of liberalism that talks of 'progress'; (2) for the country at large, which needs to have before it some strong example of, and if possible an active set of partisans for, agrarianism (country life and economy) as opposed to centralization."[21]

As Davidson explained and at least a few of the twelve essayists demonstrated, the South—and specifically *not* the Old South of myth ("sentimental and romantic") but rather the real South both "historical and contemporary"—needed to be understood as an example of something more abstract: a society that had "guarded its local and provincial ways of life against a too rapid modernization." That society now faced a great danger that came primarily from within, namely, from the "'New South' people" who, for the sake of economic development, would sacrifice "local integrity"—a phrase that for Davidson encompassed racial segregation as well as political control.

From the Agrarians' standpoint, preserving local control was far more important than achieving "prosperity" or "progress"—words that Davidson put in quotation marks to suggest not simply that they were the bywords of New South boosters but also that they were false promises. Meanwhile, the United States "at large" might also benefit from the redefinition and promotion of the South as an exemplar because of the inherent value of the form in which it had guarded localism and a provincial way of life—that is, the South's "agrarianism," which needed to be understood as both an economic arrangement centering on farms ("economy") and a slower, preindustrial pace of living ("country life"). Agrarianism was the opposite of "centralization," which was actually more of a problem than industry in and of itself.

Davidson did not say what was wrong with centralization in his letter, but the underlying idea is perhaps most succinctly explained as a pitting of Thomas Jefferson against Karl Marx.[22] Like Jefferson, the Agrarians promoted independently owned small farms, but they did so because of a very present-minded fear that the *opposite* of the agrarian republic—that is, the concentration of ownership of the means of production in the hands of a few—might lead to (even more) unchecked industrial capitalism, on the one hand, or state-centered socialism, on the other. In the latter case, the idea was that the "Sovietists" of the world could take control all the more easily in an economy that was already centralized. Thus, "the Communist menace" was not simply "a Red one," as *I'll Take My Stand* would assert, but could be found in the "blind drift of our industrial development."[23] Either outcome of centralization was anathema to individualists and artists. Only an economy in which ownership was widely distributed was safe from oligarchy or dictatorship, whether from the left or the right.

In his letter to Nixon, Davidson remained too caught up in the southern example to be able to articulate an Agrarian vision in such cool, theoretical terms. He and the other contributors did not want "to come out as rabid pro-Southerners (though we may be such, in a way)," he conceded. Instead, their goal was "to make the ideas we believe in, which are and have long been in essence Southern, go deep and carry far, and have a philosophy behind them that we hope is important for the times."[24]

As true as it may have been that the Agrarians' ideas were "in essence Southern," their thinking was characteristic of *their* "South," not that of Jonathan or even Josephus Daniels, much less that of the Scottsboro Boys or any *woman*, given that Agrarianism was an all-male as well as all-white movement. The absence of women's voices and lack of discussion of gender issues are striking differences between the culture wars of the 1930s and those of the late twentieth century and beyond. Nevertheless, the Agrarians' vision was highly gendered in the sense that it was very traditional: the Jeffersonian small farm seemed to require a male head of household and a hard-working but economically dependent farm wife, however little discussed.

Similarly, blacks' place within the ideal Agrarian society was never quite clear, except to the extent that it was clearly segregated. During the planning stages for *I'll Take My Stand*, Davidson assigned Warren the task of proving "that Negroes are country folks . . . 'born and bred in a briar patch.'" Then he gasped in horror when he read Warren's moderate essay titled "The Briar Patch," which supported Booker T. Washington's demands for equality and opportunity within a segregated system but transplanted that conception of racial justice from Washington's intended setting, the New South factory, to the Agrarian small farm. "What is he after?" Davidson demanded in a letter to Tate. Warren's essay not only had "progressive" implications but went so far as to refer to a black woman as "Mrs."—a signifier of social equality that Davidson promptly deleted from the manuscript even as he failed to persuade Tate to cut the essay entirely.[25] Needless to say, no black intellectuals were even considered as possible contributors to the volume authored by "Twelve Southerners."[26]

Regardless of the race, gender, and ideological specificity (as opposed to universality) of their thinking, it was the way the Agrarians' ideas *meshed* with their identities that made them so controversial and likely to be misunderstood, on the one hand, and yet so lasting an influence among conservatives, on the other. They claimed to speak as organic southerners representing an organic society. It is a claim that has proved appealing to many even though it belies the true diversity across a landscape that cannot be defined as *anyone's* "South" except through the tools of history and culture. As Daniels and other Depression-era documentarians showed, one did not have to be a postmodernist to recognize that there were many Souths—"as many Souths, perhaps, as there are people living in it."

Despite competing claims, the Agrarians' traditional, antimodernist definition of "*the* South" and what it meant to be "Southern" (like the regionalist liberals, they always capitalized the S) has continued well into the twenty-first century to appeal to audiences both within and outside the geographic space at issue. This definition's greatest appeal has been for those sensing a loss of cultural identity and political power, particularly whites facing integration and the transformations, both political and cultural, of the long civil rights era. Although the concerns of the 1920s and 1930s were different, the Agrarians were early practitioners of identity politics against the "psychic and social tensions" of modern life.[27] Or, as Davidson himself put it a few years after *I'll Take My Stand* appeared, the Agrarians "took for granted that we might speak as Southerners" and were surprised to find that, "for all that some of our [at least geographically southern] critics and we had in common in the way of premises, we might as well have been addressing Mr. Henry Ford" (the personification of modern industry) "or Mr. Granville Hicks" (a Marxist intellectual from New York).[28]

Even if they took their right to "speak as Southerners" for granted, Davidson, Ransom, and Tate did anticipate the need for more coherence in their collection of essays. Tate was the first to call for an introductory "Statement of Principles," which he envisioned as a sort of credo to which all of the contributors would have to pledge. Ransom ultimately wrote the declaration that became the book's preface, with tacit agreement but only minimal input from the others.[29] It might have been better, or at least clearer, if the more down-to-earth Davidson had written it.

Even in their final form the book's opening pages, which were key to its critical reception, were not as straightforward or carefully qualified as Davidson's letter to Nixon had been. First, there was a certain neo-Confederate tone that, along with the book's title, did seem to "advocate a restoration of the 'Old South' scheme." "Nobody now proposes for the South, or for any other community in this country, an independent political destiny," the manifesto began. "That idea is thought to have been finished in 1865. But how far shall the South surrender its moral, social, and economic autonomy to the victorious principles of Union? That question remains open."[30] Davidson would remember "*thought to have been* finished" as a "last-minute change of wording." But this added suggestion of doubt hardly mattered because words like "surrender" and "victorious principles of Union" already evoked the Civil War and implied that, protestations aside, even the possibility of secession remained an "open question" in the minds of the Agrarians.[31] Chattanooga editor George Fort Milton, for one, wasted no time in labeling them the "Young Confederates," while others drew comparisons with the Ku Klux Klan.[32]

If the Agrarians' Old South loyalties seemed clear enough, their ideas about contemporary society and economics were, in Ransom's handling, far less so. Where Davidson had written about "centralization," Ransom used the term "industrialism," which unintentionally suggested that any and all industry was a problem and that the Agrarians merely wanted "a much simpler economy to live by." The bulk of the introduction was devoted to enumerating the evils of industrialism or, as Ransom took pains to explain it, faith in "applied science."[33] It was a picture of industrialization's dark side that many intellectuals had painted from varying perspectives, one that achieved iconographic status in grim scenes of factory regimentation in the 1927 film *Metropolis*, directed by German Expressionist Fritz Lang. Ransom devoted several pages to fleshing out the Agrarians' understanding of the problem. First of all, labor-saving devices had made work into drudgery, something to be avoided rather than something that, under proper circumstances, could be "one of the happy functions of human life." Industrial capitalism brought "overproduction, unemployment, and a growing inequality in the distribution of wealth." Religion and the arts suffered "under the curse of a strictly-business or industrial civilization." The advertising that was necessary to create demand for overabundant products tried "to persuade the consumers to want exactly what the applied sciences are able to furnish them." Ransom professed bewilderment. It was strange "that a majority of men anywhere could ever as with one mind become enamored of industrialism: a system that has so little regard for individual wants."[34] Conversely, the farm was where individualism, a love for labor, and devotion to religion and the arts could grow.

It was too bad that the single paragraph devoted to depicting the Agrarian ideal was so inadequate and so opaque. "Opposed to the industrial society is the agrarian, which does not stand in particular need of definition," Ransom posited. "An agrarian society is hardly one that has no use at all for industries, for professional vocations, for scholars and artists, and for the life of cities."[35] Yet this negative phrasing offered no insight as to *what* use an Agrarian society might have for these things—what balance it might achieve between agriculture and other economic sectors. Nor did Ransom explain how Agrarianism would reverse long-standing economic trends—the agricultural depressions, cycles of debt, and other problems that had resulted in poverty for millions and had been pushing Americans from farms to cities for decades.

Having already made the Agrarians sound like out-of-touch academics or perhaps gentleman farmers, the "Statement of Principles" concluded by eschewing any responsibility for "proposing any practical measures." Only this much was clear: "If a community, or a section, or a race, or an age, is groaning under industrialism, and well aware that it is an evil dispensation, it must find the way to throw it off."[36] The one thing lacking, in the wry observation of historian Paul Conkin, was "the appropriate ending: 'Farmers and poets of the world unite.'"[37]

The Agrarians' decision to leave out any specific policy recommendations made satirical reactions all but inevitable. So did their decision to keep the provocative title *I'll Take My Stand*. Tate, who wanted to call the book "Tracts against Communism," anticipated the drubbing. Even before the book appeared, he observed, the *Nashville Tennesseean* had taken one look at the title and reduced "our real aims to nonsense." By "not making our appeal through the title to ideas," the Agrarians were "at the mercy of all" the reviewers. They "need only to draw portraits of us plowing or cleaning the spring to make hash of us before we get a hearing."[38] This is more or less what happened. *I'll Take My Stand* created a great deal of controversy and was reviewed in dozens of newspapers and magazines, but virtually every reviewer was at least somewhat critical, and many were downright dismissive. The composite picture was of the Agrarians as unreconstructed rebel nostalgics who were tilting at windmills (or cotton mills) with a book in one hand and a hoe (which they might or might not know how to use) in the other.[39]

Rehashing the critical response was Jonathan Daniels's main interest in *A Southerner Discovers the South*. When he met Davidson in Nashville, he must have asked him about the Agrarians' knowledge of farming in order to get the answer he recorded in his journal: "says all of his group come from agricultural origins." He also wrote to Davidson after the interview to ask for biographical information on himself and the others.[40] But even though he allowed Davidson to present the "calloused palms and soles" of his compatriots, Daniels's chapter on his "Night in Nashville" focused on making his own opinion clear. It was the opinion of an open-minded but engaged documentarian. The Agrarians deserved a hearing—they were "useful boys" who "made the South at least contemplate its problems," as he would put it with the authority of hindsight and old age in a 1972 interview. Nevertheless, he thought they had little to offer.[41]

The reviews of *I'll Take My Stand* had been somewhat unfair, Daniels conceded. More laughter "than was ever deserved" had been expended on its authors. "The South thought, even other intellectuals thought—or pretended to think—that the poetic-professorial gentlemen of Vanderbilt urged a retreat in force to the Old South." This was not what they had intended, and surely it was true that "in the alteration from the old plantation system to the new factory system," the South need not "swallow without smelling all of the aspects of industrialism." But the Agrarians were nonetheless "easy to satirize. They did seem a little like a quaint and quixotic group of gentlemen singing down from the ivory tower." On a more serious note, they had "antagonized important 'Liberal' Southern writers by declaring that their work was 'palpably tinged with latter-day abolitionism'"—a phrase that Daniels quoted from Davidson's own contribution to *I'll Take My Stand*. He did not mention that, in his essay, Davidson had been criticizing Daniels's old friend from college days, dramatist Paul Green.[42]

Because he had been in Europe working on his unpublished novel when *I'll Take My Stand* appeared, Daniels had missed the early controversy, just as he had in the Scottsboro case. He had had little significant contact with the Agrarians prior to interviewing Davidson. Still, as Davidson's criticism and his defense of Paul Green indicated, they were destined to disagree with one another, not only because of their differing intellectual temperaments but also because Daniels's loyalties lay in Chapel Hill.

IN THE 1930S, the Agrarians' chief competition for the right to "speak as Southerners" with a vision for the South came from both literary figures like Green and, most important, the Regionalist sociologists affiliated with the University of North Carolina. "If one had asked most well-read Southerners of the 1930s, Who is making the greatest contribution to the understanding of Southern society?" writes historian Michael O'Brien, "most would have answered 'Howard Odum.'"[43] Odum was Kenan Professor of Sociology and the founding director of the UNC School of Public Welfare. In 1922 (the year Daniels graduated with his master's degree), Odum started the influential journal *Social Forces*, and in 1924, he established the Institute for Research in Social Science, which he would direct for two decades. While the former Fugitives were struggling to make ends meet on meager assistant professors' salaries or, in Tate's case, trying to survive as a writer, Odum was building an academic empire based on funding from the Rockefeller Foundation and other northern philanthropies. Stipends for graduate students helped him nurture talented young social scientists and develop the school of thought in sociology known as Regionalism. In a number of books and articles published in the 1920s and 1930s, Odum and his students used extensive, largely quantitative research to argue that the United States was actually composed of several distinct economic and cultural regions. In his comprehensive, 700-page summation of their work, *Southern Regions of the United States*, published in 1936, Odum also advocated the creation of regional and national planning boards to coordinate economic and social policies appropriate for each region's development—starting, of course, with the South, where, though he did not state it so plainly, the existing political structure was least responsive to the needs of the people.[44]

With the publication of *Southern Regions*, Odum's analysis of and vision for the South gained a hearing at the highest levels of the federal government, in which he also served in various capacities. In short, in the 1930s, and in comparison with the Agrarians, the Regionalists' influence was great.

Odum and his most accomplished students—Rupert Vance, Arthur Raper, and Harriet Herring, to name a few—were southerners. Odum himself was from central Georgia, from a background not very different from the middle Tennessee roots of Donald Davidson. Both could point to pre-Revolutionary ancestors; neither grew up with the advantages of wealth, although Odum's mother felt the bitterness of a lost fortune along with the memories of the Civil War that both families passed on to their intellectual sons. Odum, whose father was a farmer, grew up even closer to the soil than did Davidson, whose father taught school. In adulthood, Odum's hobby was raising prize Jersey cattle.

Given these similarities, it is no surprise that there was a significant agrarian bent in Odum's and other Regionalists' thinking. The biggest difference between them and the Nashville Agrarians was in sensibility: social scientists versus humanists, forward thinkers and planners versus those insisting on the importance of things past. Odum accused the Agrarians of being romantic Old South apologists. Vance urged them to come up with the "practical measures" they had omitted from *I'll Take My Stand*.[45] As the Agrarians did, in fact, try to develop a political agenda, the Regionalists debated with them in the press and occasionally face to face. Sometimes, they also tried to work together.

The organization most responsible for bringing the Agrarians and the Regionalists together was the Southern Policy Committee (SPC), in which Jonathan Daniels also participated. In fact, though he did not attend the founding meeting in April 1935, Daniels was elected one of only eleven official members of this group, which functioned as a coordinating committee for local- and state-level affiliates. He would visit at least six of the men (it was initially all men, all of them white) who helped found the SPC during his 1937 travels.[46] The work and especially the reading he did for the group also provided much of the intellectual context for his journey of discovery.

As Daniels himself acknowledged, the SPC was not a well-known organization. The call for public-spirited southerners to get together and talk had issued from an unexpected quarter: the Foreign Policy Association based in Washington, D.C. Although its primary mission was to educate U.S. citizens about foreign affairs, the association's president, Raymond Leslie Buell, had become concerned about Americans' lack of engagement with domestic policy making, with which foreign policy making was inextricably linked. In 1934, he recruited Francis Pickens Miller, a Virginian who had worked in international Christian organizations, for a pilot project. Miller spent much of that fall touring the country to organize "Committees of Correspondence" inspired by the networks among patriots in the Revolutionary era. His efforts to convince audiences that well-organized and informed citizens could help shape national policy were particularly successful in the South, especially in both Nashville and Chapel Hill. Not one to give up even when the Foreign Policy Association withdrew support for the project because of its domestic focus, in the spring of 1935 Miller called together a conference of delegates from nine southern states, inviting them to form an independent regional organization.[47]

Because of shared personnel, most notably Commission on Interracial Cooperation (CIC) chairman Will Alexander, the SPC's founding session opened in Atlanta on April 25, immediately after the close of the CIC's annual meeting. The CIC event had resulted in the endorsement of the Costigan-Wagner antilynching bill, a distinct step toward a more federally focused southern liberalism. The significance of the SPC meeting would be less clear. Before the conference, Miller had ordered 100 copies of historian Frank Owsley's 1935 article "The Pillars of Agrarianism" to be printed and distributed.[48] Owsley taught at Vanderbilt and had been a contributor to *I'll Take My Stand*. Along with Davidson, he seemed to be the one most committed to answering the book's critics. He drafted "The Pillars of Agrarianism" as a rebuttal to H. L. Mencken, who had published a searing critique of the book and the subsequent Agrarian movement in the *Virginia Quarterly Review* in January 1935. Although Ransom and Davidson persuaded him to edit out a lengthy personal attack, Owsley's forceful tone made his essay the closest thing to a concrete policy agenda the Nashville Agrarians ever produced. Endorsed almost unanimously by his brethren (it was impossible for all of the Agrarians ever to agree completely about anything), the essay showed how the Agrarians' thinking had developed since 1930.[49]

First, Owsley clarified the Agrarians' basic argument. The "enemy," as he put it, was "a system which allows a relatively few men to control most of the nation's wealth and to regiment virtually the whole population under their anonymous holding companies and corporations, and to control government by bribery or intimidation." The Agrarians "agreed with the English Distributists that the most desirable objective is to break [giant organizations] down into small units owned and controlled by real people. We want to see property restored and the proletariat thus abolished and communism made impossible." Could this sort of "decentralization" be achieved? Owsley asked rhetorically. The Agrarians believed that it could, but only through an energetic effort on the part of government.

Although some of the Agrarians, particularly Davidson, would decry the overreach of the federal government in other areas, Owsley's plan called for an aggressive, government-mandated redistribution of wealth. The first of his five "pillars of Agrarianism" was "the restoration of the people to the land and the land to the people by the government purchasing lands held by loan companies, insurance companies, banks, absentee landlords, and [insolvent] planters . . . and granting to the landless tenants . . . a homestead of 80 acres with sufficient stock to cultivate the farm, and cash enough to feed and clothe the family one year." Owsley specified that not all tenant farmers but only those "who are sufficiently able and responsible to own and conserve the land" should be given these homesteads. This would help ensure the realization of his second pillar: "The preservation and restoration of the soil." Owsley's emphasis on soil erosion and other ecological concerns in addition to the "tenant problem" were what made his essay so relevant.[50] The science of ecology was still in its infancy and yet suddenly crucial in those Dust Bowl days, while sharecropping was widely acknowledged to be the South's biggest problem of all—one that was only getting worse as a result of early New Deal policies.

It was a problem that had been brewing since the end of the Civil War. Emancipation had loosened physical and spiritual bonds but tightened credit. In the dehumanizing antebellum order, slaves had been the form of property that planters put up for collateral on loans, as well as the principal form on which they had been taxed. After the war, with little cash or credit available, landowners had failed to recreate the gang-labor system of slavery chiefly because they could not pay wages and because former slaves had insisted on a measure of autonomy, away from an overseer's whip. The result was a new labor system, sharecropping, with plantations divided into the thirty- and forty-acre plots that individual tenant families could work. Drawing up annual contracts (or, in many cases, making only a verbal agreement), landlords took their rent in the form of a share—sometimes 50 percent or more—of the harvested crop. Cotton and tobacco were the main crops for which marketing structures existed—the ones that ensured the landlord a payoff—while time and acreage devoted even to growing food benefited the sharecropper family but took away from the landlord's potential profit. And so, many poor southern farmers, though blessed with a hothouse climate,

Dorothea Lange, "Sharecropper's cabin, cotton and corn, near Jackson, Mississippi,"
June 1937. Lange was on the road taking pictures for the Farm Security Administration
during the same months when Jonathan Daniels traveled. This image suggests how
much pressure sharecroppers were under to grow cash crops rather than devoting
time and acreage to subsistence farming. Farm Security Administration / Office
of War Information Photograph Collection, Library of Congress, Prints and
Photographs Division, Washington, D.C. [LC-DIG-fsa-8b32021].

suffered from inadequate food as they planted the same ground in cotton or
tobacco year after year, exhausting the soil.[51]

Meanwhile, continuing credit woes, the fluctuations of world markets, the
struggle to come up with cash to pay taxes that were now based on land
— over the decades, a variety of economic factors pushed tens of thousands
of *white* southern farmers into the ranks of the landless alongside the former slaves and their descendants. By 1920, nearly 40 percent of white farm
operators across eleven southern states stood on one rung or another of the
tenancy "ladder," either as "cash tenants" (who paid a fixed rent), "share tenants" (who provided their own mules and tools and sometimes kept as much
as three-quarters of the cash crops they produced), or true "croppers" (who

supplied only their families' labor and typically kept only half, or less, of the annual returns). Together with the three-quarters of black farm operators who owned no land, white tenant and sharecropper families had heard the 1920s economy "roar" only from a distance. Then the crash had made a bad situation truly desperate as cotton and tobacco, each of which had sold for about twenty cents a pound in 1927, dropped to five and eight cents a pound, respectively, in 1931.[52]

The most recent chapter in the history of southern agriculture had begun in 1933 with the passage of the Agricultural Adjustment Act during Roosevelt's first hundred days. Reflecting the conventional wisdom that the crisis on America's farms was primarily a matter of overproduction that kept commodity prices too low, the new Agricultural Adjustment Administration paid farmers to let land lie fallow and kill off livestock, namely, some six million baby pigs, mostly in the Midwest. In the South, more than ten million acres of already-planted cotton were plowed under in 1933, and by 1935 cotton acreage had dropped by nearly 30 percent. Cotton prices had risen and stabilized at about eleven cents per pound.[53] But human hardship had also increased as the higher prices and the subsidies went to landlords, while tenants became expendable. The law's stated requirement that landlords share the subsidy payments with their tenants—though easily and often ignored—was all the more incentive not to sign on tenants in the first place. Landowners made more by working their reduced acreage themselves and hiring additional labor as needed, especially during picking season. In cotton, the need for hands at the harvest had always been a significant constraint, requiring landlords to "furnish" tenants with food, housing, and other necessities year-round (at interest, of course) because an efficient mechanical cotton picker had yet to be perfected. Now the year-round burden could be shifted to government relief agencies, while extreme poverty and a lack of other options meant that evicted tenants were unlikely to go far, creating a pool of casual laborers. The local officials who administered federal programs could easily be persuaded to empty the relief rolls in the late summer and early fall, when planters needed pickers. National leaders, including Roosevelt and his head of relief operations, Harry Hopkins, saw what was happening but found it politically expedient to look the other way. In practice, southern offices of the Federal Emergency Relief Administration and other New Deal agencies prevented starvation but often made sure unemployed farm workers were "good and hungry," as one assistant to Hopkins complained, precisely when their labor was needed.[54]

What all of this meant in human terms and from the perspective of dis-

placed tenants themselves were aspects of the problem that Jonathan Daniels and his contemporaries were beginning to grasp more fully, thanks to
farm workers' protests and the publication of documentary photographs and
exposés. Meanwhile, what to do about federal farm policy was a vexing
conundrum. Frank Owsley's calls for "balanced agriculture" and the "establishment of a just political economy" in his third and fourth "pillars of
Agrarianism" were innocuous, even with his strong emphasis on subsistence
farming. His fifth pillar, which called for the "creation of regional governments possessed of more autonomy than the states," struck most SPC delegates as disturbingly sectionalist, even if it sounded rather Regionalist.[55] As
a policy proposal that would have to be decided upon by current politicians
and contemporary public opinion, which heavily favored the New Deal, it
seemed less like a pillar than a matchstick, both flimsy and incendiary. Then
there was the question of what to make of Owsley's first pillar, the idea that
the federal government ought to homestead the landless. And, if such a plan
were enacted, what kind of farms should the government create?

This was the key question that delegates at the first SPC meeting debated
in April 1935. They were unanimous in endorsing the Bankhead-Jones Farm
Tenant bill, which an Alabama senator and a Texas congressman had recently introduced and which promised to establish a new federal agency
responsible for buying up land and reselling it affordably to displaced tenant
farmers. But their discussions grew heated whenever they got to the next
question: what kind of farming should this new federal agency promote?
This was a question of ideology, where the Agrarians' Jeffersonian vision
contrasted sharply with that of the Regionalists, who anticipated a larger
role for industry and, more broadly, modernity in the South's economic development. There were also those who favored a more collectivist approach:
cooperative farming and the introduction of other elements of socialism into
the political economy of the United States. At the Atlanta meeting, social
scientist H. C. Nixon, who had been a contributor to *I'll Take My Stand* and
who was elected chairman of the SPC, made it clear that he was moving in
this direction. He and a few others advocated the "formation of producers'
and consumers' cooperatives" as well as "government ownership of natural
resources, public utilities, . . . insurance and credit structures, and all industries of a monopolistic nature." They also argued that "medical and hospital
services should . . . be socialized."[56]

Meanwhile, Donald Davidson and James Waller, a Nashville attorney,
argued so forcefully for the Agrarian view that one delegate tried unsuccessfully to have them censured.[57] In the absence of Odum or Vance, it was up

to Daniels's friend W. T. Couch of the University of North Carolina Press to stand up for Chapel Hill. He was joined by Virginius Dabney of the *Richmond Times-Dispatch* and a number of other delegates in a pointed dissent from the Agrarians' "unhistoric and emotional" vision. They not only opposed the "sectionalism" of Agrarian rhetoric but also believed the South already suffered "from extreme ruralism, a condition which the agrarians would not only perpetuate but would intensify." To them, "the great need of the region [was] to achieve a better-balanced economy, by the encouragement of industry and the professions, with adequate political safeguards in the interest of the public."[58] Their liberal, Regionalist position was not as fully articulated as that of the Agrarians (and Couch also joined Nixon in the call for cooperatives), but the extent of the disagreement between the two views was becoming clear.

The divergence would become clearer still in a public debate in Nashville in 1936. Allen Tate had joined forces with Herbert Agar, the editor of the *Louisville Courier-Journal* and a Pulitzer Prize–winning historian, to put together a new collection of essays, *Who Owns America? A New Declaration of Independence*, that could serve as a sequel to *I'll Take My Stand*. Eight of the original Twelve Southerners had contributed, along with three other men with Nashville connections who had entered their ranks. There were also essays by Agar and half a dozen other writers who either shared the distributist view that ownership of the means of production must be widespread or else espoused a conservative Catholicism that was increasingly appealing to Tate. The collection was somewhat scattered, but like Owsley's "Pillars of Agrarianism," several essays offered specific policy recommendations. Tate and Agar were rushing the book to publication in hopes of influencing Roosevelt during his reelection campaign.[59] Tate was also eager for publicity and a showdown with the Regionalists.

Apparently, no reporters turned out that spring evening when Odum, Vance, and Couch all came to Vanderbilt. Accounts of the event come from the memories of audience members, including a Vanderbilt graduate student who recalled that "Odum and Vance tried to pour scientific oil upon the troubled waters" and that Tate was "hot for a fight."[60] Another person who witnessed the confrontation was a young graduate student in history who had come over from Chapel Hill with the Regionalists, C. Vann Woodward. The Regionalists' main speaker, Couch, "had his hands full," Woodward remembered, "because the front row was filled with Agrarians, authors of *I'll Take My Stand*, and several of them joined in the attack." After a while, "voices and tempers rose to a high pitch, and the exchange ended suddenly with the dramatic withdrawal of the Agrarians led by Allen Tate." In one version of the story, Woodward remembered Tate pompously pronouncing, "I shall withdraw my presence."[61]

From what Daniels had heard, the volatile Tate had put on a similar performance several weeks later at the second annual meeting of the Southern Policy Committee at the Lookout Mountain Hotel. There, Tate had tried to shout down a Socialist, William R. Amberson, but had evidently gotten some comeuppance. Daniels was eager to hear more but seems to have refrained from asking Tate's friend, the sensitive and soft-spoken Davidson, about the episode during their interview. He would wait to hear about it from Amberson in Memphis.

In deference to Davidson, whom he respected as a "very fine honest man," and in keeping with his documentary approach, Daniels also pulled some of his punches in *A Southerner Discovers the South*, even as he made his own Regionalist leanings clear.[62] The Agrarians had spoken "a little more loudly" in *Who Owns America?* than in *I'll Take My Stand*, he suggested—although actually the book had received little attention and few reviews.[63] But no matter how loudly or clearly the Agrarians spoke, *how*, Daniels asked, "How should the Southern people listen?" They were too poor to have any choice between an Agrarian and some other philosophical vision. They moved "only instinctively to eat" and too often went hungry. By 1930, "the South had sent 3,500,000 people to other regions," he wrote. "And now in other regions the unemployed are still being counted and fed." With this and a few more statistics, Daniels played the social science trump card of facts against the Agrarians' romanticism. It was an ace dealt to him by a 1936 SPC study, *Industrial Social Security in the South*, which he even cited, in good scholarly fashion, in his text.[64] *Of course* the southern people were hungry for industry, his tone implied. They were hungry period. Economic development and scientific planning such as the Regionalists and Roosevelt's New Deal advocated were—as he would argue all the more forcefully in his book's final chapter—the people's best hope.

DANIELS TRIED TO TEMPER his criticisms, but the Agrarian reaction to *A Southerner Discovers the South* was bound to be angry, no matter what. It did not help that his book overshadowed Davidson's *The Attack on Leviathan: Regionalism and Nationalism in the United States*, which was published "to a resounding silence" at the same time Daniels's best seller appeared.[65] But fame and sales were only part of it. There was also the very spirit of his book, which conflicted with the Agrarian view of the South as a unitary, organic society. How could there be just "one man's South"? And how could Daniels's South contain so many contradictions? The book was "superficial" and lacked "a consistent point of view," complained Owsley, who wrote by far the most negative critique Daniels's book ever received. To those who might retort that "a travel book" was "under no special obligation to be profound," Owsley asserted (correctly) that *A Southerner Discovers the South* was "a more ambitious undertaking than a book of travel; it is also a commentary, an interpretation." As such, it was of "uneven value."

Taking the book first as if it were primarily a travel book, Owsley criticized Daniels's "inadequate reporting," suggesting "the word *incompetent* might be a better adjective." He calculated that Daniels had spent "barely three weeks" on the road and must have covered the long stretch from New Orleans to Raleigh "at the rate of five hundred miles a day."[66] Daniels's journey *was* quick, if not quite that quick, and Owsley would surely have been even more annoyed if he had known that Daniels had fibbed about its starting point. Although he started from his home in Raleigh, in *A Southerner Discovers the South* he pretended to have begun at the Potomac River, gazing up at Arlington National Cemetery and Robert E. Lee's former home. The white-columned Custis-Lee Mansion was the "façade of the South" by his reckoning—a double entendre that could only rile Owsley and other patriotic southerners.[67]

Historian that he was, Owsley skewered Daniels for a mistake about Alabama history. He also criticized his writing style—"his amateurish dialogue, irrelevant vulgarities, and smart-aleck mannerisms," which "definitely dated 1920–25" (the Mencken period, as Daniels himself elsewhere observed). More substantively, Owsley charged Daniels with being an intellectual lightweight. "I have the feeling that his excursions into [serious or scholarly] literature on the South have too often been not unlike his marathon of four thousand miles," he jabbed. Then, after a few more pages on other topics, Owsley got to the heart of the matter, which was Daniels's treatment of the Agrarians.

His "account of his interview with Davidson is not clear to me," Owsley wrote, "except that he seems to be more worried over the philosophy and implications of agrarianism than he is over those of fascism, communism, or military despotism." A better summary of "the economic and political doctrines" of the Agrarians was clearly in order, and Owsley was happy to provide it. As in his "Pillars of Agrarianism," he mostly avoided the neo-Confederate language of *I'll Take My Stand* and assured readers that Agrarianism was really about "land reform." The Agrarians "strongly advocated that tenant farmers and share croppers be homesteaded at government expense." Next came "advocacy of the decentralization, wherever feasible, of industry both as to ownership and physical structure." In cases where decentralization threatened national defense (an issue more on people's minds in the late 1930s than it had been a few years earlier), some, though not all, of the Agrarians accepted the need for "government ownership or government control." Contrary to popular misunderstandings, the Agrarians had "always advocated a balanced economy . . . where there would be industry enough for regional self-sufficiency." Like Daniels himself, the Agrarians objected to "a high tariff, freight rate discrimination, and most passionately to absentee ownership of Southern industry and resources." "In all matters," Owsley concluded, the Agrarians "are regionalists and are opposed to the exploitation of one section by any other."

With this invocation of reasonableness and, indeed, Regionalism, Owsley finally got back to Daniels. "Just why Mr. Daniels objects so violently to agrarian philosophy never appears in his book," he mused, "unless the implication is found in his excessive amiability towards Marxians. It is possible, too, that he has confused the Fugitive poets with the agrarian movement." In this case, part of his opposition undoubtedly arose "from the difficulty with which he comprehends poetry."[68]

It was a stinging review—although one that Daniels evidently got over, given that he could not remember who wrote it when asked about it in an interview many years later.[69] Incidentally, Owsley's critique was also a telling glimpse of the Agrarian movement as it stood by early 1939. For, in addition to providing his concise explanation of Agrarian politics, he noted that the Nashville group was "now almost completely dispersed."[70]

The departures were intellectual as well as physical. Robert Penn Warren and others had left Nashville years earlier, but the influence of Ransom, Davidson, and Tate had held the movement together. Now Tate was gone too, to a teaching job in North Carolina from which he would later move to Princeton. He never renounced Agrarianism but increasingly saw it as a philosophical position, even a kind of religious faith, rather than a viable political alternative.

Ransom's break was more complete. He saw Agrarianism as a politics, but it was a politics that had failed. Meanwhile, the middle way of the New Deal had succeeded, at least in terms of public support. After 1937, when a feud with the Vanderbilt administration pushed him to accept a job offer from Kenyon College, Ransom made his peace with industrialism as regulated by New Deal agencies and softened by welfare provisions such as the Social Security Act of 1935. Like Tate, he turned his attention back to literature and went on to have a very successful career as a New Critic. Although Davidson and a few of the others kept the faith and kept writing essays, Agrarianism was essentially dead by the end of the decade.[71]

No wonder Daniels found Davidson, who both loved and needed his friends and who had invested so much in the cause, to be "a very sad man" in 1937. The final three decades of his life would bring an even deeper sadness.

✦ ✦ ✦

IN THE ESSAYS he collected in *The Attack on Leviathan* (1938), Donald Davidson constructed an Agrarianism that shared the "pillars" Owsley had enumerated but also had some distinctive architectural features. Unlike most of the other Agrarians, who opposed some aspects of the New Deal but supported others, Davidson was notably quick to reject the entire package as representing a centralization in government that was equally or more dangerous than the centralization of industrialism. His book's title was a reference to philosopher Thomas Hobbes's 1651 treatise *Leviathan,* which had argued for the necessity of a strong central government to prevent "the war of all against all." In Davidson's reading of American history, the U.S. government had, over the decades, served less as a peacekeeper and more as a weapon in a long and continuing war of North against South. The tariff and other national policies that favored northern industrial interests over southern agriculture were proof. Like many of his contemporaries, including Daniels and the Regionalists, Davidson lamented the post-Reconstruction South's "colonial" economy and second-class status in national politics. Rather than arguing for scientifically planned economic development to bring the South more fully into the nation, however, Davidson wanted to see regionalism carried to what he saw as its logical conclusion: "political sectionalism" and a "New Federalism" in which regional commonwealths would supplant state governments and have enough power and autonomy to compete with and prevent any further growth of the Leviathan.[72]

Although one could continue the architectural metaphor to suggest that, for Davidson, Owsley's fifth pillar had come to bear the most weight, it was actually the other way around: it was Davidson's influence that had encouraged Owsley to include that pillar in his 1935 essay in the first place. Politically, Owsley remained a nervous supporter of the New Deal in 1935, although he would gradually follow Davidson into a bitter politics that he himself was calling "reactionary" by the middle of World War II.[73] Several more of the original Twelve Southerners would feel politically disillusioned in later life, but it is important to emphasize that, from roughly 1937 on, Davidson was no longer speaking for an Agrarian movement. Instead, as his band of brothers mostly withdrew, he chose an increasingly lonely path in-country as the 1930s "war of cultures in our time" gradually gave way to the hot fights of the *Brown v. Board of Education* era.

In his clearest proposal for a New Federalism, first published in *Who Owns America?* in 1936, Davidson argued for the need to "safeguard" the various regions of the United States "at two points: first, in their economic pursuits . . . and second, in their cultural and social institutions." Economically, regional governments should have the power "to tax or at least regulate 'foreign' capital and enterprises that attempt national monopoly." They should also have some control over the region's credit systems and money supply, allowing them to limit industrial development and promote agriculture and small businesses if they chose. Socially and culturally, New Federalism would mean the "power to safeguard educational systems against the rule of external interests." In the South, this would mean the power "to preserve its bi-racial social system without the furtive evasion or raw violence" to which white southerners were "now driven when sniped at with weapons of Federal legality." Perhaps the regional commonwealths should even "be given a veto power in certain instances, some modern equivalent of [antebellum South Carolina senator John C.] Calhoun's principle of nullification." That long-coveted right to reject federal laws was, Davidson wrote, "worth considering."[74]

Although the mid-1930s fight over a federal antilynching law had shown the strength of the southern resistance in Congress, Davidson clearly and correctly saw that more challenges were coming. Like Jonathan Daniels pondering the individual paper cups the TVA supplied its black workers, Davidson did not have to look long at the New Deal to anticipate the social changes that federal involvement in the South was likely to bring. Among the Agrarians, he had always been one of the two or three most committed to preserving white supremacy, which he saw as absolutely necessary if the purity of the white race was to be maintained. Davidson wrote with great candor about his racial views from the mid-1940s on, when blacks' demands for equality were finally starting to be heard and when Ransom, Tate, and the others were no longer on hand to encourage him to avoid the "race question." In earlier years, he had discussed his racial fears mostly in private, as when he wrote to fellow Agrarian John Donald Wade in 1934 with a dystopic vision of what would happen if Franklin Roosevelt's liberalism failed and the leftists took over. Then Wade would have to teach classes "where kinky-heads and blond tresses mix in critical appraisal, and do not even nod politely—and all this for a pittance, or for nothing, while you live with your aged mother (for whom you cannot get medicine), in an apartment designated by the local committee."[75]

Twenty years later, the *Brown* decision would feel to Davidson like a nightmare come true and rouse him to fight for his conception of the South more aggressively than ever. In 1955, while still a professor at Vanderbilt, he became the founding president of the Tennessee Federation for Constitutional Government, an organization dedicated to resisting the desegregation of public schools. The federation lobbied candidates and tried to rally white opposition through pamphlets and speeches. It also turned to the courts. In 1956, when Clinton High School became the first Tennessee public school to desegregrate, Davidson's organization filed a lawsuit and then appealed when it was dismissed. Ironically, the case gave the Tennessee Supreme Court an opportunity to declare segregation in the state's public schools unconstitutional sooner than it could have if the federation had not gotten involved.

As biographer Mark Winchell observes, Donald Davidson's "political crusade" against integration was "spectacularly unsuccessful."[76] It also hurt his reputation as a scholar and poet and strained his relationships with Vanderbilt University and even his oldest friends. The two Agrarians who would have been most likely to agree with him, Frank Owsley and John Gould Fletcher (whose opinions on the Scottsboro case Daniels had criticized in his 1934 letter to the *Nation*), were dead. Allen Tate was ambivalent about integration but did not share Davidson's zealotry. He thought the Supreme Court had made a mistake by starting with schools rather than voting rights, but he accepted social change stoically as inevitable even though he admitted that he "would not know how to conduct myself" in an integrated world.[77] John Crowe Ransom supported integration more enthusiastically than Tate did. He and Davidson remained friendly but had to avoid sensitive topics. Similarly, Robert Penn Warren sometimes visited his old friend but could not abide Davidson's segregationism. The rift may have been deeper than Davidson realized. According to Warren's daughter, "Donald Davidson was a racist whose name was never spoken in our home."[78]

In the final years of his life, Davidson's "periodic bouts of depression" got worse, and he suffered from both insomnia and disturbing, vivid dreams. One dream that he recorded in a diary entry for June 29, 1960, involved a bulldozer. He dreamed that he had bought a house with a large backyard where he intended to plant a garden. As he looked out over his property, he saw a bulldozer digging up and carrying away his soil. When he confronted its operator, the man smiled and asked him how carefully he had read his deed. Davidson told the man to leave but was racing away himself to review the terms of his ownership when he jolted awake, very upset.[79]

It was only a dream but one that was intriguingly coincident with C. Vann Woodward's daytime thoughts about the South's "Bulldozer Revolution." Woodward's classic essay "The Search for Southern Identity" had appeared in the *Virginia Quarterly Review* in 1958 and was republished in 1960. In it, he pondered whether the rapid urbanization and modernization that had been taking place in the South since World War II were going to erode white southerners' sense of themselves as distinct from other Americans. Already the "overwhelmingly rural" region that in 1930 had employed 5.5 million people in agriculture was becoming a place of cities and suburbs. By 1950, only 3.2 million people worked on southern farms, while economic growth in other sectors was taking place at a much faster rate than it had in older industrialized zones. The symbol for all this innovation was the bulldozer. The bulldozer was "the advance agent of the metropolis," Woodward declared. It encroached "upon rural life to expand urban life." It demolished "the old to make way for the new."[80]

If the decline in the rural population was not enough to trouble the dreams of a still-faithful Agrarian, there were also the concurrent challenges to traditional notions of southern identity. Woodward certainly saw them. The very first sentence of his essay was: "The time is coming, if indeed it has not already arrived, when the Southerner will begin to ask himself whether there is really any longer very much point in calling himself a Southerner." Perhaps "the Southern heritage" had already become "an old hunting jacket that one slips on comfortably while at home but discards when he ventures abroad in favor of some more conventional or modish garb." As a long-ago friend of the Regionalists and a current supporter of civil rights activism, Woodward went on in the essay to pass judgment on Agrarianism as a failed attempt "to dig in and define a perimeter of defense against further encroachment." If southern distinctiveness depended on the South's rural character, then "the Southerner as a distinctive species of American" was already doomed. Moreover, Woodward argued, "if Southernism is allowed to become identified with a last ditch defense of segregation, it will increasingly lose its appeal among the younger generation." He predicted that many would "be tempted to reject their entire regional identification, even the name 'Southern,' in order to dissociate themselves from the one discredited aspect." If Agrarianism had "proved to be a second lost cause," Woodward concluded, "segregation is a likely prospect for a third."[81]

The Jim Crow system was eventually dismantled. Davidson himself remained bitterly opposed to integration but stopping trying to fight it by the early 1960s, when his Tennessee Federation for Constitutional Government dissolved.[82] Nevertheless, Woodward's suggestion that "Southern heritage" might become no more than an old hunting jacket, worn for comfort and in private, would prove incorrect—or, rather, like other definitions of southern identity, applicable to some southerners but not to all. Even when he wrote "The Search for Southern Identity," Woodward could see another way things might go. "Southern heritage" had always had political as well as personal meanings. Rather than being an old hunting jacket, perhaps southern identity was or would become "an attic full of ancestral wardrobes useful only in connection with costume balls and play acting—staged primarily in Washington, D. C."[83]

The Southernization of American politics that Woodward seems to have been predicting was still in the future in 1960. Meanwhile, the final decade of Davidson's life was proving an unhappy present. He retired from Vanderbilt in 1964 but continued to take up an annual residency at the Bread Loaf Writers' Conference in Vermont through the summer of 1967 and remained mentally sharp to the end. He lived through enough of 1968 to see the Tet offensive in the Vietnam War and the assassination of Martin Luther King Jr. in nearby Memphis, as well as the riots that King's death sparked. Many of America's cities were still smoldering when he died on April 25 at the age of eighty-four.[84]

AS LONELY AND DEPRESSING as his final years were, Donald Davidson was not as much of a relic even in the late 1960s as he felt Daniels had portrayed him to be. Knowing that the Agrarians would be rediscovered by an ascendant New Right in the decades after his death puts Davidson's decades-old response to *A Southerner Discovers the South* in a new light. In a 1939 article, he described the interview with Daniels. He claimed to have not yet read Daniels's book, but he had read Owsley's review and could "bear witness" to Daniels's "perturbation" about his philosophy. "Mr. Daniels called me out one evening from a none too inspiring Ph.D. oral examination, and we sat down to discuss agrarianism," he reported. "It was not long before I discovered that, to Mr. Daniels' mind, I was virtually entombed, either among nostalgias or actually dead things. He was gentle with me, and sympathetically inquiring, but it was evident that he was a little uneasy. He would have been happiest if he could go on thinking of agrarians as *only* ghosts; but it would be a bother to be haunted by ideas in the flesh."[85]

In contrast to the sadness that Daniels attributed to the Agrarians' failure to be heard, Davidson suggested he had actually felt "a pleasure, known to romantic poets as 'the pleasures of melancholy.'" He had simply been playing along, not wanting to ruin the fun Daniels was having "in visiting a ghost — in studying it, watching it shake its gory locks, hearing it talk history and economics; in being a little frightened yet not really hurt. . . . We played ghost; and I was the ghost," Davidson wrote. "It was a pensive evening. We mourned a good deal and were properly nostalgic."[86] But this did not mean that Davidson was truly sad or that Agrarianism was dead. He could not accept that. Indeed, he was so determined to keep his intellectual circle together that he used the rest of the essay to try to prove that even H. C Nixon, despite his socialistic calls for cooperatives, was still an Agrarian.

On one level, Davidson was protesting too much: the Agrarian movement was dead by 1939. On another level, however, the final decades of the twentieth century would show that he was right: the Agrarians' cultural views (though not their specific ideas about government-sponsored land reform) proved remarkably capable of rising again along with other sources of late twentieth-century conservative thought. By the 1990s, as the new culture wars heated up, there would be many liberals, North and South, who, like Daniels, would have been happier if they could have gone on "thinking of agrarians as *only* ghosts." At the end of the twentieth century and into the twenty-first, it was indeed troubling to many people "to be haunted . . . in the flesh" by antiscientific, traditionalist ways of thinking wrapped up in notions of southern identity and heritage that were still (or even more) tinged with neo-Confederatism.[87]

At least Daniels could escape to documentary reportage. He "watched Davidson's red tail light disappear down the street" and into the rainy night before he went into his hotel. It would still be raining the next day when he got to the Memphis headquarters of the Southern Tenant Farmers Union, where he would hear a very different perspective on many of the same issues he and Davidson had discussed.

— CHAPTER FIVE —

Tenants Are Able to Hold Their
Heads a Little Higher

✦

MEMPHIS, TENNESSEE

IN MEMPHIS, WHERE he hoped to learn more about the plight of the
sharecropper, Jonathan Daniels of course stayed at the luxurious Peabody Hotel. The Peabody was famous for CBS radio's weekly big band
jazz broadcasts and for the ornate marble fountain in the center of its lobby.
In 1933, or so the legend went, the hotel's general manager had jokingly
stocked the fountain with some tame ducks, used as decoys in a recent hunting trip. Soon several mallards were living as permanent guests on the hotel
roof. At eleven o'clock each morning, a designated "duck master" escorted
them from an elevator to the fountain to the tune of John Philip Sousa's
"King Cotton March." At 5 P.M., he walked them back again. "The Mississippi Delta begins in the lobby of The Peabody Hotel and ends on Catfish
Row in Vicksburg," wrote David L. Cohn, the vernacular-speaking white
writer whom Daniels would meet in Greenville, Mississippi. "The Peabody
is the Paris Ritz, the Cairo Shepheard's, the London Savoy of this section,"
Cohn famously asserted. "If you stand near its fountain in the middle of
the lobby, where ducks waddle and turtles drowse, ultimately you will see
everybody who is anybody in the Delta."[1]

The man Daniels was glad to see, after dropping off the seventeen-year-
old hitchhiker he had picked up on his way from Nashville, was Dayton
Moore, a United Press correspondent who had agreed to guide him around
the city.[2] It would take local knowledge to find the headquarters of the Southern Tenant Farmers Union (STFU) "at 2529 1/2 Broad Avenue — out where
the town straggles to an end in neighborhood stores," as Daniels wrote, getting the address wrong, in his journal. The two-room office was "upstairs
over an Easy Way grocery and an M & C Market — [off] an ill-lit hall where

a tin tub sits to catch water from a leak in the ceiling (another such tub inside office). On the door crudely scrawled: Office of the S. T. F. U."[3]

When union president J. R. Butler opened the door, it was probably the one-time novelist in Daniels who noticed that it "let light into the dark hall." Darkness and light have symbolic meaning in *A Southerner Discovers the South*, the last two sentences of which conclude that all southerners are "in the warm dark, and whether they like it or not—white man, black man, big man—they are in the dark together. None of them will ever get to day alone."[4] Daniels had arranged to interview the STFU's president in order to learn more about the union's efforts to help some of the nation's littlest men, both black and white, and their families "get to day"—or at least get food to eat and jobs to work at a time when landowners were evicting tenant farmers by the thousands and beating or even killing those who dared to challenge their command over the labor force by organizing. The STFU's well-publicized strikes in 1935 and 1936 and its many other activities on behalf of farm workers would be the main subject of Daniels's conversation with Butler, as well as a later conversation with union adviser William R. Amberson and subsequent visits to eastern Arkansas and the Delta Cooperative Farm in Mississippi.

In fact, on no other topic in *A Southerner Discovers the South* did Daniels spend more time or do more reading. The STFU was one of the most important organizations seeking social and economic change in the South, and Daniels meant to capture its significance. He stayed at the Peabody for three nights and devoted two full days to driving around and exploring the Arkansas-Mississippi Delta counties where the union was most active. He also read and quoted from STFU publications, telling some of the union's history from its leaders' own point of view. Sympathetically, if unromantically, he pieced together the story of an interracial, socialist union that, like the Communist Party and the Popular Front, was helping to steer American politics and culture leftward into the long civil rights era.

✦ ✦ ✦

LONG BEFORE HE GOT TO Memphis, Daniels had come to admire Norman Thomas and the other socialists (several of whom were capital-S Socialists in the sense that they were members of Thomas's Socialist Party of America) who formed the STFU's mostly white slate of officers and executive board. "No Socialist, I am one who heartily respects the good intentions of

Mr. Thomas," he wrote. "My quarrel has been that [he and other socialists] have sometimes been men who think with their hearts instead of their heads. But often the choice has been between them and men who think with nothing, neither head nor heart. . . . The Northeast Arkansas country (and much of the other plantation South) is entitled to both." Daniels was happy to acknowledge that, in helping tenants "hold their heads a little higher," as Butler put it, the STFU had accomplished a great deal. Nevertheless, he reflected a heartbeat later, the South's tenant farmers "were probably slowly starving still," despite the STFU's efforts. "Organization had not interrupted that."[5]

In truth, neither unionization nor New Deal relief and resettlement plans would be enough to alleviate more than a small part of the human suffering that accompanied the fundamental transformation in southern agriculture. Between 1935 and 1940, the number of people making their living as tenant farmers declined by 25 percent.[6] As bad as sharecropping and other forms of farm tenancy could be, this massive displacement was devastating for the thousands of men, women, and children who experienced it. It was all the more bitter when they recognized the role of federal policy, particularly the Agricultural Adjustment Act of 1933, in making them expendable.

It was partially in hopes of influencing New Deal policies that the STFU was founded. The union succeeded in this to some extent while influencing American culture to a much greater extent. Thanks to the socialists and the STFU, Depression-era Americans developed considerable sympathy for tenant farmers that helped to counteract degrading depictions like Erskine Caldwell's *Tobacco Road*.

The STFU accomplished what it did despite both enormous external pressures and internal tensions. As Daniels would see for himself when he reached the Arkansas-Mississippi Delta, STFU members faced not only a level of violence but also a level of poverty that were almost unfathomable to an upper-class white American. The misnamed "tenant problem" was also intractable, having as much to do with efficiencies of scale and advances in technology as it did with landlords—which is not to excuse the many landowners who cheated their tenants out of the crop reduction payments that they, too, were supposed to receive, or the landlords, "riding bosses," and law enforcement officials who used violence and terror to try to keep the union from winning higher wages and better conditions for farm workers.

Internally, the STFU's greatest strength—its interracialism—was also its biggest challenge. Although the union's membership was predominantly black and in some areas included Native Americans, the STFU's most visible and visionary leaders were white men, most of them southerners as well as socialists. Organization across race lines was both less unusual in the working-class South and more difficult to achieve and maintain than many historical accounts of the STFU have suggested. Like the Populist Party and numerous other examples of interracial organizing that have captured historians' attention in recent years, the STFU was, unsurprisingly, susceptible to many of the same racial conflicts that characterized the society around it. Indeed, the union faced what historian Jason Manthorne has called a "common paradox": "African Americans often expressed the most enthusiasm for joining, but that enthusiasm—which could buoy a foundering organization and potentially turn it in to a vehicle for black empowerment—drove away the whites."[7]

In the STFU's case, there was also considerable tension between leaders' socialist, cooperative vision and the goals of rank-and-file members, who tended to see the union as a sort of fraternal aid organization whose political and labor activism might help them achieve their own primary objective: to become independent landowners themselves within the capitalist system.[8]

Following his usual practice of talking almost exclusively to white people, preferably educated ones like Amberson, Daniels heard about some, but by no means all, of the STFU's internal and external challenges, as well as its achievements, as of the time of his visit. He listened carefully and also *looked*, seeing social conditions in the Arkansas-Mississippi Delta and both socialist and New Deal efforts to improve them with his own perceptive eyes.

He also relied on his reading. Daniels's understanding of the early history of the STFU was shaped by Howard Kester's *Revolt among the Sharecroppers*, published in 1936. Kester was a graduate of the Vanderbilt University School of Religion, where an aging theologian named Alva Taylor was teaching the Social Gospel and thereby cultivating "radicals" right under the noses of Donald Davidson and the other Agrarians. A native of Virginia, as a college student Kester had gotten a chance to travel through Europe as part of the Young Men's Christian Association's American Pilgrimage of Friendship. The trip awakened him to politics. Seeing a chain drawn across the entrance to a Warsaw ghetto gave him the shocking realization that "this is exactly what we do to Negroes in the United States." He came home ready to push the limits of the association's cautious interracialism. A 1926 retreat allowed him to develop an unlikely friendship with George Washington Carver, the famous Tuskegee scientist who was forty years his senior. He went to Alabama and lived in Carver's home for two months in a blunt rejection of segregation. His letters to his fiancée, Alice Howard, reveal the spiritual and social questions he was grappling with. "I see all the sorrow, all the pain, all the suffering," he wrote. "What is to be done? How am I to use my life," he asked.

In 1927, Kester got a job with the Fellowship of Reconciliation, a pacifist organization based in New York. He kept this job while studying at Vanderbilt, and he also began investigating lynchings for the NAACP. By the time he graduated, he had become a committed socialist. He was one of the first people contacted in the summer of 1934 when other nearby Socialist Party members helped the STFU get started.[9]

In *Revolt among the Sharecroppers*, Kester told the story of the union's founding. "Just south of the little town of Tyronza, in Poinsett County, Arkansas," he wrote, "the Southern Tenant Farmers' Union had its beginning." Two dozen overall-clad men, black and white, gathered in a kerosene-lit schoolhouse to discuss the benefits of organizing. Then the "inevitable question" arose: Was there to be one union or two? Would the STFU be segregated or not? A few spoke tentatively. Then "an old man with cotton-white hair overhanging an ebony face rose to his feet."

> He had been in unions before, he said. In his seventy years of struggle the Negro had built many unions only to have them broken up by the planters and the law. He had been a member of a black man's union at Elaine, Arkansas. He had seen the union with its membership wiped out in the bloody Elaine Massacre of 1919. "We colored people can't organize without you," he said, "and you white folks can't organize without us." Continuing he said, "Aren't we all brothers and ain't God the Father of us all? . . . The same chain that holds my people holds your people too. If we're chained together on the outside we ought to stay chained together in the union."

Because of the wise old man's words (so reminiscent of the chain drawn across the Warsaw ghetto), the men in attendance decided their union would be integrated; it "would welcome Negro and white sharecroppers, tenant farmers and day laborers alike into its fold."[10]

Of course, Kester did not actually attend the founding meeting. In his telling, neither did H. L. Mitchell, the STFU's secretary-treasurer and the most central figure in its entire history. Like Kester, Harry Leland "Mitch" Mitchell was a white man and a member of the Socialist Party. Unlike Kester, he did not have much formal education but had educated himself by reading socialist books and newspapers. Born in western Tennessee to a tenant farm family that was perpetually on the move, Mitchell was working as a dry cleaner in Tyronza when the first crop-reduction payments from

H. L. Mitchell in the Memphis headquarters of the Southern Tenant Farmers Union, June 1938. Photograph by Dorothea Lange. Farm Security Administration / Office of War Information Photograph Collection, Library of Congress, Prints and Photographs Division, Washington, D.C. [LC-DIG-fsa-8b32351].

the Agricultural Adjustment Administration arrived and the mass evictions of sharecroppers began. In early 1934, he and his friend and fellow Socialist Party member Clay East were escorting Norman Thomas around the countryside when Thomas suggested that, more than a political party, what the sharecroppers needed was a union. "This was the real beginning of the Southern Tenant Farmers Union," Mitchell would explain.[11] The impetus for the meeting at the Sunnyside schoolhouse was the eviction of twenty-three tenant families by an absentee landlord named Hiram Norcross. According to Kester, the men who gathered that night appealed to Mitchell and East for help *after* they decided to form a union. According to Mitchell, he and East were there from the start.

In 1936, the same year Kester's book appeared, Mitchell wrote his own, never-published account of the Sunnyside meeting. It contradicted Kester's version in several important ways. To begin with, Mitchell indicated that the two main speakers that night were both white sharecroppers. Alvin Nunnally was a socialist and spoke forcefully for an integrated union. Burt Williams was something of a bully. He used his 250 pounds to intimidate his audience and suggested they "ought to start the Klan again and . . . this time instead [of] the niggers they ought to go after the big planters." Only in an afterthought did Williams ask the black men who were present for their opinions. A few African Americans spoke, notably John Allen, a veteran labor organizer, and C. H. Smith, a local minister.

Like the venerable old man Kester described, Smith was a survivor of the Elaine massacre. That slaughter of more than 100 black men, women, and children in Phillips County, Arkansas, had been precipitated by whites' efforts to suppress an emergent, all-black labor organization, the Progressive Farmers and Household Union of America. A gunfight between sheriff deputies and men standing guard at a union meeting on the night of September 30, 1919, had left one white man dead and another white man wounded. It had also set off a pogrom against black residents.[12] Survivors like Smith were not the only ones who would remember the events at Elaine as the STFU got started. Landlords remembered it too, but with a different take-away message about how violence could be used to break up unions.

If Smith was the basis for Kester's unnamed "old man with cotton-white hair," it is hard to explain why Mitchell began calling him "Isaac Shaw" in later accounts. Both Smith and "Ike" Shaw appear in Mitchell's "The Founding and Early History of the Southern Tenant Farmers Union," a talk he gave in 1973. The cotton-haired, ebony-faced elder Kester described was now, in Mitchell's words, "a man with one of the most beautiful speaking voices I ever heard." Meanwhile, Burt Williams had become an advocate for nonviolence. "You know my pappy rode with the KKK," he announces in this version of the story, but "time has passed and we have to forget this stuff." Lest anyone miss the point he was trying to make, Mitchell drove it home, observing that "when Martin L. King was a little boy, so high, . . . sharecroppers adopted the policy of non-violence. . . . The record will show that there was no violence on the part of the union men, though we were often threatened. There were people jailed and meetings broken up; there were attempts to assassinate leaders, including me. There were churches burned and everything that happened during the civil rights movement."[13] When King was just a child, the STFU had been on the front lines, fighting the nonviolent fight, with black and white sharecroppers leading the way.

Jonathan Daniels did not meet Howard Kester or H. L. Mitchell during his southern tour. If he had, he would have been meeting them long before King became the symbol of nonviolence and interracial fellowship that Mitchell referred to in his 1973 speech. Nevertheless, Mitchell's direct comparison between the STFU and the "classical phase" of the civil rights movement is worth examining. On the one hand, Daniels did not need such historicism to recognize that the STFU was an important social movement to emancipate the "oppressed tenant," who "is also the oppressed Negro," he noted, "since [the majority] of these tenants are black men."[14]

On the other hand, Daniels was wise not to dwell on Kester's romantic account of the STFU's founding, as a number of later historians would. The emotional, lamp-lit scene at the Sunnyside schoolhouse obscured the union's *struggle to achieve* interracial fellowship by suggesting it was there from the start. Some aspects of that struggle were evident in Mitchell's unpublished 1936 description of the founding meeting, but his willingness to acknowledge the union's internal racial conflicts may have faded over time as he became increasingly invested in portraying the STFU as a precursor to later phases of the civil rights movement.

Recent scholarship has made the civil rights movement "harder," to use Jacquelyn Dowd Hall's word, by telling its history in less simplistic and therefore less simply heroic terms.[15] The STFU was part of a longer, more complex civil rights struggle that began in the 1930s and achieved its greatest victories thirty years later. Allowed its internal conflicts, the union seems less like a "beautiful and doomed aberration," as Manthorne writes, and more like a work in progress.[16] The telling of its history might properly begin with a different founding story altogether—one the cynical Daniels could have appreciated.

✦ ✦ ✦

IN DECEMBER 1934, a few months after the STFU was established, H. L. Mitchell and four other union men drove nearly 1,000 miles to Washington, D.C., in Mitchell's 1926 Moon car, which he had bought used for $40.[17] Mitchell did all of the driving. Two of his passengers were white, Alvin Nunnally and Walter Moskop, and two were African Americans, E. B. McKinney and N. W. Webb. With little money and an acute awareness that no hotel would accept an integrated group, they drove straight through. At one point, they got lost in the dark of night and stopped for directions at what they thought might be a CCC camp. It turned out to be a prison farm. Arriving at the National Mall in the early morning hours, they slept in the car. Unfolding arms and legs after the long night, they walked over to the Department of Agriculture building at about seven o'clock, not realizing that the "Washington farmers," as Mitchell joked, would not get there until nine.

The goal of the trip was to meet with Secretary of Agriculture Henry A. Wallace. The STFU's leaders had written several unanswered letters asking for a thorough and unbiased investigation of how New Deal farm policies were affecting tenant farmers. Now they were putting themselves on Wallace's doorstep. They did not have an appointment. As a black man from the Jim Crow South who knew everything there was to know about being served last, if at all, McKinney had a ready reply when a secretary informed them that Wallace was in conference and could not be disturbed. "Ma'am, that's all right," he said, "we will just sit down here and wait until Mr. Wallace gets through." Flustered, she went to find a boss. What Mitchell would later describe as "the first sit-down ever to occur in the Department of Agriculture" actually worked. The STFU representatives got Wallace's attention and his promise to send an investigator to the Arkansas-Mississippi Delta.[18]

As a foundational story for the STFU, this episode has much to recommend it: the hard trip through a dangerous Jim Crow environment, Mitchell's and McKinney's central roles, and the goal of getting the government onto the union's side. The cramped car also temporarily contained tensions that would eventually be strong enough to blow the doors off. Two of Mitchell's four passengers would become adversaries within a few short years. A former bootlegger and an all-around tough customer, Moskop would try to shoot Mitchell in the fall of 1936 for reasons that were not entirely clear but may have involved personal jealousy as well as bitterness about losing a couple of union elections to blacks.[19]

McKinney's complaints were not so idiosyncratic. A Baptist preacher who was one of the STFU's most important leaders, he would gradually come to feel that the large black majority among the union's members were playing too small a part in its decision making while bearing the brunt of antiunion violence — both legitimate critiques.

Born in 1872 and thus a full thirty years older than Mitchell and Kester, Edward Britt McKinney was a proud man and a complicated one. Though he worked for the interracial union, he was also been a member of Marcus Garvey's Universal Negro Improvement Association, a black nationalist organization that had seen its heyday in the 1920s. A resident of Tyronza as well as an itinerant preacher who tended to more than thirty congregations, McKinney knew Mitchell and Clay East personally and was an early participant in the local branch of the Socialist Party they had started. As the STFU took off, he "struggled for three years between his faith in Mitchell's sincerity and his passionate dislike for J. R. Butler . . . and the white rank-and-file members, whom he never trusted," writes historian Mary G. Rolinson.[20] One of the white men McKinney trusted least was the erratic Walter Moskop, who became the president of a white STFU local in the town of Marked Tree, Arkansas, where McKinney was the president of a black local and the most important organizer.[21]

Allowing members to establish segregated locals was a pragmatic STFU policy that troubled socialists like Kester but suited the rank and file. In a society that taught whites to value their supposed racial superiority above virtually all else, neither whites nor blacks could easily trust or feel comfortable with people of the opposite race, regardless of how well they understood the similarities in their current economic conditions. Although tenant farmers of both races were facing eviction and unemployment during the Great Depression, there was still the possibility that the labor market would function as it always had, elevating whites at blacks' expense. Even impoverished white southerners' comparative economic and social advantages had long reinforced their society's lessons in white supremacy, making it all the more difficult for them to choose to align themselves with even poorer and less powerful people. Surely it was the planter, the politician, the town elite who could help them get ahead, they thought, not the black people who were even more down-and-out and less respected than they were.

For their part, black men like McKinney could overcome their suspicions about whites' racism and economic self-interest for a while, but not if it meant that blacks were to be expendable foot soldiers in a movement over which they had little control. From the start, McKinney tried and, to some extent, succeeded in getting whites to attend black-led union meetings and accept his and other black leaders' authority.[22] Just how difficult this was in the context of Jim Crow is suggested by the fact that a white speaker's respectful "mistering" of McKinney at a public meeting in early 1935 played a part in one of the first episodes that drew national attention to the union.

The meeting, held in a town square in Marked Tree, was intended to give the five men who had gone to Washington a chance to report on their trip. Moskop spoke first, followed by Nunnally. Then it was time for the black speakers. When white union organizer Ward Rodgers called for

"Mr. McKinney" to come to the platform, a murmur went through the crowd. Mitchell overheard a deputy county prosecutor fume, "Did you hear that Yankee agitator calling that nigger 'Mister' McKinney?" Then Rodgers created an even bigger stir when he got carried away and said he could "lead a mob to lynch any planter in Poinsett County" if he wanted to. The assembled sharecroppers "threw their hats in the air and roared their approval. There were shouts of, 'Come on, Rodgers! Let's go get them!'"[23]

With the prosecutor and other lawmen in the audience, Rodgers was gotten instead, arrested for anarchy and barratry, a charge usually reserved for lawyers who stir up trouble to get clients. He was tried and sentenced to six months in jail and a $500 fine. The case made the *New York Times* and other national newspapers, giving the union the first of the publicity and outside support that would prove crucial to its existence over the next few years. The American Civil Liberties Union joined the NAACP and a variety of liberal Protestant and labor organizations in befriending the STFU. As a result, more than three-quarters of the union's income for 1935 came from outside sources, while dues from its impoverished members amounted to less than $500.[24]

Among those who observed Rodgers's trial was, in Mitchell's words, "a lovely red-haired woman lawyer from Washington, D.C., Mrs. Mary Connor Meyers." Meyers was the investigator whom Secretary of Agriculture Wallace had promised to send. She spent weeks in the region, setting up an office in Marked Tree's one office building (Daniels would not find it impressive) and hiring drivers to show her around the countryside so she could take affidavits from sharecroppers. Because Marked Tree lacked an adequate hotel, she slept thirty-five miles away in Memphis at the Peabody.[25]

In a word, Meyers was appalled by what she saw. "HAVE HEARD ONE LONG STORY [of] HUMAN GREED," she wired Jerome Frank, the general counsel of the Agricultural Adjustment Administration (AAA). More than one section of the AAA cotton contract was "BEING OPENLY AND GENERALLY VIOLATED."[26] When Meyers returned to Washington and submitted her report, it was so damaging to the large landowners whose interests and representatives dominated the Department of Agriculture that the only copy simply disappeared. Its suppression sparked an outcry, but the power of the planters became evident in a simultaneous purge of liberal lawyers like Frank.

The issue was how to interpret section 7 of the AAA cotton contract—the standard contract signed by each farmer who agreed to reduce the number of acres to be planted. "The producer shall endeavor in good faith to bring about the reduction of acreage . . . in such a manner as to cause the least possible amount of labor, economic and social disturbance," section 7 read. The landowner "shall, insofar as possible, maintain on this farm the normal number of tenants and other employees" and "shall permit all tenants to continue in the occupancy of their houses on this farm, rent free for the years 1934 and 1935 (unless any such tenant shall conduct himself as to become a nuisance or a menace to the welfare of the producer)."[27] As he received Meyers's telegrams and sample affidavits from Arkansas, Jerome Frank became increasingly concerned about all the loopholes in this wording. What was "possible" and who determined who was a "nuisance" or a "menace"? Frank particularly wanted a revision to ensure that not only the "normal number" but the *same tenants* were employed and could not be evicted without cause. He gave the job of drafting new wording to one of the young lawyers in his division, Alger Hiss.

Later remembered as either a successfully prosecuted Soviet spy or else a victim of Cold War fears, in 1935 Hiss was a recent Harvard Law School graduate working at one of his first government jobs. He had already come under fire for his first draft of the cotton contract back in 1933, which had required AAA checks to go directly to tenants in addition to landlords. South Carolina senator Ellison "Cotton Ed" Smith had stormed into his office. "Young fella," he had boomed, "you can't do this to my niggers, paying checks to them. They don't know what to do with the money. The money should come to me. I'll take care of them. They're mine."[28] The final version of the 1933 contract had indeed sent checks only to landlords, with the feeble admonition that they must share the crop-reduction payments with their tenants. But most instead shared Cotton Ed's perspective and pocketed the money themselves. Hiss expected no better outcome from the revisions Frank instructed him to write, and unlike his boss, he would manage to keep his job when Frank and several others were fired over the issue.[29]

Henry Wallace agreed to the firings, and President Roosevelt did not object. When Norman Thomas appealed to him on behalf of the tenant farmers in a White House meeting, Roosevelt looked at the wording of section 7 in the copy of the cotton contract that Thomas slid across his desk. He admitted he had never read it. "That can mean anything or nothing, can't it?" he asked. Roosevelt "expressed the correct moral disapproval of Arkansas planters but quite frankly acknowledged his political dependence on the support of Southern Congressmen," Thomas explained in a letter to Kester. The power and seniority of politicians like Smith and Arkansas's Joseph Robinson, the Senate majority leader, tied his hands. "Now come, Norman,"

Similarities in the composition of John Vachon's 1936 photograph of evicted sharecroppers (top) and Marion Post Wolcott's 1939 photograph of day laborers being hired for cotton picking highlight the impact of the Agricultural Adjustment Act and the collapse of the tenant-farming system. As early as 4 a.m. near the Hallan Bridge in Memphis, Wolcott wrote, "crowds of Negroes in the streets gather and are loaded into trucks by drivers who bid, and offer them anywhere from fifty cents to one dollar per day." Farm Security Administration / Office of War Information Photograph Collection, Library of Congress, Prints and Photographs Division, Washington, D.C. [LC-DIG-fsa-8b30944 and LC-DIG-fsa-8a41363].

Roosevelt reportedly also said, "I'm a damned sight better politician than you are. I know the South, and there is arising a new generation of leaders and we've got to be patient."[30]

A new generation of leaders was not what Thomas had been seeing in Arkansas. In March 1935 he toured the state's northeastern counties, speaking in every town of any size. There were always hecklers, but in a small community called Birdsong he encountered worse. In a crowd of about 500 tenant farmers gathered at a black church, there were also "thirty to forty armed and drunken planters led by a man who later turned out to be the sheriff of Mississippi County." When Kester opened the meeting with the words, "Ladies and gentlemen," the planters shouted, "There ain't no ladies in the audience and there ain't no gentlemen on the platform." They jerked Kester down from the pulpit, prompting Thomas to pull out a copy of the U.S. Constitution and point to the Bill of Rights. The planters agreed that the meeting was "legal all right" but said "there ain't goin' to be no speakin' here." Then they bullied Thomas and his companions out the door and into their cars. An Associated Press correspondent who was just pulling up was told to "get the hell out of here and don't you write a line."[31]

What Jonathan Daniels, quoting from *Revolt among the Sharecroppers*, called the "famous 'Birdsong incident'" got a lot of publicity and helped the union gain much-needed funds.[32] But it was just a small part of the violence that planters were beginning to unleash against the union. Already there had been beatings and arrests, and the homes of prominent organizers had been invaded or strafed with gunfire. Two of E. B. McKinney's sons were wounded in one shooting, and even the upper-class home of the union's white lawyer, C. T. Carpenter, was not spared. Blacks were targeted indiscriminately —while walking home from church, for example—and African American women took some of the worst beatings. In one case, sheriff's deputies demanded that a black woman tell them where a well-known organizer was hiding, and when she refused, they pistol-whipped her so brutally that her ear was sliced off.[33]

When the drunken planters at Birdsong said there were no "ladies" present, they were delivering an insult to the black women who *were* in attendance but did not, in their minds, qualify as ladies. Often serving as secretaries of union locals, black women played important roles in the STFU, whose membership may have been as much as three-quarters African American.[34]

Although their numbers were smaller, white women also contributed. One of the most valuable was Evelyn Smith, an earnest young socialist from New Orleans who, in the fall of 1935, became the office manager at the Memphis headquarters, a job she held for more than five years. This self-described "Girl Friday of the STFU" participated in all sorts of union activities, including an undercover investigation of an Earle, Arkansas, labor camp where black workers were rumored to be kept behind bars. Smith and Clay East's wife, Maxine, took a picnic and a camera to go find out for sure, possibly risking their lives. Smith was also the key figure in a 1936 push to revise the STFU constitution to clarify women's roles, particularly their eligibility for union offices. Yet she was not an STFU member herself, according to Mitchell. She was "ineligible . . . being only a hired hand who had never seen a cotton plantation until she came to work for us."[35]

Mitchell's description of Smith as a "hired hand"—a designation he used for himself as well—spoke to a concern that he and others seem to have felt from the union's earliest days.[36] As much as they appreciated and needed outside support, the STFU's predominately white, socialist leadership seems to have been committed to making the organization a "real union," meaning its power had to emanate from workers' ability to strike.

The obvious time to strike was cotton-picking season, when the demand for labor was highest. Catching planters by surprise, a 1935 cotton pickers' strike was a tremendous success. Despite violent reprisals, the union was able to hold the strike together for a month, calling it off only after the prevailing wage rose to 75 cents per 100 pounds. This near-doubling of wages attracted the attention of farm workers throughout the Arkansas-Mississippi Delta in a way that speeches and handbills never could. "Over thirty new locals have been organized within the past 45 days," Mitchell wrote jubilantly. By the end of the year, he would claim the union's membership had reached 25,000.[37]

Although a subsequent strike in the spring of 1936 proved less effective, the STFU was still on the rise throughout the year. One tangible success was the arrest of deputy sheriff Paul Peacher, whose Crittenden County land Evelyn Smith and Maxine East had sneaked onto in search of a stockade. They and other investigators found one, and Peacher was convicted of violating federal laws against peonage: the unlawful practice of holding workers against their will, usually on the grounds that they had to pay off a debt before they could leave or seek other employment. The $3,500 fine assessed against Peacher was small, but the significance of seeing a widespread practice actually punished, as well as discredited, was great. With the incentives of mechanization and day labor and the disincentive of being vulnerable to a federal trial, white southern planters became less inclined to restrict black farm workers' movements, as many had done in the seven decades since slavery had supposedly ended.[38]

Other STFU successes in 1936 had to do with the power of publicity. For example, there was the February fund-raising dinner at Washington's exclusive Cosmos Club. Orchestrated by Gardner Jackson, one of the lawyers purged from the Agricultural Adjustment Administration and now an STFU lobbyist, the dinner featured a number of speakers. One was Howard Kester, who described the brutal violence STFU members had faced in Arkansas's ongoing labor wars. Another was John L. Lewis of the Congress of Industrial Organizations (CIO). A powerful orator, Lewis demanded federal protection for workers and predicted that "not until blood is flowing in the streets will Congress realize the menace to civil liberties!" Finishing up the evening, Wisconsin senator Robert M. La Follette Jr. vowed to answer Lewis's call by forming a Senate subcommittee to investigate antiunion violence. Although the La Follette committee proved more valuable for industrial workers than for farmers, the Cosmos Club event demonstrated the extent to which Jackson, Kester, Norman Thomas, and the STFU's many other friends—as well as its two widely publicized strikes and the extensive coverage journalists gave to the violence directed against its members—had managed to get the plight of the sharecroppers onto the national agenda.[39]

By the spring of 1936, Roosevelt himself was showing a greater willingness to act on the tenant problem. He had not lent his support to the Bankhead-Jones Farm Tenant bill—the proposal to aid displaced tenants that Donald Davidson and the rest of the delegates at the first Southern Policy Committee meeting had endorsed back in April 1935. The bill had not passed, but now, a year later, it appeared that Roosevelt was ready to put his weight behind it.[40] Even in the absence of such a law, the president had taken some initiative for the nation's rural as well as urban poor by creating the Resettlement Administration (RA) through a 1935 executive order. Under "Brains Trust" economist Rexford Tugwell, the RA would build new, planned communities in both suburban and rural areas and relocate destitute and low-income Americans into them. The agency would also provide loans "to finance, in whole or in part, the purchase of farm lands and necessary equipment by farmers, farm tenants, croppers or farm laborers."[41] When the Southern Policy Committee met again in May 1936 at Lookout Mountain, the work of the RA was one of the topics under discussion. Although he was glad to see the federal government finally addressing the tenant problem in some manner, the STFU's representative at the meeting, William R. Amberson, was not impressed by what he had seen of the agency's work thus far. After his conversation with Butler at the STFU headquarters, Jonathan Daniels would meet Amberson and find out why.

✦ ✦ ✦

AS HE AND BUTLER TALKED, Daniels could hear someone moving around in the second of the STFU's two leaky offices. "She was obviously entering [the] conversation by little intervening noises," he wrote in his journal. "Finally she came out and turned out to be a petite, dark and pretty girl, Evelyn Smith, a New Orleans socialist. . . . [A]s a high school and business school graduate she had volunteered to act as a stenographer. . . . Now quite a figure in the union."

And quite a figure in another sense. Jonathan took one look at Evelyn Smith and decided she was of an "entirely different world and race" from the "dumpy hill billy blond" who was also working in the office and was finally introduced as Butler's niece.[42] Full of class assumptions, Daniels attributed to Smith characteristics she did not have. The daughter of a long-unemployed railroad telegrapher, she had not finished high school, much less business college, and did not know shorthand.[43] But she was by all accounts an attractive person. In *A Southerner Discovers the South*, Daniels would mention the "plump and phlegmatic" niece but subtly use Smith's beauty to make a point. "She looked less like the conventional intervening idealist than anyone I ever saw," he wrote, drawing an implicit contrast with the kind of moralizing, Yankee-schoolmarm reformer he had criticized in his earlier discussion of the TVA. Daniels expected many of his readers to be biased against reformers of any kind, and he frankly shared some of their biases, especially against high-minded women. He liked women to be young, pretty, and cheerful, and Evelyn Smith was pleasantly all three — which spoke well for the whole concept of socialism, in his view. "On the way down the dark stair . . . Dayton [Moore, the United Press correspondent] and I agreed that Evelyn Smith was as pretty as she was enthusiastic," he wrote. A few more such Socialists and no one could tell what might not happen to the always susceptible South."[44]

Still acting as local guide, Moore seems to have taken Daniels next to see William Amberson, probably at his home since they also met his wife. From Amberson, Daniels would learn more about the Lookout Mountain quarrel over cooperatives versus private ownership in agriculture that he had been pondering since Chattanooga. During the second Southern Policy Committee (SPC) meeting, Allen Tate had done "the most reprehensible thing" Amberson had "ever [seen] a college man do." In the midst of a discussion of the tenant problem, Tate had complained about Communist agitators from the North who were exploiting the South's hardships for publicity. He cited the STFU as an example. Amberson, a northerner as well as a prominent STFU adviser, objected to the charge of Communism, but Tate pressed the issue. According to Amberson as quoted in Daniels's journal, Tate "said [the] S.T.F.U. [is] communistic and I know it because I went to Arkansas with a Communist organizer."[45]

For Tate to mention his trip to Arkansas was a mistake because Amberson had heard the true story and laughingly told it at the SPC meeting. In April 1935, leftist intellectual James Rorty, a writer for the *Nation*, had been in Memphis. Aware of the Arkansas labor wars from newspaper coverage, he wanted "to get someone to go out to Arkansas with him [and] finally got Tate to go." They had driven out to Marked Tree, and Rorty had asked a lot of questions, attracting the attention of the same upstanding citizens who had recently convicted Ward Rodgers of anarchy. From what Amberson had heard, Tate and Rorty were seized and held incommunicado for several hours before being released unharmed.[46]

The version of the story that came down through the Rorty family was a little different. Rorty's son Richard, who became a well-known philosopher, heard that "Tate was concerned that the white folks in the area weren't behaving like Southern gentlemen, and he proceeded to make a stump speech in the local courthouse square." James Rorty "claimed to have saved Tate's life by dragging him into the car and speeding back across the bridge into the next state before a mob could be organized to lynch Tate as a 'nigger-lover.'"[47]

The idea that even Allen Tate could seem like a radical to Arkansas planters was enough to generate laughter at the SPC meeting. When Amberson told his version of the story, "Tate was left hysterically speechless." Those who considered Tate arrogant—a view that Daniels would share, at least by later life—were amused at his comeuppance. Even former Agrarian H. C. Nixon told Daniels he thought Amberson "got the best of the exchange" because he "kept his head and Tate did not."[48]

One thing Amberson may not have realized is that Tate was not only embarrassed but afraid of losing his job. Deep in debt after years of trying to live by his pen and that of his wife, novelist Caroline Gordon, he had been teaching at Southwestern College in Memphis for less than a year when its president, Charles Edward Diehl, got word of his adventure with Rorty. A delegation from Marked Tree was soon in Diehl's office, where their spokesman threatened "that if any story is written [he] will give a story to the A.P. saying as how this northern agitator accompanied by a Southwestern professor stopped him on the street . . . and questioned him against his will," wrote

Gordon. Tate was furious, but he felt obligated to Diehl "not to get him on the spot, where a crowd of village idiots could blackmail him." Getting word to Rorty before he filed his story was a challenge, but Tate eventually reached him by telegram.[49] Hearing the incident made public anyway—in a room full of college professors who were bound to get it back to Diehl—was a shock.

As a politically engaged academic, Amberson might have been sympathetic to Tate's predicament. Born in Harrisburg, Pennsylvania, in 1894, he was a Harvard-educated physiologist who had become attracted to socialism while studying in Germany in the 1920s. In 1930, he became the chair of the physiology department at the University of Tennessee Medical School in Memphis. He joined the Socialist Party and, in 1932, helped form a local Unemployed Citizens League. When the mass evictions of tenant farmers began after the passage of the Agricultural Adjustment Act of 1933, he heard about it from the displaced tenants themselves, many of whom came to Memphis seeking relief.[50]

As Mitchell and others did the on-the-ground organizing that resulted in the STFU, Amberson became one of the union's most important publicists. "He admits that he has had to ghost write most of the [union's] pronunciamentoes etc.," Daniels jotted in his journal. His notes on their conversation make it clear that one thing he was trying to figure out was how an educated man like Amberson—a man of his own social class—could relate so fully with sharecroppers. Daniels himself felt a tremendous distance, and he wondered whether Amberson felt it too. His questions elicited Amberson's belief "that white men, Northern or Southern, cannot know what is going on in [the] heads of Negroes," but that "Negroes gradually confide to strangers about their affairs."[51] Daniels wrote down this observation without comment; he would experience the phenomenon himself at least once, later in his travels.

Ultimately, Daniels could attribute Amberson's deep commitment to the STFU only to politics and personality. His notes on their interview reveal his ambivalence. "Amberson is a socialist but denies any Communistic taint though calls Communists he mentions by their first names," he wrote. "He is a typical uplifter—sincere—smug—self-satisfied—and his wife, a rather pretty, gray-haired woman, thinks he is almost as wonderful as he thinks he is—deserves credit for courage and good will."[52]

The bulk of Daniels's conversation with Amberson had to do with cooperative farming. Amberson enjoyed his victory over Tate but lamented that both the "New Deal and [the] Southern Policy people" were "trying to carry out the Agrarian philosophy." Exhibit A was the "Dyess Colony experiment in Mississippi County, Arkansas—where," Daniels jotted, "behind nice little houses—wired though electricity not yet available, with baths though running water not yet running—government is following individualism along lines of 40 acres and a mule." The Dyess Colony was an RA project that had its origins in the vision of an Arkansas relief administrator. Even before the RA was created, William Dyess had used federal funds to buy thousands of acres of land with the idea of building a town and resettling relief clients there and on surrounding farms of twenty to forty acres apiece. The RA assumed responsibility for the project in 1935 and continued more or less according to Dyess's original plan—which, according to Amberson, was the problem. "Amberson says that with the lumber used in building an individual barn for each individual farm they could have built a barn to take care of half [of] Arkansas."[53]

Large-scale cooperative farming was the only good option for the Arkansas-Mississippi Delta and its people, in Amberson's view. Mechanization was coming, and already small farmers were losing out in competition with big planters, even if they did own their own land. "Forty acres of good rich land are enough to maintain any family in normal years. But some years are not normal," he explained in an article for the *Nation*. Plus, the "big planter across the road" had all the advantages. He, "with his tractor and four-row equipment and his superior credit facilities, cultivates his cotton for $5 an acre." Meanwhile, the small farmer with one mule "dragging a half-row plow, runs the bill up to over $14." Sooner or later a crop failure would sweep away "the little man's reserves." His mortgage would be foreclosed, and "the next year the little man is a tenant on the big farm, which now includes his own former acres. So tenants are made," Amberson concluded, "and so they will surely continue to be made, as surely as God makes little green apples and cotton bolls, unless we, as a nation, do some deep and serious thinking and some wise and careful planning."

Attempting to recapture some "Golden Age of the Republic," when "all men were little men," was not wise, Amberson argued. The Agrarian vision failed to see that "the big planter across the road is a stubborn fact." In addition, decades of poverty, poor health, and minimal education meant that "the majority of Southern rural workers are not ready for land ownership." The nation was "dealing with a vast rural population of no fewer than five million whites and three million Negroes who are so thoroughly demoralized, so ignorant and irresponsible, so dirty, ragged, and diseased, that one may well doubt whether they can ever be reclaimed."

Given all these factors, cooperative farming was the best solution. It was the way to steer "between plantation exploitation on the one hand and the inefficiency of the small homestead on the other." Whether one began "with an emphasis on technical efficiency" or "an appreciation of the low culture of these laboring masses," the logical conclusion was the same. "Large-scale cooperative farming ventures are in this region the only hope for the majority. The efficiency of the large plantation must be retained and increased, not destroyed," but its profits must be distributed more equitably. Rather than attempting to own their own farms and compete with "the big planter across the road," the rural poor should be helped to own shares in cooperative plantations that would divide their profits among members. "Group ownership of land presents new legal, as well as new psychological, problems," Amberson acknowledged, but it was the best possible solution for the plantation South.[54]

Amberson's brief reference to "new psychological problems" betrayed a concern that he avoided in his *Nation* article, as well as in his conversation with Daniels. Like the other socialists involved in the STFU, he understood how deep the American commitment to landownership and the independent family farm was, even among sharecroppers for whom farming had proved to be a miserable way of life. In 1935, the STFU surveyed its rank-and-file members to get their views on what a federal resettlement program for displaced farm tenants ought to offer. Even though the union's socialist leaders advocated cooperatives and described individual ownership plans as "every man for himself," rank-and-file members made their preferences clear. More than half of the survey's nearly 500 respondents selected ownership as their first choice, while only one in six preferred cooperatives. A long-term lease option that would have felt much like ownership was also popular.[55]

In the view of socialists like Amberson, tenant farmers would undoubtedly come to prefer cooperatives if only they could see how successful a cooperative farm could be. The STFU had taken a step in this direction in early 1936 by founding the Delta Cooperative Farm at Hillhouse, Mississippi. Protestant missionary and philanthropist Sherwood Eddy had provided $17,500 to purchase a 2,138-acre tract of land. A Parkin, Arkansas, planter who evicted approximately 100 sharecroppers that January provided some of the first residents. Delta Cooperative was a biracial community with a Christian socialist vision and manager, a man named Sam Franklin. By early 1937, it was home to nearly thirty families, who were all members of the cooperative and would share any profits it cleared. The newly built settlement had a community center, a rudimentary medical clinic, a post office, and rows of small, simple houses in which black member-families lived on one side of the main street and white ones lived on the other. It was, at minimum, a very unusual place.[56]

With a net profit of more than $8,000 for the year 1936, Delta Cooperative Farm seemed to be succeeding. Amberson was proud of it, and he urged Daniels to go and see for himself. In fact, he encouraged him to visit the RA's Dyess Colony first and then visit Delta and draw his own conclusions. It was true that Delta needed more money. "We can't demonstrate a successful new pattern of life for the agrarian South unless we can get the very latest and best equipment." But Amberson was optimistic, and an hour or two earlier Evelyn Smith had been truly passionate. "She is sure tenants can go forward, she says, after seeing cooperative farm at Hillhouse," Daniels noted in his journal.[57] After his conversation with Amberson, he decided he should take a look.

✦ ✦ ✦

BREAKFAST AT THE PEABODY made the poverty of rural Arkansas seem all the more shocking as Daniels drove to the Dyess Colony on May 13, 1937. As he went, he wondered where in the countryside lived a black man named George Wells, whom he had read about in one of the STFU publications Evelyn Smith had pressed upon him as he left the Memphis office. A thirty-page book, *The Disinherited Speak: Letters from Sharecroppers*, opened with a letter about Wells's desperation for food—desperation so great that he had fought off a water snake for a turtle and scavenged a dead pig he found alongside the road.[58]

Although he would have been curious to talk to someone like Wells, Daniels assumed that he would not get very far if he tried to drop in on any of the black families whose homes he passed. Beside the road, across "a land as flat as a floor," he saw one- and two-room tenant cabins with cotton planted "almost to the door" and no trees allowed to stand, lest their shade stunt the cotton's growth. The "pretty, painted houses of the Dyess Colony . . . seemed almost designed to emphasize [the cabins'] sunburnt littleness and dusty squalor" by comparison. These government-built houses looked to him "like debutantes in the slums."[59]

Daniels's overall assessment of the Dyess Colony would prove little different from this visual first impression. He admitted that the settlement's three-, four-, and five-room wooden houses with their electricity and running water were "by no means extravagant dwellings." He found the administrative buildings and other public spaces pleasant but not at all luxurious. "But the 500 houses on the 500 farms [at Dyess] come to an average cost per house of $1,885, while the average farm house in Arkansas . . . has been recently valued at an average cost of only $391," he wrote. Like Amberson and a host of other critics on both the left and the right, Daniels could see that the RA's attempt to give poor families their own individual homesteads was too expensive to be a practical solution to the South's massive tenant problem. Federal officials "had been merely playing doll house" in Arkansas. "I say it sadly and with the expectation that I shall be answered swiftly and sharply," Daniels concluded, but "Dyess seemed to me to be a toytown cut out of the jungle." It was so small an experiment and so impossible to extend region-wide that it "means nothing to the South." He would have to "look further" for any "solution of the dark problem of the little man on the land."[60]

The next day, Daniels drove to the Delta Cooperative Farm. He found a far less developed community than he had expected. General manager Sam Franklin gave him a thorough tour. "Sam Franklin—sparrow-like, jumpy-step, tired individual, booted and good natured, who runs the place even to telling the manager of the poultry farm that the chickens need water," Daniels noted in his journal. "He showed me saw mill, chicken yard, store, community building, garden and a tenant house. . . . Each 'member' (not tenant) gets an unceiled two-room house with little unscreened porch . . . no lights—no plumbing—he can add to it as he will at his own expense and with this own time. Behind each house is a 'modern' fly-proof privy."[61]

Although Delta was far more rustic than Dyess, Daniels's impressions of it were more favorable. To him, the "economic set-up" there seemed more realistic. Sounding a lot like Amberson, he observed that the "cotton plantation has always been a collective and its transfer from cotton capitalism to cotton cooperative is far simpler than a transfer from the collective plantation to the collection of little independent farms at Dyess." The primitive living conditions at Delta were also "within the possibility of men working in cotton fields."[62] The lack of electricity and plumbing might be lamentable, but at least they avoided the falsehood of providing a standard of living that was so much higher than the local average that it could only be given to a few—the false promise of planting debutantes in the slums.

The problem at Delta Cooperative was a different kind of debutante: the well-meaning but ignorant reformer whose worst manifestation, in Daniels's mind, was always female and well-to-do, if rarely young. He would laugh about one or two such types at Delta, including the wealthy female visitor who "slipped and fell on her behind in the mud." More soberly, Daniels

Dorothea Lange photographed this house at the Delta Cooperative Farm in Hillhouse, Mississippi, when she visited there in June 1937, shortly after Jonathan Daniels visited in May. Farm Security Administration / Office of War Information Photograph Collection, Library of Congress, Prints and Photographs Division, Washington, D.C. [LC-DIG-fsa-8b32082].

recognized a "tragic flaw" in Delta's otherwise commendable arrangement: the fact that there were no *farmers* among those in charge. Director Sam Franklin was an ordained minister who had been a Protestant missionary and a close associate of donor Sherwood Eddy. He had a cousin who was an agronomist and offered advice from far away in Georgia, Daniels reported with wry skepticism. Franklin had also paid a local farmer to visit regularly, but there were definitely limits to his ability to provide scientific management. Plus, knowing he had never farmed himself, cooperative members did not always take kindly to his anxious overseeing. The "whole place seems to me to be a pathetic and almost ludicrous piece of play acting," Daniels wrote in his journal. "Christian amateurism disregards the real difficulties in farming even by practical men—and obviously [Delta's] best crop is the philanthropy of the East."[63]

With its tragic flaw and dependence on Yankee charity, Delta had not "even begun to test the cooperative plan," in Daniels's view. In *A South-*

erner Discovers the South, he cited a September 1937 article from the *New Republic* that examined Delta's finances, including its claim that, for 1936, its member-families had earned a significantly higher income than the average sharecropper household. But what of Franklin's salary, which was not on the books because it was paid by Sherwood Eddy? And what of Eddy's other contributions and the unpaid services of Amberson and other volunteers? As long as Delta's success "hangs dependent upon capitalistic philanthropy," Daniels argued, "it does not rest upon the cooperation in brotherhood of the common man."[64] He did not ask whether Delta's success should be measured by economic criteria alone.

Somewhat surprisingly, he did not dwell on Delta's biracialism either. He was very conscious of it—and very self-conscious about it, as indicated by the fact that, once in his journal and twice in his book, he mentioned that he had washed his hands before lunch and dried them on a common towel (a towel that black people might have used). Daniels's annoyance at being put on the spot by the volunteer who offered him the towel may account for his mean-spirited description of her in his journal. She was a "buxom but young looking blond," and her olive-colored, pajama-like outfit gave her "a vivid appearance among the tenant farmers," he wrote. She was "a little fat for such a costume—especially in the tail. Brown scars like cured pimples on one side of her face."[65]

Despite his own discomfort, Daniels described Delta's racial practices as simply a "queer compromise" that seemed to have little to do with the viability of the cooperative approach. Franklin and the other staff members "want to take the Christian attitude toward race, but they do not want to complicate the cooperative experiment unduly by unnecessarily alarming Mississippi." Other than "Mississippi's" possible reaction, however, there seemed to be no problem. "Negro houses in one row—whites in another—Negroes voted for this—but no segregation," Daniels wrote in his journal. "Negroes treated as if they were as good as whites," he added (the "as if" seeming to betray his own unconsciously racist view).[66]

Like the STFU's pragmatic policy of establishing separate black and white locals, Delta's "queer compromise" on race was based on more than just concern about external repercussions. It was also an effort to address internal tensions that resulted not only from the racial divide but also from a class and educational divide between cooperative members and managers like Franklin. When Delta began to lose money in its second year, the losses led to disagreements and misunderstandings. "White cooperative residents were unsure what to make of black residents advocating for rights they had here-tofore been denied," writes historian Robert Hunt Ferguson, "while black ex-sharecroppers were concerned that whites were getting better financial returns and preferential housing at Delta. Additionally, Resident Director Sam Franklin and the Board of Trustees often viewed former sharecroppers as a primitive community who needed to be shepherded along the path to socialism and were not yet capable of running the cooperative."[67]

By 1939, these internal tensions would compel William Amberson to re-sign from Delta's board of trustees. He cited a lack of democratic decision making and argued that Franklin and Eddy had been misleading donors about the farm's financial health, as well as mismanaging funds. Somewhat like Daniels, Amberson attributed many of the problems at Delta to reli-gious attitudes, if not exactly "Christian amateurism." "Never before have I seen with such blinding clarity . . . the essential and irreconcilable conflict [between] the scientific and ecclesiastical approach[es] to social problems," declared Amberson. Franklin's self-perception as a missionary or a pastor tending a flock allowed "the pattern of plantation thought which he (Frank-lin) had meant to break" to "grip his own mind."[68] It was a sad outcome for the effort to "demonstrate a successful new pattern of life for the agrarian South" that he had so enthusiastically described to Daniels in May 1937. But it was not the end of the story.

Even before Amberson resigned, operations at Delta were being shifted to another location: the 2,800-acre Providence Farm in Holmes County, Mississippi. Although the Delta Cooperative was a failed experiment that would end with the sale of the last of its land in 1943, Providence turned out to have a longer and more positive history. For two decades it provided an institutional base for the sort of "local people" who led the civil rights move-ment at the grassroots level. But it was not a cooperative farm of the sort that Amberson and other Depression-era socialists had envisioned. It employed comparatively few farm workers and instead centered on a credit union and educational and health initiatives. As white former sharecroppers dispropor-tionately left the Arkansas-Mississippi Delta for military service and factory work during and after World War II, Providence became a haven of black self-help. Holmes County native Fannye Booker was a particularly powerful presence who ran a school and summer camps for black children into the 1970s—long after Providence Farm itself fell victim to the post-*Brown* de-cision anxieties of white Holmes County residents. In 1955, the Providence Cooperative Federal Credit Union was forced to dissolve, and in 1956 the final white staff members left, ending the experiment in biracial socialist cooperatives that had started twenty years earlier.[69]

✦ ✦ ✦

"IT ISN'T SIMPLE," Jonathan Daniels remarked to Dayton Moore as they drove back to the Peabody Hotel after the interview with Amberson. "The tenants are organizing. But plantation and landlord are changing, too. . . . And the old-fashioned plantation, a profit enterprise. Now the cooperative plantation. And still in the plantation South the free yeoman on the little farm. It isn't simple at all."

"Who the hell said it was simple?" Moore demands in *A Southerner Discovers the South*.[70] Like other recounted or imagined conversations in the book, Daniels was using it to make a point — except in this case the point was the very lack of any resolution to the "dark problem of the little man on the land."

By the time he wrote this dialogue, Daniels would have known that, at a convention held in Memphis in September 1937, the STFU had decided to affiliate with a new CIO union, the United Cannery, Agricultural, Packing, and Allied Workers of America (UCAPAWA). But he could not know what a disaster the alliance would be. The UCAPAWA's founding documents promised to preserve the "identity and administrative self-government" of the STFU but failed to work out the details. It was unclear who would set the union dues and whether or not they could still be sent directly to the Memphis office, as H. L. Mitchell and J. R. Butler, who became vice president of the UCAPAWA while continuing to serve as president of the STFU, preferred. And, although the UCAPAWA stated lofty goals — goals that would still define agricultural workers' struggles in the twenty-first century, including the right to collective bargaining, old-age pensions, workers' compensation, unemployment insurance, and equal pay for equal work — the reality was that organizing farm workers was not a top priority for the CIO.[71] The UCAPAWA got far less money and far fewer organizers than it requested. Meanwhile, the CIO and UCAPAWA wanted more in dues than most STFU members could possibly pay.

Financial disagreements made tempers run high, as did ideological conflicts between socialists like Mitchell and Donald Henderson, the UCAPAWA's president, who was a member of the Communist Party. The party's declaration of a Popular Front had not erased old animosities or allayed all fears that association with Communists would hurt the reputations of non-Communist liberal and socialist organizations. As their frustrations with

UCAPAWA policies mounted, STFU leaders became convinced that, as Kester put it, "the CP controlled UCAPAWA is out to liquidate the STFU," which must either resist or be "smashed like a potato bug."[72] Although Kester was reluctant to believe it of an old friend, Mitchell thought he knew who was at the center of the perceived conspiracy: STFU executive council member Claude Williams.

Williams was a white clergyman who had become friends with Kester and Ward Rodgers while they were all students at Vanderbilt. He had recently become the director of Commonwealth College, an Arkansas school for labor organizers. Both his own radical, egalitarian take on Christian theology and his need for a broad base of financial supporters for Commonwealth made him a ready convert to Popular Front ideology and the Communist Party's aggressively antiracist stance. He was strongly in favor of the STFU-UCAPAWA alliance and used powerful oratory at the fall 1937 convention to encourage STFU members to "Go forward, FORWARD INTO THE CIO!"

Williams's enthusiasm put him at odds with Mitchell, who was reluctant about the merger from the start. When Williams nominated a black challenger for Mitchell's position as secretary-treasurer and criticized the STFU's policy of allowing segregated locals, Mitchell was furious. He won reelection to his office by a wide margin but became convinced that Williams was an enemy within.[73] He also grew newly anxious about Britt McKinney, whose black nationalism was becoming more pronounced.

E. B. McKinney was vice president of the STFU but increasingly felt that he and other blacks were the "goat" of the organization. He distrusted Butler and the rest of the union's white leadership, usually excepting Mitchell. In a letter to a fellow black STFU member, he described the Memphis headquarters that Daniels had visited as "an office full of poor white people, who had nothing before this organization was set up but now in a time when a man can hardly live they are buying big fine car[s and] sending their children to school . . . while your old servant must walk and work to build up the union." McKinney feared that "at the rate we are now thinking . . . we are just manufacturing some new masters who have always wanted to get the opportunity to handle the Negro." He assured his friend that his views did not "come from any prejudice . . . towards the white people . . . but I must admit that I am very suspicious of them."[74]

Apart from any personal animosities, McKinney was justified in thinking that blacks had taken the worst of planter violence while occupying fewer leadership roles than they should have in an overwhelmingly black union.

His deeply felt black nationalism had probably also been stirred by his participation in the National Negro Congress, a civil rights group founded in 1935 that strongly embraced the Popular Front. Rather than sharing Kester's and Mitchell's suspicions about Henderson and the UCAPAWA, McKinney may have been attracted to the Communists.[75] Certainly, he believed that working through the CIO—which was not Communist but shared much of the party's commitment to racial justice—was the best option for black former sharecroppers seeking support from the labor movement. He may well have been right. "In the long run," historian Nan Elizabeth Woodruff concludes, "given the acceleration following World War II of land consolidation, labor displacement, mechanization, and crop diversification, black sharecroppers were right to insist that their future lay with a national body like the CIO, one that was committed in principle to interracial equality and one that had the clout to counter the power exercised on the national level by the planters. The STFU had proven no match for the landowners' authority in Washington."[76]

Still, what historians can see in retrospect was less clear to McKinney or anyone else trying to look ahead from the vantage point of the late 1930s. The STFU's leadership struggle did not play out with any great wisdom or foresight on the part of anyone. First, McKinney tried and failed to get an all-black slate of officers elected at an STFU convention in early 1938. Then, a few months later, Williams inadvertently allowed Butler to find a document that proposed using Communist Party funds to organize sympathetic STFU locals, "establishing a real party base in the STFU" and making it possible to "capture the union for our line at the next convention." Butler was so angry that he immediately released the document to the press and denounced Williams as a Communist. At a special meeting of the STFU's executive council, both Williams and McKinney, whose personal letters criticizing the union's white officers had come to light, were stripped of their membership. Grief stricken, Williams appealed his expulsion and drew up what he called "A Program for a United, Democratic, and Effective STFU." McKinney initially signed on but then renounced Williams's plan in time to allow Mitchell and his allies to reinstate him to the union, although not to his former position as vice president. Williams's expulsion was upheld, ending his association with the STFU, although not with the UCAPAWA. When the STFU decided to withdraw its affiliation from the UCAPAWA in early 1939, he and McKinney encouraged black farm workers to stick with the UCAPAWA and CIO.

These bitter internal fights all but destroyed the STFU, which had reached a peak of about 31,000 members in several states in 1937. By the end of 1939, union membership had plummeted. The number of locals dropped from a high of about 200 down to 40, and the STFU's reach was limited almost exclusively to eastern Arkansas.[77] Butler continued to serve as president, while Evelyn Smith left in 1941 to join the staff of the International Ladies' Garment Workers' Union and later the Workers Defense League.[78] Mitchell had taken a job with the National Youth Administration in 1938 but remained devoted to farm workers' struggles. In 1946, he helped the STFU turn itself into the National Farm Labor Union, which became most active in California and which a next-generation labor leader, Cesar Chavez, joined during a cotton pickers' strike in 1948, when he was twenty-one years old. Howard Kester continued his work for social justice through religious organizations such as the Fellowship of Southern Churchmen, and he also taught and served as headmaster of various schools. Disenchanted with a struggling Socialist Party as well as the Delta Cooperative Farm, William Amberson had already left Memphis by the time Daniels wrote *A Southerner Discovers the South*, taking positions at the University of Maryland School of Medicine and the Marine Biological Laboratory in Woods Hole, Massachusetts.[79]

Even by the summer of 1938, when Daniels's book appeared, most of the STFU's story was already finished, not because of the union's internal conflicts or because of its ill-fated affiliation with UCAPAWA, but because the moment when decisive action might have been possible had essentially passed. Like the five union men who drove to Washington in Mitchell's Moon car, the STFU—and the South's entire population of destitute and displaced farm workers—needed the federal government's help if the costs of the region's transition away from the sharecropping system were not to be borne solely by those who were already poor and disadvantaged, the expendable laborers in a mechanizing, modernizing world. New Deal policy had exacerbated landless farmers' problems, but the federal government was also the only authority with enough power to challenge the power of the planters. Despite planter dominance in the Department of Agriculture, there were those in government who tried to ease the sharecroppers' plight after the STFU succeeded in raising their awareness of it. Franklin Roosevelt was one such government official, as indicated by his executive order creating the Resettlement Administration in 1935 and his appointment of a President's Committee on Farm Tenancy in the fall of 1936.

In February 1937, the president's new committee presented its report, endorsing the work of the Resettlement Administration and recommending that it be put on a firmer basis through the creation of a new Farm Security Administration (FSA) within the Department of Agriculture. The FSA would administer a "tenant purchase" program much like the one proposed in the Bankhead-Jones Farm Tenant bill, which had still not passed in Congress. With the backing of the president, in July 1937 the Bankhead-Jones bill finally did become law, appropriating $85 million over its first three years for long-term, low-interest loans for tenants purchasing farms. Bankhead-Jones also allowed for existing resettlement programs, including a small number of cooperatives, to be completed and maintained. Although these were comparatively small measures given the magnitude of the tenant problem, with the passage of Bankhead-Jones and the creation of the FSA all discussion of land reform—a burning issue for political thinkers as different as William Amberson and Frank Owsley in the mid-1930s—"abruptly ended."[80]

The man appointed to head the FSA was Will Alexander, who had already taken charge of the Resettlement Administration from Rexford Tugwell at the end of 1936. As a member of the Southern Policy Committee as well as the chairman of the Commission on Interracial Cooperation, Alexander had participated in the heated debates over Agrarianism versus cooperatives versus other forms of regional planning. With the help of another white southern liberal, his deputy administrator C. B. "Beanie" Baldwin, he did what he could to make the FSA a transformative force in the South.

Not surprisingly, however, the agency's efforts to promote social change ran up against fierce conservative opposition. Those who represented planter interests in Congress and the Department of Agriculture "tolerated the FSA as a temporary relief measure during the late 1930s," writes Patricia Sullivan, but in 1940, when Baldwin succeeded the widely admired Alexander, their toleration gave way to a bitter, two-year assault. A Democratic congressman from Georgia began the attack with a proposal to reduce the agency's budget and charges that some FSA programs were "very suspiciously related" to "sovietism." Many others who spoke for the planters joined the crusade, and by early 1943, the agency was "virtually crippled."[81]

Jonathan Daniels learned a lot during his tour about what the STFU and its allies had accomplished. But the power of the planters was another, equally poignant lesson. The furor and effectiveness of planters' violent resistance to any effort to empower farm workers were the clearest part of the STFU's whole complicated history. "It is not necessary to believe all the atrocity tales," Daniels mused. "But certain it is that here [in eastern Arkansas] so conservative a Southerner as Allen Tate was made to seem a sansculotte merely for being there looking as I was looking."[82] Like the Communist-led mobilization in defense of the Scottsboro Boys and the NAACP's fight for antilynching legislation, the STFU was one of the earliest signs of organized dissent in the South that would gradually come together in the long civil rights movement. But the planter opposition was even more organized. The "long backlash" arguably began first, as soon as the organizational stirrings of black and white farmworkers became visible. Rooted in the labor oppression of the rural South, the fight for the status quo would become more specifically a "long *segregationist* movement" after World War II, when the legal framework of separation and exclusion was threatened. By that time, a changing economy and the growth of the Sunbelt would result in shifting emphases, tactics, and leadership—in changes that some have called "smart" segregationism—although the rural South still saw an enormous amount of old-fashioned racial violence in the post–World War II years.[83]

Even for someone as socially secure as Daniels, the hostile climate of the Arkansas-Mississippi Delta felt oppressive. Angry little towns like Marked Tree were a short drive and yet a very long way from the genteel South of the Peabody Hotel.

— CHAPTER SIX —

Naked and Hot as If She Were
Stripped in the Sun

✦

MARKED TREE, ARKANSAS

UNLIKE THE HIGHWAYS he had taken from Raleigh to Memphis, many of the roads Jonathan relied on to travel around the Arkansas-Mississippi Delta countryside were of poor quality and poorly maintained. They were "choking gravel roads," as he wrote in his journal. When he had a tire blow out "in the empty, dusty backwoods of Arkansas on the hottest day so far," he "got her changed but nearly burned up in the process."[1]

Even more noteworthy than the roads were the "back settlements and little towns" and "the white men sitting in idleness as if there were nothing creative to be done."[2] Daniels wrote with acute sensitivity about how it felt to be the object of southern white men's suspicious gaze. "Anyone who as a stranger has been in one of these small Arkansas-Mississippi towns will feel the possible crime of his presence," he reflected. "I was put in no jail but when I rode in the back country I was forever aware of the arresting eyes." He must have mentioned this "strange sensation" of being looked at to someone he met. A woman, she told him "that in such little towns she always felt naked and hot as if she were stripped in the sun."[3]

It would be interesting to know which woman told Daniels of this feeling. He talked to many, all of them white and most of them the wives of men he had made arrangements to see. One likely candidate was Effie Leigh of Little Rock, whose husband, Gilbert, was a distant relative and Daniels's contact in the city. Daniels's notes make it clear that he discussed his impressions of the Arkansas-Mississippi Delta with the Leighs once he got to their house on May 15.[4] He may have also discussed Delta social conditions with Mary Rose Bradford, the wife of writer Roark Bradford, whom he met a few days later in Greenville, Mississippi, and saw again in New Orleans. In one of his uglier moments, Daniels wrote in his journal that she was "a kike if I ever saw one." Despite his anti-Semitic tendencies, however, he seems to have had deep, intimate conversations with Mary Rose, to the point where she informed him that, in her opinion, the daughter of a mutual acquaintance was "a Lesbian who doesn't know it."[5] Although Daniels's journal does not provide any evidence, it is easy to imagine Bradford being the woman who told him about feeling naked in little Delta towns.

Jonathan would have had to be a more empathetic man and one well ahead of his times to be able to analyze his society in self-consciously gendered terms in 1937. Nevertheless, he was able to recognize an appropriate metaphor when he heard one. The unidentified woman's comment bespoke a breakdown in southern convention that had become quite apparent in the midst of the Arkansas labor wars. The South's old order of honor, "chivalry," and racial paternalism—no matter how rarely realized and inherently unjust—had given way to something more raw, a brutality that could leave even the supposedly pedestaled white southern lady feeling naked and exposed.

This was the point of a widely reported story that Daniels was reminded of when he visited Marked Tree, Arkansas, on May 13. Together with the weight and heat of fellow white male southerners' surveillance, the visit and what he learned about Delta violence made him feel, perhaps more fully than ever, that questions about the South's future were not merely academic even though his own best answers were to be found in books. It would prove quite a relief to *see* some of those books and discover at least one man who shared his faith in them in the embattled Delta.

✦ ✦ ✦

THE STORY THAT Daniels was reminded about in Marked Tree—the story of Willie Sue Blagden—was one that he undoubtedly already knew, whether from newspaper and magazine articles or from a *March of Time* newsreel that had opened in 6,000 theaters nationwide in August 1936.[6] During a strike earlier that spring, one tactic the Southern Tenant Farmers Union (STFU) had employed was long, single-file marches along eastern Arkansas's dusty roads. Strikers maintained a distance of six or eight feet between them to make their numbers look larger, and they called out to workers in the fields to lay down their hoes and join them. Plantation owners and their "riding bosses" took to the roads as well, driving up and down the countryside to break up the pickets.[7] In early June, a march near the town of Earle, Arkansas, was "broken up by two carloads of plantation guards swinging baseball bats, [a] sledge hammer and axe handles." The STFU newspaper, the *Share-cropper's Voice*, reported that "J. M. Reese, leader of the 'march,' and Eliza Nolden were among those beaten. But the most badly beaten was Frank Weems. It was reported that he had died of the beating."[8]

Just what had happened to Weems, a middle-aged black sharecropper who lived near Earle, was unclear. Left unconscious by the side of the road, he had not come home, but no one had been able to find his body either. H. L. Mitchell and Evelyn Smith had spent two nights searching, an experience that for Smith became the subject of a recurring dream. "Great material for dreams was there," she acknowledged, "terror and nightmare, adventure and romance, heroes and villains, and always long rows of cotton, with men, women and children dragging behind them long sacks to hold the cotton they picked."[9]

The villains in this case were John "Boss" Dulaney, a planter and president of the local board of education; Earl Cherry, a deputy sheriff and bookkeeper for a cotton gin; Ernest Richards, the owner of a 500-acre plantation north of Earle; and L. L. Barham and Percy Mangus, a planter and "just a farmer," respectively. These were all men whom Mitchell and others in the STFU leadership knew to be among the union's chief antagonists. Dulaney, Barham, and Richards had been part of a planter mob that Howard Kester had seen indiscriminately attack black men, women, and children with ax handles and pistol butts at a meeting at a Methodist church earlier that year.[10]

As Weems's disappearance made national headlines, generating interest in the strike, Mitchell tried to keep the story in the news. He dispatched one of the STFU's best orators—white, Vanderbilt-trained Claude Williams (still a friend at this point)—to conduct a funeral, despite the uncertainty over whether or not Weems was actually dead. On Monday, June 15, 1936, Williams, who lived in Little Rock, stopped by the Memphis office before heading out to Earle. A middle-class white woman who happened to be visiting—twenty-nine-year-old Willie Sue Blagden—asked if she could come along. Williams felt "the presence of a white woman might be some protection," Mitchell recalled. "Southern chivalry was still presumably alive even in Arkansas." He reluctantly agreed to let Blagden go but warned Williams that she "was young and impetuous."[11]

When they got to Earle, Williams and Blagden had to wait while a local contact went to find Weems's wife. At about four o'clock, they stopped at a grocery store on Highway 75 and bought Coca-Colas. They were sitting in Williams's car drinking them when another car pulled up. "Boss" Dulaney and five other "well dressed white men" got out. They demanded to know what Williams and Blagden were doing in Crittenden County and then forced them to drive "out Highway 75 until we came to two buildings." Blagden described what happened next in an article for the *New Republic*. "We turned up a dirt road, crossed a wooden bridge over a ravine and drove around a soybean field," she wrote. "To the left was the overgrown bank of a river." Parking the two cars near the riverbank, Dulaney and his men questioned Williams and Blagden and searched Williams's car. Then they took Williams down to the riverbank and flogged him with a four-inch-wide leather mule harness. Blagden heard fourteen cracks before Williams was brought back to his car, "pale and shaken."

"Now it's your turn," one of the men said to Blagden. "I could hardly believe what I had seen and heard, and I did not believe they would beat me," she reported. "But I was forced to go with them. One of them held the barbed wire fence apart, stepping down on the wire below, so that I wouldn't tear my dress as I crawled through. Branches of shrubbery were held back to save my stockings." But the men beat her nevertheless. A "slender, tanned young man, with brown hair and eyes, . . . and wearing a straw hat" gave her four strokes with the mule harness on her buttocks and thighs, leaving her badly bruised. Then, after driving her and Williams around for a while in uncertainty, the men took her to the Earle depot and told her to take the train to Memphis.[12] They finally let Williams go too, following his car as he left the county. Williams drove all the way back to Little Rock, where he collapsed in his wife's arms at about two o'clock in the morning.[13]

Arriving in Memphis, Blagden immediately called Mitchell. "She was hysterical," he later wrote. "She said that Williams had been killed and that she was so badly beaten she could hardly walk." Mitchell telegraphed the U.S. attorney general's office and demanded an investigation. Then he called the newspapers and wire services. "I was asked to bring Willie Sue to the office of the *Memphis Press Scimitar* for an interview and pictures. Pictures of the black and blue welts on Willie Sue's prominent thighs appeared in newspapers all over the country."[14]

A widely distributed photograph of Blagden raising her dress to reveal her bruises, plus reports that she belonged to a prominent white Memphis family, made the story a sensation. "Woman Flogged" was the *Literary Digest* headline, indicating the extent to which it was the attack on her and not the beating of Williams, much less the far more vicious assaults on Weems, Reese, and Nolden, that mattered. The bitter truth was that black men, women, and children could be and long had been beaten, even beaten to

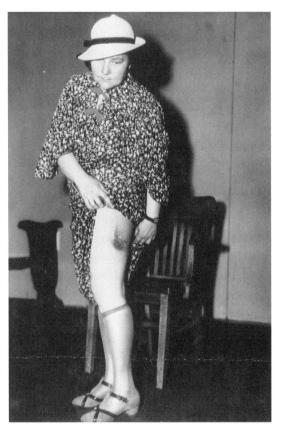

Willie Sue Blagden raising her dress to show her bruised thigh
after she and Southern Tenant Farmers Union representative Claude
Williams were flogged by antiunion planters in June 1936. Courtesy
of Tennessee State Library and Archives, Nashville, Tenn.

death, without white newspapers or magazines taking much notice. The
beating of a white clergyman might have attracted some attention, although
once Williams's radical views became public, he might well have been dismissed as an "outside agitator" who had been asking for trouble.

Blagden, too, was a socialist. In fact, her views were to the left of the Socialist Party and the STFU leadership. She wanted to use the publicity her
story generated to start a mass movement—"to build around the flogging of
the Union members, Preacher Williams and myself a Joint Committee for
Sharecropper Defense which would begin an organized movement to establish the right of union members and their allies in this section of the South to
the protection of the Constitution of the United States." Frustrated by their

refusal to cooperate with Communists in the Popular Front (she called it a "United Front" and a "Democratic Front"), Blagden would eventually break with the STFU and the Socialist Party—which casts a different light on Mitchell's, other contemporaries', and subsequent historians' often-negative descriptions of her, including the dismissive suggestion that she was "young and impetuous." Instead, Blagden could be incisive. "To not believe in the effectiveness of mass action, of building the broadest front for working class objectives, is not to believe in the working class itself," she wrote. In 1938, two years after the flogging, she informed the STFU leadership that she was joining the Communist Party because—unlike the socialists, in her view—the party and the Popular Front were "leading the fight to maintain and extend the democracy we now have."[15]

Despite Blagden's Popular Front views and her impressive education (she had studied anthropology at Columbia University under Franz Boas), most newspaper accounts of the flogging identified her only as white, female, and middle class or, at most, as a "social worker."[16] Her political ideas and even her precise background were of little importance compared with a vague profile of her as a white southern lady. "Arkansas: Chivalry Has Flown," the *Washington Post* charged in a headline that captured the cultural context in which the story became a national outrage.[17] Hoisted on the white South's own petard of supposed chivalry, even the local *Earle Enterprise* had to admit that the planters had crossed a line when they flogged a white woman.

Usually, the *Enterprise* approved of planter violence. For months, "foreign agitators" had been "stirring up unrest and causing much ado about nothing among the laboring classes." Fortunately, tenants were now "all on the job and day laborers are plentiful and glad to work for 75 cents a day, instead of the $1.50 demanded by the union." It was true "that a few foreign agitators representing the Southern Tenant Farmers Union have felt the strong sting of a backhand applied where it would do the most good. This method has produced results where all other remedies less drastic have failed." The recent "hue and cry" had arisen "from the fact that a white woman was forced to endure the indignity of a light whipping." Opinions varied "as to the wisdom of this act," but it "is hard for us to condone" it. "However, there is no doubt but what the woman was completely out of her place. Assisting in conducting a Negro funeral is no job for a white woman in the South."[18]

Reported by the Associated Press, the *Enterprise* editor's views became almost as much of a scandal as the flogging itself. The *Chicago Tribune*'s response was particularly acid. "Citizens of our region . . . may have jumped to the conclusion that southern chivalry is, if not dead, then moribund," an editorial titled "Arkansas Chivalry" chided. "We are happy to reproduce evidence from the columns of the Earle Enterprise to show that this conclusion is unwarranted." Chivalrous "to his marrow," the Earle editor agreed that "even so delicate" a beating—a beating that was "scarcely more than a ceremonial assault and battery"—was "to be condemned. . . . Granted that the lash only bruised and that little or no blood was drawn, granted that Miss Blagden did not lose consciousness and that no one so much as suggested kicking her in the face, the gallant editor still asserts that the efforts to persuade were carried altogether too far." Continuing in the same ironic tone, the *Tribune* editor took up the assertion that helping with a black man's funeral was "no job for a white woman." "Obviously it is not," he concluded, "for a white woman who thinks otherwise must expect to be flogged for her opinion."[19]

The impact of all the publicity was stunning. "More than any other single event," according to historian Donald Grubbs, the Blagden flogging "made the nation demand action on behalf of sharecroppers; little more than six weeks elapsed between the bruising of Miss Blagden's bottom and the appointment by President Roosevelt of a special commission on farm tenancy, and the proximity in time was not coincidental."[20] Although Grubbs's claim was somewhat exaggerated, the episode did give union supporters like Norman Thomas a dramatic story to put before the nation's most powerful politicians. Plus, even though ideologically it was a bit of a mish-mash, the *March of Time* newsreel "King Cotton's Slaves" reached far more Americans than any STFU publicity effort possibly could. Blagden and Williams's dramatic reenactment of their kidnapping was the short film's climax, while shots of newspaper headlines supported the authoritative narrator's claim that "the violent end of the Blagden-Williams attempted investigation brings into sharp focus for the entire nation eastern Arkansas' planter-cropper troubles."[21]

Still, as Grubbs's condescending reference to "the bruising of Miss Blagden's bottom" suggests, Blagden hardly emerged from the experience as an STFU heroine. "We used to call [her] 'Willie Sue Flogden' after the incident. I shouldn't mention that," Evelyn Smith laughingly told an interviewer many years later. Conflicting views on the Popular Front explain some of this disdain, along with the fact that Blagden was an unaffiliated "fellow traveler" rather than a STFU stalwart. As someone who "just sort of showed up," in Smith's words, she did not deserve her sudden stardom in the eyes of the STFU leadership.[22] It was also infuriating that, as Mitchell later wrote, "no attention was paid to Eliza Nolden, a black woman . . . nor to the serious condition of white sharecropper Jim Reese, injured for life, or to the fact that Frank Weems, a black sharecropper, had presumably been beaten to death. After all," Mitchell added bitterly, "these three people were just sharecroppers."[23]

Of course, it was Mitchell, not Blagden, who had first publicized her beating. She used the publicity to make his very point "that floggings of union members had been going on for months" but "the attack upon her was the first to draw national attention." All of the previous victims "had been men or colored women," she told a *Washington Post* reporter. "'The fact that I was a white southern woman naturally attracted attention.'"[24]

Blagden's words were not as cavalier as the word "naturally" made them sound. In her article for the *New Republic*, published only two weeks after the flogging, she did her best to expose the ugly race, class, and gender relations that lay behind southern white men's paeans to chivalry. Even after the "well dressed" young man landed his first blow, "I could not believe it," she wrote. "What crimes have been committed for the 'Honor of Southern White Womanhood'! A Negro is lynched if any white woman can be found who will say 'He attacked me.' Is it womanhood they are protecting when they flogged me?" She went on to explain that "in the South we enjoy thinking our men folk chivalrous. Yet these were men I might meet at any of a number of my friends' homes."[25] In other words, it was well-dressed, good-looking, *respectable* men—men who represented the white southern establishment—who assaulted her. Clearly, the establishment itself must be violent and unjust.

Blagden's hastily written article sketched the gender dynamics of white supremacy. To flesh out the picture, she could have drawn comparisons with the ongoing Scottsboro case, which exposed the hypocrisy of southern gender conventions in a different way. Whereas Victoria Price and Ruby Bates had succeeded in wrapping themselves in the cloak of white men's professed chivalry to hide their own crimes, she herself, an innocent, had been denied the protection of her race, class, and gender because of her sympathy for sharecroppers. Both cases revealed that it was not, in fact, *womanhood* that southern white men were protecting; rather, it was a social order that guaranteed elite white male privilege and economic power.

Like Mitchell, Blagden understood that Eliza Nolden, Jim Reese, and Frank Weems had done more courageous work and suffered greater consequences for it than she had. Weems, it would turn out, had not died from his beating but had been thoroughly terrorized. After recovering consciousness, he had hidden in the woods for a week and then fled north in such fear that he did not even stop to see his wife and children. He resurfaced, coincidentally, one week after Jonathan Daniels visited the STFU headquarters in Memphis.[26]

Reese, a white sharecropper originally from Bolivar County, Mississippi, had also suffered greatly. As part of an abortive lawsuit the STFU initiated against Dulaney and the other planters, he and Blagden gave affidavits. Reese described how, while walking along a highway near Earle, he had been stopped by several white men who beat him with axe handles and took him to a store, where they searched him and imprisoned him for more than an hour. He experienced "great mental and physical anguish and humiliation" and "still suffers as a result of [the] injury." In fact, by September 1938, Reese had lost his sanity because of the beating. His lawsuit had to be dropped because he was "non compos mentis."[27]

Eliza Nolden's case was the most serious. A middle-aged black woman who was participating in the march led by Reese, she died as a result of the attack. The STFU's brief press release and funeral notice reveal painfully little about her. Union president J. R. Butler asserted that "there is no doubt in my mind that the death of Eliza Nolden was hastened by the brutal beating she received at the hands of this planter mob. As yet we do not have conclusive proof," he admitted, "but we do know that up to the time she was assaulted she was in good health and that since the beating she has been confined to her bed almost continuously." Her weakened state had required her to move from Earle to Memphis. She died in Memphis on May 16, 1938, at the John Gaston Hospital—a recently opened charity hospital whose morgue would also house the body of Martin Luther King Jr. thirty years later.[28]

Although the nation's most prominent white newspapers, including the *New York Times* and *Chicago Tribune*, had mentioned Nolden in relation to the lawsuits that she, Reese, and Blagden had filed, the black *Chicago Defender* may have been the only national newspaper to report her death.[29] Evidence from the 1930 federal census indicates she was a widow but would have been mourned by two sons, James, who was twenty-one, and William, who was eighteen. That census record also shows that Nolden was born in Mississippi to parents who were from Tennessee. She had married at the age of fifteen to a man from Arkansas. In 1930, she was a head of household and a tenant farmer growing cotton on a plantation near Earle.[30] Perhaps it was for the sake of her two sons that Nolden got involved in labor activism. Public records and even the union's own archives provide little information about her, but the fact that she was murdered because of her support for the STFU is worth remembering.

✦ ✦ ✦

NEEDLESS TO SAY, Jonathan Daniels never wrote a word in his journal or his book about Eliza Nolden, or Jim Reese, or Frank Weems. He almost certainly skipped the town of Earle, which would have been twenty miles out of his way as he drove from Memphis to Marked Tree on May 13, 1937. When he arrived, he was surprised to find the little town crowded with people. Usually, small towns in the South were busy only on Saturdays, when farm families drove in to do their shopping. "Why so many Negroes and white men in town on a Thursday morning[?]," he jotted, adding "found out later that in this low country work [is] impossible if [it] rains when water is high as it now is in this 'spring rise.'"[31] In fact, the first few months of 1937 had seen some severe flooding, as the people of the Delta Cooperative Farm would explain when he visited there the next day.

In Marked Tree, Daniels got at least some of his local knowledge from Jack Bryan, a fellow journalist who had "covered [the] Tenant farming story from the beginning for the [Memphis] Press-Scimitar." It was Bryan who refreshed Daniels's memory about the Blagden-Williams flogging and led him to describe her in his journal as a "left wing socialist"—a more accurate picture of her than the dismissive one that has appeared in decades of STFU scholarship.[32]

The visit with Bryan may have also helped Daniels understand some of the aspects of the Arkansas countryside that he was finding curious. For one thing, where were the big houses? "Wealth has been taken out of this land in both timber and cotton but it has been completely taken out and away," he explained in *A Southerner Discovers the South.* "There are few, if any, big houses and no evidence of planter grandeur beside the tenant poverty. The unscreened cabin is everywhere but I saw not one house before which the familiar white columns rose in even the pretense of classic responsibility"— the pretense of honor and paternalism, as he might equally have put it.[33]

The absence of traditional southern pretense—of the "façade of the South," as he would pointedly describe the white columns of Robert E. Lee's mansion at Arlington—left Daniels feeling a bit unnerved.[34] "I walked by

Ben Shahn, "Main Street, Marked Tree, Arkansas" (top) and "Inhabitants of Marked Tree, Arkansas," October 1935. Farm Security Administration / Office of War Information Photograph Collection, Library of Congress, Prints and Photographs Division, Washington, D.C. [LC-DIG-fsa-8a16286 and LC-DIG-fsa-8a16245].

Marked Tree's stores and Marked Tree's eyes," he wrote. "It was impressive how directly the town's merchants made their appeal to poverty with the heavy necessities of living—the three M's, meat, meal, and molasses." The only "luxuries" they carried were "the rawer, cheaper brands of liquor, the more florid rayons (not all women make their shifts out of flour sacks) and the most sweetly stinking soaps." "Of course," Daniels realized, "if there were rich men living on this land, they would buy in Memphis."[35]

Or they would do their shopping even farther away in places like Kansas City or St. Louis, where some of them actually lived. A substantial amount of Delta land was owned by corporations, particularly in the lumber and insurance industries. The really wealthy men were absentee landlords or, at most, recent arrivals—men who had made their money in banking or some other profession and then swept in looking for investments. That had certainly been the case with St. Louis financier Hiram Norcross, whose profit-minded decision to evict twenty-three tenant families from his Fairview plantation near Tyronza had resulted in the meeting at the Sunnyside schoolhouse where the STFU was founded. As Daniels was coming to understand, the area around Marked Tree had its own distinctive history. It was not *unlike* the rest of the plantation South but was a newer and rougher-edged version of it.

"At the end of the nineteenth century, the northeastern Arkansas delta included one of the last frontiers in the United States," writes historian Jeannie M. Whayne. "Majestic stands of virgin timber covered hundreds of thousands of acres, but the presence of swamps made this timber virtually inaccessible to the lumber industry." Railroads and massive clearing and drainage efforts changed that, and once the trees were gone, it "became readily apparent that this final frontier included some of the most fertile soil remaining uncultivated in the country. Thus began the exploitation of the region's last resource: the land itself." As people from other places poured in, they fought for competing visions of northeastern Arkansas's development. Small businessmen "in towns like Marked Tree insisted on plantation agriculture and its satellites—cotton, sharecropping, the crop lien, and the commissary." Meanwhile, "other men clamored for the opportunity to homestead a few hundred acres and carve out an independent existence for themselves"—the hunger for land and autonomy that the STFU's 1935 survey found still very much alive in the hearts of its rank-and-file members.[36]

Even by the late 1920s, however, the plantation had prevailed. Although the impact of the Great Depression and New Deal farm policies would give businessmen-planters like Norcross even more power over their workers, the fact was that a relative few had already consolidated their wealth, while many others had overreached or had bad luck and come up short.

The story of Alex East read almost like the parable of the "big planter across the road" that William Amberson later published in the *Nation*. East, an uncle of the STFU's Clay East, had been a respected small farmer who gradually acquired more and more land. In the late 1920s, he made a deal with Hiram Norcross to buy nearly 2,000 additional acres, and the Bank of Tyronza handled the loan. When the bank collapsed in 1930, East was unable to make his payments. Norcross not only reclaimed the land but also got 560 acres that East had put up for collateral on the purchase. Other debts took an additional 170 acres, leaving East with only 120 acres to farm. He decided to become the manager on Norcross's new Fairview plantation instead. "Hence, some of the acres Alex East was managing were those he had once owned."[37]

Both East's long history in Poinsett County and Norcross's short one were important factors in the events that led up to the STFU's founding. As Norcross's manager, East responded to the crop reduction policy under the Agricultural Adjustment Act of 1933 not by evicting tenant farmers but by reducing the amount of land he allotted to each tenant family to farm. Their reduced acreage should have meant a reduced "furnish." As Clay East explained, "a man was allowed $1 per month for each acre he was working and could buy that much groceries at the Tyronza Supply Store," which belonged, in part, to Norcross. Even though he must have known that Norcross's tenants would not be able to make enough money from their smaller plots to pay off their grocery bills at the end of the season, Alex East chose not to make these families go hungry. Norcross was not so generous. When he examined his books and realized his tenants were buying more in groceries than they could pay off in cotton, he chose to reduce his excess labor costs by evicting twenty-three families, both black and white.[38] In making this decision, he was by no means alone among planters, nor was the situation in Poinsett County fundamentally different from the collapse of farm tenancy in other parts of the South. But there was a difference of degree, both the degree of Arkansas planters' coldness and the heat of the labor wars that ensued.

The STFU's battle was not yet over when Daniels visited Marked Tree in May 1937, but it did rather feel that way. The union's first and most famous lawyer, C. T. Carpenter, certainly seemed to speak of the STFU in the past tense. Carpenter had become famous in news coverage of the Arkansas violence, most notably in a six-part series by F. Raymond Daniell of the *New York*

Times. Daniell described a planter raid that left Carpenter's home riddled with bullets as "the climax to a series of similar attacks upon the homes of Negro members of the union."[39] He also reported on how, in a bid to see section 7 of the Agricultural Adjustment Administration's cotton contract interpreted in tenants' favor, Carpenter sought an injunction against Norcross's mass evictions at Fairview.

Carpenter lost the case, as he expected, in the Chancery Court of Poinsett County, but he appealed to the Arkansas Supreme Court. Despite the support and simultaneous efforts of Mary Connor Meyers, Jerome Frank, and others, the STFU's legal challenge was a failure. The Arkansas Supreme Court denied the injunction and "held that since share-croppers were not parties to the contract, they had no cause of action."[40]

The suppression of the Meyers report and the firing of Frank and other Agricultural Adjustment Administration liberals made it obvious that any additional legal fight against sharecropper evictions would be a losing battle. In February 1935 (on Abraham Lincoln's birthday, no less), Secretary of Agriculture Henry Wallace drove home the point in a telegram to the Memphis Chamber of Commerce: "SECTION SEVEN OF COTTON CONTRACT DOES NOT BIND LANDOWNERS TO KEEP THE SAME TENANTS. . . . THAT IS THE OFFICIAL AND FINAL INTERPRETATION OF THE SOLICITOR OF THE DEPARTMENT OF AGRICULTURE AND NO OTHER INTERPRETATION WILL BE GIVEN."[41]

For Carpenter, the failed suit against Norcross was still a point of pride. Jonathan Daniels was struck by the impression that Carpenter was, at heart, a greater man than his surroundings could accommodate. He had wavy gray hair, "rimless, fairly thick spectacles," and looked "like the kindly, good, if not brilliant family physician."[42] Born in Virginia and a graduate of the University of Kentucky, he had moved to Arkansas in 1903 and served as president of Woodland College, a Baptist school in Jonesboro, before taking up the law in 1912. Until he agreed to represent the STFU, he was "one of the most respected citizens of Marked Tree."[43]

"Oh, it almost ruined me," Carpenter confided to Daniels. "He threw up his hands but," Jonathan thought, "without any sign of real regret." No one could talk to him "without feeling that his appearance for the tenants . . . gave him a chance for bigness and accomplishment which he otherwise could not have had."

As to whether or not Carpenter minded local disapproval, he "snorted at the suggestion that members of the planter-lawyer-merchant-doctor class" who had taken their legal business elsewhere "might also have undertaken to ostracize his family socially. Without saying so he suggested that so far as most of the local folk were concerned the idea of social ostracism of his family by them was a vast foolishness."[44] *He* was the Virginian. While "the Ritters who own most of the land in Marked Tree [were the] children of [a] German [immigrant] who came from Iowa as a day laborer," *his* father had studied under Robert E. Lee at Washington College after the Civil War.

Daniels smiled, thinking the lawyer "a little vain, a trifle pompous," but "a nice old fellow" and "undoubtedly decent and courageous." Later, as he re-viewed his notes about their conversation, he penciled in another comment: "The South and America need more like him."[45] The best thing, in Daniels's view, was how Carpenter combined a southern aristocratic tradition with a defense of democracy and the common man. He was a Roosevelt Democrat but unafraid to take the side of socialists and stand up for a racially mixed union of sharecroppers and tenants. Titling his chapter about Marked Tree "Arkansas Gentleman," Daniels concluded that C. T. Carpenter embodied "as few men do in the modern South—or the modern world—the patrician ideal."[46]

In the context of the Arkansas Delta, with its disturbing eyes and lack of "even the pretense of classic responsibility"—or, if one thought of Wil-lie Sue Blagden, even the pretense of chivalry—Carpenter's very existence was reassuring. Daniels had found him at the end of "a dismal dark hall" in an ugly, squat office building. Yet, to his great pleasure, he had discovered a shelf of books by Howard Odum, Rupert Vance, and other Chapel Hill Regionalists in the lawyer's bookcase. "Carpenter thinks U.N.C. [the] most liberal college in [the] South," he recorded approvingly. He "[is] proud of a shelf of contemporary books on tenantry etc."[47]

At some point, Daniels would have to ask himself whether Regionalist books, with their sociological analyses and calls for scientific planning, could be any more successful at improving the lives or guaranteeing the civil rights of poor black and white southerners than Carpenter's law books had been in the face of planter dominance in the courts and the Department of Agri-culture. For the moment, however, it was simply nice to find a "man of the virtues" in one of the rawest places in the deeply troubled South.[48] He would be able to drive on to Little Rock and eventually to Hot Springs, where he was to attend a Southern Newspaper Publishers Association conference, feel-ing much more relaxed than he had felt under the weight and heat of Delta white men's gaze.

— CHAPTER SEVEN —

The Most Interesting Man I Met

✦

FROM HOT SPRINGS, ARKANSAS,

TO TUSKEGEE, ALABAMA

I N THE RESORT TOWN of Hot Springs, Arkansas, Jonathan Daniels's optimism for the South's future got a boost from an interview with Governor Carl Edward Bailey. A "thick man, not handsome," with blond hair and "weather-toughened skin," Bailey was forty-three years old and relatively new to politics.[1] He had been governor for only a few months, but his support for the New Deal and enthusiasm for government planning encouraged Daniels to think of him as representative of the new generation of leaders that he, along with President Roosevelt, hoped was arising in the South.

This governor had a different attitude toward the South's problems than the older generation of southern politicians. He acknowledged that "a few years—even a few months—ago it would have been politically suicidal for a State official to talk out loud about the tenant problem. . . . State officials were supposed to be devoted to proving that everything was beautiful and everybody was happy."[2]

Now, however, the South's many problems were in the news and on the agendas of both state and national governments. He and other governors could finally speak plainly about their states' desperate need for economic development. He also wanted to "protect the forests—develop the parks—aid in the development of the State's water power and protection against floods." It is no wonder he reminded Daniels of David Lilienthal, the young TVA commissioner who had impressed him so much when they met in Norris, Tennessee. "Like Lilienthal," Daniels wrote, Bailey "does not believe in doing for the people but in making it possible for the people to do for themselves."[3] He was, in short, Daniels's very definition of a small-d democrat and wise leader, conscious of the need to think about the long-term and protect the South's human and natural resources.

Unfortunately, actually achieving the goals of planned development was difficult, and not all of the South's governors were like Carl Bailey. In Jackson, Mississippi, a week later, Daniels found Governor Hugh L. White a lot less impressive. "A stout man with a big stomach, straight graying hair, and brown hairy arms, [who] chewed and gesticulated with a cigar [in an] emphatic manner," White seemed to be "an honest man but not a very smart one or a very sensitive one." His much ballyhooed Balance Agriculture with Industry plan appeared to be nothing more than a "naked subsidy" that could only bring sweatshops.[4] According to the governor, the plan was simple: with approval from the new State Industrial Commission and two-thirds of local voters, any Mississippi community could issue bonds to offer tax exemptions and low- or no-rent buildings to any manufacturer who promised to move in and create jobs. "Do you really think you're going to get industries worth having by subsidizing them?" Daniels asked provocatively. To him, White's plan seemed "almost designed to secure for Mississippi the worst types of industry" and the lowest possible wages while providing "a veritable picnic for promoters."[5]

Daniels's opposition to Governor White's plan softened only a little when L. J. Folse, the director of the Mississippi State Planning Commission, assured him that he actually did care about natural resources and regretted seeing people sell their labor so cheaply. It was discouraging but hard to argue with Folse's claim that Mississipians' poverty gave them few alternatives to the sweatshop. The people "did not always possess the free choice that David Lilienthal demanded for them," Daniels thought with chagrin.[6]

If contemplating Mississippi's Balance Agriculture with Industry plan was not enough to check Daniels's optimism for the future, there was also the specter of the state's haunting past. Much of his meandering, ten-day journey from Hot Springs to New Orleans was devoted to visiting graveyards, some literal, some figurative. First, in Greenville, Mississippi, there was William Alexander Percy's house and the bronze statue of a knight that Percy had erected over the grave of his father, whom Daniels understood to have been "a great defender of the aristocratic ideal," now dead and gone.[7] Then, in Vicksburg, he arrived at his hotel on a day when "patriotic ladies" wearing bright sashes were welcoming visitors to a meeting of the Descendants of the Participants of the Campaign, Siege, and Defense of Vicksburg. The Civil War was more alive in Vicksburg than elsewhere in the South, he noted, but the town itself was "commercially dying." On one side was the Mississippi River "on which the great boats no longer move," and on every other side there were cemeteries "crowded with the dead."[8]

The highlight of Daniels's stay in Vicksburg was drinking beer in a brothel that was said to be 100 years old. "It's old. I don't know how old," the disappointingly dull madam assured him. "I was a girl here twenty—twenty-five years ago. And one night I was with a man who said he was in the house during the siege. He told me he paid for his entertainment with a silver spur he'd found where some Yankee dropped it. . . . They'd have loved him better for bread, he said. Everybody was hungry then, soldiers and girls."[9] As Daniels could see, many Mississippians were hungry still.

From Vicksburg, Daniels drove on to Jackson and then to Natchez. There he drove around the countryside with Mrs. Balfour Miller, who had organized the first Natchez Pilgrimage under the auspices of the Natchez Garden Club in 1932. She showed him some of the antebellum mansions that had made the annual event a success, even as a "schism" ran "like a crack in old masonry" through the community. A policeman walking his beat explained it: the garden club "took in folks that didn't even have a flower pot . . . and some of the folks that own the biggest places" would be starving if they did not get "the fees the tourists pay" to see their homes. The desperation that underlay some people's commitment to the "preservation, beautification, and restoration of historic Natchez" was bound to create controversy over how much pilgrimage revenue went to the garden club and how much to the homeowners. Daniels would remember the frustration of a young woman in high heels who stood on the steps of a once-grand mansion and cried, "Damn antique! Damn ante-bellum! I want some modern conveniences. I want to live!" He came to think of Natchez as a place where "the living occupy the past."[10]

After the "Lost Present" of Natchez, Daniels drove on to look for a "Ghost in Louisiana," namely, that of Huey Long, the Louisiana governor and senator whose populist appeal and demagogic tendencies had been a thorn in the side of the Roosevelt administration until his habit of slandering his local political opponents caught up with him in the form of an assassin's bullet in 1935. In Louisiana, Daniels debated with various people over whether or not Long's Share Our Wealth movement, which had boasted 7.5 million members in 1935, had truly died with him. His plan had been to cap personal fortunes and redistribute the wealth of the nation's multimillionaires to give every American household a minimum income that would make "Every Man a King." Long had claimed to be promoting change in order to prevent violent revolution, but after visiting Baton Rouge and seeing his grave in the garden of the state capitol, Daniels came away with the feeling that his spirit still moved "as John Brown's spirit moved." Like that of the abolitionist whose radicalism outlived him, Long's legacy might still have consequences. His stirring of populist passions had not yet created an American Hitler, but his ghost did seem to pose a threat at "the big house door." Though hardly a desirable alternative, he and other populist demagogues did at least indicate "a Southern unwillingness to leave government entirely to the political gentlemen of the gentlemen of business"—those "persisting and ineradicable Bourbons and Brigadiers who are devoted to a class before a region."[11] The challenge was to promote democracy without promoting demagogues—to persuade southern voters to replace the Bourbons and Brigadiers with Carl Baileys rather than Huey Longs.

By the time he reached New Orleans, Daniels felt he needed the mint julep that a black waiter at the Boston Club prepared for him as he chatted about the South's problems with yet another group of educated white men. He was tired. He had been on the road for twenty-three days and had seen more than he could possibly have imagined when he set out from Raleigh. It was hard to make sense of the South he was discovering. Although he did diligently visit Southern Policy Committee colleague H. C. Nixon, who taught at Tulane University, Daniels spent most of his two days in New Orleans seeing the sights and making small talk. He was drawn to the city's legendary culture of drunken lassitude. A sign on an ice house pleased him for what he read into it, not only about Gulf Coast heat but also about the South's many and seemingly intractable problems: "Ice is best / Forget the rest." He read it and "laughed and went looking for [ice], broken and packed in a glass," he wrote, ending his chapter on New Orleans.[12]

Nevertheless, there were still important people and places to visit. One of these was Tuskegee Institute, the famous school devoted to training black southerners in scientific farming and other vocations that Booker T. Washington had founded in Tuskegee, Alabama, in 1881. Daniels drove quickly from New Orleans, through Gulfport and Biloxi, Mississippi, and Mobile, Alabama, to reach Montgomery, the state capital, on May 31. The next morning, he interviewed Governor Bibb Graves and then drove the forty miles east to Tuskegee. It was the one place he went with the deliberate intention of interviewing educated African Americans. It is ironic, given his proud but false claim to have spoken "everywhere to Negroes," that he would feel compelled to omit the story of his visit to Tuskegee from his book.[13] Only briefly, in his chapter on Birmingham, would he mention that he had gone there. The notes in his journal, plus the fact that he reported on a Tuskegee conversation as if it had taken place elsewhere, help to explain why.

Weary as he was from nearly a month of nonstop discovery, with his hopes for the South rising and falling depending on whom he had just been talking to, Jonathan Daniels suddenly did discover that straight talk from a knowledgeable black man could be something new—and unsettling. What he learned at Tuskegee would provoke him to ask questions and engage in a literary subterfuge that—along with the suggestion that he began his travels near Robert E. Lee's house at Arlington—was the biggest lie in his whole book. Whether he would lie to himself along with his readers or allow the truths he learned in the Alabama Black Belt to persuade him of the need for more aggressive federal action on behalf of black citizens remained to be seen. Like what he had learned about planter violence in the Delta, Daniels's explorations in Alabama uncovered the extent to which control over a cheap and dependent labor force was the central feature of the white southern power structure. If this was the nature of the South's white elite, then what besides outside influences, perhaps even federal *pressure*, could bring social change?

✦ ✦ ✦

BORN A SLAVE IN 1856, Booker T. Washington had been dead for more than twenty years by the time Daniels visited Tuskegee Institute in 1937. But his legacy lived on, not only in the school and its pragmatic educational philosophy but also in the son who showed Daniels around the red-brick campus. Ernest Davidson Washington seemed "to be in charge of public relations and is a very pleasant man of 45," Daniels noted in his journal. He introduced him to the school's most famous faculty member, elderly George Washington Carver, whose "piping high voice" and feeble frame seemed at odds with his reputation as a brilliant scientist.[14]

"But the most interesting man I met," Daniels wrote, was not Dr. Carver but a man named Turner—a man whose first name he seems never to have learned, probably because a refined black southerner like Washington would undoubtedly have introduced him as "Mr. Turner," whether a white visitor like Daniels liked it or not. Indeed, one of the reasons Turner was so interesting to Daniels was the shifting racial etiquette of their encounter. At first, Turner "would not talk about the share crop tenant situation—pretending ignorance behind loud cackling Negro laughter." But, "reassured by Washington," he soon decided to drop the mask and went on to tell Daniels more troubling truths about racial violence than he and most other white southerners were accustomed to hear.[15]

Turner was definitely an expert on the tenant problem. An employee of the Negro Cooperative Extension System funded by the U.S. Department of Agriculture, his job was to teach practical skills and scientific techniques to black farmers all over the state.[16] He was also well educated. Daniels found it hard to reconcile his racist first impression of the man with even the small amount he learned about his background. He described Turner insultingly in his journal as "black as night, thick lipped, burr headed, drawl talking but a graduate of the University of Michigan. Such a man—a nigger of cotton field niggers in appearance—could easily go down into the jungle and emerge with [the] ability to understand and discuss in civilized terms."[17]

It was a profoundly racist description, even though Daniels presumably meant the word "jungle" to refer to the plantations of the Alabama Black Belt rather than some imagined darkest Africa. Arkansas's Dyess Colony was "a toytown cut out of the jungle," plus he had been known to describe the reactionary white South as an "intellectual jungle" and had even admitted to his friend W. T. Couch that his opposition to blacks and whites eating together made him "seem a jungle creature myself."[18]

Daniels's comparative sensitivity—the fact that, at his best, he knew racism was uncivilized—makes his description of Turner surprising. He was rarely a slinger of epithets. Like many white southern children of the middle and upper classes, he had been taught not to engage in vulgar name-calling on pain of punishment. He understood, as he wrote to NAACP Executive Secretary Walter White in a 1941 letter, "how the word 'nigger' can be as offensive as any word on earth."

Daniels's letter to White helps explain his notes about Turner. He had learned of an NAACP campaign against the word "nigger" and was "puzzled about it" and wanted "to ask [White] in confidence for your opinion . . . as a writer as well as a crusader." Though offensive, "isn't it often an irreplaceable word," he asked, "as used, for instance, in 'nigger town' indicating not merely a slum but the worst kind of ghetto? Haven't Negro poets found it a word carrying a special impact in the harshness of its meaning? Finally, isn't it an indispensable word not for social use, of course, but in all colorful discussion of American life?" Daniels wanted his words to be colorful and hard-hitting. He "believed, and hoped others would agree," writes biographer Charles W. Eagles, "that when he used the word 'nigger' or 'pickaninny,' he used them with sympathy and not malice and to describe more accurately the condition of many black people."[19]

It may have been a specious argument, but it was what Daniels told himself. And it is true that his description of Turner in his journal was a commentary on conditions and facades. Turner was "a nigger of cotton field niggers *in appearance*." He was "drawl talking *but* a graduate of the University of Michigan." When he dropped the drawl along with the mask of defensive humor, Daniels remarked on it. Perhaps he used the offensive language in his notes precisely because he wanted to make sure he remembered how much of a divergence there was between the mask and the man behind it.

Still, he must have been exaggerating because it is hard to imagine the man he met "cackling" in a minstrel-like performance, no matter what the circumstances, for he was a dignified fellow. In 1937, the only Turner at Tuskegee who worked for the Extension Service was Victor Caesar Turner Sr., an impressive fifty-two-year-old whose biography epitomized the struggles and triumphs of the Jim Crow–era black middle class. Born in 1885 near the town of Crawfordville in Taliaferro County, Georgia, Turner was the son of two former slaves, Jake and Mariah Turner, who, though illiterate, managed to buy land. He grew up farming and started his education at local schools in the Crawfordville area. He went on to Atlanta Baptist Seminary (now Morehouse College), where he spent ten years, starting in the elementary and secondary grades that the college provided to compensate for the dismal state of black public education in the South. He earned his Bachelor of Arts degree in 1911, when he was twenty-six years old.[20]

After graduation, Turner taught for three years at Americus Institute, a high school for black youths operated by the Southwestern Georgia Baptist Association. Then he enrolled at the University of Wisconsin (not Michigan, as Daniels mistook), where he graduated with a Bachelor of Science degree from the School of Agriculture in 1917. Now thirty-two, he volunteered for World War I and was sent to a new Army training camp for black officers at Fort Des Moines, Iowa. After the war, he returned to the South, where he taught briefly in Jackson, Mississippi, and Orangeburg, South Carolina, before landing a job at Tuskegee Institute.[21]

Working for Tuskegee from 1922 to 1928, Turner supervised a dairy herd and taught classes on soils and fertilizers, animal husbandry, and other topics. Then he got a job with the Extension Service as state supervisor of Negro 4-H Clubs for boys, the youth program that complemented Extension agents' work with adult farmers. For seventeen years, Turner "traveled over most of the state, especially where Negro County and Home Demonstration Agents were stationed." But his home base was Tuskegee, where he lived with his wife, Katie, and their three sons.[22] The oldest, Victor Jr., remembered his father in this period as the kind of strict and respectability-minded parent who was characteristic of the segregated South's black middle class—the

Victor C. Turner Sr. in later years. He was fifty-two
when Jonathan Daniels stopped by Tuskegee Institute
on June 1, 1937. Courtesy of Alabama State University
Archives, Montgomery, Alabama.

kind who would whip a boy for taking three pecans from a neighbor's tree.
But Victor Turner Sr. was also loving and protective. In retrospect, Victor Jr.
was sure that both his parents "shielded us from a lot of contact with whites
in Tuskegee, downtown."[23]

Victor Turner's principles as a father paralleled his philosophy as an educator. He was known for encouraging people "to learn to love the hard
work that goes with Agriculture." His personal motto was "to make the best
better."[24] He continued his own self-improvement by taking a leave from the
Extension Service and earning a master's degree at Cornell University in
1931. He wrote a thesis titled "An Agricultural Program for Alabama," and
his Master of Science degree was reported and his photograph published
in the Crisis, the monthly magazine of the NAACP.[25] In short, Turner was
even better educated than Daniels realized, while the stories he told of social
conditions in Alabama were set against a wider experience of the world than
Daniels probably could have guessed.

Turner's stories relating to the "share crop tenant situation" were the main
reason Daniels found him so interesting. "He said that both the meanest

white folks and the meanest 'Neegroes' live in Lown[d]es county," Daniels wrote in his journal, misspelling the name of the county and adding the extra 'e' to the word "Negroes" as a reminder of how Turner pronounced it. White southerners' tendency to pronounce "Negro" as "nigra" struck many blacks as a deliberate approximation of word "nigger." To elongate the vowel as Turner did was to reject whites' preferred way of speaking. Daniels picked up on the difference, as well as on Turner's good grammar and swift, sober (no longer "drawl talking") style of speech once he dropped his defensive mask and decided to talk man-to-man.[26]

Having identified Lowndes County as the worst in the state for share-croppers and tenants, Turner went on to give examples. "One planter there, Mr. Joe Dixon (Dickson)," Daniels jotted, unsure of the spelling, "had killed 14 men, Negroes and white men," but had never been convicted of murder. He had also stolen the payments his tenants were supposed to receive under the Agricultural Adjustment Act. "When government checks came to tenants he made them sign them and give them to him," Daniels recorded. This planter kept his tenants "in debt and terror," and he was not unusual. "Turner says he has twice himself been forced to look down gun barrels of white men." The implications of such terrorism went well beyond even the personal safety of individuals. "In such counties where conditions are worse, union organizers and communists are at work," Turner lamented, expressing a concern that reflected his own antiradical, Tuskegee-style, hard work and uplift approach to black advancement. Daniels did his best to recall the exact words Turner used in summary, quoting: "'I don't see why white folks haven't got sense enough to spend the money so we can have enough farm agents to teach the Negroes how to make more so they could have more and the planter more, instead [of] keeping them hungry and making them ready for the union and the communists.'" Friendly to unions but suspicious of Communists, Daniels seems to have been listening intently. Turner's analysis of and anxieties about rural blacks' attraction to the Communist Party may have been what he meant when he noted that Turner had the "ability to understand and discuss in civilized terms."[27]

It was an upsetting conversation, and Daniels would find himself thinking about it and telling other people about it for days. He particularly wanted to learn more about the murderous planter. That same evening, when he was back in Montgomery at a dinner party, he met a white man maned Murray who was from Lowndes County and who "verified Dixon's reputation as a bad man." Murray even added a story of his own about "one Negro who came back to Lown[d]es after being away and told Negroes if they were not treated right to move." The man was "given [a] ride in Dixon's car and never seen again." The dinner party hostess was shocked and insisted that Dixon was a "most inoffensive looking man" whose wife she had met when they went together "to Richmond to a [Parent-Teacher Association] meeting." Yet "none seem to question his violent reputation," Daniels wrote in his journal.[28] Nor should they.

✦ ✦ ✦

IT IS IMPOSSIBLE TO BE completely certain about the identity of the violent planter whom Turner called Joe Dixon or Dickson. But there was one Dickson family that had the worst reputation for meanness. Other contemporary observers and historians familiar with Lowndes County describe Robert S. "Bob" Dickson as the most fearsome planter there in the period when Daniels traveled, while his older brother John, known as J.W., the local sheriff, was notorious in earlier decades. The eldest brother in the family was named Joe.[29] Turner (or Daniels) may have gotten Bob Dickson's first name wrong, or he may have been referring to somebody else. It is worth remembering that Turner's point was not to single out any one man or family anyway; he was merely providing an example of a type of violence and repression that was widespread. The Dickson brothers were extreme but not unique in their treatment of farm workers. Recorded in not one but two U.S. Department of Justice investigations for peonage, their story is both chilling and brutally ordinary. Although Daniels learned only a few pieces of that story during his travels, a fuller accounting of the facts (facts that Daniels himself longed to know) shows why it was so important that he listened to what Turner, Murray, and others who knew Lowndes County had to say.

The Dickson brothers traced their lineage back to David Dickson of South Carolina, who served as an officer in the Revolutionary War.[30] Their father, John Calhoun Dickson, was born in Georgia in about 1827 and moved to Alabama as a young man. By 1860, he and his wife, Sarah, had settled in Lowndes County to farm. They had five children by then, including two daughters and an infant son. Their two oldest sons, Joseph T. and John W., had been born in 1853 and 1854. Although relatively young and not yet landowners, John and Sarah Dickson were sufficiently well established by 1860 to provide room and board for a minister and his wife and their one-year-old child. They held more than $5,000 in personal property, including one adult female slave and three slave children.[31]

Like any other antebellum farm family on the rise, the Dicksons would have their work cut out for them if they aspired to join the planter class. The population and wealth of Lowndes County had grown quickly between 1840 and 1860 as settlers learned how to grow cotton in the area's sticky black soil. Slave labor was the key to success, and by 1860 there were 19,340 slaves in the county along with 8,362 white residents. Sixty percent of Lowndes County whites who were engaged in agriculture owned some slaves, and perhaps 20 percent of these slaveholders owned thirty slaves or more. A few of the wealthiest white families had built sumptuous, white-columned mansions as early as the 1820s, turning the little town of Lowndesboro, twenty-five miles southwest of Montgomery, into "the jewel of Alabama's planter villages."[32] With only one adult slave and eight young children to feed (three enslaved and five of their own, not counting the minister's family), John and Sarah Dickson had a long way to climb.

Then came the war. During the Civil War, John Dickson enlisted in the Montgomery County militia unit of the Confederate Home Guard.[33] Afterward, he, Sarah, and their children tried to pick up their lives amidst the chaos of Reconstruction. The war had mostly passed over Lowndes County in the sense that there were no major battles nearby. But it was economically devastating and, in the words of historian Charles W. Eagles, "a nightmare, nonetheless, as the whites' vaunted Black Belt culture was severely damaged, if not completely destroyed."[34]

How the Civil War and Reconstruction affected the Dickson family is suggested in the 1870 census, which found John and Sarah Dickson with real estate valued at $2,700 but only $800 in personal property. The land they had purchased was near Letohatchee (sometimes spelled Letohatchie), a small community that lay a dozen miles southeast of Lowndesboro and a half-dozen miles southeast of Hayneville, the county seat. Letohatchee would be home territory for the Dickson family, particularly the two oldest brothers, Joe and J.W., for decades.[35]

Like other Lowndes County landowners, the Dicksons may have struggled even to hold onto their farm because of the effects of the war and declining cotton prices. The 1870 cotton crop was less than half as large as the one Lowndes County farmers had grown in 1860, and production continued to lag for more than a decade. Meanwhile, John and Sarah Dickson's family grew, with two more sons, Edwin and Lewis, born in 1865 and 1868, and their youngest child, Robert Stiles Dickson, born in 1873.[36]

The five Dickson brothers who survived to adulthood (Joseph T., John W. or J.W., John G., Edwin, and Robert, known as Bob) undoubtedly worked hard to turn their parents' post–Civil War holdings into the comparative wealth and status that defined the family by the early twentieth century. Joe took over the family farm after his father died in the 1870s. J.W. became sheriff in addition to farming, and Bob dropped out of school and went to work "clerking and being handy in a general store." He saved "every cent possible" and eventually bought the store, as well as land for farming, timber, and a cattle business.[37] He achieved a deeply held ambition and also signaled his family's economic rise in 1901 when he bought an antebellum, Greek-revival mansion in Lowndesboro. Built in 1830 and remodeled in 1856, the house Bob Dickson named "Dicksonia" was painted white and had a two-story portico held up by a dozen fluted Doric columns. Stately and impressive, it was the very picture of "planter grandeur" and "the pretense of classic responsibility" that Jonathan Daniels had been looking for when he noticed the absence of big houses in the area around Marked Tree, Arkansas.[38]

Bob Dickson was still in his twenties when he bought Dicksonia and the 400 acres surrounding it. He would eventually own more than 10,000 acres, becoming "one of the great figures of Alabama's Black Belt farm economy." His operation was "as close an approach to the plantations of old as is to be found in all Alabama," wrote one admirer, who went on to claim that Dicksonia's "dozens of Negro families . . . had medical care, personal attention, intelligent direction and all the things which tied the old plantation master to those dependent upon him."[39]

Dickson seems to have heartily embraced the role of plantation master and landed gentleman. A Baptist, a Mason, and a Shriner, he was also a passionate fox hunter and breeder of hunting dogs and was even better known for his hospitality and love of his plantation home. When Dicksonia burned in an accidental fire in 1939, he had the house rebuilt according to the original plans except that, instead of wood, he chose cast-concrete over a steel frame.[40] Dickson wanted his house to be fireproof, but his choice of building materials also says something about his worldview. He aspired to permanence as well as antebellum prestige.

According to a U.S. district attorney writing at the turn of the twentieth century, the Dickson brothers' worldview was indeed antebellum, at least where the management of their black laborers was concerned. Unfortunately, they were not alone. In 1903, a young white attorney's attempt to free a black client from a fraudulent prosecution up in Shelby County near Birmingham set off a minor earthquake in the Alabama justice system. When the lawyer turned to U.S. district attorney Warren S. Reese Jr. of Montgomery for help, Reese was suddenly made to realize that, even though he had lived in Alabama for his "entire life of thirty-seven years," he had

The Turner-Dickson House, also known as Dicksonia, in 1934. It burned
in 1939, was rebuilt, burned again in 1964, and stands in ruins today.
Photograph by W. N. Manning, Library of Congress, Prints and Photographs
Division, Washington, D.C. [HABS ALA,43-LOWB.V,1].

"never comprehended until now the extent of the present method of slavery
through this peonage system."[41] He and a federal judge named Thomas
Goode Jones—also an Alabama native as well as a Confederate hero and
former two-term governor—became concerned that peonage was not only
common in Alabama but truly endemic. In March, Jones persuaded the U.S.
attorney general to send federal agents to investigate. By June, their inquiry
had reached Lowndes County.

In a June 1903 letter summarizing the investigation, Reese explained how
the peonage system worked. The practice of keeping workers in involuntary
servitude had "not been confined to one or two periodical or independent instances," he wrote, but had "developed into a miserable business and custom
to catch up ignorant and helpless negro men and women upon the flimsiest
and the most baseless charges and carry them before a justice of the peace
who is usually a paid hireling of these wealthy dealers. The form of a trial is
sometimes gone through, but usually that even is dispensed with. The victim is found guilty and a fine is assessed . . . and then it is that one of these
slave dealers steps up, pretends to be the friend of the negro, and [offers to]

pay him out if he will sign a contract to work for him on his farm." On the farm "or mine or mill or quarry of the employer," the black worker was typically "locked up at nights in a cell, worked under guards during the day . . . whipped in a most cruel manner, [and] insufficiently fed and poorly clad." In some cases, workers had been beaten to death. "When the time of a good working negro is nearing an end, he is rearrested upon some trumped up charge and again carried before some bribed justice and resentenced to an additional time." Thus, blacks were held, often for many years, "in abject slavery without any knowledge of what goes on in the outside world."[42]

Lowndes County was "really the center where it is charged these practices are more freely indulged than anywhere else," Reese's letter continued. It was a county "honeycombed with slavery" where the local sheriff, "a large land owner," was one of the worst offenders. "One of the most severe cases" was "that of Dillard Freeman, who after being convicted before the Justice upon some flimsy charge, was fined, and the Sheriff of the county paid his fine."[43] Reese reported the sheriff's name as J. W. Dixon, the same alternate spelling of "Dickson" that Jonathan Daniels later scribbled in his journal.

Once he had signed Dillard Freeman to a labor contract, J. W. Dickson "compelled [him] to work by force," according to Reese, and refused to let him leave his farm. When Freeman slipped off one Sunday to visit his family, Dickson tracked him down. He "drove up with one of his men and beat the boy in the presence of his mother unmercifully with a pistol until he was bloody." Then he and his men tied Freeman "around the neck, just as you tie an animal, his hands were handcuffed behind him, and the other end of the rope was placed in the hands of one of the men who was on a mule, and the boy was compelled to run afoot for six or seven miles behind this mule, while Mr. Dixon himself followed [on] horseback whipping him whenever he would lag behind." When they reached the farm, four men held Freeman down while Dickson whipped him until his back was "one mass of [sores] from his thighs to his neck."

Reese's letter did not explain how Freeman had gotten free or how his case had come to light. But he did make it clear that, when Freeman came to Montgomery to testify, one of the five Dickson brothers, Bob, "followed the boy to the grand jury room . . . and it was impossible to get anything out of him because of his fear of death." He finally gave his testimony only "upon the assurance that he will not be made to go back to Lowndes county."

"These Dixons are men of the highest political and financial influence not only in Lowndes county but in the state of Alabama," Reese observed in his long letter to the U.S. attorney general. "They are said to be dangerous men. They are said to have killed several men." If the government wanted to put an end to peonage in Lowndes County, "some provision will have to be made for the protection of . . . witnesses, as well as their preservation after they have given up the truth at Montgomery."[44]

Even though Dillard Freeman risked his life by testifying, J. W. Dickson was not indicted in the case. Reese did succeed in prosecuting a few other Alabama planters for peonage in 1903, but Judge Jones handed down lenient sentences and fines, apparently on the theory that once an evil had been exposed he should, as historian Pete Daniel dryly observes, allow "men's consciences to be their guides."[45] Peonage remained a common practice throughout the South, particularly in plantation regions, turpentine camps, and the coal-mining area around Birmingham. Very few bosses were ever tried, much less convicted, for practicing slavery in the decades between 1903 and 1936 when, with the help of the Southern Tenant Farmers Union and Evelyn Smith and Maxine East's courageous "picnic," the Justice Department managed to get a conviction in the case of Arkansas sheriff Paul Peacher. Meanwhile, after the brief tremor of 1903, Lowndes County remained "inviolate" to demands for social change. In early 1904, a federal official found that one of the special agents Reese had employed to investigate peonage was "spending a considerable portion of his time" sitting at home while "charging the Government with his meals and lodging." Behind the fraud was his fear that, if he continued his lonely inquiry in Lowndes and other Black Belt counties, some white planter would kill him.[46]

Although one might think that forcing a tied-up young black man to run behind a mule for several miles would attract some attention from the neighbors, white residents of Lowndes County did not necessarily think of the Dickson brothers as violent or mean. Bob Dickson's family was especially well regarded in the white community. In a memoir, one Lowndesboro resident remembered Dickson primarily as the father of some of her childhood friends. He had a "big, beautiful two story home" and "offered a place near his fish pond" where a shelter for the Girl Scouts' various activities could be built.[47] The family's social prominence was such that, in the 1940s, the engagements and marriages of Bob Dickson's three daughters were reported in the newspapers of several Alabama cities. His son, Robert Stiles Dickson Jr., born in 1926, was elected to the Alabama state legislature in 1955.[48]

Still, not all of the white residents of Lowndes County were willing to let members of the Dickson family treat black workers however they pleased. In January 1946, a Lowndesboro couple named Frank and Clyde Gordon escorted Aaron "Champ" Smith to the office of an assistant U.S. attorney in Montgomery, initiating the second federal investigation for peonage to center on one of the five Dickson brothers.[49] At least three of the five were dead by this time, and Bob, the youngest and the subject of this second investigation, was seventy-three years old.[50] According to statements taken by two FBI agents, Champ Smith was in his forties and had been working on Dickson's farm for about twenty years. For the previous two years, 1944 and 1945, he had been given only half of the twenty-dollars-a-month wage he had been promised. Because he "could not get by on what Dickson was paying," Smith begged Clyde Gordon to let him work for her at her store, which was about two miles from Dicksonia. He already lived on the property in the home of a black woman who was one of Gordon's employees. Eventually, Gordon agreed to hire him too, starting in January 1946.

When Bob Dickson heard about their agreement, he called Smith into the garage at Dicksonia and told him that, in Smith's words, "I could not work for any such little woman as that[,] that close under him." He also threatened to have Smith put in jail, saying he "had had three other boys put in jail for trying to stop working for him and that he would have me put in jail also." Smith was scared and lied about his intentions, but Dickson seemed not to believe him. He "said that no man in Lowndes County could work me unless he had more land or more money than he had."[51]

A week later, Dickson told Smith that he was in debt for $170 and had better not try to change jobs. Smith appealed to Gordon, and she and her mother, who owned the store, decided to try to reason with Dickson. They offered to pay off Smith's $170 debt, but Dickson now claimed the debt was $400 or $500, and they were unable to come to terms. On January 2, 1946, Smith signed a contract to work for Gordon. On January 14 at about eight o'clock in the morning, he was at work in the back of the store when Bob Dickson walked in.

In front of Gordon and two other witnesses, Dickson demanded that Smith come with him to Dicksonia. Then he grabbed Smith by the strap of his overalls. Gordon tried to intervene, but Dickson ignored her and claimed he had a warrant. He pulled Smith out the door and pushed him into the backseat of his car. Gordon thought they were going to the jail in Hayneville and tried to follow in her car but gave up when Dickson's car turned into the driveway at Dicksonia. During the short drive, Dickson told Smith that he "ought to shoot your God-damn heart out." With the help of his driver, a black man named Julius Johnson, he then took Smith into a room in the house and locked the door. He cursed and threatened him further, drawing a nickel-plated pistol out of his pocket and cocking it. "Boss, don't shoot that nigger," Smith reported Johnson as saying. "Dickson then reached across Julius and grabbed me by the collar and shook me and said he ought to kill me. . . . He then said, 'If I ever have any more trouble with you this year, I'll put you in a hole.'"

Apparently satisfied that Smith was too frightened to try to leave again, Dickson told him to get to work. Smith was "so afraid that Mr. Bob would get to thinking about me again and get mad and come and shoot me" that he slipped off through the woods to the Gordons' house, at which point they drove him to Montgomery to file a complaint.[52]

After hearing Smith's story, assistant U.S. attorney Hartwell Davis immediately called the U.S. attorney general's office. He explained "that Robert Dickson is reported to have killed several people" and predicted "that unless action is taken immediately, he will kill Aaron Smith."[53] The attorney general's office called the FBI, whose investigation showed that, according to Lowndes County records, Dickson had been arrested twice for fatal shootings. In 1894, he was arrested but not prosecuted for shooting John A. Sanderson and Lamar Sanderson, who were presumably white. In 1942, he was arraigned "for the shooting and killing of C. C. Coleman (c[olored]) . . . but was released for lack of evidence."[54]

In the Champ Smith case, Bob Dickson was arrested on January 15, 1946, and released on a $5,000 bond. On January 25, he pleaded not guilty and asked to waive the preliminary hearing. However, prosecutor Davis insisted that the witnesses' testimony be recorded "on account of the character and reputation of the defendant for killing six negroes and three white men prior to this time." The case was then bound over to a grand jury and scheduled for mid-March.[55]

Although the U.S. attorney general's office considered the evidence sufficient to indict Dickson on a single count for arresting Aaron Smith "to a condition of peonage in violation of Section 444, Title 18, U.S. Code," the grand jury that met in March "declined to indict" him and the case was dismissed.[56] Like his older brother J.W., Bob Dickson escaped prosecution for peonage.

✦ ✦ ✦

OF ALL THE BITS of information Jonathan Daniels learned about the Dickson family during his tour, one that he took to heart was that they were powerful enough to be dangerous. If he were to write about his conversation with Turner exactly as it happened, not only Turner but he himself might be vulnerable to reprisals. As his correspondence with his publisher confirms, this is why Daniels chose to leave both Turner and Dickson anonymous in his book and to camouflage his encounter with Turner in such a way that it seemed to have nothing to do with Tuskegee Institute. He recognized that he "was dealing with dangerous material and tried to eliminate any possibility of identification." He also assured his editor that he had "told practically everybody I met on the road that I was writing a book and if anybody spoke out of turn it was not because they were not warned."[57]

In *A Southerner Discovers the South*, Daniels puts Turner's words in the mouth of an unidentified black man whom he supposedly meets "by chance at a school" shortly after passing through Mobile. In physical appearance, the man is a pure minstrel stereotype. He is "as black as asphalt," his hair "short and kinky," and his lips "as wide as my thumbs." His arms are long, and he has "tremendous hands." His laughter is "loud and cackling like defensive idiocy which," Daniels informs readers, "Negroes erect against the danger-ous answering of white men's questions." He is "cousin to the jungle" but also college educated, and he has the ability to discuss what he has seen in the "Negro lower depths of America . . . in the civilized terms common to all educated men."[58]

Daniels was making the same distinction between intellect and appear-ance that he had made in his journal, but it is hard to see what he hoped to accomplish with such an offensive description. It is also troubling to think about Victor Turner's reaction to it, if he read Daniels's book, as he probably did. (Turner's boss in the Extension Service, Thomas Monroe Campbell, definitely read it and wrote to Daniels with praise, although there may have been more to his comment that "fortunately, I know many of the people to whom you referred" than there appeared.)[59]

Despite his insults, Daniels seems to have wanted readers to understand and believe what Turner had told him. Otherwise, why even write about their meeting? There is a great deal of ambivalence in his published account of the conversations with Turner and at the dinner party in Montgomery. Even a careful comparison of his book and his notes leaves many unanswered questions about his authorial choices and intentions. Some of his tailoring was designed to fit his audience, which he anticipated to be white, largely southern, and generally less enlightened on racial matters than he prided himself in being. Other choices seem to have had less to do with audience than with Daniels's own uncertainties. He had heard Turner's story verified and even supplemented by white men, but he still felt it was necessary to cast doubt on Turner's credibility and maintain an emotional distance. He even added elements of fiction, inventing a character—a southern "Colonel" no less—who could have the last word so that he himself could avoid making a definitive statement. Together, his creation of the Colonel and minstreliza-tion of Turner undercut and falsify a powerful moment of truth telling that, his journal reveals, had actually affected him deeply.

In keeping with the general tone of his book, Daniels wrote about Turner from the noncommittal perspective of a traveler seeking facts and asking provocative questions. He presented more dialogue between himself and Turner than he had recorded in his journal. As in real life, the Turner char-acter drops his mask of laughing ignorance after being reassured that Dan-iels can be trusted. He describes how planters terrorize and cheat their ten-ants in clear, precise language that includes the pronunciation "Neegroes." He also adds a point that Daniels may have imported from his earlier con-versations with activists from the Southern Tenant Farmers Union: that "the government knows" that planters steal the money their tenants are supposed to receive under the Agricultural Adjustment Act, "but I haven't heard of anything being done about it." On this point, Daniels suggests he tried to debate with Turner in a back-and-forth engagement:

> "But some landlords are fair."
> "Of course."
> "Is it true that even on such places the Negro tenants are lazy?"
> He laughed.
> "That's what the white folks say when they're sittin' on the porch."
> "That's where I heard it," I admitted, grinning.[60]

Daniels's effort to work in laughter and jokes seems meant to disarm, while the Turner character's admission that some landlords are fair suggests he is reasonable and not an agitator. Unlike the real Turner, who spoke boldly of Dickson's brutality, the fictional character names names only when asked. "Where are the worst places?" Daniels questions.

> "All over Alabama. But the meanest Neegroes and the meanest white folks live in Nonesuch County."
> He looked about him, instinctively fearful, as an Italian might look in Italy who had said Mussolini's name out loud. He lowered his voice.
> "There's one planter there who's killed something like fourteen men—Neegroes and whites—and never been to jail for it."
> "What's his name?"
> He all but whispered it.[61]

The Turner character is more timid than the man Daniels wrote about in his journal, but he does voice the real Turner's concerns about Communist organizing. His insistence on the need for more black farm agents "to teach the Negroes how to make more so they could have more and the planter more" also comes across.[62]

The idea that Lowndes County violence resulted from "Negroes and white men sharing an insufficiency" is a key point that Daniels attributed in his journal not only to Turner but also to the Montgomery dinner party guest named Murray.[63] Murray appears anonymously in *A Southerner Discovers the South* as "a young lawyer" who adds "a little light to darkness" by observing that "Nonesuch County" is "largely made up of worn out land." The lawyer turns for confirmation to the Colonel, a character who seems to have no basis in reality as recorded in Daniels's notes. None of the men who attended the Montgomery dinner party is an obvious match for the Colonel character, and nothing the Colonel says is based on Daniels's journal. Daniels's description of him is also thin. He is about fifty years old, has brown eyes, and looks "merry, self-indulgent, wise and kind." He assures Daniels there are "several counties" like Nonesuch and "several men like the one your nigra described. . . . Every nigra that slips off from his wife may be whispered around as murdered. Still and yet and under all the whispers there's some truth. I'm not the counsel for the defense of this man or his county," he concedes, adding that "slavery is still in force there, but not generally profitable."[64]

In his earlier chapter on Hot Springs, Daniels had attributed the words "slavery is still in force but not generally profitable" to some journalists he had chatted with during the Southern Newspaper Publishers Association meeting.[65] Clearly, he was not only inventing dialogue for the Colonel but repeating a line he had heard somewhere else. By allowing the Colonel to take over the dinner party conversation, he avoids taking a stand on whether or not Turner's accusations are true and whether his call for more black farm agents makes sense. The issue of Communist organizing in the Alabama cotton fields drops away entirely. Instead, the Colonel encourages his listeners—and therefore Daniels's readers—not to take the situation too seriously. His attitude is like that of "an intelligent physician discussing a malignant condition, but enjoying his cigar nevertheless."[66] If Daniels was attempting satire—if he hoped to persuade readers that they *should* take the South's "malignant condition" more seriously than the Colonel did—then he was not very successful. The well-informed but complacent Colonel comes off far more favorably than the caricature of Turner. Allegations of mur-

der are reduced to "whispers" behind which there may be "some truth."
The Colonel says the planter in question "may be a killer" but "I doubt it.
Certainly he is a nigger whipper." With a genteel apology for his language,
the Colonel concludes by stating that this particular planter is "the greatest
sonofabitch that I ever heard of, but if you say anything about him, he may
drive to Raleigh in his car and shoot you on sight. . . . After which . . . he
will buy the jury, paying, I hear, a fair price." Daniels ends the chapter by
claiming to have "laughed, not wanting to be shot."[67]

Unfortunately, Daniels's fear was genuine. His correspondence with his
editor indicates that he had gone so far as to write "his car" instead of "his
Lincoln" in order to further obscure the planter's identity. This was after
he had already "made the automobile [a] Lincoln instead of [a] Cadillac,"
which is what the planter actually drove.[68] Daniels probably did believe that
if he wrote more explicitly, Dickson might shoot him—or sue him, or try to
locate Turner, or raise a hue and cry against Tuskegee Institute or the Negro
Cooperative Extension System. Daniels also believed, much like the Colonel, that some of the South's "malignancies" were inoperable. He believed
criticizing white southerners directly would only make them recalcitrant.
The same worry about local opposition that constrained his views on federal antilynching legislation seems evident here and throughout the book.
He wanted to attract readers, not anger them. Like other white southern
liberals, he thought only moderate opposition to the worst injustices could
gain a hearing among white southerners, and even then it had to be voiced
through spokesmen whose southern credentials could not be questioned. If
those spokesmen were wise, genteel "Colonels," that was all the better.

Below the surface, Daniels's telling of Turner's story did include a comparison between southern racism and European fascism. The Turner character
looks around after naming Nonesuch County just "as an Italian might look
in Italy who had said Mussolini's name out loud." The analogy sets the stage
for Turner's comments about the growing appeal of union organizers and
Communists among black tenants and sharecroppers. The failure of "white
folks" to provide more black farm agents to educate the ignorant and hungry
black masses is "pushing them toward the unions and the Communists."
The real Turner, as quoted in Daniels's journal, had used the words "making them ready," a milder verb than "pushing." Either way, Turner shows
himself to be a man looking for a moderate solution. Perhaps without even
realizing it, Daniels thus captured the concerns of a black middle class that
saw danger and also loss of its own authority in the agitation and organizing
campaigns of the Communist Party. As of the late 1930s, Tuskegee had never

even had a branch of the NAACP—a legacy of Booker T. Washington's conflicts with the organization and its commitment to confronting, rather than coaxing, the nation's white power structure. Left and labor approaches to race progress were even more antithetical to the Washingtonian tradition of accommodation, respectability, and uplift.[69] Daniels heard and approved of Turner's anti-Communism. To what extent he understood it within the context of philosophical and class divisions among African Americans is less clear.

Meanwhile, by invoking fascism as well as Communism, Daniels's published version of his conversation with Turner suggests that ignoring the South's problems could have dire consequences for white people and the nation as a whole. Although such a suggestion seems at odds with the Colonel's complacency, Daniels acknowledges—briefly, before handing the scene over to the Colonel—that Turner's call for more black farm agents ought to appeal to whites' "enlightened self-interest."[70] His own voice is quieter than that of the Colonel, but like the fictional version of Turner, he manages a truthful whisper in the midst of a scene that echoes with ambivalence.

The fact is that Daniels had found the whole encounter with Turner unsettling. Otherwise, he would not have kept telling people about it and asking for more information. He was not satisfied to hear white southerners like Murray confirm Dickson's reputation for violence and then move on to other topics. He brought up the subject again in conversations in Birmingham. The stories he heard there added a few more ounces to his internal moral-political scale, which would eventually tip in favor of racial liberalism and support for black civil rights.

✦ ✦ ✦

AFTER HE REACHED BIRMINGHAM on the morning of June 2, Jonathan walked from his fifteen-story hotel, the Bankhead, to the Thomas Jefferson Hotel, which was even taller and more modern and had a mooring for dirigibles on its roof. He had lunch in the hotel coffee shop and then took a taxi to the offices of the *Birmingham Age-Herald* to visit editor James E. Chappell.[71] A balding man with cheery eyes and a warm smile, Chappell was someone with whom Daniels could talk freely. They did not know each other well, but both were open-minded intellectuals who were politically liberal. In 1936, Chappell had served on the President's Committee on Farm Tenancy, the advisory group Roosevelt appointed just weeks after the flogging of Willie Sue Blagden and Claude Williams. He was also the local contact whose willingness to listen to the arguments of the leftists and liberals of the Scottsboro Defense Committee allowed the Alabama Scottsboro Fair Trial Committee to be formed.

Born in 1885, James E. "Jim" Chappell was from Cadiz, Kentucky, although many people, including Daniels, thought he was from Tennessee. He did study at Vanderbilt and started his newspaper career in Nashville before joining the *Birmingham News* in 1910. By 1936, he had become president and general manager of both the *News* and the *Age-Herald*, making him a busy administrator. Fellow journalists wished he had more time to write because he was such a fine "student of literature and of limping human beings." He was also "a gifted raconteur, a ready wit, a good egg."[72]

Chappell was known for working closely with his columnists. On the afternoon of June 2, Daniels found him in his office "reading editorials . . . in a big room kept shady by Venetian blinds." The editorial writer waited patiently, sprawled across an armchair, and Daniels sat down to wait as well. Once Chappell had approved the editorials and dismissed the columnist, he and Daniels talked of many things. "We talked . . . about the Scottsboro boys, about steel and unions in Birmingham, and about white men and black men in the Deep South."[73]

Perhaps most interesting, Daniels's journal entry for June 2 shows that he and Chappell talked at length about Lowndes County. The fact that Daniels told the Birmingham editor what he had heard about the county and the planter named Dickson suggests he was still trying to figure out what to think. Chappell "verified" the "essential facts" of Turner's and Murray's stories and added some observations of his own. He "says that the Sup[erintendent] of Education in Lown[d]es requires all Negro teachers to submit to him as he wishes them and though none of them can vote they must contribute to his campaign fund." Daniels responded by asking "how general such black-white intercourse was." Confronted with the bugaboo of interracial sex, he seems hardly to have registered the white school superintendent's abuse of his power over black teachers, whose jobs he controlled.[74]

If the Birmingham editor seemed surprisingly familiar with a distant, rural county, it was because his daughter Mary had recently worked there. "Chappell says that in this same Lown[d]es county his own daughter has taught and is going to teach again in the mixed white and black faculty of the Calhoun School—a school somewhat like Tuskegee which was started by [a] New Englander and is almost a New England village today."[75]

The Calhoun Colored School was indeed modeled on Tuskegee, as well as on *its* model, the Hampton Institute. Booker T. Washington had been on a visit to Hampton, his alma mater, when he met two young white women from New England, Charlotte Thorn and Mabel Dillingham, who were teaching there. Thorn and Dillingham were so moved by Washington's account of conditions in the Alabama Black Belt that they decided to open a school for black students in the area. It was Washington himself who directed them to Lowndes County. With support from the General Education Board of the Rockefeller Foundation and other northern philanthropists, they began their work in 1892, and after Dillingham died in 1894, Thorn continued it until her own death forty years later. During that time, the Calhoun School grew from a single building to a bustling campus that offered a high school curriculum, agricultural and vocational training, adult education, and, especially noteworthy, a land bank that eventually held more than 4,000 acres. The Calhoun School's land-purchase program allowed black farmers to escape tenancy and buy land at low interest rates provided by the school's charitable donors. In its first thirteen years, the program resulted in ninety-two deeds issued to eighty-five people.[76]

Despite its successes, the Calhoun School always faced obstacles, including white neighbors' hatred and suspicion. For an Alabama-born white woman like Mary Chappell to live and teach there in the mid-1930s was extraordinary. Even Chappell's close friend Virginia Van Der Veer, who would grow up to be respected Alabama historian Virginia Van Der Veer Hamilton, pondered whether Chappell was a "contemporary 'do-gooder,'" worthy of scorn like the Reconstruction-era northern missionaries her high school history teacher had ridiculed.[77]

Though he shared some of this widespread white southern skepticism about do-gooders, Jonathan Daniels considered twenty-one-year-old Mary Chappell a hopeful sign. He thought she might represent "a new youngness and intelligence in the South," but he was also "puzzled to place her between missionary Christianity and a hard-headed wish to be of use in a difficult world." Chappell was neither overtly religious nor singularly serious. Daniels found her pretty "in her straight long evening dress" and noted that she had "a forthright and interesting stride." She seemed quite comfortable at the Shades Mountain Country Club, where the Chappells took him for dinner, and her appreciation of an occasional cocktail made her even more likable in his eyes. It was hard to know what to make of her decision to teach English and economics at the Calhoun School. Her "striding legs were carrying her like a missionary into darkest Alabama. But she moved with no lugubrious Christianity"—which made her different from other high-minded women he had known (or stereotyped) in the past.[78]

Mary Chappell of Birmingham, who Jonathan Daniels
hoped "may be representative of new youngness and intelligence
in the South." Courtesy of William C. Barclift.

In truth, Daniels seems to have gained little insight into Mary Chappell's personality. One thing he did notice was that, like her parents and
others in Birmingham's less than cosmopolitan scene, she seemed "almost
pathetically interested in writers, writing and what passes for literature."[79]
Yet it was Daniels himself who made a literary mistake in the first edition
of *A Southerner Discovers the South*. As he explained to his editor, he "meant
to imply" that Chappell was "the type of awakening woman as portrayed
in Nora Helmer," the protagonist of Henrik Ibsen's play *A Doll's House*. Instead, he compared her to Hedda Gabler, a potentially insulting analogy.
Daniels asked for the reference to be removed from the second and all other
printings, with the sentence "A new belle moved in Alabama" inserted in its
place. He wondered whether he should make the change quietly or write the
Chappells to apologize "and call attention to my error."[80]

Daniels was sensitive to the Chappells' reaction, not only because Jim
Chappell was a colleague who ran two important newspapers but also be-

cause he knew that Mary's decision to teach at the Calhoun School had cost them some friends. "John Temple Graves II says Chappell and [his] daughter [are] being talked about because of her teaching in [a] Negro school," he had jotted in his journal. A columnist for the *Age-Herald*, Graves felt that Chappell, not being from the state, had "never been able to understand [the] Alabama feeling about the Negro."[81]

✦ ✦ ✦

IF GRAVES'S GOSSIP deflated Daniels's hopes for Mary Chappell as a "new belle" who could maintain both a social life and a social conscience, his conversation with another Birmingham newspaperman punctured his optimism for change in the South even more thoroughly. Charles F. Edmundson, the managing editor of the *Birmingham Post*, "told a terrible story." He had been a reporter back in 1932, "when farmers in Iowa were resisting foreclosures [and] something of the same sort happened in Alabama but to a different tragic ending."[82] The story Edmundson told was a bare-bones version of the same story an elderly black man named Ned Cobb would tell a researcher in the late 1960s, resulting in Theodore Rosengarten's classic book *All God's Dangers: The Life of Nate Shaw.* Shaw was a pseudonym for Cobb, whose hundreds of hours of interviews with Rosengarten resulted in a powerful as-told-to autobiography, at the center of which was the story of how he and a dozen other black men in Tallapoosa County resisted foreclosure on a neighbor's farm.

Cobb and his companions belonged to the Share Croppers' Union (SCU), an all-black labor union that was affiliated with the Communist Party. As Victor Turner suggested, Communist organizing had taken off among Alabama blacks after the party intervened in the Scottsboro case in 1931. Struggling farmers like Cobb and his friend Clifford James were particularly attracted to SCU policies that advocated "the abolition of all debts owed by poor farmers and tenants, as well as interest charged on necessary items such as food, clothes, and seed." Weighed down by a mortgage and the cost of three mules he had bought on credit, James "threw himself into the movement," writes historian Robin D. G. Kelley. He joined the Communist Party and became the leader of an SCU local.[83]

On December 19, 1932, Cobb and other SCU members assembled on James's farm with pistols and shotguns at the ready to prevent a deputy sheriff from taking his livestock. The eloquent and respected Cobb, the group's natural spokesman, pleaded with the sheriff not to serve the writ of attachment because it would "dispossess [James] of bein able to feed his family."[84] Seeing the black men's guns, the deputy left without the animals but returned with reinforcements. When he and three other armed white men stepped onto James's property, a shootout started that left one SCU member dead and several others, including James and Cobb, wounded. The white men suffered no significant injuries before fleeing in the deputy's car.

After the shootout, the inevitable roundup began. Local whites formed posses and arrested and terrorized all the SCU members they could find, as well as many other black people who had nothing to do with the union.[85] It was the manhunt that drew Edmundson and other reporters. Daniels described it as a "reign of terror" in which "white men in school buses hunted Negroes down." He found it particularly upsetting to learn that "two of the Negroes who had been wounded in the original clash went to the hospital at Tuskegee and Tuskegee turned them over to [the] sheriff who took them gasping and dying away from the hospital to jail. . . . They both died."[86]

In truth, although two men did die of their wounds in the county jail, only one of them, Clifford James, had gotten there by way of Tuskegee. "Despite severe injuries to his back," writes Kelley, "James managed to walk seventeen miles" to the Tuskegee hospital, where Dr. Eugene Dibble dressed his gunshot wounds and then called the local sheriff. The sheriff "removed James to a cold, damp cell." He and another prisoner, Milo Bentley, who had been shot in the head, neck, and arms, reportedly received no medical care, and both were found "lying on filthy and flimsy blankets on the floor . . . delirious from the loss of blood." James died from infection and pneumonia on December 27, and Bentley died soon thereafter. Ned Cobb survived but ended up going to prison for thirteen years.[87]

Edmundson told Daniels this terrible story as an illustration of the "lengths to which Tuskegee goes in keeping good white relations." He "was afraid the incident was typical even if unusual"—an idea that made Daniels sad because "Tuskegee had seemed rather impressive . . . and realistic."[88] It had seemed to offer a pragmatic approach to meeting blacks' desperate educational and economic needs. It also employed men like Turner, whose intellect Daniels had appreciated and whose passionate request for more farm agents he had thought rather sensible. Daniels might have been even more impressed by Turner's analysis of conditions in the Black Belt if Edmundson had explained, as he apparently did not, that the men who died in jail had been members of a Communist union. Debt and hunger were indeed making African Americans "ready for the union and the communists."

Jonathan may not have gotten that bit of confirmation, but he did learn enough from his conversations in and about the Alabama Black Belt to feel compelled to ask himself what it must be like to face the ever-present threat of white brutality. He also reflected on the elite social status of some of those who committed terrible violence—men like the Lowndes County planter who could drive to Raleigh and shoot him and then "buy the jury," as his invented character, the "Colonel," suggests. Little did Daniels know that, in the actual peonage investigations of the two Dickson brothers, juries did not even have to be bought because the cases never got that far. Rarely even investigated, planter violence was endemic to the Black Belt, making it impossible to distinguish between law enforcement and labor oppression, the posse and the mob. Daniels realized as much himself in a moment of particular clarity as he was writing his Birmingham chapter. It would be fascinating to know whether Victor Turner, the "most interesting man [he] met," was in the back of Daniels's mind when he "wondered" whether he or Edmundson—or, it would seem, any white person—"could appreciate the dry hysteria which probably touches even the Negroes most remote from the danger of the mob in the Black Belt when mobs (or 'posses') run past—in school buses."[89]

CHAPTER EIGHT

As Furious as the Last Horseman
of a Legion of the Bitter-End

✦

BIRMINGHAM, ALABAMA

ON HIS SECOND DAY in Birmingham, Jonathan noticed there were "special elevators for Negroes" in the Brown-Marx building, where the Tennessee Coal, Iron and Railroad Company (TCI) had its offices. It was one of the few times he remarked on segregation in his notes. Perhaps he saw the symbolism instantly, given that his main goal in Birmingham was to learn more about union efforts to "elevate" black and white workers together in a single, organized body. He and Jim Chappell had already discussed "the great job done in unionizing together the Negro and white miners of Jefferson and Walker counties"—a job done primarily by the United Mine Workers of America (UMW) even before UMW president John L. Lewis spearheaded the formation of the Congress of Industrial Organizations (CIO).[1]

Daniels was eager to meet William Mitch, the UMW organizer who had cracked the Birmingham coal industry and was now the CIO's chief representative in steel. First, however, he was to hear from the bosses' side of the table, namely, from Ernest D. Le May, the director of public relations for TCI. Le May turned out to be a "thin, pleasant-faced man" who assured Daniels that he "had nothing against unionism." "I'm only against Communism," he insisted, even acknowledging that "most communism . . . grows from reaction." Birmingham employers "were far from enlightened in matters of social justice. . . . The whole South has much to learn." But such criticism "did not in any sense apply to TCI." His company was "trying to build up the South," regardless of the fact that, as a subsidiary of Pittsburgh-based U.S. Steel, TCI was a prime example of the South's subordinate, even "colonial" economic status. If Daniels really wanted to understand the labor conflicts in Birmingham, he should interview Charles F. DeBardeleben, an employer who was as local as could be.[2]

For, as Daniels would soon discover, Charles DeBardeleben was one of the staunchest antiunionists and angriest opponents of the New Deal in the entire United States. He was "a gentleman who spits his words out of bitter lips," Daniels wrote, but also one who said "openly and honestly what a good many business men in Birmingham and the South believed but as good politicians did not say."[3] Like Bob Dickson in the Black Belt, DeBardeleben represented the South's system of racial capitalism in a particularly explicit form. He thought of himself as a paternalist but was even more devoted to mastery. He was extreme but unique among southern industrialists for his belief in his absolute right to run his business, including the lives of his workers, as he saw fit.

Suddenly confronted with political and economic change in the 1930s, DeBardeleben denounced both labor organizing and New Deal regulations and reforms as Communist and un-American. He refused to negotiate with unions and only slowly and grudgingly complied with federal wage and hour laws and other mandates. He also shifted his loyalties away from the national Democratic Party because, in his view, Franklin Roosevelt's "infernal administration" was "turning the country over to John L. Lewis." Lewis was "a thug and a redneck" whose "racket amounts to $16,000,000." The South was "worse off as a result of the Roosevelt Administration than it was as a result of the Civil War." The New Deal was "sending the country to hell as straight as the martin to its gourd."[4]

Daniels could respect the honesty, even in someone he disagreed with and, in this case, disliked. In contrast to the conservative Donald Davidson, who had impressed him as a fine, honest man who deserved sympathy for his sadness, DeBardeleben seemed "foolish and mistaken" in his off-putting anger.[5] His epithets only made Daniels all the more confident in his own pro-labor and pro–New Deal views, even as he tried to comprehend a man and an industrial scene that was no less wracked by change in the 1930s than southern agriculture. "In the South the collision of collapsing agriculture and rising industry is not merely private tragedy infinitely repeated, but also a spectacle which should be terrifying to America," he wrote. Even though organized labor experienced a new moment of hope in the 1930s, there were ample reasons for fear, as his portrait of the angry industrialist would show.[6]

✦ ✦ ✦

CHARLES FAIRCHILD DEBARDELEBEN SR. was sixty years old in 1937, "a thin faced man with thin white hair" above his "bitter lips." His story began with his grandfather, Daniel Pratt, an Alabama pioneer and, as Daniels observed in a long paragraph on the family history, "a Yankee." Pratt was born in New Hampshire in 1799, the son of a farmer. He apprenticed under an architect. Then, in 1819—a "wandering time"—he moved to Georgia. For several years he lived in Milledgeville, where he designed and built plantation homes with wide hallways, elegant staircases, and the requisite white columns. In the late 1820s, a friend drew him into the cotton gin business, which he quickly mastered. Pratt tried to convince his partner to expand westward into central Alabama, but ongoing conflicts between settlers and Creek Indians dissuaded him. So, in 1833, Pratt struck out on his own with his wife, Esther, plus two slaves and enough materials to make fifty cotton gins. He founded the town of Prattville along the Autauga Creek northwest of Montgomery. By the late 1850s, the Pratt Gin Company was producing 1,500 cotton gins a year and selling them worldwide, while Pratt himself became a prominent spokesman for industrial expansion in the South and state aid for railroads and other internal improvements.[7]

It was during the 1850s that Daniel and Esther Pratt took in Henry Fairchild DeBardeleben, the adolescent son of a deceased neighbor. Born in 1840, DeBardeleben married the Pratts' only child, a daughter named Ellen, in 1863. He was then serving in the Confederate army. After the war, DeBardeleben worked in his father-in-law's various businesses and joined in Pratt's ongoing efforts to promote industry and railroads. In 1872, Pratt and DeBardeleben acquired a controlling interest in the Red Mountain Iron and Coal Company. The Panic of 1873 brought a quick end to their first foray into mining, but DeBardeleben had "caught the speculative fever." After Daniel and Esther Pratt both died in the 1870s, he had plenty of money with which to speculate.[8]

His larger-than-life personality also emerged from behind Pratt's temperate New England shadow. "Savagely energetic, restless, impatient," Henry DeBardeleben "seemed to have one foot always in the stirrup, and to be itching to mount and be off and away," wrote one local historian. To him, there was nothing more exciting than "taking a wild piece of land, all rock and woods . . . and turning it into a settlement of men and women, making pay rolls, bringing the railroads in, and starting things going. There's nothing like boring a hillside through." He liked to "use money as I use a horse—to ride!"[9]

Exuberant, impatient, Henry DeBardeleben used his inheritance to ride up and down a boom-and-bust business cycle with the whole population of the Birmingham area riding along with him. He bought huge tracts of land for mining and started Alabama's first big coal company, Pratt Coal and Coke, in 1878. Pratt Coal fueled a local iron boom in the 1880s, which DeBardeleben helped along by investing in the Alice Furnace Company (named after his oldest daughter) and other iron and steel ventures. By the end of 1881, however, he was feeling exhausted and worried he might have tuberculosis. He sold Pratt Coal and Coke to a group of Tennessee investors and took a sabbatical. A few years later, the company he had founded became the centerpiece of the rapidly expanding TCI.

After recovering his health during a year of sheep ranching in Mexico, Henry DeBardeleben was ready to get back into the "big game of poker" that, to his mind, was what life was all about. He returned to Birmingham and invested in another blast furnace, this one named for his second daughter, Mary Pratt (who would soon marry TCI lawyer Walker Percy, eventually becoming the grandmother of the well-known novelist of the same name). Next came the DeBardeleben Coal and Iron Company and the founding of the town of Bessemer, a dozen miles southwest of Birmingham. In 1889, DeBardeleben consolidated his holdings under DeBardeleben Coal and Iron. Its growth made TCI anxious to buy out the competition. An 1892 corporate merger turned TCI into the largest coal and iron company in the South but left Henry DeBardeleben feeling discontented as its first vice president. He saw himself as "the eagle" and "wanted to eat up all the crawfish I could — swallow up all the little fellows." But an attempt to gain control of TCI by buying vast quantities of stock on margin failed, and in 1893 DeBardeleben got swallowed up instead. Forced to sell out his TCI shares to rival John Inman, who was in turn swallowed up by J. P. Morgan ("the biggest eagle of them all," notes C. Vann Woodward), DeBardeleben was directly responsible for at least some of the loss of local control over Birmingham's coal, iron, and steel industry.[10] His gamble "not only cost him his fortune," writes a biographer; "it also ended Southern ownership and management of the principal coal and iron company in the South. Within a few years all of the Southerners would be ousted, and control of TCI would pass entirely into Northern hands."[11]

Those northerners imposed a "Pittsburgh Plus" pricing scheme that put Birmingham steel at a competitive disadvantage against steel produced in the older industrial areas where U.S. Steel was based. Southerners, including Jonathan Daniels, would lament the South's "colonial" economy for decades to come. Yet even Daniels described Henry DeBardeleben as a builder whose "fortune rose and fell with Birmingham's." In truth, it was largely vice versa: Birmingham's fortunes rose and fell with men like DeBardeleben.[12]

As a builder, Henry DeBardeleben may or may not have been an eagle, but he was by definition a "Big Mule." Politician Bibb Graves popularized this term for Alabama's industrial elite during his successful bid for the governor's seat in 1926.[13] But the reality of a Black Belt–Big Mule coalition in Alabama politics went back decades. As historian Robert J. Norrell explains, "Since the 1880s Birmingham industrialists had coalesced with planters from the predominately black counties in south central Alabama" (counties like Lowndes and planters like Dickson) "to preserve a political system that featured a strong state government dominated by a malapportioned legislature, weak local government, and a highly restricted ballot." The Big Mules did not win every political battle from the 1880s to the 1930s, "but they almost always prevailed on issues that really mattered to them—low taxes, freedom from government interference, and use of the state militia to control striking workers. The latter was particularly important to them: Alabama governors . . . dispatched the National Guard to help break coal miners' strikes in 1894, 1908, and 1919–1921."[14]

By the 1910s, it was Henry DeBardeleben's sons who benefited from Alabama's Black Belt–Big Mule version of racial capitalism. Born in Prattville on the historic Fourth of July, 1876, Charles was the fifth of Henry and Ellen Pratt DeBardeleben's eight children. He grew up in Birmingham and was educated at home and at the Alabama Polytechnic Institute (now Auburn University). He went on to work in a variety of jobs in the multiple, intertwined coal and iron companies of the Birmingham area. He also married, and he and his wife, Margaret Prince DeBardeleben, had three sons: one called Prince, his wife's family name; one named after himself, Charles F. DeBardeleben Jr.; and one honoring his brother-in-law, Walker Percy. In 1908, Charles Sr. became the vice president and general manager of his father's Alabama Fuel and Iron Company, which owned mines at Overton in Jefferson County and Acmar and Margaret in St. Clair County. After Henry DeBardeleben died in 1910, Charles was named president of Alabama Fuel and Iron in 1921.[15] He was also a member of several clubs and civic organizations and served terms as president of the Birmingham Chamber of Commerce and the exclusive Country Club of Birmingham (far more exclusive than the Shades Mountain Country Club, where the Chappells took Daniels).[16]

In personality, Charles was steadier and less boisterous than his father, but they still shared a great deal. Like Henry, he prided himself on being a rugged individualist and expected the same of others, which of course meant no unions. Henry DeBardeleben's antiunion sentiments had been legendary. He was not only an enthusiastic early adopter of convict labor but, in 1890, was also responsible for introducing a "new inflammatory element" into Alabama labor politics: the recruitment of black strikebreakers. Although coal operators already used violent armed guards, an antiunion press, and mass evictions from company housing to defeat strikers, DeBardeleben's systematic recruitment of black workers from outside the mines proved even more devastating. The labor force in coal had been racially mixed from the start, and the UMW's first organizers had tried and largely succeeded in promoting unity between black and white miners. Nevertheless, the availability of a vast pool of rural black workers who were eager to escape sharecropping undercut the union's bargaining power while exacerbating underlying racial tensions in the coal mines.[17]

In 1894, Henry DeBardeleben responded to a UMW strike with an even more explicit appeal to blacks who were willing to cross picket lines and renounce any desire for union representation. If they went to work for him, blacks could have "their own churches, schools and societies, and conduct their social affairs in a manner to suit themselves," he promised. Each of his mining communities could be "a colored man's colony"—a prospect that had a certain appeal at a time when frequent lynchings, the loss of political rights, and the hardening of segregation made the chances for black advancement within the wider community seem slim indeed.[18]

Henry DeBardeleben's promise to create "colored man's colonies" prefigured the "welfare capitalism" or industrial paternalism that Birmingham bosses would practice in the 1910s and 1920s. By that time, a failed 1908 strike had wiped out the UMW: membership in the Birmingham area (the UMW's District 20) had dropped from a peak of nearly 20,000 in 1908 to only 278 the following year.[19] Because so many skilled miners moved away, however, the 1908 strike proved to be a turning point for industrialists as well. They soon realized that the only way to maintain stable productivity was to cultivate the existing labor force, which by this time was predominantly African American. TCI led the way by investing in technology, training, and better housing and other facilities for workers. The company also moved black workers into skilled and semiskilled jobs—"though less out of a commitment to racial fairness," as historian Brian Kelly explains, "than from an appreciation of the necessity of developing a layer of skilled black miners."[20] Necessity *and advantage*: coal operators insisted they were "friends

Like Jonathan Daniels, photographer Arthur Rothstein sought a mountaintop view to take in Birmingham's coal and iron mines and company housing when he visited the city in 1937. Farm Security Administration / Office of War Information Photograph Collection, Library of Congress, Prints and Photographs Division, Washington, D.C. [LC-DIG-fsa-8b36032].

of the Negro" and discouraged black workers from joining a "white man's union" like the struggling UMW. Meanwhile, white employees got higher wages than black ones, but they also got the not-so-subtle message that they could be replaced.

In short, welfare capitalism as practiced in Birmingham had a strong racial component. It also came with many entangling strings attached. In return for improved conditions on the job and in company-owned communities, employers demanded absolute loyalty. They also tried to dominate workers' very thoughts, as well as many aspects of their lives. Company schools came with company teachers; company clinics, with company doctors. Even the clergymen employed in company-built churches preached the company line. Workers were denied an independent voice and were "subjected to a near-constant barrage of middle-class morality," particularly lessons in personal responsibility, thrift, sobriety, and hard work. Meanwhile, armed guards patrolled mining towns to keep out union organizers, and bosses claimed the right to limit workers' travel and to fire and evict anyone who challenged their authority or broke company rules.[21]

No Birmingham industrialist engaged in welfare capitalism more eagerly than Charles DeBardeleben. He encouraged his 6,500 employees to call him "Uncle Charlie" and prided himself on his paternalism. "Julius Caesar, who could call every one of his soldiers by his first name, had nothing on Charles DeBardeleben," wrote one sympathetic columnist. A 1939 company history titled *Alabama Fuel and Iron Company and Its People: A Story of a Visit to Happy Communities* touted the schools, churches, and leisure activities that DeBardeleben and his managers supplied. Even racism had supposedly yielded to their wise oversight. Blacks made up 60 percent of the workforce and were "given the same consideration as the whites in reference to rates of pay, working conditions and schooling," claimed author Fred Richard Marvin, and "there have not been any racial difficulties in twenty-five years." Marvin, supposedly an independent journalist but actually a veteran union baiter, also insisted that Alabama Fuel and Iron employees had "enjoyed collective bargaining" through their racially segregated welfare societies—their company unions—since 1914.[22] Yet, as Marvin chose not to mention, Alabama Fuel and Iron's all-white management used spies and a private police force to keep workers isolated from outside influences. Anyone who joined an independent union was promptly fired, evicted from company housing, and put outside the gates of Acmar, Margaret, and other "happy" towns.[23]

Charles DeBardeleben was vocal about his antiunion philosophy. In a 1922 letter to the *Manufacturer's Record*, he equated "the principles of Americanism" with "the open shop policy" and insisted that any government that refused a man "the privilege of working when he wants to work" was not "the right kind of government."[24] At company picnics and in frequent speeches at his mining camps, DeBardeleben pounded these ideas into his workers and tried "to create a cult of personality" around his own paternalism.[25] He wanted employees to think of him as someone who would treat them fairly and even generously as long as they approached him individually or as part of his collective (his company family) rather than through a union.

When the New Deal and especially section 7(a) of the National Industrial Recovery Act of 1933 gave explicit support for workers' right to organize in independent unions, DeBardeleben was outraged. When the Social Security Act of 1935 imposed a corporate tax to pay for unemployment insurance provided by the government, he was apoplectic and fought the constitutionality of it, unsuccessfully, all the way to the Supreme Court.[26] By the time

Jonathan Daniels met him in 1937, the New Deal and organized labor were clearly winning in the Alabama coalfields, making DeBardeleben "as furious as the last horseman of a Legion of the Bitter-End."[27]

Daniels recognized in DeBardeleben the kind of Old South paternalist he had been looking for since at least Marked Tree, Arkansas. It was no mere coincidence that the best example he had so far found was DeBardeleben's kinsman by marriage, William Alexander Percy of Greenville, Mississippi. It was through marriage as well as mythmaking that families like DeBardeleben's connected themselves to the plantation tradition. Even after digging at the industrialist's Yankee roots, Daniels described him as "one of the last of the old time masters of men out of the old time South." He had heard that DeBardeleben was "a paternalist who has succeeded in paternalism. During the whole depression, people said, no DeBardeleben employee . . . was ever on the relief rolls. . . . Instead [he] marshaled his 'big family' in self-support. He put his miners to gardening while other miners elsewhere depended on the government."[28]

What Daniels had heard about DeBardeleben's decision not to lay off his miners during the depths of the Great Depression was partially true and distinguished him from other bosses. Like planters who evicted their sharecroppers to eliminate overproduction, most coal, iron, and steel operators responded to the low prices and reduced demand for their products by drastically cutting their numbers of employees. The unemployment rate in Birmingham was crippling, with nearly 25 percent of the city's workforce unemployed by early 1932 and most of the rest employed part-time. The Depression left "more than one third" of the city's population "prostrate before an economic altar of idled coal and ore mines and steel mills," writes historian Glenn T. Eskew. Daniels made the same point: the Depression "hit Birmingham perhaps harder and swifter than any city except Detroit," he wrote. "It is a Birmingham proverb: 'Hard times come here first and stay longest.'"[29]

In addition to laying off workers, most companies responded to the hard times by dismantling their systems of welfare capitalism. In 1933, TCI stopped paying for company schools and rented out its buildings to the Jefferson County Board of Education. Laid-off employees were allowed to remain in company housing, but TCI turned off the water and electricity. Other companies such as Republic Steel evicted workers who were no longer needed and posted armed guards "with orders to shoot if the people returned."[30]

Charles DeBardeleben's agricultural program seemed compassionate by comparison. He supplied his idled workers with mules, tools, and seeds and wrote glowingly in company reports about the bushels of corn, potatoes, and peas his miners produced and the blue ribbons "our people" won at the state fair.[31] Ever the cynic, Jonathan Daniels must have snickered at the cover of the March 29, 1937, issue of *Alabama* magazine, which featured an obviously pasted-in picture of DeBardeleben smiling over a group of smiling black schoolchildren—"Ol' Man Charlie an' His Chillun," the caption read. But Daniels did pay attention to the accompanying article, "The Debardeleben Oasis—Unionism's Last Frontier," from which he quoted extensively in *A Southerner Discovers the South*. "Through four years of business stagnation," De-Bardeleben "carried 1200 mining families, and not a penny of relief money was spent among them," the magazine praised.[32]

Daniels formed his own opinion. He was wise enough to know that *Alabama* magazine was financed by local industrialists, including DeBardeleben. He acknowledged the practical benefits of the agricultural program, suggesting that Uncle Charlie, "as a benevolent despot in charge of miners growing cabbages, did an excellent depression job in paternalism."[33] But he was a "despot" nevertheless.

Like his conversations about lynching and planter violence during his tour, Daniels's face-to-face encounter with the bitterness of the Birmingham industrial scene was unsettling. He did not enjoy the short time he spent being harangued in Charles DeBardeleben's office. The industrialist lived up to his claim that his door was always open, even "to the lowest paid worker in the mines," but he made no promise to restrain the "quality of excitement" in his character—no promise not to spit his words, raise his voice, or bang his fist.[34] Finally able to get a word in edgewise, Daniels asked him, "If your miners wanted to join [a] union, could they do it without being fired?"

"What are you doing coming here catechizing me about my personal business?" DeBardeleben roared. Then he turned to his desk and Daniels understood that he was "dismissed without his saying so but clearly and angrily dismissed."[35]

Daniels left "less angry than aware that I had met a personality." His long-standing support for labor unions made solutions to the South's industrial problems seem more obvious than any solution to "the dark problem of the little man on the land." Paternalism was the way of the past and in any case had seldom been practiced with DeBardeleben's level of commitment. Plus, "whatever may have been the results of the DeBardeleben system during the depression, I found no convincing evidence that his 'people' were better off . . . in paternalism than they would be in unions." Without going into detail, Daniels also acknowledged that "blood had already been shed at Acmar and more blood would probably have to be before paternalism gave way to unionism in the DeBardeleben mines."[36] It was the violence, the anger, that showed that paternalism was a lie. It might even be a self-deception on the part of some paternalists, but it would inevitably collapse when push came to shove.

Meanwhile, Daniels reflected, the "foreign agitator" he had met an hour or two before he talked to DeBardeleben seemed "far less agitated" than the bosses.[37] That "agitator" (not Daniels's word but definitely one of DeBardeleben's) was William Mitch of the UMW and CIO.

✦ ✦ ✦

"MITCH HAS THE RESPECT of newspaper men in Birmingham," Daniels wrote, offering a high compliment as he introduced the union organizer in *A Southerner Discovers the South*. His physical description was less complimentary. Sitting in his office at the Comer Building, where Daniels had been forced to wait in a room filled with miners, Mitch looked, he thought, like "a Methodist preacher with a predilection for costume jewelry. A man of fifty, dark-haired and sallow, he wore . . . a tie pin, a tie clasp, a watch chain and, I think, a ring." In his journal, Daniels also noted "white silk socks with black up and down stripes"—socks that apparently struck him as flashy or perhaps simply soft for a labor leader. If he intended to make a metaphor around Mitch's "silk stockings"   long a symbol of affluence and thus potentially the start of a union fat-cat image—he never got around to it. Perhaps listening to Mitch or hearing DeBardeleben sputter about UMW president John L. Lewis's $16 million "racket" made him change his mind.[38]

The onset of the Great Depression had presented new opportunities for the UMW in Birmingham. Mass unemployment after the 1929 crash made coal miners, as one man put it, "restless and rareing to go."[39] The passage of the National Industrial Recovery Act (NIRA) offered further encouragement. Section 7(a) of the new law said quite clearly that "employees shall have the right to organize and bargain collectively through representatives of their own choosing," without "interference, restraint, or coercion" on the part of employers.[40] Lewis understood that the support of federal law could spur unionization, and he entrusted UMW District 20 to Mitch, a veteran organizer from the Midwest who had worked his way up through the ranks after entering a coal mine himself at the age of twelve. Mitch "had, of course, been labeled a carpetbagger and a foreign agitator," Daniels wrote. The bosses had tried "to make his unionization of the white and Negro miners

The CIO presence was visible in Birmingham in 1937, as Arthur Rothstein's photograph of the New Idea Barber Shop's window suggests. Farm Security Administration / Office of War Information Photograph Collection, Library of Congress, Prints and Photographs Division, Washington, D.C. [LC-DIG-fsa-8b28538].

in the same unions appear as somehow wicked and anti-Southern and a betrayal to the white race." But Mitch "had replied that the operators had not regarded it as wicked to work them together" in the mines.[41] Decades-old tactics for dividing and conquering the workforce were proving ineffective. Mitch enrolled more than 6,000 new members in the UMW by the time the NIRA was officially signed.[42]

As he rebuilt District 20, Mitch also participated in negotiations over an industry-wide code for coal companies, which the NIRA required and the new National Recovery Administration (NRA) would implement for coal and a number of other industries. One key question was whether or not existing racial disparities in wages would be sanctioned by federal policy.

Southern manufacturers and conservative southern congressmen fought hard for a racial differential, inaugurating "the first major contest over the New Deal in the South."[43] It took energetic lobbying on the part of national black leaders and organizations like the NAACP and the National Urban League to prevent southern industrialists and their allies from inscribing racial wage discrimination into the NRA codes.

Instead, *regional* disparities in wages were allowed to serve as something of a proxy. In the particular case of coal, Alabama operators, including Charles and his brother Henry T. DeBardeleben, argued vigorously that wages had to be kept low because both geological and economic factors made the labor costs involved in producing coal in Alabama higher per ton than for coal produced elsewhere. Alabama coal companies could not compete with northern producers or with natural gas or hydroelectric power, especially that of the TVA, unless they could save money on wages, they warned. The very survival of the Alabama coal industry and the tens of thousands of jobs it provided were at stake.[44]

Mitch and other labor leaders quickly pointed out that Alabama coal operators had *relied* on cheap labor rather than investing in better machinery and other innovations. But, given the economic realities, a regional disparity in the NRA codes was probably inevitable. The coal code that took effect in October 1933 maintained a North-South differential, with southern workers' wages set significantly lower than those of their northern counterparts. Even so, Alabama miners started so far behind that they still saw a huge percentage increase in their pay as a result of the NRA code. For some, the raise was more than 64 percent.[45]

The wage increase was a great victory for workers, but it did not solve all of Mitch's problems. A number of coal operators were disregarding section 7(a) and firing employees for joining the UMW. A federal negotiator named L. C. Richardson was sent to Birmingham in July 1933 to persuade coal executives to meet with UMW representatives. "The Alabama Fuel and Iron Company of which Charles DeBardeleben is president, and the DeBardeleben Coal Corporation of which Henry DeBardeleben is president and Mr. Milton Fies, vice president, will require more than conciliation to stop them from coercing and interfering with their employees (whom they have in corrals)," Richardson wrote to a supervisor, presumably referring to the high fences around the DeBardeleben camps. "In my opinion, if these two companies could be straightened out and could be shown that their idea of rule or ruin would not be tolerated, it would greatly clear up the condition in this part of Alabama."[46]

The DeBardelebens' recalcitrance contributed to labor unrest in District 20 throughout the next year. Mitch had his hands full resolving disputes and working out contracts with a multitude of companies that, unlike Alabama Fuel and Iron and DeBardeleben Coal, decided to negotiate. In addition, Mitch faced ongoing conflicts over the NRA code. In the spring of 1934, a revision to the code angered Alabama coal bosses so much that they temporarily closed the mines until they could get a restraining order and a more favorable revision.[47]

Meanwhile, antilabor violence was an ever-present threat. Some operators "have dynamite planted on the roadway leading to and from their coal mining camps and this dynamite is connected with electric wires so it can be set off," Mitch wrote to Secretary of Labor Frances Perkins in August 1934. Alabama Fuel and Iron was found to have constructed an "organizer trap" on the only road leading to its Overton mine. "Buried in the road between [two telegraph] poles was a gallon syrup can containing approximately 20 sticks of dynamite." A black employee named John Jones "was assigned to the job of watching the road and throwing the switch in the event organizers or union men attempted to come into the camp." DeBardeleben's men also positioned machine-gun nests around the mines and his St. Clair County home, which was now surrounded by an electrified barbed-wire fence. "As evidence of its lethal qualities," wrote a federal investigator, "three dogs who ran into it . . . were killed."[48]

Charles DeBardeleben's annual report to stockholders for 1934 reads as if it were written from behind a barricade. "The year was filled with many trying problems, many of which at the time seemed to be almost insurmountable," he began. He reflected on the "many weeks of hard work" that it took to get a "satisfactory compromise with the N. R. A. . . . We were also taken from an eight hour work day to a seven hour work day, and the new wage scale and hours of work became effective on April 1st." All these changes "were most demoralizing, and much effort was put forth . . . towards stimulating the men to acquire a faster gait to compensate for the one hour less working time." In other words, Alabama Fuel and Iron had been busy implementing a speed-up. Because of financial losses and the workers' decision to join the UMW, the company was also in the process of closing its Overton mine and evicting "these undesirables" from their company-owned homes.

Meanwhile, the mines had proven even more dangerous than usual. "Our Personal Injury record for the year is really shameful," DeBardeleben admitted to shareholders. "We had a total of five fatalities during the year, one of which occurred at Margaret and four at Acmar. . . . This terrible record is largely accounted for by the fact that we brought in so many new men during the year." As DeBardeleben had explained elsewhere in his report, in 1934 Alabama Fuel and Iron recruited "approximately 300 negroes from South Alabama who had never seen coal mines." "We have greatly increased the ratio of our negro employees," he added, describing the company's workforce as 70 to 75 percent black and 25 to 30 percent white at its various mines. "Our past experience has taught us that this is about the right ratio in order to maintain the proper loyalty and cooperative spirit." Yet even such a careful racial policy could not keep "our men" from being "more occupied with thinking of their welfare and protection from outside invasion than of the dangers they were being subjected to in the mines."[49] In DeBardeleben's view, even the fatal accidents of 1934 could be blamed on the UMW and NRA.

As bad as 1934 was for Charles DeBardeleben, 1935 would be worse. While other coal operators and even his own brother gradually and grudgingly gave way to federal pressure and negotiated contracts with the UMW, he dug in his heels. He vowed to "die and go to Hell"—or at least quit the coal mining business—"before he would deal with the union."[50] When a national coal strike in the fall of 1935 idled other mines in the Birmingham area, DeBardeleben kept his mines open and resorted to his usual tactics for keeping organizers out of his camps.

On October 28, 1935, when two carloads of union men approached Alabama Fuel and Iron's Acmar mine in St. Clair County, one of the company's machine-gun nests erupted in gunfire. A union member named Virgil Thomas died from thirty bullet wounds. Six other men were also shot but survived. The union men did not return fire, and an eyewitness said she did not see any of them carrying guns.[51] The company admitted there had been no provocation other than alleged trespassing on company property, but a statement signed by DeBardeleben himself still asserted that "there was no rightful ground for criticism of this company or its employees in defending and persisting in defending their lives, homes, and jobs against the continuing attacks of armed Union mobsters."[52]

In the wake of the Acmar shooting, DeBardeleben and several other company men were indicted, and Charles Shepherd, the superintendent of the Acmar mine, was tried for first-degree murder. Company lawyers defended him, and he was acquitted in a trial that Mitch later described as a "farce comedy."[53] All other charges were dropped. In late 1936, Alabama Fuel and Iron's board of directors passed a resolution thanking the two lead lawyers for their "masterly and brilliant conduct" of Shepherd's trial.[54] The lawyers' successful defense against a damages suit several months later earned them another resolution of gratitude for a "legal victory of great financial importance" that, the board felt, also marked "a brilliant epoch in the labor history of this Company. It vindicates . . . the right to work without interference from outside agitators," as well as "the right to defend this right against all those who seek to destroy it."[55]

Charles DeBardeleben was still waiting for this second bit of vindication from the courts when he agreed to meet with Jonathan Daniels. By the time Daniels arrived in Birmingham, the UMW had succeeded in negotiating union contracts with all the other coal operators in District 20. The CIO had also won a tremendous victory nationwide when the chairman of U.S. Steel, Myron Taylor, agreed in March 1937 to recognize workers' right to collective bargaining. "Taylor betrayed his associates for a steel price," DeBardeleben fumed and Daniels jotted in his notes on the interview.[56]

As angry as he was, DeBardeleben could at least take comfort in the fact that his murder charge had been dropped about five months earlier. The *Alabama* magazine article that Daniels quoted was an even more recent effort to defend his public image as a paternalist. Over the next few years, DeBardeleben would continue to promote that image in the local media and by employing men like Fred Marvin, the so-called independent journalist who wrote *Alabama Fuel and Iron Company and Its People*.

The connection with Marvin was significant. Fred Richard Marvin was a Minnesota native and former newspaperman who had become fiercely anti-union after seeing members of the Western Federation of Miners dynamite mines during an 1899 labor dispute in Coeur d'Alene, Idaho. By the late 1930s, he had become "the granddaddy of America's right-wing pamphleteers."[57] His recent titles included *Our Government and Its Enemies* (1932) and *Fool's Gold: An Exposé of Un-American Activities and Political Action in the United States since 1860* (1936). From an office in the Webb-Crawford Building, where DeBardeleben had his offices, Marvin ran the Birmingham branch of the Constitutional Educational League, an anti-Communist organization that had been founded in 1919 during the post–World War I red scare. In 1942, a National Labor Relations Board investigation of Alabama Fuel and Iron found that Charles DeBardeleben had been a financial benefactor of the league.[58] That same year, a special grand jury in Washington identified it as one of twenty-eight organizations supposedly linked to an international fascist plot against the U.S. military.[59] Little came of the charge, but in 1944 the league's vice president, Joseph P. Kamp, published an incendiary pamphlet titled *Vote CIO and Get a Soviet America* that resulted in a congressional investigation into the league's activities. Kamp refused to disclose the names of donors and eventually went to prison for a few months for contempt of Congress.[60]

Other than his association with Marvin, the extent of Charles DeBardeleben's ties to domestic or international fascism is unclear. His financial support for the Constitutional Educational League suggests that he was "more than just an angry capitalist championing the principles of free enterprise," as Birmingham author Diane McWhorter has argued. His campaign against labor may have been rooted in fascism—"in the most extreme anti-democratic movement of the century," as McWhorter claims.[61]

Even more to the point is one of Daniels's observations: that it seems "absurd to use a foreign term" like fascism "for a condition that was American before Mussolini was born."[62] Daniels thought DeBardeleben was more typical than atypical of southern industrialists, except for the fact that he said "openly and honestly" what others kept to themselves. He also acted on his antipathy for the New Deal by voting for a Republican for president in 1936. Daniels watched him bang his fist on his desk and was intrigued to see an Alf Landon campaign flyer preserved beneath the glass.

After his "Breakfast with a Democrat," David Lilienthal, in Norris, Tennessee, Jonathan had reflected on how bewildering politics were in the South, "where the toughest Bourbons are often the noisiest Jeffersonians and all slaveholder-thinkers vote the straight Democratic ticket."[63] But Charles DeBardeleben was no longer voting for the Democratic Party, at least not at the national level. Like other arch-conservative southern industrialists who, as historian Jason Morgan Ward writes, were really "the first southerners to question the racial implications of the New Deal," he had renounced the national party and started to vote Republican.[64] He made his loyalties clear in advertisements in *Alabama* magazine—ads that earned him yet another federal investigation.

In 1940, DeBardeleben paid for nine ads supporting Republican presidential candidate Wendell Willkie that may have been in violation of the Federal Corrupt Practices Act because they "appeared to be corporate expenditures." Looking into them, investigators found other problems, including coercion of voters. About a month before the 1940 election, DeBardeleben had called a meeting of Alabama Fuel and Iron employees, telling them "it was their privilege to vote as they pleased, but he did want to show them how to vote." He held up a sample ballot and instructed his workers "to place a cross (x) in front of the names of electors for the Republican candidate for President and then to switch to the other side of the ballot and place a cross (x) in front of the names of all State and county Democratic candidates."[65]

This was not the first time DeBardeleben had been accused of pressuring his miners to vote a certain way. After a controversy erupted over a 1930 U.S. Senate race, two men testified before a Senate hearing that they had been fired for voting against DeBardeleben's wishes.[66] In 1940, the Senate would look closely at election results in the relevant precincts. In the town of Margaret, the presidential race went 210 to 96 for Willkie over Roosevelt, yet the Republican candidate for county probate judge lost to his Democratic opponent by 7 to 314. Results in Acmar were similar, and in both communities the polling place was "located on company-owned property, and there was present in each polling place an armed deputy sheriff who is on the company pay roll and who was present ostensibly to maintain order. In many instances this officer marked the ballots of company employees or assisted them in voting." Though the Senate committee reported other facts "offered in substantiation of charges that the president of Alabama Fuel & Iron Co. controls elections in the county," there was no legal follow-up.[67] Nothing was done to prevent DeBardeleben from coercing his employees to vote according to his shifting political preferences.

After Charles DeBardeleben died in 1941, his descendants and eventually much of the white South followed his lead as a "pioneering modern southern Republican."[68] Of all the people Daniels met during his tour, the industrialist was perhaps the most indicative of where the "long backlash" in response to the long civil rights movement would end up.

Writing at the start of the long contest between conservatives like DeBardeleben and the forces of black, left, and labor dissent that the New Deal had unchained, Daniels could not foresee the white South's full-scale political realignment, which would proceed in fits and starts over the next thirty years. Instead, he understood DeBardeleben's support for Alf Landon as a look backward, not forward, sensing a nostalgia in his preservation of the Republican campaign flyer that, for him, could only evoke the capital-S "Southern" and usually Democratic Party–affiliated Lost Cause. Under DeBardeleben's "violent fist and his violent words, the label seemed to me a little touching," he wrote, "like a Confederate flag flying where no longer any Confederacy is. The past is sweet."[69]

Nostalgia for the past explained Charles DeBardeleben, in Daniels's view. He was an Old South paternalist—a feudalist who proved Franklin Roosevelt's point that there was "little difference between the feudal system and the Fascist system. If you believe in the one, you lean to the other."[70] Perhaps he really was ready to die for his lost cause, as "Southerners have died for lost causes before . . . and been heroes for it." Daniels could not know that DeBardeleben would die just four years after they met and without ever having signed a union contract or acknowledged his workers' right to organize. A funeral notice suggested his long illness "began eight years ago"—in the early days of Roosevelt's first term.[71] Born on the 4th of July, 1876, DeBardeleben was buried—appropriately, as he might see things—on Labor Day.[72]

"Suddenly and very sadly," Daniels felt he had "come in Birmingham to the other side of something remembered." That memory was of Joe Poe, the hitchhiker he had picked up on the road to Scottsboro. "Old man DeBardeleben and old Joe Poe . . . make an interesting old pair in a strange new world," he noted in his journal. It was not simply that the two men were close in age and that Joe had been on his way to Birmingham to look for work. It was also the fact that both were so upset—Joe "querulous and confused," too old and weak to support himself, and DeBardeleben white with anger at a world he could no longer control. They had "grown old together and one is no more satisfied with these times than the other is." It was "a bad present for both." DeBardeleben was "a mountain and Joe Poe is a mouse and both are equally lost in these times." Both "seemed old in a world as brash as Lewis, hopeful as Roosevelt, pragmatic as Taylor. The two are brothers of each other and of the past." [73]

CHAPTER NINE

A Red-Headed Woman Immaculate and Immediate from the Beauty Parlor

✦

ATLANTA, GEORGIA

VISITING ATLANTA made Jonathan Daniels mad. He arrived on June 4 in time for a late lunch of salmon and mayonnaise at the Biltmore Hotel, an eleven-story luxury hotel that had been financed by the son of Coca-Cola magnate Asa Griggs Candler. From there an old college friend, Garland Burns Porter, drove him around to see the sights. Porter "took me through North Atlanta where there is more money in evidence than anywhere else in the South I have been," he wrote. Then they "doubl[ed] back" through some of the city's poorest black and white neighborhoods. That was the problem with Atlanta: the ride from wealth to poverty was "too brief and too far."[1] The social distance between nearby neighborhoods was distressingly great.

Atlanta's white elites also seemed pretentious. North Atlanta and, specifically, Paces Ferry Road featured "the palaces of the new masters of Dixie. Never in any earlier South were there such or so many mansions." Even if the James River shore of Virginia "were extended along the Battery and Bull Street [of Charleston] through Prytannia Street in old New Orl-yuns and all the fine houses of the older South were set upon that way, they would make no such show as that which Atlanta does now on the hills where dwell the aristocrats of Coca-Cola, the lord of golf, the baron of chocolates, and all the rich, fat city burghers and their sleek pretty wives who grew in the years after the landed folk were cut down like the lilacs."[2]

Daniels "had no time to trace out how much of Atlanta's array of palaces came from Coca-Cola," as he wrote in *A Southerner Discovers the South*. "But as Chattanooga had taken its greatest wealth from a combination of Coca-Cola and Cardui," a medicinal syrup for menstrual cramps, "so at least some Atlanta money had come from the revived Ku Klux Klan which for a while seemed to serve men, as Cardui eased women, as tonic for disturbed, uncertain or deranged virility.

"'They don't have lynchings on Paces Ferry Road, do they?'" Daniels claimed to have abruptly asked his old friend Porter. If not, it seemed "a pity . . . with so many trees and so much room for the congregation of the indignant. If there are going to be lynchings in the South there could be no better place for them," he observed with caustic irony. He imagined a scene that "might look perilously similar to that famous scene in which Marie Antoinette spoke of bread and cake in hungry, angry days. I wondered who, if anybody, in Atlanta would have a witticism for the poor if they should come clamoring at these gates for bread. Probably," he concluded, "some practical plutocrat would throw them a nigger instead. It has been done before."[3]

Nearly 300 pages into an affable, moderate book, Daniels's suddenly acerbic tone could be expected to shock some of his intended audience. "I am no roaring radical," he insisted, adding that "most of the leftists whom I know in the South are both as violent in their talk and as rigid in their thinking as old Uncle Charlie DeBardeleben of Birmingham."[4] Nevertheless, in Atlanta the disparity between rich and poor, white and black, was so large and potentially dangerous that it demanded fiery words (and even some nascent gender analysis about masculinity and the Klan). Revolution — a Marie Antoinette moment — seemed possible and could only result in violence when some "practical plutocrat" threw the white masses a black scapegoat to save his own hide. In Atlanta, it certainly had "been done before," most horrendously in a three-day, white-on-black massacre in 1906.[5]

Daniels's anger at Atlanta was a cry of disappointment: old social patterns were all too evident in the capital of the "New South." Much of the city's wealth had come from northern capital lured south, just as Henry Grady and other late nineteenth-century proponents of the "New South creed" had promised. Unlike the Arkansas-Mississippi Delta's wealth in timber and cotton that had "been completely taken out and away," Atlanta's wealth in railroads, textile mills, and banking had built *local* fortunes, even if they were the fortunes of "overseers" rather than owners.

The success of the New South movement had brought wealth for a managerial class but very little change for white or black workers. Instead, the "new overseers, faithful to the absentee owners," continued to "beg and plead and promise for more absentee investment and control while simultaneously they cry to hysteria in condemnation of foreign agitators among nice native labor." Politically, the rise of the absentee owners and their overseers had meant oligarchy, not the small-d democracy Daniels hoped for. The "native Bourbon" had "steadily served the large propertied classes, absentee or local, in the exploitation of the South." Their thinking was "still patterned in that master-slave concept which in sense of superiority applied not only to slaves but to white men lacking slaves." The new "aristocrats in the South—and that is the name for both the Coca-Cola bottler and the member of the Society of Cincinnati—do not believe and never have believed that the people should—if they could—govern the South." Such opposition to democracy "leads to the unincorporated mill village and the company union. Included under it are both the kindliest paternalism and the most vicious and careless exploitation."[6] If there had ever been a moment in the post-emancipation South's history when master-slave thinking could have given way to something truly new, that moment had not been realized. The promise of democracy and social change remained unfulfilled.

Unrealized potential for change was the dominant theme of Daniels's angry Atlanta musings. It was an impression he had gotten not only from the city itself but also from the most exciting interview he had conducted there, one that, frustratingly, he was not allowed to use. All he dared extract from it was a "parable of our times in Atlanta and the South" that he placed as an opening vignette at the start of his Atlanta chapter, ironically titled "Overseer's Capital." It was a gossipy story that seemed, on the surface, to have nothing to do with plutocrats or an imagined, compensatory lynching on Paces Ferry Road.

The story began with a "young thing" arriving home from a party in a taxi without her date. Her aunt explains that she "ran upstairs weeping and threw herself down on the bed sobbing as if her heart would break." Eventually the young woman reveals the reason for her tears: "I've been insulted," she says.

Suddenly alarmed and ready to assemble the men of the family or even "reach for a shotgun myself," the aunt quickly learns that the "insult" was not the rape or attempted rape she feared but merely the smell of liquor on her niece's date's breath. "My God," she responds, "when I was coming along—that was about 1924—the only way a man could insult a woman was to try to pull her pants off and if she knew how to act it was some time before he got out of the hospital." The prim and proper niece "let out a wail at that." "God knows I can't understand these children growing up in Georgia now," the aunt concludes ruefully. "It's a different world."

"Certainly Atlanta is," Daniels confirms. "Long before I heard this parable of our times in Atlanta and the South from an Atlantan of my own age, a red-headed woman immaculate and immediate from the beauty parlor, I had concluded that. She clinched it."[7] She clinched it because, as Daniels was not allowed to mention, *she* was Margaret Mitchell.

As his placement of this anecdote suggests, a "parable" that Daniels could not discuss — that of Mitchell and her one-year-old blockbuster novel *Gone with the Wind* and the impact it was having on Americans' popular conceptions of the South — was part of the reason he found Atlanta's New South plutocracy so infuriating. Mitchell and her niece stood in implicit contrast to Calhoun School teacher Mary Chappell of Birmingham, whom he had seen as "representative of a new youngness and intelligence in the South." Socially conscious and intellectually engaged, Chappell was a "new belle," while the priggish niece seemed much more like the silly yet demanding belles of old.[8] Even though Mitchell forbade Daniels to write about their interview, she and her niece and another "young thing," Scarlett O'Hara, stayed on his mind as he considered how much had really changed in Atlanta and the so-called New South.

✦ ✦ ✦

BORN IN ATLANTA IN 1900, Margaret Mitchell was only seventeen months older than Jonathan Daniels and came from a similar background of wealth and social prominence. Her father, Eugene Mitchell, was a lawyer. Her mother, May Belle Stephens Mitchell, was a suffragist and a formidable society matron who had grown up on Atlanta's distinguished Jackson Hill. Margaret spent her first dozen years on Jackson Hill as well, until her family moved a few miles north to an even more elegant Peachtree Street address. Educated in local public schools and Atlanta's Washington Seminary, she left for Smith College in 1918 but came home a few months later when her mother died of the Spanish flu.

Compelled to remain in Atlanta after her mother's death, Mitchell made her formal debut in society in the winter of 1920. In 1922, she married one of her many beaus, Berrien Upshaw, but it turned out to be a bad match. Upshaw was an ill-tempered alcoholic who soon became physically abusive. A petite woman, 4 feet, 11 inches tall and weighing less than 100 pounds, Mitchell responded by buying a gun, which she kept on her bedside table for years, long after she and Upshaw divorced in 1924.[9]

In 1925, Mitchell married John Marsh, who had been Upshaw's best friend and, poignantly, the best man at her first wedding. Although many in their social circle found Marsh, a public relations specialist, exceedingly dull (and he was often sick and virtually always dyspeptic), he and Mitchell stayed together for the rest of her life.[10] Indeed, they seem to have grown ever more dependent on each other as they matured. No dashing Rhett Butler, Marsh provided the stability that Mitchell needed to be able to write her one epic novel, which she drafted almost in its entirety between 1926 and 1929.

In the early days of her disastrous first marriage, Mitchell had decided she needed her own income and got a job writing features for the *Atlanta Journal*'s Sunday magazine. She enjoyed the work and kept her job for nearly a year after she and John Marsh married, even though she felt some ambivalence about whether or not she should. Her father and her brother, Stephens Mitchell, had always opposed her employment, and most of her friends considered it unseemly for a married woman to work outside the home. The low pay and the misogyny of the newsroom were added disincentives. Mitchell boiled at her bosses' sexist diatribes and petty restrictions, such as the one that prohibited her from using the dictionary that was kept beside the city desk because the sight of her legs as she stood on tiptoe to reach it "upset" the male reporters.[11] Finally, in the spring of 1926, a badly sprained ankle that refused to heal persuaded her to resign. Mitchell never held another job and seems increasingly to have embraced the traditional gender roles of dutiful wife and daughter.

Yet, as a number of biographers and critics have argued, this was only a facade. Her public persona as a modest southern housewife who just happened to write one of the best-selling novels of all time belied her suppressed ambitions and internal struggle against the mores of white southern womanhood—a struggle in which she was hardly alone as she came of age in the 1920s. "In striking contrast to her later claims to satisfaction with southern life," writes historian Kathleen Clark, "Mitchell struggled throughout her adolescence and young adulthood to define an independent white female identity, a struggle that was nourished and ultimately stymied within the social order of Jim Crow."[12] Her own personality as well as that of her famous protagonist, Scarlett O'Hara, embodied many unresolved tensions, as a perceptive observer like Jonathan Daniels could recognize even in a first meeting. While most of the scholarship on Mitchell has emphasized either gender and sexuality issues or Mitchell's treatment of black characters and the history of slavery and Reconstruction, Daniels took in Mitchell whole. Lacking a vocabulary for gender analysis and sharing Mitchell's own racial paternalism, Daniels nonetheless wrote perceptively about her personality and political views in his journal. He intuitively discerned, if only telegraphically described, the internal conflicts that showed (or, more accurately, sounded) in Mitchell's outward demeanor. "Talks with the vulgarity

Margaret Mitchell, ca. 1938. *World-Telegram* photograph
by William F. Warnecke. *New York World-Telegram* & *Sun* Newspaper Photograph Collection, Library of Congress, Prints and
Photographs Division, Washington, D.C. [LC-USZ62-109613].

of newspaper women," he jotted in his notes.[13] It was his first indication that
the Margaret Mitchell of the 1920s — the "newspaper woman" — was still a
big part of the Mitchell he met in 1937. Nevertheless, like Atlanta and the
New South, she had not turned out quite as he might have hoped.

Along with her "vulgarity" and verbal swagger, Mitchell's deep conservatism was the characteristic that struck Daniels the most when he met her
on Saturday, June 5, 1937 — almost exactly one year after the publication of
Gone with the Wind had catapulted her to international fame. With the help
of a mutual friend, Daniels had managed to score an interview, but Mitchell
would not give him permission to write about it, either in a *Saturday Review
of Literature* article, as he had suggested, or in *A Southerner Discovers the South*.
Instead, she absolutely prohibited him to quote her or refer to her in any way.

The fact that Daniels was not supposed to write about Mitchell heightens the significance of the anecdote with which he began his Atlanta chapter. Why break his word unless there was some larger point he was trying to make? And what made the story of the niece "a parable of our times in Atlanta and the South"? The answer to that question seems to lie in the identification between a much more famous young woman, Scarlett O'Hara, and the city of Atlanta that Mitchell herself had invited. "Atlanta was of [Scarlett's] own generation," she had written. The city was "crude with the crudities of youth and as headstrong and impetuous as herself. . . . In a space of time but little longer than Scarlett's seventeen years, Atlanta had grown from a single stake driven in the ground into a thriving small city . . . Moreover, there was something personal, exciting about a town that was born—or at least christened—the same year she was christened."[14]

Forced to keep his storyteller anonymous, Daniels forged a similar identification between Atlanta and the unidentified niece. But to truly understand Mitchell's "parables" of her niece and of Scarlett would have required a more thorough understanding of white southern women's struggle to carve out a new gender role—to define a "new belle" identity—than Daniels possessed. His interview with Mitchell irritated more than it enlightened him. In part, this was because, by 1937, Mitchell was feeling pretty irritable herself.

"MARGARET MITCHELL STILL LIVES in [an] apartment . . . and still has a party line telephone," Daniels marveled in his journal. John Marsh answered when he called and "told me he would go to Mrs. Marsh's office which does not have a telephone and get in touch with me within an hour." No one was allowed to know where Mitchell's office was "except her husband and a good secretary." She "has a couch there," Daniels learned, "so that she can sleep in the afternoons [and] escape from callers."[15]

In truth, however, Mitchell had found little escape from publicity and social obligations, particularly answering letters, for a whole long year, and there were several more such years to come. Even before *Gone with the Wind*'s official release date of June 30, 1936, word had gotten out that she and her publisher, Macmillan, had a hot property on their hands. In April 1936, the Book-of-the-Month Club had selected the novel for its July offering, delaying publication for a month and heightening anticipation still further. In May, Kay Brown, the New York agent of Hollywood producer David O. Selznick, had acquired page proofs and, after reading the novel over the telephone long-distance to actor Ronald Coleman, who was as deeply moved as she was, she advised Selznick to "DROP EVERYTHING AND BUY IT."[16] Although the premiere of the film version of *Gone with the Wind*, with the even greater fanfare it brought, was still two and a half years away when Daniels telephoned Mitchell's apartment, he was fortunate to find her husband so accommodating. Just a few weeks earlier, on May 4, 1937, it had been announced that Mitchell's novel had won a Pulitzer Prize. One year, one Pulitzer, and 1.7 million sales into the *Gone with the Wind* phenomenon, an out-of-town journalist who was less well connected than Daniels might not have received a return phone call.[17]

"Half an hour later Margaret Mitchell calls me up and invites me to lunch at the Athletic Club," Jonathan wrote in his journal, almost as if he were telling the story over cocktails among friends. "Her husband could not come as he had to finish working on details of Polish (or some such) rights for G W the W — M. M. says agents are not to be trusted — they are merely brokers not really agents — and her father and husband have to watch to see that all the fillings are not stolen from her teeth." It was the first of several, rather churlish references to money that Daniels recorded disapprovingly.

Mitchell "is a very small woman," he wrote, and "red headed though I cannot swear it is natural." She "had just come from the beauty parlor." Showing no appreciation for the square jaw, pointed chin, and expressive face that intrigued others or the striking eyes that seemed to change from gray to violet to blue depending on her mood, Daniels judged Mitchell "a plain little thing but attractive and in morality rather than in vice [as] hard as nails."[18]

The observation was cryptic enough to be misleading: it was not Mitchell's "morality" that interested Daniels so much as her hardness. Perhaps her swaggering talk did raise questions of vice and virtue, for in 1937 what more familiar model was there for a hard-talking woman than the prostitute, the gun moll, or the fallen angel of the dime novel and Hollywood screen? But to say that Mitchell was hard "in morality rather than in vice" was merely to set aside such images. Though Daniels did not use the word, a decade or so earlier, when he and Mitchell had both been a good bit younger, there had been another persona, the "flapper," who might very well embody the seeming contradiction of being essentially virtuous and yet "hard as nails." *The Hard-Boiled Virgin* was the title that another best-selling Atlanta novelist writing in the 1920s, Frances Newman, chose for a 1926 book featuring such a character. Surely, as he listened to Mitchell produce such daring words as "pants" and "S. O. B.," the former "Dice" Daniels could recognize a Jazz

Age and newsroom sensibility, however indelicate or perpetually surprising it might seem in a woman, especially one so "immaculate and immediate from the beauty parlor."[19]

As Daniels may or may not have known, even after the publication of *Gone with the Wind*—and a full decade after she seems to have settled down into more conventional gender roles—Mitchell considered herself "a product of the Jazz Age, being one of those short-haired, short-skirted, hard-boiled young women who preachers said would go to hell or be hanged before they were thirty." She had shocked Atlanta society with her behavior and dress during her debutante days, most famously in a sexually charged dance routine that she and a beau had performed at a charity ball in the spring of 1921. Copied from a Rudolph Valentino film, the "Apache Dance" was supposed to depict an Indian brave's violent seduction of his mate and included slapping and other rough play. Mitchell and her partner "threw one another around like rag dolls," a society columnist reported. "Margaret would hit the floor with a thump," then crawl back to her man in submission, and her partner also kissed her passionately onstage. Mitchell's father was appalled and thought the dance "a little too—strenuous is the only word," the columnist euphemized.[20] But Mitchell was a modern woman—or had been and still claimed to be in the late 1930s, even after her novel was published. As such, she was "a little embarrassed," as she told one correspondent, at finding that the publication of *Gone with the Wind* had made her "the incarnate spirit of the old South!"[21]

And yet Mitchell had written of the Old South with admiration if also with realism—the aspect of her carefully researched novel that *she* tried most to emphasize. "However lousy the book may be as far as style, subject, plot, characters, it's as accurate historically as I can get it," she wrote to respected newspaper editor Julian Harris. "I didn't want to get caught out on anything that any Confederate Vet could nail me on, or any historian either."[22] All her life, Confederate veterans and local historians including her father had been a big part of Mitchell's cultural milieu. "I had thought for years of the historical background but not in connection with putting it into a book," she wrote to another correspondent, Norman Berg, Macmillan's representative in Atlanta. "It was not so much that I thought of this background as that I was raised up on it. . . . And of course I had always thought the campaign between Johnston and Sherman the most dramatic of the war. So that day when I sat down to write I did not have to bother about my background for it had been with me all my life."[23] The Civil War and Reconstruction background, as understood and interpreted by white Atlantans, was "with her," regardless of how much of a flapper or "newspaper woman" she might become.

And therein lay the contradiction. Margaret Mitchell was "part and parcel of the Southern Scott Fitzgerald era . . . of Frances Newman and The Hardboiled Virgin . . . of the rebellion of young southern women against the mores and patterns and restrictions of the past," as Berg reflected in a 1962 memorandum. "She was the flaming flapper of the 20s" and "yet an unreconstructed southerner."[24] While critics of a later era might debate Berg's adjective (some denouncing *Gone with the Wind* as racist and retrograde, while others argue that Mitchell was more "reconstructed" than many of her white southern contemporaries), the paradox still holds. Both Mitchell herself and her book blended new attitudes and old ideals in ways that seem contradictory and ultimately untenable.

And so, the most interesting question about Mitchell was not about "morality"—especially not for Daniels, who was no conventional moralist—but about what lay behind her "hard as nails" persona and strutting tongue. What did a Jazz Age demeanor actually mean? Mitchell's generation, which was also Daniels's, may have been "the coarsest since the restoration"—words Mitchell attributed to her niece "with mincing voice" in response to what she said about how women of her generation handled "insults."[25] But to what extent had her generation's coarseness—or, more generously, its rebellion against stifling Victorian propriety—promoted a greater liberality of spirit? What did it mean to be a "so-called free modern," as Daniels had asked himself at various times in various words?[26]

It was in relation to this sort of question that Mitchell struck Daniels as not only "hard" but also rigid and petty. It was a question that did, ultimately, matter in relation to race and politics—although Daniels was as little troubled by the racial stereotypes and biased depictions of slavery and Reconstruction in Mitchell's novel as most other contemporary white readers, with the exception of committed leftists. Indeed, Daniels thought it "absurd . . . for Communist critics to condemn 'Gone with the Wind' because the mammy part did not conform to Communist ideas of the dignity in independence of the Negro race."[27] For him, the question of Mitchell's political and racial views was broader and vaguer than the question of how she portrayed former slaves or Reconstruction-era politicians. It was a question of her own character—a question that he never fully articulated but on which he seems, based on the notes in his journal, to have judged Mitchell wanting.

"M.M. has as her ideal the man of property type," Daniels wrote critically, "and she is a hard little holder on to property," as her frequent references to money showed. "My guess is that while she may lack Scarlett's looks her heroine was never more hard headed than herself."[28]

It was an insult, an offhand comparison that Daniels would have acknowledged to be overly simplistic, and yet it did contain a kernel of truth. Scarlett O'Hara is definitely a hard-headed heroine. She begins Mitchell's novel as a self-absorbed, willful child interested only in her own romantic obsession with Ashley Wilkes, who does not return her affection and marries Melanie Hamilton instead. Across more than 1,000 pages, Scarlett is forced by the exigencies of the Civil War and Reconstruction to learn to survive. Yet she becomes only *more* self-centered, materialistic, grasping, while remaining thoroughly insensitive to other people's feelings and incapable of understanding their thoughts. "Hard as a hickory nut" since childhood, she becomes "hard as nails" in her effort to survive.[29] She is not above lying, seducing men for their money, employing convict labor, or deliberately hurting others to get what she wants, and she is more successful at turning a profit than any man in the novel except Rhett Butler.

It is the all-knowing Rhett who best articulates the novel's major theme, survival, specifically an amoral survival of the fittest. "This isn't the first time the world's been upside down, and it won't be the last," he tells Scarlett. Such upheaval has "happened before and it'll happen again. And when it does happen, everyone loses everything and everyone is equal. And then they all start again at taw, with nothing at all. That is, nothing except the cunning of their brains and the strength of their hands." Those who "have neither cunning nor strength or, having them, scruple to use them . . . go under," Rhett continues, "and they should go under. It's a natural law and the world is better off without them."[30]

Of course, Rhett expects Scarlett to be one of those "hardy few who come through" and admires her for it, realizing only too late that she is too self-centered to be capable of returning his love. For, although Scarlett is hardy, she cannot avoid becoming *hardened* as she uses her strength and especially her cunning to carry herself and her family, including her loyal slaves, through the hardest of times. A "shell of hardness" begins "to form about her heart" when she collapses in the garden at Twelve Oaks, in the famous scene when she vows, "as God is my witness," never to be hungry again.[31]

Along with the book's romance, drama, and compelling characters, Mitchell's theme of survival resonated with her Depression-era audience. She had used every "known and proved device to stir sentiment and sobs," but the "real stroke of genius," wrote one perceptive early reader, "is in the

story of Scarlett's struggles to survive—it is the story of thousands of young
(& older) women during the depression. It is so very *modern*—and yet it is
set in the most romantic period of America's past. . . . *It is a very modern story.*
Thousands of women have lived it since the crash in October, 1929."[32]

Written almost entirely before the crash, the novel's modernity sprang,
as biographer Darden Asbury Pyron has argued, from a different source.
Gone with the Wind's critical scene mirrored "the most critical episode" of
Mitchell's childhood.[33] It was a connection she herself explained in a letter
to historian Henry Steele Commager after he reviewed the novel in the *New
York Herald Tribune*. "And how happy I was that you were impressed enough
by Rhett's remarks about the upside-down world to quote them in full," she
wrote. "For in that paragraph lies the genesis of my book and that genesis lies
years back when I was six years old and those words . . . were said to me."

> They were said to me not by a materialist but by . . . an idealist with a
> very wide streak of common sense, my mother. I didn't want to go to
> school. . . . I saw no value at all in an education. And Mother took me
> out on the hottest September day I ever saw and drove me down the
> road toward Jonesboro—"the road to Tara" and showed me the old
> ruins of houses where fine and wealthy people had once lived. . . .
>
>   And she talked about the world those people had lived in, such a
> secure world, and how it had exploded beneath them. And she told me
> that my own world was going to explode under me, some day, and God
> help me if I didn't have some weapon to meet the new world. She was
> talking about the necessity of having an education, both classical and
> practical. For she said that all that would be left after a world ended
> would be what you could do with your hands and what you had in your
> head.

Unlike Rhett Butler, Mitchell's mother, the woman suffragist, added an explicitly gendered point to her story (which was truly a parable). "The strength
of women's hands isn't worth anything," she said, "but what they've got in
their heads will carry them as far as they need to go."[34]

Gone with the Wind was "a very modern story" that "thousands of women
had lived," but they had lived it in good economic times as well as bad. It
was the story of a woman's coming of age and trying to establish an independent identity that was at odds with women's—specifically, elite white
southern women's—traditional, dependent role. Scarlett's biography was
both a timeless tale and a Jazz Age story of "the flaming flapper" who was

nevertheless "an unreconstructed southerner." Mitchell's protagonist was no ideal but rather a vicarious experiment in living and being, both for many readers and for the author herself.

In her voluminous correspondence, Mitchell always discussed Scarlett's character with ambivalence. "My central woman character does practically every thing that a lady of the old school should not do. And so do many of the characters," she wrote to an older friend, Julia Collier Harris, two months before the novel was released. "But whatever their shortcomings they are the shortcomings of strength and exuberant health and tough mental fibres. For when I look back on the survivors of those hard days of war and reconstruction they all impressed me as a remarkably tough bunch of people. I don't mean tough in the modern slang meaning of the word. But tough in its older meaning, hard, resistant, strong. The old ladies were certainly not lavender and old lace ladies. They had more drive at eighty than their children and grandchildren."[35]

After the novel came out and many readers criticized Scarlett for her lack of morals, Mitchell started making more of a point to distance herself from her heroine but continued to reject harsh moral judgments of her. "Thank you for your kind words about poor Scarlett," she wrote to a reviewer who had been especially sympathetic. "It never occurred to me . . . that such a storm of hard words would descend upon the poor creature's head. She just seemed to me to be a normal person thrown into abnormal circumstances and doing the best she could, doing what seemed to her the practical thing." In this letter, Mitchell separated her character from her historical setting, suggesting the traits she had seen in "the survivors of those hard days of war and reconstruction" came from within, regardless of historical circumstances. "The normal human being in a jam thinks, primarily, of saving his own hide," she wrote, and Scarlett "valued her hide in a thoroughly normal way."[36]

If Scarlett O'Hara is a social Darwinist's darling—a natural or "normal human being" concerned primarily with her own survival—she is not the only woman in Mitchell's book. Her alter ego, Melanie Wilkes, is singularly admirable, except for her feminine weakness, which predetermines her death from a miscarriage near the novel's end. Melanie was "so honorable that she could not conceive of dishonor in others," as Mitchell explained to one correspondent, and Scarlett's mother, Ellen O'Hara, was another of the "wonderful women of the Old South."[37] Yet Ellen, too, dies in the novel, a victim of her own benevolence when she catches typhoid while nursing a poor white neighbor. She performs the duties of the southern lady to deadly perfection, but even she has a guilty secret: a girlhood romance that she has successfully hidden until deathbed delirium gives her away. The implication is that her southern ladyhood has been something of an act all along, not her true or whole self. Only for the saintly Melanie have the role and the self been inseparable, and her death, even more than Ellen's, leaves Scarlett completely bereft. "Suddenly it was as if Ellen were lying behind that closed door, leaving the world for a second time," Mitchell wrote. "Suddenly [Scarlett] was standing at Tara again with the world about her ears, desolate with the knowledge that she could not face life without the terrible strength of the weak, the gentle, the tender hearted."[38] Melanie, the softest of all women and one who would never have survived if Scarlett had not been so hard, turns out to have been crucial for Scarlett's survival as well. Becoming as hard as nails has made Scarlett unhappy and unlovable, as her desertion by her true love, Rhett Butler, in the book's final scene underscores. Though Scarlett holds out hope that she can get Rhett back, there is nothing but uncertainty in the book's closing words, Scarlett's oft-repeated mantra that "tomorrow is another day."

✦ ✦ ✦

ALTHOUGH JONATHAN DANIELS recognized that both Margaret Mitchell and Scarlett O'Hara were "hard-headed," he did not ponder whether, in the South's stultifying, patriarchal culture, ambitious women had to be in order to survive. In truth, he was never as interested in Scarlett as in Tara. Writing in the early 1940s, he remembered that when he "first read the story of Tara" (a novel most readers consider the story of Scarlett), he was very much impressed "that a woman novelist should speak of the furrows on the Georgia hill farms where life seemed, as she wrote it, so good." Mitchell had described hill-country plowing with unusual attention to detail. "She spoke of the fresh-cut furrows of red Georgia clay. They were not cut at Tara . . . in the long, straight furrows of the flat fields of middle Georgia or in the lush black earth of the coastal plantations." To prevent soil erosion, "the rolling foothills" at Tara "were plowed in a million curves."[39]

   In other words, Daniels appreciated the care Mitchell had taken in differentiating the various landscapes in the South. Even when he read novels, it was the *real* South he cared about most. Like other writers and intellectuals of the Southern Renaissance, Daniels wanted to jettison the romanticism of the plantation myth that had dominated southern literature and continued to play out in American popular culture, particularly in advertising and

Hollywood films. He complained about the fact that, "like cotton, Southern literature is for the export trade." "Almost anything can happen to a book about the South except to be read in the South." he wrote pithily in 1936. But was the South "uniquely romantic," as readers elsewhere seemed to think? "I doubt it," he said, explaining that his southern neighbors were like "all men everywhere so far as I have been able to judge." Jeeter Lester of Erskine Caldwell's *Tobacco Road* "is a true picture of a man," he added, "but with slight differences in stage set he might be found living in a degradation and poverty as deep in Jersey as in Georgia."[40] So, too, Daniels might have argued, was Scarlett O'Hara a true picture of a woman who "with slight differences in stage set" could have been found someplace other than Tara. But Tara itself, with its red clay and contour plowing, was distinctive not just to Georgia but to a particular place within the state.

Daniels's reference to Jeeter Lester reflects the extent to which, in the mid-1930s, Caldwell's degraded sharecropper was a dominant—perhaps *the* dominant—cultural representation of the South. *Gone with the Wind* reinvigorated an older romantic image, and Daniels was just as astounded by the novel's popularity as other contemporary intellectuals. "Atlanta has demonstrated that if the Lost Cause is gone with the wind, it still sells like Coca-Cola," he jeered (a line that, in context, made the city of Atlanta a stand-in for Mitchell).[41]

A few years later, Daniels would still be thinking about the comparison between *Gone with the Wind* and *Tobacco Road* and the enormous popularity of these two fictional representations. He considered both somewhat realistic and somewhat romantic. One was a romance of the high and mighty, the other a dark romance of the lowest of the low. "Nearly five years ago Scarlett O'Hara began to get into America's head beside Jeeter Lester," he wrote. "Both are still there. Out of Georgia have come the two best-known symbols for the South. And one is about as typical as the other." Neither Jeeter nor Scarlett should be taken as representative, but both were useful in their way. "It is the miracle of the South that both are true. . . . As outside limits they provide the possibility of understanding the South and understanding it whole." For, as Daniels argued, the "dramatic thing about the South today is that not only in literature but in life, the distance between grandeur and the gutters is absolute but a remarkably short way all the same."

It was the same complaint he had leveled against the city of Atlanta: the distance from the palaces to the slums was "too brief and too far." Similarly, *Gone with the Wind* and *Tobacco Road* "were each of them extreme legends of the right and the left in our emotions." The real and diverse people of the real and diverse South existed somewhere "between obscene legends and elegant ones." It was up to readers to make sense of it all. "Sensible people, of course, know that Jeeter Lester is not Georgia or the South, just as they know that Scarlett never was the South, nor Ashley nor Rhett nor any little group of the others. But if romance serves dignity, it is well. We need it. If realism makes us aware that men lack dignity and decency, that is good too. . . . The writers have given us the symbols but it is the job of the readers to make sense — a sense for everybody in being as well as in print."[42]

Unfortunately, few readers paid as much attention to the plowing and other elements of realism in Mitchell's epic as he had. "Nobody listened," he complained, when she observed that "life in the county of Clayton around Tara was, by aristocratic low country standards, even in 1861 'a little crude' at its best." The luxurious film version of *Gone with the Wind* was completely unrealistic, and Daniels wisely considered it even more responsible than the novel for making the story of Scarlett O'Hara into a paean to the Lost Cause. But Mitchell was responsible also; she had contributed mightily to an "emotional revival of faith in that old gone South." It was especially regrettable that her backward-looking novel had appeared and become popular when it did, "almost at the same time that the country re-elected Roosevelt to continue change in our times which seemed a wind blowing, too, to some of the comfortable and content."[43]

MITCHELL "SAYS SHE was content with her life, her husband, her apartment and does not mean to give them up," Daniels wrote in his journal after the interview. Yet their conversation also revealed her deep discontent with the current state of politics. "She feels that [the] present theory of government is to destroy just such people as herself and her family, people of property, and to lift up and exalt the propertyless." She "does not like paying so much of her money in income taxes to go to [the] TVA to destroy her husband's job. [It is an] important job, she insists, with 60 people working under him. [She] keeps reiterating his importance as if it were in doubt comparatively."[44]

John Marsh's job was with the Georgia Power Company, where he was the director of the publicity department. As such, he was thoroughly caught up in the politics of the Depression-era public versus private utilities debate. While Daniels considered the TVA a blessing for the South, Marsh and Mitchell opposed it. The fact that she explained her opposition in terms of her husband's job security seemed a bit self-centered. Daniels disliked

Mitchell for being "a hard little holder on to property," just like Scarlett O'Hara. Though by no definition a feminist, he also felt uncomfortable about her apparent need to puff up her husband, a trait for which she was notorious among Atlanta friends.[45]

Jonathan Daniels was an astute observer and captured much of Mitchell's personality. But he could not know that her anti-New Deal politics would become increasingly reactionary over the remaining twelve years of her life. Always protective of her privacy, Mitchell rarely spoke out in public, but friends saw her rightward trend. "I practiced silence during Margaret's vituperative denunciations of FDR and all his works," fellow southern writer Clifford Dowdey later recalled. When Roosevelt tried to "purge" conservative southern senator Walter F. George by endorsing a more liberal candidate in Georgia's 1938 Democratic primary, Mitchell and her husband responded by supporting a racist demagogue, Eugene Talmadge, in the three-way race.[46]

After 1938, as the newly formed House Un-American Activities Committee became a force to be reckoned with, Mitchell kept a private "Red" file on other southern intellectuals such as Lillian Smith and Katharine Du Pre Lumpkin. She took up the cry of anti-Communism with a passion, not least because left-leaning critics had so thoroughly castigated her book. From the moment of the novel's publication, "the Communists, the Left Wingers, the Pinks and the Liberals loathed me and my works, and, even after ten years, a Mr. David Platt on the *Daily Worker* scarcely lets a week go by without writing an anti-'Gone with the Wind' editorial," she complained to a Macmillan executive in 1948. Even more insidious, to her mind, was the way in which "ultra radical statements about 'Gone With the Wind' and the South which appeared in publications such as the Daily Worker in 1936 traveled toward the Right and by 1946 were appearing as newly hatched ideas in the Saturday Review of Literature, Harper's and magazines heretofore considered conservative." Although she acknowledged that "it's the style to low-rate 'Gone With the Wind,'" she wanted to set the record straight on its initial reception among the intellectual elite. In 1936, the "sudden skyrocketing sale" of the book and "the good words of the big critics" had "caught our Left Wing friends off their balance," she told a correspondent, "and it was several weeks before The Nation and the New Republic and the Daily Worker et cetera could unlimber and get into action about this Fascist anti-Negro book, this false picture of the South, this distorted retelling of the 'plantation myth' et cetera."[47]

Though Mitchell might have sneered at Daniels's vague characterization of *Gone with the Wind* as "an extreme legend of the right," she could at least appreciate the extent to which his liberal ideas were grounded in a shared love for their native land. She heartily agreed with his view that the South had long suffered from economic injustices—"tariff, freight rates, etc."—though her term for it, "economic slavery," took his and others' colonial economy argument to a further extreme than he would have himself. "There is a good paragraph on this subject in Jonathan Daniels's 'A Southerner Discovers the South,'" Mitchell wrote to her friend Dowdey. "It's where he compares the South with Carthage and remarks that the Romans, after all, were politer than the Northern conquerors, for after they had sown Carthage with salt they never rode through it on railroad trains and made snooty remarks about the degeneracy of the people who liked to live in such poor circumstances. Please read that paragraph," Mitchell concluded, cautioning Dowdey (though he was more liberal than she was) that "you may not like the rest of the book."[48]

Certainly she did not like it, but how could she? Even during the interview, Mitchell had found Daniels interesting but thought their political ideas were "diametrically opposite," as she confided to another friend, Herschel Brickell. "I do my best to be polite to the opinions of Leftwingers and to be as tolerant as possible, for I expect tolerance of my own opinions," she explained. "However," she admitted, "occasions arose" during the interview "when, instead of being the retiring Southern gentlewoman, I made such crude remarks as 'applesauce.'"

As for seeing that Daniels had, in fact, used part of the interview despite their agreement, Mitchell was furious. "I am back on my hind legs pawing the air, wondering how many other people will recognize me if you did," she wrote to Brickell—although apparently she had little to worry about, given that only one review of *A Southerner Discovers the South* publicly identified her. Mitchell told Brickell she had avoided discussing Daniels's book with anyone because she "was bursting with wrath about it." He had been "under no misapprehension about not quoting me," she added. "I had thought I could rely upon his word, but it seems these days when honor is up against money or good copy, honor very naturally bites the dust."[49]

Perhaps most infuriating of all, Mitchell had caught a glimpse of Daniels's private thoughts about her, including her hardness. After the interview, Jonathan wrote to their mutual friend, Hunt Clement, to thank him for his help in securing it. He included a few lines about his impressions of Mitchell's "very interesting character," not considering the possibility that Clement might forward his letter to Mitchell. The letter remains among Mitchell's papers, and she quoted from it in her letter to Brickell. "Mr. D's opinions" had not been very flattering. He had said she had "'a mind that seemed to me to be as hard and definitely formed as a jewel.' You may gather from this that the young man did not think too highly of me," she wrote Brickell, adding, "It will be a cold day in August before I meet any other writer."[50]

Jonathan had to know that using Mitchell's anecdote, even anonymously, in *A Southerner Discovers the South* would annoy her and might even land him in legal trouble. He had thought her petty and paranoid—a celebrity author who felt in danger of having "all the fillings . . . stolen from her teeth." So why use the story, and what did he mean by it? Certainly, his intentions are less than perfectly clear. But his reflections on another young white woman, Mary Chappell, plus his tendency to equate Mitchell with Scarlett and Scarlett with Atlanta and the New South offer some clues. Here, in a story about a sacred subject, alcohol (the subject on which he had first decisively broken with his father in his own desire to be "modern"), Daniels found a young woman, the niece, who was *not* representative of "a new youngness and intelligence in the South." Nor, as the rest of his chapter showed, was the city of Atlanta. Just as Margaret Mitchell was somehow both a "flaming flapper of the 20s" and "yet an unreconstructed southerner," so the capital of the New South was an "Overseer's Capital." Ruled by an oligarchy and home to the new revival of the old plantation myth, Atlanta revealed a South that seemed almost impervious to political and cultural change.

— CHAPTER TEN —

The Newly Exciting Question of the Possibility of Democracy

✦

FROM ATLANTA TO

RALEIGH, NORTH CAROLINA

ONATHAN DANIELS peeled out of Atlanta before dawn on the morning of June 6 with the goal of completing his southern tour as quickly as he could. He visited the federal cemetery at Andersonville, Georgia, site of a notorious Confederate prison camp, to satisfy his own curiosity. He doubted whether the place had "the least significance so far as the present South is concerned." A 150-foot-deep gulley near the town of Lumpkin was more relevant, showing at its worst the problem of soil erosion in the older plantation districts where cotton had been king. The result of such intensive, single-crop agriculture was that "no less than 61 per cent of the country's eroded lands are in its Southern regions," as Daniels gleaned from Howard Odum's 1936 masterwork of Regionalist sociology, *Southern Regions of the United States*. Attempting to replace the soil's lost nutrients with commercial fertilizers cost southern farmers $161 million a year—only slightly less than the entire South spent annually, he noted, "for the education of all its children," who needed a lot more education than they got.[1]

Nevertheless, Daniels did not see the South's children as hopeless; instead, their resilience inspired faith. "Perhaps it was only Sunday finery," he wrote in his journal, "but [the] whole people in this land looked well off to me—The women and children particularly." The dusty back roads around Andersonville and Lumpkin were full of families walking to church, all of whom "seemed handsome" to his eyes. "White girls dressed [the same] as white girls in New York and colored girls dressed [the same] as white girls—[a] Negro woman with white gloves and pocketbook to match!"[2] These people were "not at all wasting survivors or wasted remnants of a human order that had departed from depleted and eroded soil," Daniels asserted in *A Southerner Discovers the South*. The words were a warm-up for his final chapter, "Dixie Destination," where he would argue for the potential of the black and white southern masses to lead a "happy, productive, peaceful life, side by side," if given a chance to govern themselves.[3]

A brief for the freer exercise of democracy turned out to be the destination to which he had been guiding readers across thousands of miles and hundreds of pages. Although he drove on for a few more days through Florida and the Carolinas to get back home to Raleigh, Daniels's 1937 journey of discovery really culminated in Georgia. There, his anger at Atlanta's New South social divisions reinforced his commitment to the small-d democracy he had first learned from his father. But unlike Josephus, Jonathan included African Americans in his democratic vision. His political musings at the end of *A Southerner Discovers the South* were racially inclusive, even if they failed to explain how disfranchised black southerners were supposed to take part in a democratic revival that would prove challenging enough for poor whites.

To what extent Daniels himself would participate in contemporary efforts to bring social change was also an open question. The summer and fall of 1938 when his book appeared and became a best seller were a pivotal moment for Franklin Roosevelt and others who saw the opening up of southern politics as vital to the expansion of the New Deal. Given the uncertainties of the moment and Daniels's own ambivalence about integration and other possible consequences of democratic reform, it was highly appropriate that he opened his "Dixie Destination" chapter with the aspirational but inconclusive words "A traveler comes to destinations. Or hopes to."[4] The urgent question in 1938 was whether the "Dixie Destination" of a more racially inclusive and egalitarian political and social order could be reached, and if so, who would lead the way.

✦ ✦ ✦

THE "HANDSOME" Georgians Daniels wrote about in his journal on June 6, 1937, were among the very last people he "discovered" on his tour. His notes end on June 7 with his impressions of St. Petersburg, Florida, and he devoted only a scant twenty-four pages of his book to his final few days on the road. In fact, there is no evidence to confirm whether the route across Florida and up the Atlantic coast that appears on the map in *A Southerner Discovers the South* is actually the route he took to get home. His brief chapter on Charleston was based on a visit "in July," while other evidence indicates that he got back to Raleigh before June 15.[5] He left again soon thereafter, heading east to a vacation house on the North Carolina coast to write. Newspaperman that he was, Daniels worked quickly. He submitted his first five chapters to Macmillan and got an anonymous reader's report back by the end of August. The entire manuscript was ready by mid-December.[6]

Daniels was able to work fast because he often used the notes in his journal almost verbatim. Early chapters of *A Southerner Discovers the South* show some attempts at artistry, as well as thoughtful engagement with contemporary issues. Later chapters tend to be short and less well formed. When he got to "Graveyard and Gully," the chapter about Andersonville and Lumpkin, he copied whole passages from his notes, which meant his tribute to ordinary southerners' democratic potential was freighted with his most immediate and uncensored thoughts from the road. Some of his impressions seem less than laudatory; others, downright lascivious. For, on that early June morning, Jonathan had not been looking at "the people" so much as he was looking at *women*, most of whom were black. He had "never seen so many good looking colored women in my life." Some were "good looking after the white pattern—slim, fragile, mulatto," but he also saw "one big young woman who might have come out of a jungle—Her hair stood out from her head—she had on a blue blouse and a red skirt and she looked beautiful as what she was." Her beauty, vigor, and sex appeal made Daniels want to know more about "the racial differences in Negroes. Africa is as big as Europe," he wrote, "and there is probably as much difference among Africans as among Europeans—Certainly anybody who rides through back country Georgia and sees the different types must realize that the conventional flap-breasted, narrow butted, straight shanked Negro woman is merely the worst of an infinite variety . . . such creatures probably predominate because they accepted slavery without struggle. Indeed in Africa for centuries they may have been the slaves[,] drones and helots of handsomer and prouder people whose very pride made them poor survivors of the slave trade. —All these people seemed handsome to me."[7] Daniels's words were remarkably crass and even more insulting to African Americans in general than his description of Victor Turner back in Tuskegee had been. And yet, he presumably meant what he wrote in his own private journal: the South's people in all their variety did seem handsome to his eyes. In the end, they were where his hopes for the region's future must rest.

Though he used the same ugly descriptions of black women's appearance in *A Southerner Discovers the South*, Daniels turned the published account of his impressions of the Georgia folk into yet another rebuttal of Erskine Caldwell's influential caricatures. "The roads of Georgia are not considered

Alfred Eisenstaedt took this photograph of an African American woman
and her daughter walking to Sunday school while he was traveling with
Jonathan Daniels for a *Life* magazine photo-essay on *A Southerner Discovers
the South* in the summer of 1938. Though they were in the Mississippi
Delta, perhaps the scene reminded Daniels of the women and children
he had admired—but also described insultingly in his journal—
in Georgia the previous year. Alfred Eisenstaedt/Pix Inc./
The LIFE Picture Collection/Getty Images.

Pomander Walks," he wrote. "Indeed, Erskine Caldwell has made them
seem instead grisly ways to the bone pile." But, if the Georgia road he
traveled "was any sample," then "the triangular-breasted Negroes and the
squirrel-mouthed whites are rare in the South as they have always been rare
in a world of vain and vigorous folk everywhere anxious to love and eat."[8]
Or, as he put it in his "Dixie Destination" chapter, in contrast to the degenerate stereotypes, the real people of the South were "awaking, scratching at
new desires." It was from this "scratching" that the "newly exciting question
of the possibility of democracy" derived.[9]

"Is democracy possible in the South?" Daniels asked. In terms of the human material on which it must be based—the innate qualities of black and white southerners—he believed that it was. "White men and black men have shared the South's too little for a long time," he wrote, "and, though there is more than a casual connection between hunger and lynchings, they have shared it in relative quiet, decency and peace." His words suggest that he had overcome or at least was overlooking his own doubts about white southerners' penchant for violence, which had peaked just a few months earlier in response to the lynching at Duck Hill.[10]

He had not overcome his preference for segregation. Daniels still believed that the blacks and whites who "shared" the South would and should remain socially apart. But, especially because he was writing for a national and not merely southern audience, he avoided the subject. Instead, like other Regionalist liberals of his day, he wrote as if blacks were to be equal partners in the determination of the South's future, ignoring racial divisions even as he linked class stratification and poverty to the undemocratic nature of southern politics. Black and white southerners "would be able to build a South in terms of the South's potentiality, if together they had a chance to make and share plenty" instead of being poor and misruled by oligarchs—the aristocrats and their "overseers" whose "capital" he had seen in Atlanta. The "saddest thing in the South is the fact that those at the top who do not believe in the intelligence of those at the bottom have not shown themselves capable of a leadership satisfactory to the people they assume to lead," he wrote. "The market for stuffed shirts is glutted. Finally, the people are not as disturbing as the patricians."[11]

Meanwhile, the "most encouraging thing" in the contemporary South was "that the ordinary Southern whites, given fair chance and training, are showing themselves capable of performing the best types of work." The TVA had "discovered" this fact, and other employers were discovering it of the millions of black as well as white southern migrants who had moved north or west and "been able to compete with the workers already on the ground."[12] Daniels had already noted the fact that, by 1930, "the South had sent 3,500,000 people to other regions."[13] These migrants of the southern diaspora, who included at least twice as many whites as African Americans, were "of course, inadequately trained, inadequately skilled." But they were "capable of vastly more training than they possess."[14] They simply needed opportunities, and they needed them *in the South*.

Planning for the South's future must begin with these ordinary working people who were proving themselves capable—and restless. Southern labor was not docile, as promoters and industrialists courting northern capital liked to claim. Daniels hoped for democracy against the alternative possibility of a demagogue. If the southern people had to "depend for guidance in government" on a "plutocrat, demagogue, or professor," he would choose the professor but anticipated that the people and their "scratching" would ultimately matter most. Jonathan had come around on the question of federal intervention in the South to the point where he unreservedly hoped to see an extension of New Deal planning. He acknowledged that "the materials" for developing a "new plan for the South" had "grown at the University of North Carolina in a huge, wise book," Odum's *Southern Regions of the United States*. An "ordered program" for the South must focus on expanding public education and improving public health and welfare. But in the end, he believed, "the new Southern plan will grow more directly from itching than from statistics."[15]

From what he could see, it was not really the planners and "not the Communists who are coming but the advertisers." The "capitalists, absentee and local," who wanted wages to remain low in the South and the capitalists "who are concerned for sales in the South" did not "seem to be acting in perfect unity" in this regard. "Even the power companies, incited by the TVA," were "filling the tow-heads and the burr-heads with glittering dreams"— dreams of joining the modern world. The South's rickety cabins were "wall papered with the pages of newspapers and magazines" full of unattainable products. Even if "all of those who see the walls cannot read them, all of them can desire. If they lack the money, they can wish for it. They can be dissatisfied with the old Do-Without Plan of the Southern regions of the United States. They are."[16]

Writing at the end of 1937, Daniels could not foresee the changes in the South's economy that would come with World War II, much less the impact of postwar prosperity and the building up of the nation's military-industrial complex. Instead, he felt the black and white southern masses had reached a "big-eyed stage" and faced "the prospect of plenty with more wish than way" at present. But wishing and dreaming were important, and if they were not held back by antidemocratic Bourbons or misled by demagogues, southerners who wanted to take part in a modern, consumer society could succeed in transforming their native land.[17]

Finally, the removal of obstacles from without must accompany the removal of oligarchs and demagogues from within. Any plan "for a new, free, fed, housed, happy South must include not merely program at home for improvement but also program in the nation for the relinquishment of advantages elsewhere over the South." The advantages Daniels named were freight rates and tariffs that benefited the industrialized North at the still-agricultural South's expense. These were the "imperial advantages which New England took as its loot after the Civil War." But now the South was starting to escape its colonial economy and needed to be allowed to do so. Daniels also wanted an end to Yankee condescension—a recognition that "the poverty of the South" was "part of the same civilization as Harvard and in a measure . . . the creation of the same people. Cato did not ride through Carthage" after its Roman conquerors planted its fields with salt "and blame its condition on the Carthaginians. That much only I ask of the Yankees."[18]

"A good deal more is necessary for the Southerners," Daniels wrote in his final paragraph. "But planning in the South must begin at the bottom where so many of its people are. There is no handle on its top by which it can be lifted." Everyone in the South—"the tyrants and the plutocrats and the poor"—needed instruction. "All are in the warm dark, and whether they like it or not—white man, black man, big man—they are in the warm dark together. None of them will ever get to day alone."[19]

✦ ✦ ✦

PUBLISHED ON JULY 12, 1938, *A Southerner Discovers the South* was reviewed widely and prominently—so prominently that the *Richmond Times-Dispatch*, edited by Daniels's friend Virginius Dabney, remarked that there had "been no such critical reception for any book in recent years." Plus, "the reviewers who presented these critiques were overwhelmingly favorable in their judgments. The consensus of several was that the book was the best which had been written about the modern South."[20]

Writing mostly for northern publications, white southern reviewers particularly appreciated Daniels's balance—his "humility before some of the more perplexing problems which confront this section," as Dabney put it. Daniels did "not rail at everybody who disagrees with him, as the Communists and the ultra-reactionaries are wont to do. He is generally favorable to the TVA, but he recognizes that the town of Norris cost entirely too much money."[21] Lambert Davis, editor of the *Virginia Quarterly Review*, said much the same thing, claiming Daniels's distrust of "final solutions" allowed him "to write a book that is far richer and more humane than any dogmatic approach would have allowed." Davis went on to suggest that "anyone who has faced candidly the South's most overshadowing problem, the Negro, knows that there are only two final solutions, disappearance or amalgamation, neither of which is entertained as an immediate practical possibility by any large group." On the race question "and on all the others that confront the South Mr. Daniels works . . . within the limits of the possible. In this he displays a wisdom that I like to think is characteristically Southern, a kind of cheerful skepticism of the possibility of making the world over in the next five days."[22]

A Southerner Discovers the South "carries its social philosophy lightly," acknowledged another regional expert, former Agrarian H. C. Nixon. But Nixon saw more "attack" and "pointed judgment" in Daniels's book than did most reviewers. "Nuggets of apt comment" were scattered throughout, but "the general thesis" was to be found in the final chapter. "The one-crop South, the tariff-ridden South, the soil-eroded South is an economic colony, which has not realized its potentiality and which, in reality, has not yet had democracy," he summarized. The South "has had the distinct disadvantage of a large amount of absentee ownership. The absentee owners have wished to keep the South in its place, 'a place in the nation geographically similar to that of the Negro in the South,'" he quoted. These words, along with Daniels's bluntly stated rejection of "human inferiority explanations," were "embattled words for the digestion or indigestion of 'ineradicable Bourbons and Brigadiers who are devoted to class before region.'"[23]

Nixon was appreciative: "Here is faith in democracy in the South," he proclaimed. But he also remained a little skeptical of Daniels as "a sort of lone-wolf critic. He criticizes the South and criticizes those who criticize the South. . . . He hits out at professional Southerners . . . and likewise at Yankee invaders, whether of the military, economic, or missionary type." Ultimately, Nixon was not sure *what* to make of Daniels's all-purpose cynicism: whether or not *A Southerner Discovers the South* carried its "social philosophy" *too lightly* was an unstated question at the end of his review.[24]

Black critic Sterling A. Brown, by contrast, put more faith in Daniels's social critique. He considered "cracks at Yankee meddling" to be part of a strategic effort on Daniels's part to "disarm southern prejudices" while he took the South "severely to task." Although his "chats with Negroes are too few," Brown complained, Daniels was "almost always fair-minded and sympathetic. He repeats again and again the idea that 'the Negro was set free, in a manner of speaking,' and he resents contemporary injustice and exploitation."[25]

Several other black critics were equally or nearly as charitable in their assessment. Indeed, blacks' response was so favorable that it makes sense to see it as self-consciously diplomatic. Black intellectuals like E. Frederic

Morrow, who reviewed the book for the NAACP's *Crisis* magazine, could see how little Daniels actually said on the subject of racial equality. But Morrow also knew that allies had to be *cultivated*, and he was willing to praise Daniels as a "liberal and enlightened" white southerner.[26] Howard University law librarian A. Mercer Daniel was even more enthusiastic, lauding Daniels for "a voice that rises above prejudice."[27] Gertrude Martin of the *Chicago Defender* regretted that he "did not devote more of his attention to the Negro directly" but praised his effort to "look upon [the South's] many diverse aspects and . . . give a realistic picture of what he has seen."[28]

Perhaps the most interesting of all the black-authored reviews came from educator, writer, and poet Benjamin Brawley. Writing in the *Journal of Negro Education* a few months after the book appeared, Brawley echoed many white critics' appreciation for Daniels's "objective and at the same time so suggestive," yet always even-keeled approach. He "does not lose balance before present-day schemes that seek to usher in the millennium," Brawley wrote. Even more important, Daniels "constantly forces one to check up on his judgments, and more than once suggests what some previous writers have failed to say, that before the South finishes solving her problems the Negro's political status will have to receive new consideration."[29]

This was, indeed, an implication of Daniels's "Dixie Destination" chapter—if one chose to see it. Brawley was unusual among black reviewers in drawing so pointed a moral, but he was not alone in wanting to push Daniels's arguments to their fullest political potential. One of the most insightful and hardest-hitting reviews came from white Communist Rob F. Hall, a Mississippi native who had grown up in Mobile. Hall described the book as an "agreeable collection of essays on the South, held together by a roadmap." But he criticized Daniels for being a "liberal aristocrat" and therefore limited in perspective and lacking in revolutionary or even reformist zeal. There was "a quality of aloofness about his observations of the South" that "weakened" their value and made them "often false and frequently superficial." Daniels "falls down" as a social critic, Hall charged, because "try as he might," he had not "dismounted from the aloof pedestal of the aristocrat and become one of the people. And he simply doesn't have faith in them."[30]

Thus far, Hall's review differed little from one published a few months earlier in the leftist magazine *New Masses*. Reviewer Barbara Giles had described Daniels as "confused" and explained that his "anti-Yankee defensiveness" and "romanticism" accounted "for some of this confusion, regionalism for more of it."[31] Perhaps because of his own southern background, however, Hall was more sympathetic to Daniels as an honest inquirer. His breakfast with a democrat, David Lilienthal, "gives us a little light on the matter," Hall interpreted. Daniels was attracted to Lilienthal's truly democratic and even (in Hall's assessment of the TVA) socialistic vision, but he would not make "wise-cracking" remarks about it if he actually shared Lilienthal's beliefs. "I think Daniels believes in democracy, if not for itself at least as an alternative to fascism. But workers, farmers and the mass of people for whom democracy is a life and death matter—the people who will spill their blood for democracy—don't wisecrack about it," he wrote.

"Mr. Daniels' attitude toward the Negro" was "a 'civilized' attitude," Hall conceded. "He abhors lynching. He wants educational opportunities for the Negro people. He is careful to avoid either the position that the Negro people are a care-free, banjo-playing lot or that they are all dangerous animals." Daniels had "affection, admiration, sympathy" for blacks—"everything, in fact, but the respect which prevails between equals." His aloofness and, in Hall's view, his *liberalism* were emotional and political barriers. "To Mr. Daniels, the Negroes, like the workers, like the South, like the capitalists, contain both good and bad, the classic liberal answer to everything important."

"Only once," in Hall's view, "did Jonathan Daniels get close to the real issues in the South today. That was in his report of the 'angry collision' of Allen Tate and William R. Amberson at the meeting of the Southern Policy Committee high on Lookout Mountain." Hall recounted the episode and explained that the issue "of the impromptu debate" was whether the problems of landless tenants and farm laborers were to be solved "through organization into militant class unions, or through a retreat to the past without organization, depending solely on the paternalism of the ruling class." Hall, of course, sided with Amberson and organizing, but Daniels "dismisses the historic occasion" with his typical liberal rejection of extremism on either side. This liberal dodge was unacceptable. "It is precisely between these 'extremes,' democracy or fascism, that Southerners must choose, Mr. Daniels," Hall admonished. "Shall we, the Southern people, unite—labor, the farmers, the middle classes, Negro and white—to preserve and extend democracy? Or shall we surrender to the absentee owners of our lands and our industries and their agents who represent feudalism and fascism?" Daniels raised the question but tried to avoid answering it. Nevertheless, like Brawley and the other black reviewers who emphasized the positive, Hall was ready to hold out hope for a potential ally. "I fancy that Daniels will be in with us, with the people, on the final solution," he wrote. "He is too honest a man and too patriotic a Southerner to remain merely a liberal aristocrat."[32]

Given Giles's disdain and Hall's feeling that he had to *fight* for Daniels's wavering soul, it is ironic that the only other deeply critical review of *A Southerner Discovers the South* was that of Agrarian Frank Owsley. Owsley accused Daniels of "excessive amiability towards Marxians," among his many other complaints. Of course, his chief complaint was with how Daniels had portrayed the Agrarians, a source of irritation for Allen Tate as well. Tate did not write a review, but he did protest in a letter to Daniels. "I am just wondering what you have found anywhere in my writings — critical essays, verse, biographies — that you could possibly describe as coming out of the 'honey-dripping' school of the Old South," he wanted to know. He had experienced "a good deal of this from many sides," but from Daniels, whom he had met socially after moving to Greensboro, North Carolina, in early 1938, it felt personal. "There should never be this kind of misunderstanding at a dinner table. Alas, Jonathan, people simply do not like to be misrepresented!"[33]

Daniels wrote back to Tate quickly to pour oil upon the waters. "'Honey-dripping' certainly is an extreme word," he admitted, "but it stood in comparison with 'the soot of industrialism and the stink of collective loss of dignity' in the same paragraph. Also as you may have noted this swift, perhaps too swift characterization of the Agrarians is modified and qualified on page 115. . . . But, as for *misrepresenting*, Allen," he concluded, "that's another big, bad word. Misinterpret may be the word that properly fits and if you feel I misinterpreted, I'm sorry."[34]

Daniels would feel misinterpreted himself when James Rorty of the *Nation* wrote him a few weeks later to complain about how *he* was portrayed in one of the same chapters that irked Tate. "First, I am neither a liberal nor a sensationalist," Rorty wrote. "As you know, the word 'Sensationalist' is unfortunate when used in connection with a journalist." As for his politics, "I am a socialist in the sense that I take the socialist view of property relations. All my writings take this view and are sharply critical of the liberal-reformist position which I consider obsolete and ineffectual in this period." Like Tate, Rorty had to assume that Daniels had not really read his books and essays. Nor did he have a good grip on the true Allen Tate. Although Tate and his wife, novelist Caroline Gordon, "have never bothered to acquaint themselves with the basic economic and social facts of life in this country" and thus deserved a certain amount of "jesting," Rorty still found Daniels's account of Tate's side of the argument with Amberson "a bit *too* unsophisticated." If Tate actually made the "amazing statement" that Daniels attributed to him, then Rorty felt released "from any obligation to keep quiet about what happened in Marked Tree." Tate's concern that publicizing the incident "might endanger his job . . . and embarrass the liberal president of his college" had compelled Rorty to kill the story. "My reward has been that I have not heard from the Tates," who seemed to be snubbing him.[35]

As with Tate, Daniels apologized to Rorty if he had "misinterpreted your attitude." But he also thought it was "a very strange thing" that he had "made a more careful effort to get this story exactly right than any other story in the book. . . .Yet you and Tate are the only two people referred to in the whole book who have made a kick."[36] (Apparently, Daniels was unaware that Margaret Mitchell was "back on [her] hind legs pawing the air" and "bursting with wrath.")[37]

There were more private grumblings in response to *A Southerner Discovers the South* than the overwhelmingly favorable reviews in newspapers and magazines suggest. Daniels received both a great deal of fan mail and many angry rebuttals from white southerners who felt he had maligned the South in some way—or in every way. A letter from Mary L. Gullette, president of the Daughters of Maryland in New York, Inc., was representative of the criticism. "I am ashamed of you for writing such low tho[ugh]ts to place before the public as being the things a Southerner would see and expose," she wrote. After "overcoming war, havoc, destruction & magnificently rising above the almost impossible," the South's "fine people want to treasure memories of the beautiful & sacred traditions." For Daniels "to write such a book, showing your ordinary channels of expression," was "a great disappointment. . . . You ought to hide yourself," she scolded. "Southerners are not proud of you."[38]

Daniels's "low thoughts" and "ordinary channels of expression" were a problem for many readers, regardless of whether they aligned their preference for old-fashioned morals and manners with patriotic feelings about the South. Readers who knew Josephus and Addie Daniels often felt Jonathan had "betray[ed] his raisin'." A North Carolinian who had collaborated with Josephus on temperance campaigns insisted that "if Jonathan ain't ashamed of his drinking wine and liquor and beer I know his Daddy ain't proud of it, and he needn't have put it in a book."[39] But in fact, Josephus and Addie Daniels were rapturously proud of Jonathan's achievement. Both had "tears of pride and happiness that other people have discovered in you what we knew existed long ago." Josephus was "preening myself" and "strutting around because you dedicated your magnum opus to me," and Addie carried clippings of book reviews in her handbag to show friends.[40]

The complaint that Jonathan had "betrayed his raisin'" was one of more than a dozen "comments picked up at random" by Frances Doak, a friend who wrote Daniels that she "could send you pages of complimentary comments" but thought he might be more interested in "a compilation of the other kind." In addition to many concerns that the book was "coarse and obscene," her notes show contemporary readers' uncertainty about its political message. Doak herself wished Daniels had written as forcefully of those southerners who loved and admired President Roosevelt as he had of the "opinion of certain types of business men to the effect that Roosevelt is a demagogue." Readers needed to know that many southerners "love . . . and believe" in Roosevelt "almost as if he were a god."

Precisely what Daniels *was* trying to say about Roosevelt and the New Deal was difficult for some readers to discern. A "conservative Democrat" thought he wrote the book "just to put a prop under the New Deal!" Doak recorded. But a conversation between two "New Dealers" revealed their disappointment. To them, Daniels's conclusions seemed to be "the same as those of the Old Guard Republicans."[41]

A Southerner Discovers the South "has been received with mixed emotions," *Atlanta Constitution* columnist Ralph McGill confirmed. "It has been condemned, praised, and screamed at"—though the published reviews contained hardly any condemnation or screaming. It was ordinary readers whom Daniels's book had set "to debating." Southerners had known "the things he discovered . . . for some time [but] had planted honeysuckle to cover some of them and had trained ourselves not to see others. It really is unimportant whether or not Mr. Daniels was correct in all his deductions," McGill wrote. "The important thing is, he put us to looking at them and to talking about them."[42]

If McGill was correct, by removing the "honeysuckle" Daniels had achieved his primary goal of compelling readers, especially white southern readers, to contemplate a truer and more complex South. The reviews by Sterling Brown, Benjamin Brawley, and others indicate that he had also reached African Americans. Just as Doak provided a glimpse of white North Carolinians' mixed response, a black librarian wrote to tell Daniels about his readership in Raleigh. "We have three copies . . . and could truthfully use several more," she wrote. "Our readers are enjoying your book" and "are interested for several reasons; first because they know you. . . . Second, because you are fair and unbiased in your treatment of the subject."[43]

More prominent African Americans who wrote to Daniels expressed similar sentiments. Walter White of the NAACP saluted him "on a superb book" that captured "the inchoate mass of contradictions which our South presents."[44] James E. Shepard of the North Carolina College for Negroes (now North Carolina Central University) wrote to say he had "always had for you the warmest personal esteem and admiration because you sought the light and truth, and after finding it have not been afraid to walk in the paths marked out."[45]

Still, in the midst of all this praise, Daniels did receive at least one letter from a black correspondent who forced him to consider a different perspective. Writing from Glendale, Ohio, in December 1938, Wilhelmina Roberts began by expressing her regret that she "did not discover your *Discovery* until after I left Raleigh six weeks ago." After living in Raleigh for five years and reading the *News and Observer* "from weather report to crossword puzzle," she felt she knew Daniels and would have liked to talk with him about his book. She hoped he would be in town the next time she visited, "for I want you to tell me whether or not I smell of wood smoke, pig fat, and perspiration. Yes, I am a Negro," she revealed.

Having gotten Daniels's attention with this sharp reproof for his persistently crude and debasing depictions of black people, Roberts went on to write four more pages around the theme of what he might have discovered if only he "had found a southerner"—implicitly, a black southerner—"who could have made the trip with you, to show you some of the real south that you missed." Roberts's vignettes describe an alternate itinerary through a South where educated blacks were achieving and advancing. "In Okolona, Mississippi, you would have found a Negro school with children as clean [and] round legged as the whites you saw when looking for hookworm specimens. . . . You might have also been interested in the Negro schools in Atlanta. Surely you have heard of Morehouse and the rest of them." Closer to home, there was "a young Negro woman at Bennett College for girls in Greensboro who needs discovering. She is Merze Tate, educated at Oxford in England. There are many more like her."

Indeed, Roberts herself aspired to be like her. She told Daniels nothing of her own background except that she was "also a Southerner. Born in Fernandina, Florida, but lived in Columbia, S.C. for 20 years."[46] Her family had moved to Columbia in 1920, when she was four years old, because her father had been transferred there by the postal service. Richard Samuel Roberts worked as a janitor at Columbia's main post office every day from 4 A.M. until noon. Then he walked to his studio "in the heart of the city's 'Little

Harlem'" district, where he took photographs, mostly luminous portraits, that documented the rise of the South's black middle class.[47] His daughter Wilhelmina grew up in this aspiring class and took pride in her own and other blacks' accomplishments. She graduated from St. Augustine College in Raleigh in 1937 and spent most of her adult life in New York, where she worked as a teacher and social worker until her death in 2009.[48]

The point of Roberts's 1938 letter to Daniels was to instruct him about black southerners like herself. "What I am trying to indicate, Mr. Daniels, is that there is a type of Negro, in the south, who should have shared in your book as much as the poor 1938 slave." She hoped that "somebody will write something sometime, somewhere, that will let the whole world know that there are Negroes who smell of something besides wood smoke and pig fat and perspiration."

"Don't you think we get tired of that, no matter who calls the author of it a liberal?!" she chastised. Roberts admitted "that I think your paper the best in Raleigh," but patience clearly had its limits. The fact that she did not respond to Daniels's insulting descriptions of black women's bodies in his "Graveyard and Gully" chapter may signal only that they were too infuriating for words. "Please find some good things to say," she urged.[49]

To his credit, Daniels did not ignore Wilhelmina Roberts's letter. He thanked her for it "and the interesting point of view it contained. To tell you the truth, I was a little surprised," he admitted, "because both Walter White and Benjamin Brawley, for whose opinions I have high regard, thought that my book was written in friendliness toward your race. I am very sorry if it seemed otherwise to you."[50]

Daniels's letter was brief, but Roberts felt conciliated. She wrote back to say she was "very glad to get your letter, for I had not expected it. I, too, am sorry if I caused you to think that I considered your book unfriendly to my race. Not that. All of what you wrote was quite true, and not unfriendly, but I simply long to see the few achievements of the Negro put into print beside the things he still has to suffer." Roberts thought Daniels could understand "that young people anywhere of any race, want to be recognized for better things, and the younger Negroes are better." She enclosed a poem she hoped the *News and Observer* might be able to use during the upcoming Epiphany season.[51] But it was not her poem so much as her letters — and the way they challenged Daniels, as the diplomatic, glass-half-full responses of Brawley, White, and other prominent African Americans did not — that held potential for epiphany.

✦ ✦ ✦

THE WIDESPREAD COMMENTARY and favorable critical reaction to *A Southerner Discovers the South* was accompanied by strong sales. Macmillan shipped 12,500 copies of the book in the first two months after its publication, and it made best seller lists in both *Publishers Weekly* and the *New York Times*. Sales in southern stores were particularly brisk. Released on July 12, Daniels's book was "leading at Washington and Atlanta stores" by August 6, and *Publishers Weekly* declared it the "non-fiction leader of the South" on September 3, "with excellent sales in other parts of the country as well."[52] It was also the top nonfiction choice of borrowers at Atlanta's Carnegie Library for the year 1938. "Here they are, folks," read the caption of an *Atlanta Constitution* photograph showing a librarian holding Daniels's book in one hand and the top fiction choice of white Atlanta readers in the other: Erskine Caldwell's *Tobacco Road*. The accompanying article mentioned that *Gone with the Wind* had also made the top ten list for fiction for the third year in a row. Clearly, Daniels's book had not managed to displace either of these polar opposite visions of the South, but it had, at least temporarily, stepped into the limelight between them.[53]

The book's staying power would be another question. Although Atlanta's Ralph McGill credited Daniels with being the kind of writer "who can set people to debating," the truth is that his book became popular, in part, because it appeared at a moment of particularly intense debate. It was "an opportune opus for Dixie," as the *Richmond Times-Dispatch* explained, because President Roosevelt had "just pronounced the South the chief economic problem of the nation."[54]

In fact, the publication of Roosevelt's famous statement preceded the publication of *A Southerner Discovers the South* by less than a week, and the *Times-Dispatch* was hardly alone in drawing a connection. The *Saturday Evening Post* titled its book review "The Problem South," while a *Boston Herald* editorial on "Our 'No. 1. Problem'" recounted Daniels's arguments in detail.[55] A columnist for the *Baltimore Sun* suggested the book's best seller status in Washington indicated that "perhaps the New Deal is really making a study of the nation's No. 1 economic problem."[56] Benjamin Brawley hoped so and argued that "members of the committee looking into [economic problem No. 1]" should consider Daniels's book "the first item to go into their knapsacks."[57] A review in the *William and Mary Quarterly* took the same idea a bit further, buttressing its discussion of Daniels's points with quotations from the National Emergency Council (NEC) *Report on Economic Conditions of the South*—the government study that had been under way when Roosevelt issued his provocative statement.[58]

The coincidence in timing that provided a boost to Daniels's sales would not have happened if a *New York Times* reporter had not sneaked into a Washington meeting room during a lunch break and pilfered and then published a letter that Roosevelt had sent to the "Members of the Conference on Economic Conditions in the South." This group of twenty-two prominent white southerners had been assembled as "a sort of sponsoring committee" for the NEC report.[59] The report itself had been the idea of Jerome Frank, one of the liberal lawyers who had been fired from the Agricultural Adjustment Administration back in 1935. Frank had landed on his feet and was working for the Power Division of the Public Works Administration when, in late 1937 or early 1938, he accompanied the head of the Power Division, Atlanta-born Clark Foreman, to a meeting of the Washington branch of the Southern Policy Committee (SPC). After listening to the discussion, Frank suggested the SPC members should publish a report summarizing their views. Foreman liked the idea and relayed Frank's suggestion to Roosevelt when he was called to the Oval Office that spring to discuss the president's goal of fostering political change in the South.

By the spring of 1938, Roosevelt had decided he had to do something to counteract the increasingly open rebellion taking shape among conservative southern congressmen. Ever since the court-packing fight, southerners in his own party had shown a greater willingness to oppose New Deal initiatives rather than merely grumbling about them and trying to limit their impact on established race-and-class hierarchies. A crucial wage and hour bill—the bill that eventually became the Fair Labor Standards Act, establishing the federal minimum wage, a forty-four-hour maximum work week, overtime pay, and a prohibition against child labor—had stalled in Congress in 1937. A deep recession that had set in by the middle of the year was going to make the renewed fight for the bill even harder because it eroded the president's ability to point to economic recovery as an indication of the New Deal's success. Embattled as he was, Roosevelt could not know that the hard-won Fair Labor Standards Act would be the last major piece of New Deal legislation he would get through Congress prior to World War II or that many historians would consider 1938 the year when the legislative phase of the New Deal ended.[60] When he called Clark Foreman to the Oval Office, Roosevelt still had hopes for expanding the New Deal, which seemed to depend on more liberal Democrats being elected to Congress from the South.

Foreman did not have a liberal candidate to recommend for the upcoming

Georgia Senate race, but he mentioned Frank's idea of publishing a report that could remind southern voters of the many benefits the New Deal had brought to the region. Roosevelt approved, with the stipulation that any such report should merely describe the South's problems rather than touting New Deal programs. "If the people understand the facts . . . they will find their own remedies," he thought.[61]

Preparation of what became *The Report on Economic Conditions of the South* fell to the NEC and its executive director, Lowell Mellett, although Foreman and other Washington-based SPC members did most of the actual writing. In sixty-four pages divided into fifteen sections, the NEC report documented the appalling waste of the South's natural and human resources: the low wages and lack of purchasing power; the soil erosion and desperate poverty on southern farms; the pellagra and other preventable diseases; the lack of education and high birth rate; the tumble-down housing in the countryside and slum conditions in cities and mill villages; the draining away of the region's most talented people as they sought a decent standard of living someplace else. The "paradox of the South" was "that while it is blessed by Nature with immense wealth, its people as a whole are the poorest in the country." The South's problems were "not beyond the power of men to solve," Mellett's preface insisted, but "there is no simple solution."[62]

Though they wrote in sadness, the NEC report's authors knew that even a matter-of-fact accounting of the South's many problems would wound southern pride. In hopes of getting the best possible reception for their efforts, Mellett and Foreman put together an advisory committee of white southerners to review and critique a near-final draft at a day-long meeting in Washington on July 5. These were the "Members of the Conference on Economic Conditions in the South" to whom Roosevelt sent a letter (written by Mellett) that included the words, "It is my conviction that the South presents right now the Nation's No. 1 economic problem—the Nation's problem, not merely the South's. For we have an economic unbalance in the Nation as a whole . . . that can and must be righted."[63]

Jonathan Daniels was among the high-profile white southerners invited to serve on this committee, which was chaired by his friend Frank Porter Graham, the president of the University of North Carolina and one of the most highly respected white liberals in the South. Had he attended the meeting, Jonathan would have seen a number of familiar faces, including fellow journalists and SPC members, Congress of Industrial Organizations (CIO) organizer Lucy Randolph Mason, and Arkansas governor Carl Bailey. H. L. Mitchell of the Southern Tenant Farmers Union was there, too, and he and

Mason, in particular, represented the inclusion of the most racially progressive elements of the non-Communist left in the South—white southerners
who were ready to fight for blacks' civil rights and not merely "separate-but-
equal" economic uplift. Nevertheless, the advisory committee's role would
be to revise the draft report's few references to social and economic problems
that particularly affected black southerners to make them seem like problems
common to both blacks and whites. Those who wrote and vetted the 1938 report believed that "the race issue was, if not exactly a red herring, certainly a
disruptive issue that stood to blast their hopes for a liberal coalition," explain
historians David L. Carlton and Peter A. Coclanis. They understood that
the worthwhile goal of mobilizing southerners "behind a common desire
for federal action to compensate for the 'colonial' past" would remain out
of reach "if southern whites allowed their fears of a new Reconstruction to
obscure their need of outside help."[64]

Jonathan Daniels shared the NEC advisory committee's regionalist liberal
perspective and would have liked to participate in the meeting. Unfortunately, he did not even see Lowell Mellett's June 25 letter inviting him to
until after it took place. He had been away from Raleigh "making a swing
around the South," but he assured Mellett that he was "more interested in
[the meeting's] subject than any other question." After the NEC report was
published, he wrote Mellett again with effusive praise for "the amount of fact
and intelligence you have packed into so brief a space." He also suggested
that Roosevelt should ignore those southerners who had been offended by
his number one economic problem statement because they were simply "the
same old Daughters of the Confederacy—though some in pants—who in
all the long years" had been "a more destructive crop than cotton."[65]

Daniels regretted missing the meeting, but he would have regretted missing his "swing around the South" even more. That trip had come about
when Mary Fraser, an associate editor at *Life* magazine, wrote to him on
June 21 asking if he could "take a couple of weeks off, to guide one of our
cameramen along the route you followed" for *A Southerner Discovers the South*.
She had been reading an advance copy of the book and felt *Life* should "il-
lustrate it." She could pay only his expenses but promised that "if the story
is used your book will be the theme."[66] Daniels jumped at the opportunity,
knowing how much a *Life* photo essay could do for his sales. Because the
Life photographer assigned to work with him was the world-famous Alfred
Eisenstaedt, the trip would result in dozens of spectacular images as well.

Daniels's eagerness to collaborate with Eisenstaedt may have been height-
ened by the great success of Erskine Caldwell and Margaret Bourke-White's

You Have Seen Their Faces, which had been published the previous November. Based on a trip through the South in the summer of 1936, Caldwell and Bourke-White's book combined text and photographs to depict the poorest of the poor: the "ten million persons on Southern tenant farms . . . living in degradation and defeat."[67] Although Caldwell's figure was too high and implied that *all* tenant farmers lived in degradation and defeat, his passionate text was really nothing new in an era that saw many exposés. Instead, it was Bourke-White's stunning photographs that made the book a sensation. Critic Malcolm Cowley called it "a new art."[68] "At one time there must have been a copy of the cheap edition of *You Have Seen Their Faces* in every 'progressive' household in America, and in many other homes as well, if only as an act of piety toward the southern poor," historian Morris Dickstein has observed. "Yet I wonder how many people actually read the book, as opposed to simply taking it in. Caldwell's modest text was not what they were looking at."[69]

Increasingly critical of Caldwell, Daniels was eager to see what a photographer could do with *his* subjects. He told reporters in Chattanooga that *Life* planned "to use the photographs along with a sort of review of the new book to show the 'real South.'"[70] Meeting him in eastern Tennessee, Daniels guided Eisenstaedt to Chickamauga Dam, Lookout Mountain, Scottsboro, and Paint Rock. In Memphis, they visited both the offices of the Southern Tenant Farmers Union and the Peabody Hotel. Crossing into Mississippi, they reached the Delta Cooperative Farm on Sunday, July 3, in time to attend a church service. They also went to Greenville, where Eisenstaedt took a picture of the bronze knight over LeRoy Percy's grave. From there, they took the quickest route east through Tuscaloosa to Birmingham, skipping Natchez, New Orleans, and the entire Gulf Coast. After Birmingham came Atlanta, where Eisenstaedt snapped a picture of the Biltmore Hotel and Daniels spoke to reporters, cheerfully promoting his soon-to-be-published book. Then they started back toward Raleigh, driving up the "Gold Avenue" of the textile industry that Daniels had driven down on the first day of his original tour. Their final stop was Arlington, Virginia, where Eisenstaedt took pictures of the white-columned mansion that had once belonged to Robert E. Lee—the "façade of the South" where, Daniels claimed, any discovery of the South must begin.[71]

"I got home last night after taking Alfred Eisenstaedt around the route you suggested," Daniels wrote to Mary Fraser on July 11. He thought they had gotten "some excellent pictures," and he wanted to encourage *Life* to include "some note of hopefulness, as expressed in the last chapter" of *A Southerner Discovers the South*, in the accompanying text. "I feel very strongly that the South as an unrelieved land of depressing problem, circumstance and people has been rather overdone and I think there is a real opportunity to give some emphasis to the advance and promise of the South and its people," he argued.[72] If this was not a self-conscious critique of Caldwell and Bourke-White's *You Have Seen Their Faces*, it might as well have been.

Eisenstaedt, too, thought his photographs were good ("which really means something," as *Life* picture editor Wilson Hicks wrote Daniels), but the magazine never found the right moment to run the story.[73] "What seems to be holding the whole thing up," according to Fraser, "is the fact that we are working on a large essay on the American Negro and cannot run the two stories too closely together."[74] Daniels was disappointed and annoyed. "I'm appreciative for your interest in my book," he wrote, "but I feel that if *Life* sent me three thousand miles to no end I have been on a long snipe hunt."[75]

Especially in the absence of the panoramic treatment *Life* had planned, *A Southerner Discovers the South* became inextricably linked to its political context—to Roosevelt's number one economic problem statement, the NEC report, and what came to be known as the "purge." On August 10, the day the *Report on Economic Conditions of the South* was released, Roosevelt endorsed a little-known Georgia politician named Lawrence Camp in his primary bid against conservative Democratic senator Walter F. George, who was running for his fourth term. The next day, in a speech in Barnesville, Georgia, Roosevelt used the NEC report to argue that the "battlefront" for fighting the South's problems "extends over thousands of miles and we must push forward along the whole front at the same time," meaning federal involvement and planning were crucial. "The task of meeting the economic and social needs of the South" called "for public servants whose hearts are sound, whose heads are sane—whose hands are strong, striving everlastingly to better the lot of their fellowmen." Senator George was *not* a public servant of this kind, in Roosevelt's estimation. With George sitting just a few feet behind him on the platform, Roosevelt said he was "confident" that he and George "shall always be good personal friends." But, "if I were able to vote in the September primaries in this State, I most assuredly should cast my ballot for Lawrence Camp."[76]

This attempt to "purge" a conservative southern Democrat (and Roosevelt's similar moves against "Cotton Ed" Smith of South Carolina and a few other congressional incumbents) backfired so badly that it hampered the administration's whole effort to promote political and economic change. Southern opinion makers deeply resented the president's "interference" in the primaries, and even Daniels expressed private doubts about Roosevelt's tendency to overreach.[77] George Fort Milton's *Chattanooga News* complained that Roosevelt was "blinking the fact that the people back home do not like to be told exactly what the White House wants them to do."[78] John Temple Graves of the *Birmingham Age-Herald* agreed that "the President's political interference in these two Southern campaigns shocked many who are inclined to follow him and to approve his economic and social philosophy. The President has called the South a No. 1 economic problem and he has made it a No. 1 political problem. For the time being the politics is likely to overshadow the economics."[79]

Graves's editorial overlooked a major political problem that already existed in the South: the fact that the southern electorate was so reduced as a result of poll taxes and other methods of disfranchisement that politicians like George and Smith were routinely elected by mere thousands of voters even though there were hundreds of thousands or millions of voting-age people living in their states. Poll taxes "arguably kept more poor whites from the polls than African-Americans," writes political scientist Ira Katznelson. "In Alabama, Georgia, Mississippi, and South Carolina turnout rates were at or below 20 percent."[80] Although Georgia counted 2.9 million residents in the 1930 federal census, Senator George ultimately won his 1938 primary with a total of only 142,074 votes. He went on to win the general election with a mere 66,987—a striking illustration of the fact that, in the one-party South, the Democratic primaries were the only elections that mattered.[81] (And even they rarely mattered much: "For the first time in more years than I can remember there's a real issue in Georgia politics, and a bitter one," observed Margaret Mitchell, who supported the third candidate and second-highest vote-getter in the primary, racist demagogue Eugene Talmadge.)[82] Given the extent to which southern states' discriminatory voting laws effectively eliminated the New Deal constituency of blacks and nonelite whites, Roosevelt's so-called purge "seemed destined to fail in the short term, and it did," writes historian Patricia Sullivan. "But," she argues, "it marked the opening battle in a growing movement to open up the political process in the South."[83]

In that battle, which overlapped the "battlefront" for fighting the South's many problems that Roosevelt had identified in his Barnesville speech, the regional identities of the combatants were key. Graves said those who considered the NEC report insulting to the South had been "naturally somewhat silenced" because it had "been prepared by Southerners and . . . approved by an advisory board of other Southerners" and because its "findings coincide with what Southern economists and sociologists have been discovering and pointing out for at least a decade."[84]

Whether or not Graves's use of the word "discovering" was a conscious allusion to Daniels (whom he had written a few weeks earlier with congratulations on his book's success), he and many other commentators understood *A Southerner Discovers the South* to be an integral part of the insider versus outsider, liberal versus conservative debate.[85] Eleanor Roosevelt made the connection when, two weeks into the firestorm set off by her husband's Barnesville speech, she quoted Daniels's book and told readers of her "My Day" column that she had been rereading it "because of much discussion on the vital needs of the South." Frank Porter Graham similarly cited it alongside Howard Odum's *Southern Regions of the United States* and Gerald Johnson's *The Wasted Land*, published in 1937, as books that had influenced the development of a homegrown movement to reform the South and open up the democratic process.[86]

By the time he expressed this view, Graham had become the president of a brand-new organization, the Southern Conference for Human Welfare (SCHW). Historians have written a great deal about the founding of the SCHW and its first meeting in Birmingham in November 1938. The meeting attracted over 1,200 delegates, who paid a one-dollar registration fee and participated in daytime sessions. An additional 1,000-plus people attended one or more of the free public plenaries, which were held in the evenings at the Birmingham Municipal Auditorium and featured such high-profile speakers as Eleanor Roosevelt and Supreme Court justice Hugo Black.[87]

During three and a half days, this multitude divided into more than a dozen committees and discussed an incredible range of topics, including labor relations and unemployment, farm tenancy, education, housing, public health, the problems of young people, freedom of speech, regional wage- and freight-rate differentials, and prison reform. Delegates also took up the question of the poll tax, advocating it be abolished wherever it existed. The resolutions presented by the Panel of Interracial Groups were particularly wide-ranging. They urged "the positive extension of the franchise to all of our citizens of proper educational qualifications," the passage of state and federal antilynching laws, an end to "the practice of wage differentials between racial groups," and a more just distribution of funds for public education, including "adequate appropriations . . . by the states for Negro graduate work in Southern state-supported Negro institutions." A separate resolution called for clemency for the five Scottsboro Boys who remained behind bars.[88]

Even more significant than the dozens of resolutions passed at the Birmingham meeting was the wide range of attendees. There had "never been such a gathering as this in the South, such a diverse convocation of progressives from every stratum of the society," writes John Egerton.[89] There were a number of prominent politicians and New Deal officials, including National Youth Administration division chief Mary McLeod Bethune, the highest-ranking member of Roosevelt's "Black Cabinet." There were SPC members, including Francis Pickens Miller, H. C. Nixon, and Daniels's friend W. T. Couch of the University of North Carolina Press. There were white southern journalists, including some whom Daniels had visited on his tour, such as Milton and Graves. There were sociologists and historians, from Arthur Raper, author of *The Tragedy of Lynching*, to C. Vann Woodward, who had just turned thirty and was teaching at the University of Florida. Some of the nation's most prominent black educators also attended, at least three of whom were current or future university presidents: Charles S. Johnson of Fisk, Frederick D. Patterson of Tuskegee, and Benjamin Mays of Morehouse. Even Swedish social scientist Gunnar Myrdal was there, though he was just getting started on the monumental research project that would result in the publication of *An American Dilemma: The Negro Problem and Modern Democracy* in 1944.

Significantly, blacks made up about a fifth of the conference participants, and "the labor movement may have had the most delegates of all."[90] William Mitch of the United Mine Workers of America (UMW) and CIO not only attended but had also helped with fund-raising and local arrangements. Lucy Randolph Mason was another prominent CIO figure, and there were also representatives from the Women's Trade Union League, the American Federation of Teachers, and other unions. The Southern Tenant Farmers Union was well represented by both rank-and-file members and H. L. Mitchell and Howard Kester, who also represented a socialist viewpoint. Some Communists were there, too. Rob Hall was one of several known Communist Party members in attendance, and—especially because this was Birmingham, where the party had gained a strong foothold through its defense of the Scottsboro Boys and advocacy for unemployed industrial workers—there were undoubtedly low-profile Communists who attended as well. But even if the number of Communist Party members far exceeded the half dozen figure that Frank Porter Graham later gave in defense of the organization, he was correct that the SCHW was by no means under Communist control.[91]

Instead, the important fact about the presence of Communists, socialists, and labor organizers was that a wide range of voices was heard. "For years I have known that the South cannot be saved by middle class liberals alone—that they must make common cause with labor, the dispossessed on the land, and the Negro," explained Mason, who believed in making the SCHW as broad based a movement as possible. "Some may find it too shocking to have the other three groups so articulate about their needs," she acknowledged. "But this is the basis of progress in democracy, economic justice, and social values in the South."[92]

It was also what made the Birmingham meeting such an exhilarating experience. Arthur Raper called it "one of the most exaggerated expressions of change in the South . . . here was a revival, a bush-shaking, something that just jumped up." In the eyes of Virginia Durr, an Alabama native who was one of the leading figures in the poll tax fight, the Birmingham meeting was "a wonderful sort of love feast because it was the first time that all of these various elements from the South had gotten together."[93]

Perhaps inevitably for the Jim Crow South, the genesis of the SCHW lay in an act of violence—one that Jonathan Daniels had learned about during his tour and that had forced him to question his own perceptions. When he met Ernest D. Le May, the director of public relations for the Tennessee Coal, Iron and Railroad Company, Daniels had thought he seemed like "an enlightened being," a "thin, pleasant-faced man" who insisted he "had nothing against unionism." But, Daniels noted in his journal, John Temple Graves subsequently told him it was "practically proved" that Le May had "organized the beating of a liberal [a] couple of years ago." The victim was Joseph Gelders, a Birmingham native from an established Jewish family and a former University of Alabama professor.[94] Long interested in social issues, Gelders had moved to the left politically in response to the devastating unemployment and antiunion violence of the early 1930s. By 1936, he had secretly joined the Communist Party and was officially a representative of the National Committee for the Defense of Political Prisoners. When a party member and union organizer named Jack Barton was arrested for sedition, Gelders tried to investigate. He was soon abducted, beaten, and left for dead by men he could identify as company thugs. Although Daniels seems to have forgotten about the story by the time he met Le May, his own newspaper and many others had reported on Gelders's and Le May's January 1937 testimonies before the La Follette committee—the senate subcommittee investigating civil liberties violations that Wisconsin senator Robert M. La Follette Jr. had promised to form when he spoke at the Cosmos Club dinner organized by supporters of the Southern Tenant Farmers Union.[95] The committee's investigation that January, plus U.S. Steel president Myron Taylor's decision to negotiate with the CIO in March, brought an end to much of the antilabor violence that had long plagued Birmingham.[96]

Ernest D. Le May of the Tennessee Coal, Iron and Railroad Company testifying
in January 1937 before a Senate civil liberties committee chaired by Robert M.
La Follette Jr. Harris and Ewing Collection, Library of Congress, Prints
and Photographs Division, Washington, D.C. [LC-DIG-hec-22002].

A year later, in the spring of 1938, Gelders convinced Lucy Randolph
Mason that the time was ripe for a major conference on the civil rights violations that, despite improvements in Birmingham, were still taking place
all across the South. The well-connected Mason arranged for Gelders to
meet with Eleanor Roosevelt, who arranged a meeting with the president.
Both endorsed the idea of a conference but argued that it should have the
broadest possible scope, encompassing the wide-angle view of the South's
problems presented in the NEC report. Franklin Roosevelt also "specifically
urged that the conference act on the issue of voting rights, beginning with an
expansion of the campaign to abolish the poll tax."[97]

Jonathan Daniels was high on the list of southerners to be invited to the
Birmingham conference. During the same week of August when the "purge"
was quickly turning into (in historian John T. Kneebone's words) "a bitter
draught for the president," he started receiving letters asking him to serve
on a planning committee.[98] Virginia Durr also wrote Daniels personally

"to arouse your interest in the Southern Conference for Human Welfare. I am sure you have been approached officially," she wrote, "but I don't know if you realize how important you have become to the liberal movement in the South. You are not only forceful but discerning, and no one seems to be scared of you!"[99]

The idea that Daniels and his well-received book had become essential to "the liberal movement" that the SCHW represented was also evident in the idioms commentators used to discuss the conference. "More Southerners Discover the South" was the title of an account Charles S. Johnson published in the *Crisis*. W. T. Couch chose a slight variation, "Southerners Inspect the South," for an article in the *New Republic*.[100]

As at least his friend Couch must have known, however, Daniels did not attend the SCHW meeting. He was not present at the "revival," the "bush-shaking," the "love feast," or, in another Virginia Durr phrase, "the New Deal come South."[101] Although several of his friends wrote afterward with surprise, it seems likely he never intended to go. He wrote Durr almost eight weeks before the conference to say he was "very much interested in its purposes, but I will not be able to make it."[102] He gave her no reason, but he had been traveling quite a bit, plus his wife, Lucy, was several months pregnant with his fourth daughter and final child, Mary Cleves. Daniels was also, as he admitted confidentially to his agent, "beginning to get a little bored with this Southern business. I'd like to write about something besides Economic Problem No. 1."[103] In fact, he was still holding out hope that he had another novel in him, and he wrote to his father for advice. Josephus thought he should take his successful travel formula to another part of the country, and indeed Daniels's next book would be a rather superficial sequel, *A Southerner Discovers New England*, published in 1940.[104]

Jonathan Daniels not only skipped the SCHW meeting, but rather perversely, he also criticized this gathering that endorsed so many ideas he believed in and that involved so many of his friends. The issue was segregation. For the first night of the conference, attendees sat where they pleased in the Birmingham auditorium, ignoring the city's segregation ordinances. Then, on Monday, November 21, the local police commissioner, forty-year-old Theophilus Eugene "Bull" Connor, arrived with more than a dozen officers and threatened to arrest anyone who violated the color line. The rest of the conference took place in an uneasy and segregated environment. Once she arrived, Eleanor Roosevelt famously sat without noticing in a black section. Told she would have to move, she asked for a chair that she could position in a space between black and white.[105]

Segregation thus became a painful and distracting topic for the SCHW within moments of its birth. The group's response was to pass a resolution condemning Birmingham city officials' enforcement of the laws and instructing its own leadership "to avoid a similar situation" in the future "by selecting a locality in which the practices of the past few days would not be applied."[106] Misled by an Associated Press report that exaggerated its breadth, Daniels considered this resolution a mistake because it "placed emphasis upon the one thing certain to angrily divide the South." A few days after the SCHW meeting ended, he published an editorial titled "An Unfortunate Beginning" in which he warned the organization not "to advocate a haste in the adjustment of racial relationships." "If progress is to be safe and sure, it must also be gradual," he insisted.[107] Here, as always, was the rejection of extremes on either side—"the classic liberal answer to everything important," as Rob Hall described it. Here was the "lone-wolf critic" who, as H. C. Nixon wrote, "criticizes the South and criticizes those who criticize the South."

Two months later, on January 20, 1939, Daniels would find himself writing apologetically to Nixon, who had become the SCHW's executive secretary. Nixon had sent him a copy of the resolution on segregation, which, Daniels admitted, "certainly is a very different resolution from that which The Associated Press gave the impression had been passed." He did not retract his "Unfortunate Beginning" editorial, but he did acknowledge that it was "a pity that publicity was not given [to] the text of the resolution at the time the story was sent out."[108]

Even before he wrote to Nixon, Daniels had been reflecting on his own commitment to segregation. The U.S. Supreme Court had issued its historic *Gaines* decision on December 12, 1938, ruling in the case of a black applicant to the University of Missouri law school that states must provide equal educational opportunities for people of all races *within the state* and could no longer get around the separate-but-equal doctrine by paying for blacks to attend out-of-state schools. The *Gaines* decision was the NAACP's first major victory on the road to *Brown v. Board of Education*—"the beginning of the end of compulsory school segregation," in the words of civil rights activist Pauli Murray.[109] Murray, who had grown up in Durham, North Carolina, and was then in her late twenties, had applied for admission to graduate school in sociology at Daniels's beloved University of North Carolina several weeks before the *Gaines* decision was announced. On January 19, the day before he wrote to Nixon, Daniels gave a talk at the campus bookstore, expressing his opinion on Murray's case. "I don't see how anybody can object to taking a graduate course at the University with a Negro," he said.[110]

Evidently, Daniels had finally discovered that black people did not all smell of wood smoke, pig fat, and perspiration. In other words, though he never explained his sudden readiness to accept integration at the university in this way, it does seem possible that, in addition to the Supreme Court ruling, Wilhelmina Roberts's December 1938 letters had sunk in. Pauli Murray would not be admitted to the University of North Carolina, but Daniels would continue to grow beyond his "classic liberal answer to everything important." He skipped and criticized the SCHW meeting in Birmingham but played a more positive if very minor role in the organization's later activities. Through *A Southerner Discovers the South*, he also provided perhaps the most widely read account not only of the South's myriad problems but also of the potential for Regionalist and New Deal approaches to ameliorate or even solve them. As Virginia Durr suggested, his book was more important "to the liberal movement in the South" than he may have realized. How far that "liberal movement" could go, especially as a world war began in Europe, is another matter.

Only All Together Shall
Any of Us Overcome

✦

SADLY, JONATHAN DANIELS was right that the Southern Conference for Human Welfare (SCHW) and the broad-based coalition it represented got off to an "unfortunate beginning." The segregation issue did angrily divide otherwise liberal white southerners. So did the charge that Communists were setting the SCHW's agenda. The reactionary politics behind the vicious race-baiting and red-baiting the organization faced were obvious. But most white southern liberals of the 1930s were too ambivalent about the coalition themselves to be able to withstand it. As Lucy Randolph Mason predicted, middle- and upper-class whites were shocked to discover that blacks and working-class whites could be "so articulate about their needs." Even those who supported labor unions almost always found the prospect of racial change deeply troubling. As Daniels himself explained in a private letter, there was "no more difficult problem" confronting white southerners in 1938 "than how we shall deal with the Negro as he becomes better educated and more insistent upon his civil rights."[1] The regionalist approach that had subsumed racial issues under a geographic and economic umbrella could no longer provide cover. By the mid-1940s, to be a liberal required a commitment to *racial* and not merely regionalist liberalism.

The departure of the racially reluctant from the coalition that had come together in Birmingham meant that it would be primarily blacks and their left and labor allies who carried forward what Virginia Durr had optimistically called "the liberal movement in the South." Instead, a civil rights movement—what historians have identified as the long civil rights movement—would grow up outside the South as well as within it. The most racially progressive members of the liberal coalition of the 1930s—people like Durr, Mason, and Frank Porter Graham—would actively participate in that struggle in various ways. But the majority of Depression-era white southern liberals, including Jonathan Daniels, would not, and some, like

Virginius Dabney, became self-styled "conservative" critics.[2] Yet the long civil rights movement was able to take off because Daniels and other "travelers" had been willing to ride along as an emerging black-left-labor–New Deal coalition steered American politics and culture slightly leftward. These politically "middle" Americans' sympathy for the Scottsboro Boys and sharecroppers and labor unions, as well as their support for the New Deal, allowed the United States to enter the long civil rights era. From 1938 on, the contest over black civil rights and ultimately the rights of other minorities would be at the very center of American politics and eventually result in fundamental cultural change.

✦ ✦ ✦

LIKE THE DELEGATION OF police commissioner Bull Connor to enforce Birmingham's segregation laws at that first SCHW meeting, the opposition to the SCHW emanated from the South's racial capitalist establishment. One of the earliest and bitterest critiques came from *Alabama* magazine, the mouthpiece of Birmingham industrialists that had featured "Ol' Man Charlie [DeBardeleben] an' His Chillun" on its cover the year before. The Birmingham meeting "was a joint enterprise of Southern radicals and left-wing members of the Roosevelt administration with a 'program vicious in its intended results,'" the magazine declared.[3] Both it and the Birmingham City Commission called for an investigation by the Dies Committee—the recently formed House Un-American Activities Committee that would become a household name during the post–World War II red scare.

Still, as the always forthright DeBardeleben made clear, it was not the alleged radicalism but the threat to the South's *racial* order—the linchpin of racial capitalism—that upset SCHW opponents the most. Writing on Alabama Fuel and Iron letterhead, DeBardeleben scolded SCHW president Frank Porter Graham. "Being a dyed in the wool Southerner, I am one of the greatest believers in White Supremacy you could find," he wrote, "and notwithstanding the supposed good that prompted the Southern Conference for Human Welfare it was all lost in the estimation of the better element of this district by the resolutions asking that the Jim Crow Law of this city be withdrawn and further [by] the desire of the leading ones of the Conference to mingle and associate with the negroes on equal social equality." DeBardeleben found it "quite amazing" that Graham had "failed to raise your voice in protest to some of the resolutions adopted at this conference. In my opinion," he concluded, "the greatest need of the South today is for our

Northern friends to attend to their own affairs and let us direct ours, as we have these many years."[4] Nowhere in his letter did DeBardeleben mention the threat of Communism.

For many SCHW attendees, the resolution on segregation that DeBardeleben abhorred was reason enough to disappear. Connor's squadron had split the white participants "into quarreling factions," as John Egerton writes: "one that resented the enforcement" of the city's segregation laws and "one that resented the resentment." Among the latter were some of the most prominent white southern liberal journalists of the day, several of whom had participated in the planning stages but, like Daniels, chose not to go to Birmingham. As historian John T. Kneebone explains, journalists like Dabney and George Fort Milton "reacted with anger" to the resolution on segregation, "which they interpreted as a general condemnation of Jim Crow laws." Although they, too, were initially misled by the Associated Press report that exaggerated the resolution's scope, the fact was that Connor's intervention had "exposed the new southern liberalism's break from the old southern liberal doctrine" that advocated greater fairness for blacks *on their own side* of the color line.[5] Few among the current generation of white southern liberals were ready to give up the segregated system they had always known; most knew no better than Allen Tate how they would conduct themselves in an integrated world.

The journalists also worried, with much justification, that other white southerners would resist any but the most gradual changes. "Until the South is prepared of its own volition to level racial barriers," cautioned Milton's *Chattanooga News*, "no Conference resolutions are going to do anything but irritate and alienate the average Southerner."[6]

As this very language revealed, *white* opinion and control over the pace of change were what mattered most to Milton and many others—so much so that the words "average Southerner" were implicitly coded white, as was "the South" itself. Not least among the reasons established white southern liberals were reluctant to participate in a broad-based "liberal movement" is that joining a coalition meant ceding some of their own authority over the race relations agenda. At best, participating in a new, national, black-left-labor-liberal coalition would diminish their stature as individual voices of reason crying out in a benighted South. At worst, it would mean having to admit that the old moral suasion approach had completely failed and allowing someone else to take the lead.

The idea that Communists might be taking the lead—might be working behind the backs of the liberals like Graham who were actually in charge

of the SCHW—drove away still more potential allies, especially the politicians. Francis Pickens Miller, who had founded the Southern Policy Committee, turned down the vice-presidency of the SCHW because it was "out
of the question for me to serve as an officer of a Southern organization which
includes among its other officers any one who is either a member of the Communist Party or regarded as working in the interests of that Party."[7] The two
men Miller was worried about were John P. Davis of the National Negro
Congress, who had been elected a vice president at large, and Donald Burke,
a delegate to the Birmingham meeting who was also executive secretary of
the Communist Party in Miller's own state of Virginia. Burke was something
of a personal nemesis. "By the way, Miller, Virginius Dabney and myself had
a very interesting talk about the recent Conference in Birmingham," Daniels wrote to Howard Odum after a visit to Richmond. "Miller tells me he
was attacked as an emissary of reactionary capitalism because he opposed a
resolution to deal with the Southern poll tax question by national action. In
Richmond last night . . . the secretary of the State Communist Party in Virginia [Burke] came to the platform and in effect jumped on Miller again."[8]
Miller not only disliked Communists himself but also worried about being
associated with them for fear that it would ruin his chances if he ever wanted
to run for office. He was right—after a distinguished career in military intelligence during World War II and with the State Department after the war,
he would run unsuccessfully for governor of Virginia in 1949 and for senator
three years later. In both races, Senator Harry F. Byrd's political machine
smeared him for his association with leftists in the 1930s.[9]

Those who were already in office when the SCHW was formed would
not have to wait to experience such mudslinging. Alabama senator Lister
Hill and others distanced themselves from the organization immediately.
Even Florida senator Claude Pepper "refused official association with the
Conference"—yet he, too, would be red-baited to defeat in a Senate race in
1950.[10]

The departure of the southern liberal politicians, who were few in number anyway, weakened the potential impact of the SCHW and the "liberal movement in the South" it hoped to spearhead. After the Birmingham
meeting, the organization decided to focus its efforts on abolishing the poll
tax "by national action," as Daniels, Miller, and Dabney discussed. The
goal was to empower Franklin Roosevelt's core constituency of blacks and
working-class whites and thus increase support for an expanded New Deal.
Plus, as historian Morton Sosna has observed, "at a time when racial liberals
still considered the disfranchisement of Southern blacks too sensitive an issue

to tamper with, it could be pointed out that the poll tax affected many more whites," at least in raw numbers, than it did African Americans. Those who favored black civil rights could see eliminating the poll tax as an important first step, while the more hesitant or politically vulnerable could make it clear that other methods for preventing blacks from voting, such as literacy tests and the whites-only primary, were not being challenged. Even Maury Maverick, the former Texas congressman who chaired the SCHW Civil Rights Committee, insisted that he was not "out on a reforming tour to help the poor, persecuted black man."[11]

In 1939, Maverick's committee, particularly its vice-chair and chief lob-byist Virginia Durr, persuaded a California congressman named Lee Geyer to introduce a bill to eliminate the poll tax in federal elections. The bill did not make it to the floor, but Geyer introduced it again in 1940 with co-sponsorship from Claude Pepper. Meanwhile, labor leader William Mitch was recruited to join the SCHW Civil Rights Committee, and the CIO began providing funds for the anti–poll tax campaign. In 1941, Geyer and his SCHW allies founded the National Committee to Abolish the Poll Tax as an umbrella organization to unite a number of groups that had joined in the cause. One of the most prominent was the NAACP, "which had waged a long legal campaign to eliminate voter restrictions," notes Patricia Sulli-van, "and which lent legal talent, lobbying support, and publicity." Other affiliates included the CIO, the American Federation of Labor, the National Farmers Union, the Young Women's Christian Association, the League of Women Voters, and the National Negro Congress. Eleanor Roosevelt served on the organization's executive board alongside Graham, Mary McLeod Bethune, labor leaders A. Philip Randolph and Philip Murray, and a num-ber of other prominent figures.[12]

Unfortunately, the fact that a number of leaders and organizations had come together in support of a civil rights issue did not mean that issue would be promptly addressed in Congress. The chair of the House Judiciary Committee, Texas congressman Hatton W. Sumners, prevented the Geyer-Pepper anti–poll tax bill from reaching the House floor for nearly three years until a discharge petition finally brought it to a vote in 1942. The bill passed by a wide margin in the House but fell victim to an eight-day filibuster in the Senate that resulted in its being tabled that fall. The SCHW would help introduce similar anti–poll tax bills repeatedly over the next few years, but none would become law, and poll taxes would remain in force in most southern states until they were prohibited, at least in federal elections, by the ratification of the Twenty-Fourth Amendment in 1964 and the passage of the Voting Rights Act of 1965.[13]

The failure of the poll tax fight and the demise of the SCHW by 1948 were disheartening but need to be understood as part of a bigger picture: one in which "the structural changes and political possibilities of the late 1930s," to use Jacquelyn Dowd Hall's words, had allowed a movement committed to expanding American democracy to form. But a long fight against those who opposed political and social change would still be necessary. When Durr described the SCHW as "the New Deal come South," she was alluding to a widely shared perception that the New Deal made democratic change possible—a perception that the discriminatory nature of actual New Deal policies and their implementation often failed to justify. As Daniels might observe, "paper cup sanitation" was in force, but the TVA still segregated its workforce and relegated blacks to menial and manual labor jobs. The model town of Norris, Tennessee, was all white. The New Deal did change Americans' attitudes about the role of the federal government, and some aspects of New Deal policy also promoted social justice, though mostly in indirect ways: by strengthening the rights of workers and by raising the expectations of activists. What Durr described as a "feeling of support," a "feeling of having the government on your side" was incredibly important, but it was mostly just a feeling.[14] It would take grassroots activism over the next three decades—a long civil rights *movement*, not just the latent potential of having entered a new era —to add substance to this New Deal–inspired sensibility.

Meanwhile, the New Deal "headed [into the] South" in a different sense from 1938 on, as historian Bruce J. Schulman has argued. Franklin Roosevelt's claim that "Dr. New Deal" gave way to "Dr. Win-the-War" was not quite accurate in the South's case; instead, his prescription changed from a "purge" of southern conservatives to a heavy diet of defense-related and infrastructure spending that required little in the way of social justice reforms. In the process, Roosevelt fostered political change of a different sort than he had hoped for when he spoke of a "new generation" of southerners. "As Keynesian fiscal policy replaced New Deal reform as the mainstay of national economic policy, and as the national security state supplanted the social welfare state as the South's principal benefactor," writes Schulman, "young southern liberals fled national service or lost their seats in the elections of the early 1950s. Meanwhile, a group of politicians dedicated to business development came to the fore."[15]

Though Schulman sees the "business progressives" of the 1950s as distinct

from the Black Belt–Big Mule or "planter-mill owner alliance" of earlier decades, other historians have connected both to a "long segregationist movement" and argue that southern conservatives changed in tone over time
more than they changed in their fundamental views.[16] Gavin Wright has lent
support for this interpretation by observing that "the core of the problem
was that the vast majority of white southerners held a vision of economic
progress in which blacks had no more than a subordinate role, if any." So,
on the one hand, Wright argues, New Deal spending "kick-started the modern southern economy" even earlier than most historians have recognized,
providing the "improvements in regional infrastructure and public health"
that "made the South much more suitable and attractive for essential defense
activity than it otherwise would have been." On the other hand, modernization did not necessarily undermine the Jim Crow system.

"Indeed," Wright concludes, "the correlation often seemed to be the opposite" as whites were able to benefit from government programs to a much
greater extent than blacks were, widening racial gaps in wealth, education,
and opportunity still further. In addition to the TVA's "sorry record on
race," Wright cites the example of the Servicemen's Readjustment Act of
1944. Although the GI Bill itself was colorblind, black veterans faced discrimination from program administrators, especially in the South. An even
bigger problem was that, because of segregation, they had fewer options to
make use of the law's benefits. As white returning veterans streamed into the
nation's colleges on GI Bill scholarships, black veterans found that small, un-
derfunded black institutions were "unable to accept even half" of the qualified applicants. Thus, a program that made a huge difference in the lives of
white Americans and also benefited some blacks outside the South resulted
in "no significant gains in educational attainment" for black southerners.[17]

The GI Bill is only one example but a good one because its legislative
history shows clearly that what might seem like unintended racial consequences were not unintentional. Instead, Mississippi congressman John E.
Rankin, who chaired the House committee that wrote the law, made sure
to insert language that limited its potential to bring social change by limit-
ing federal oversight. "No Department or Agency, or Offices of the United
States . . . shall exercise any supervision or control whatsoever over any state
educational agency," a part of the law read. Schools would get federal tuition
dollars with no strings attached—and certainly no requirement that they
integrate. The same principle held true for many other federal policies that
helped transform the South from "the nation's No. 1 economic problem" into
the thriving "Sunbelt" of the postwar years.[18]

Southern Democrats' seniority in Congress is one reason for this outcome, and Roosevelt's need for white southerners' support to win the war
is another. Ira Katznelson has highlighted the fundamental importance of
these two factors in a study that both extends the timeline of the New Deal
through the Truman years and broadens its scope to include international
affairs. Even as southern congressmen increasingly allied with conservative
Republicans against New Deal social reforms, they also emerged as leaders of an "interventionist coalition" against the isolationism of the Republican Party. "Combined with southern control of the key foreign relations
and military affairs committees," Katznelson writes, southern Democrats'
"nearly unanimous support for activist overseas policies made it possible
for the House and Senate to endorse a massive buildup of warships and
planes, make thousands available to America's allies, and sponsor the swift
conscription of some 900,000 Americans." Without southern support for
the Lend-Lease Act and other policies, "Britain would have found it more
difficult to resist a Nazi invasion, and the United States would have been far
more vulnerable when Japan attacked and Germany declared war early in
December 1941."[19]

Thus, U.S. mobilization for World War II, like the very creation of the
New Deal from 1933 on, took place within what Katznelson calls a "southern
cage." With the election of Roosevelt and the rise of their party to power,
southern Democrats in Congress became "the most important 'veto players'
in American politics." They set the terms "not just for their constituencies but
for the country as a whole," and those terms included a reduction of "the full
repertoire of possibilities for policy to a narrower set of feasible options that
met with their approval, or at least their forbearance." They and the shrunken
southern electorate that kept returning them to office "permitted American
liberal democracy the space within which to proceed, but . . . restricted American policymaking to . . . a 'southern cage' from which there was no escape."[20]

The fact that Roosevelt even tried to escape—or at least remove a few
bars from this cage through the "purge"—is a testament both to his own
commitment to New Deal liberalism and to blacks' refusal to be caged themselves. Even beyond organized activism, it was blacks' having voted with
their feet in the Great Migration, as well as their subsequent votes for the
Democratic Party, that made it possible for Roosevelt and others to imagine
a new Democratic Party coalition that was not dependent on conservative
white southerners.

To see blacks as allies and constituents was not an obvious viewpoint for
most white Americans. Instead, they considered the "Negro problem" to

be a southern problem. The southern cage had been long in the making and was built with cultural as well as political tools. The very process by which "the South" and "Southern" identity came to be synonymous with the interests and prejudices of white, especially elite white, southerners contributed to a nationwide perception that the United States had a problem that was not only regional in scope but racial in character. It was culture — ideology—that made Americans think there were innate, biological differences between blacks and whites rather than historical ones emanating from slavery and its aftermath. History *mattered* and had devastating results for blacks' health, education, and material circumstances. But history was not biology, and whatever "race problem" existed was the long-term consequence of the fact that economic and cultural elites had worked, since the earliest days of slavery, to make the very *idea* of race seem like a natural, biological category to justify the creation and perpetuation of a permanent underclass. Much as the notion of "white supremacy" masked the reality of white-elite supremacy, the idea of a "Negro problem" or "race problem" masked the ways in which class had created caste.

As historian Barbara Jeanne Fields has astutely observed, "A commonplace that few stop to examine holds that people are more readily oppressed when they are already perceived as inferior by nature. The reverse is more to the point. People are more readily perceived as inferior by nature when they are already seen as oppressed."[21] This is all the more true when an oppressed people are thought to have been happy as slaves rather than resistant. It was in relation to the cultural construction of "race" itself, as well as the construction of the southern cage, that the popularity of a book and movie like *Gone with the Wind* was so significant. As a cultural product that traded in racial stereotypes and the moonlight-and-magnolias mythology of the Old South, Mitchell's beloved novel had a much longer reach and more lasting impact than her own participation in politics—her capital-P politics of voting for a racist demagogue like Eugene Talmadge.

Sharing many of white southerners' racial and cultural biases, most white Americans outside the South were perfectly willing "to attend to their own affairs and let us direct ours," just as white southern elites like Charles De-Bardeleben had long insisted. Even such committed reformers as Secretary of the Interior Harold L. Ickes thought it was "up to the states to work out their own social problems if possible," as he noted in his diary, "and while I have been interested in seeing that the Negro has a square deal," he added, "I have never dissipated my strength against the particular stone wall of segregation." Like many liberals, Ickes believed that segregation "will crumble when the Negro has brought himself to a higher educational and economic status. After all, we can't force people on each other who do not like each other, even when no question of color is involved. Moreover, while there are no segregation laws in the North, there is segregation in fact and we might as well recognize this."[22]

Set against white Americans' indifference to, tacit support for, or feelings of impotence against the "stone wall of segregation," efforts like those of the SCHW look more impressive. For example, the Geyer-Pepper anti–poll tax bill "initiated the first full-scale congressional debate over federal protection of voting rights in the southern states since the defeat of the Lodge elections bill in 1890."[23] After fending off what they called the Lodge "Force Bill," white southerners had gotten even more assurance that the federal government was not going to act to protect blacks' rights when the U.S. Supreme Court handed down its "separate but equal" decision in *Plessy v. Ferguson* in 1896 — the decision that *Brown v. Board of Education* finally overturned half a century later.

Under these circumstances, it really was up to blacks to "become better educated and more insistent upon their civil rights," as Jonathan Daniels put it. Only this could compel the nation to deal with what he and most other white Americans perceived not as a matter of simple justice but as a "difficult problem." A big step forward came in 1909 with the creation of the National Association for the Advancement of Colored People — an organization whose very name (like that of the National Urban League and later the National Negro Congress) denied, if not the southernness of the problem, certainly the demands of white southerners to have control over solutions.

Even so, many of the first issues the NAACP tackled were predominately southern, particularly lynching and local and state authorities' refusal to prosecute those who took part in mob violence. While it makes sense to locate the origins of the "long backlash" against the "long civil rights movement" in the mid-to-late 1930s, the filibuster and solid South opposition to the Dyer antilynching bill in the early 1920s could be seen as at least "the dress rehearsal for the dress rehearsal," as Jason Sokol has written.[24]

Nevertheless, the start of the Great Depression *was* the start of a new drama. For one thing, a new player managed to get onto the stage, stealing the first act from the NAACP. That player was the Communist Party, whose defense of the Scottsboro Boys made an international cause célèbre out of something that had long been all too ordinary: the deadly workings of the Jim Crow justice system in relation to economically expendable young black men. The Scottsboro defense was part of a larger Communist Party agenda that "considered the South crucial to their success in elevating labor and overthrowing the capitalist system," explains Glenda Elizabeth Gilmore. "By brooking no compromise with full social equality for a decade after they entered the South in 1929, the Communists gave Southerners a vision and a threat. Their small numbers mattered less than their very existence. It was Communists who stood up to say that black and white people should organize together, eat together, go to school together, and marry each other if they chose."[25]

For a few years between 1935 and 1939, the Communists pursued the strategy of the Popular Front, attempting to forge alliances with liberals and socialists against the threat of fascism. As flogging victim Willie Sue Blagden found out, liberals and socialists were not always willing. The Southern Tenant Farmers Union leaders who dismissed Blagden's hopes for a "United Front" and a "Democratic Front" on behalf of sharecroppers were hardly alone in their fear that Communists could not be trusted.

Such fears seemed to be fully borne out in August 1939 when the signing of the German-Soviet nonaggression pact was announced. This abrupt change in Soviet policy not only cleared the way for the Nazi invasion of Poland and the start of World War II but also "undercut the southern Left by undermining the strongest argument of non-Communist Southerners for associating with Communists: anti-Fascism." Meanwhile, white supremacists "leaped to the moral high ground, even if they balanced precariously there," Gilmore writes. "They quickly equated Fascism and Communism to convince Southerners that all '-isms' were antidemocratic." The "glimmers" of another "illogical equation" also became visible: "Communists supported black equality; therefore, any supporter of black equality might be a Communist."[26]

Embattled as they were, Popular Front efforts to forge a broad coalition were important for connecting activists across racial as well as ideological lines. As historian Doug Rossinow observes, "Before about 1935, there was no such thing as racial liberalism, and political liberalism up to that time was a white political tendency. Occasionally an African-American, most notably W. E. B. Du Bois, had sought to involve himself in liberal politics in earlier times, but such efforts had met with frustration over the unwillingness of (white) liberals to extend their stated values to questions of race." Communists' uncompromising stand on black equality made it clear that "the liberal movement could not be true to itself if it did not move to a position favoring civil rights and opportunity for black Americans and opposing Jim Crow segregation in the South. . . . Of the Popular Front's entire agenda," concludes Rossinow, "its racial egalitarianism was the element that, by far, was absorbed most fully and durably into the American political mainstream."[27]

To be sure, the Communists' moral challenge was not the only reason for this important change. Anthropologists and other intellectuals were developing new ways of thinking about race in this period, making some white Americans more willing to extend the principle of equality.[28] Plus, on a more pragmatic level, the process of implementing the New Deal had made the effects of racial injustice more visible to those in power than ever before. "New Deal liberals, often prompted by the rapidly learning Mrs. Roosevelt, soon realized that general economic assistance to the poor was not enough, that blacks had to be specifically targeted," explains historian Anthony J. Badger. Often, "the racial limitations of the New Deal were revealed by the government's own field investigations," and government officials sought help from black experts, including New Deal critics — hence the piecemeal hiring of Roosevelt's "Black Cabinet" of advisers.[29]

Clearly, the Communists were not alone, but they did relentlessly press the issue of racial equality, as did black organizations such as the NAACP. The NAACP's victory in the *Gaines* case at the end of 1938 indicated that a "showdown situation" was coming, as one white southern liberal observed.[30] While Daniels drove around in ten of the eleven states of the former Confederacy to discover his region's prospects, NAACP lawyers were busy in a border state, Missouri, and in New York and Washington pursuing a legal strategy designed to change the whole picture. Lloyd Gaines's suit for admission to the University of Missouri law school was an important victory for the NAACP and a stepping stone toward *Brown*. Another big win came in 1944 in *Smith v. Allwright*, a Supreme Court decision outlawing the whites-only primaries that had long made a mockery of black voting rights.

Although the NAACP's legal strategy achieved some of the most important civil rights victories of the World War II era, it was not the only way to get results. Black labor leader A. Philip Randolph proved this point dramatically in 1941. Randolph was a Socialist and the long-time president of a black railroad workers' union, the Brotherhood of Sleeping Car Porters. He had also been the president of the National Negro Congress until he resigned in 1940 because he felt the group had been taken over by Communists, who failed to see the dangers of Stalinism. He considered the Soviet Union a "death prison where democracy and liberty have walked their last mile."[31] He also hated fascists and supported U.S. intervention in World War II.

As the United States began to mobilize, Randolph, like other black leaders, was frustrated to see blacks Jim Crowed in the military and turned away from defense industry jobs. When all other attempts to get Roosevelt's support for an antidiscrimination policy failed, he started the March on Washington Movement. He vowed to lead a march of 50,000 African Americans into the nation's segregated capital city unless Roosevelt issued an executive order prohibiting discrimination in the armed forces, among government contractors, and in federal jobs. On June 25, 1941, Roosevelt compromised. He did not desegregate the military, but he did issue Executive Order 8802, prohibiting "discrimination in the employment of workers in defense in-dustries or government because of race, creed, color, or national origin." The order also created a temporary Fair Employment Practices Committee (FEPC) to address discrimination complaints and "take appropriate steps to redress grievances which it finds to be valid." Roosevelt's order was enough to convince Randolph to call off his proposed march, though he would be the man of the hour, if not the most celebrated speaker, when the idea of a march on Washington was revived in 1963. In recognition of its origins and the continuing problem of economic inequality, the 1963 March on Wash-ington where Martin Luther King Jr. gave his famous "I Have a Dream" speech was officially titled a March for *Jobs* and Freedom.[32]

Executive Order 8802 was the first presidential decree on race and civil rights since the Emancipation Proclamation. It was also a direct blow to the practice of job discrimination and segregation in the labor force—the practice on which the South's system of racial capitalism was based. Aggres-sive federal enforcement could have made real the promise of fair treatment that the TVA's paper cups only ephemerally suggested. Equality of oppor-tunity during the long boom of the post–World War II years could have made blacks and other minority populations more economically secure than proved to be the case. Although enforcement of Executive Order 8802 was not aggressive and the effectiveness of the FEPC should not be overstated, it is nonetheless true that both Roosevelt and the prospects for social change in the South had come a long way in the three short years since the "purge." The United States had not just entered the long civil rights era but, with the *Gaines* case and the March on Washington Movement, the activist drive toward the Second Reconstruction—the long civil rights *movement*—was under way and beginning to gain ground.

✦ ✦ ✦

A YEAR AND A HALF AFTER he issued Executive Order 8802, Frank-lin Roosevelt faced another decision point with regard to the FEPC. As weak as it was, the federal committee had sparked enormous controversy and was particularly loathed by southern industrialists.[33] As he considered what to do—whether to strengthen the FEPC or perhaps let it quietly die—Roosevelt sought advice from several White House staff members, one of whom was Jonathan Daniels.

After the publication of *A Southerner Discovers the South*, Daniels had continued as editor of the *Raleigh News and Observer*. He had also kept up his "discoveries," publishing *A Southerner Discovers New England* in 1940 and *Tar Heels*, an interesting look at his home state of North Carolina, in 1941. From the middle of 1940 through early 1942, Daniels wrote a weekly column for the *Nation*. He also volunteered in civilian defense planning that began several months before the Japanese attack on Pearl Harbor. In the fall of 1941, Addie Daniels's poor health led Josephus to resign his ambassadorship and return to Raleigh, where, though he was turning eighty, he naturally expected to resume command of the *News and Observer*. Father and son quickly "found that the newspaper was not big enough" for both of them, and as one family member put it, "when Josephus came back, Jonathan left."[34] He went to Washington, taking over from Eleanor Roosevelt as the director of the Division of Civilian Mobilization of the Office of Civilian Defense under director James M. Landis. Largely because he and Landis did not get along, Daniels's first year in government service proved unhappy. Then, in March 1943, Roosevelt chose him to become one of his six administrative assistants, who had the job of "gathering, condensing, and summarizing information" for the president.[35] For the next two years, Daniels's areas of responsibility included three government agencies that were of particular importance to the South: the Tennessee Valley Authority, the Rural Electrification Administration, and the Department of Agriculture. He also became an expert on the rationing of newsprint, wartime baseball, and other topics. But, in keeping with his discoveries of 1937 and beyond, his most passionate area of interest was race relations.[36]

Although he maintained his friendships with liberal stalwarts like Frank Porter Graham, Daniels was never an activist. He opposed the SCHW's main objective in the early 1940s, federal anti–poll tax legislation, for the same reason he had opposed a federal antilynching law: because he wanted state-level action instead. He understood how undemocratic poll taxes were and how difficult it would be to get them repealed. Writing about Virginia's forty-year-old law in the *Nation*, he acknowledged that repeal required approval by legislators who had been "elected by voters who have paid their poll taxes." Then it would be up to "the people—but 'the people' will be only those who paid their poll taxes (cumulative for three years) six months in advance." He could see that "the Virginia pattern shows that it is easy for the people to lose their liberties in this American democracy, but even in democracy it is hard as hell to get them back."[37] Yet he still remained skeptical about the use of federal power to restore democracy in the states, even as he pointed out the contradiction in pro–states' rights southerners' eagerness to use American power to preserve democracy in Europe. "I have the feeling . . . that if we cannot trust democracy below the Potomac River, we are fools to hope to save it along the English Channel," he wrote.[38]

Most of all, Daniels hoped for a "growth of enlightenment in the South" to end poll taxes, just as he had once hoped Alabama officials would do the right thing in the Scottsboro case.[39] Change from within would be more genuine and provoke less backlash, he thought, and he had long used his editorials and other writings to try to educate white southern audiences. Like Milton, Dabney, and other fellow white southern liberal journalists, he wanted social change but in a manner and at a pace that white southerners could accept without resorting to violence or a politics of resentment. Unlike these other white editors, however, Daniels would be encouraged through his work in Washington to subordinate white southerners' preferences to other concerns: first, to the cares and commitments of the Roosevelt administration and, eventually, to the just demands of civil rights activists. As much as his tour of the South in 1937 had taught him, in his longer, moral and political journey these Washington years were an equally important leg.

Daniels's continued emphasis on winning over the white South was evident in his response to Roosevelt's question about the FEPC. He wanted it to survive but urged the president to limit its responsibilities to redressing "discrimination which prevents the employment of Negroes at a time when all the manpower the nation possesses is needed." The emphasis should be on employment rather than fairness, and the FEPC should have "nothing to do with housing, with state and local Jim Crow laws, with the non-employment aspects of the color question." Daniels hoped patriotic white southerners could accept a limited FEPC that was presented as a wartime necessity. If that proved not to be the case, he was willing to see the FEPC eliminated and antidiscrimination efforts moved into a quieter corner of government — perhaps even his own office, where he could serve as an informal goad to employers on the president's behalf.[40]

As Roosevelt understood far better than Daniels, the symbolic importance of the FEPC to black Americans outweighed the opposition of white southerners and other critics. In May 1943, the president issued another executive order to make the FEPC stronger and more independent and to give it a larger budget and a full-time director and staff.⁴¹ "Only reluctantly, tardily, inadequately, and under coercion did Roosevelt take these steps," writes historian William E. Leuchtenburg, but the fact remains that he did take them, and "perhaps in no other act of Roosevelt's four administrations was the president so politically in advance of the majority of his own party" and his advisers.⁴² As Daniels later reflected of those advisers, including himself, "I don't know anybody around the President who was a strong Negrophile; I don't know *anybody*."⁴³

Daniels's word choice is revealing, if also condescending, for to be in advance on race issues *was* to be a "Negrophile" in the minds of most white Americans of the day (and not merely white southerners). What else would make someone willing to dissipate his strength, as Harold Ickes put it, "against the particular stone wall of segregation"? Apart from Eleanor, whose role as First Lady allowed for a more open advocacy, Roosevelt had no close associates who were especially eager to join him in the difficult task of prying apart the bars of the southern cage. Yet, as difficult as the task was and as distracted as *he was* by the national emergency of World War II, Roosevelt did make efforts. As Leuchtenburg notes, "A powerful northern congressman later remembered that FDR's last request to him came on the morning of his death when Jonathan Daniels called on him to say that Roosevelt wanted him to do his utmost to get legislation for a permanent FEPC through the Rules Committee."⁴⁴ Instead, and despite Harry Truman's support, the FEPC died just a year after Roosevelt in 1946.

While serving as Roosevelt's liaison and aide, Jonathan Daniels developed a new perspective on race and civil rights. "He gained a greater appreciation of the magnitude of the nation's racial problems and the difficulties in overcoming prejudice and discrimination, and he became more closely acquainted with many black leaders such as Walter White, Mary McLeod Bethune, and Robert Weaver," writes Charles W. Eagles, whose biography of Daniels provides a thorough and detailed analysis of his wartime work and evolving racial views. Perhaps most important, Daniels came to understand that the nation had a "majority problem as well as a minority problem"—that it was not blacks' poverty or lack of education or any other incapacity but, rather, whites' prejudices that prevented change. Daniels also accepted the fact that blacks' demands for equal citizenship were legitimate, not premature, even if he worried about the social disorder that efforts to promote equality and redress grievances might bring. For, as he observed in a 1942 letter, "in many places white men are so fixed in their emotional

attitudes that their morale may seem to depend upon the maintenance of
those attitudes. Sometimes it is easier to ask people to give their lives than to
give up their prejudices."[45]

Slowly but surely, Daniels was making a transition from white southern
liberal to racial liberal, from an emphasis on regional identity and ameliora-
tion within limits to seeing the nation's racial dilemmas more fully through
black activists' own eyes. There were even times when he, the cautious and
conflicted white southerner, advised Roosevelt to take a bolder stand. For
example, he urged the president to issue a "disciplinary statement" to the
American people in response to the terrible Detroit race riot in June 1943.
Conscious that racial tensions were building in the nation's cities as black
and white industrial workers, many of whom were recent migrants from the
rural South, competed for housing and jobs, Daniels wanted Roosevelt to
call for "freedom from fear" at home and appeal to Americans' patriotism
in support of the war effort. Yet Roosevelt said nothing, and proposals for an
official response to the Detroit riot such as Ickes's call for a national committee on race relations went nowhere. The administration also turned down
Attorney General Francis Biddle's recommendation for a less public, inter-
departmental committee "to collect and exchange information concerning
racial problems"—a committee that Biddle thought Daniels should head
because of his acknowledged expertise on the subject.[46]

Roosevelt rejected the idea of a committee but approved Daniels's own
proposal to become his "fact-finder in the background" with the goal of
preventing further racial violence that could embarrass the administration
and hinder wartime production and morale. From the start, the president
could spare little time or attention for Daniels's efforts, which involved positioning himself at the center of an information-gathering web and bringing
the power of persuasion to bear wherever he could. "One month after the
Detroit outburst, the President approved Daniels's plan with a curt, handwritten 'J.D. O.K. F.D.R.,'" writes Eagles.[47] The brevity and informality of
his reply speak volumes about where domestic racial tensions ranked in the
president's long list of concerns.

The task itself also required sensitivity and a willingness to work without
recognition. The wartime administration not only lacked a coherent and
decisive racial policy but also worried that any perception of such a policy
would provoke a negative response. As Eagles observes, "Although many
people knew that Daniels advised Roosevelt on race relations, only a few in
the government were familiar with the details of his work. . . . By working
behind the scenes and through existing governmental bodies, he hoped to

avoid becoming the target of the pressures of politicians and agitators that had plagued the FEPC."[48]

For almost two years from 1943 to 1945, Jonathan made phone calls and drew on contacts within more than a dozen federal agencies who could supply him with information about simmering racial conflicts and how they were being addressed. He also worked closely with the Office of War Information (OWI) to comb through newspapers and news wires. Indeed, the very idea of preemptive information gathering had come to Daniels from former anthropology professor Philleo Nash, who worked as a special assistant to the deputy director of the OWI's domestic branch. Nash was aware of Daniels's interest in race issues and had used *A Southerner Discovers the South* in courses at the University of Toronto before he took the OWI job. After the Detroit riot, he and Ted Poston, a black journalist who was the head of the OWI's Negro Press Section, helped Daniels collect information about all kinds of racial frictions, including conflicts on military bases and many nascent labor disputes. They tried "to watch for the tension spots," as Daniels later explained, and "avoid the development of violence."[49]

"The absence of major interruptions in war production because of racial conflict indicates that the Daniels operation had no notable major failures," concludes Eagles. Yet "Daniels's work ignored many of the problems of blacks except as they impinged on production," he adds.[50] Like others in the administration, Daniels was less concerned about racial justice or black advancement than about maintaining domestic peace in order to win the world war.

He also felt the constraints of the southern cage. In his role as aide, Daniels was unable to win approval for even very modest proposals, such as a request for more black agricultural extension agents that came from Frederick D. Patterson, the president of Tuskegee Institute, and Claude Barnett, the founder of the Associated Negro Press. He had heard such a request before, from Victor C. Turner of Tuskegee, who wondered "'why white folks haven't got sense enough to spend the money so we can have enough farm agents to teach the Negroes how to make more so they could have more and the planter more, instead [of] keeping them hungry and making them ready for the union and the communists.'"[51] Perhaps Daniels thought of Turner in the fall of 1943 when Patterson and Barnett approached the White House. An increasingly sophisticated political adviser, he assured Roosevelt that more farm agents would not only "give real assistance to the Negroes" but also "demonstrate" the influence of "conservative Negro leaders," which could elevate their status among potentially restless blacks. Roosevelt supported the idea, but the Department of Agriculture rejected it, claiming budget constraints.[52] Black farm agents like Turner would have to continue their work unaided, and Turner himself would resign from his position as Alabama state supervisor of Negro 4-H Clubs in 1945. He went on to teach at State A&M College (now Alabama A&M University) and then returned to Tuskegee, where he died at the age of eighty in 1964.[53]

Seeing even modest proposals like the one for black farm agents shot down forced Daniels to confront, in Eagles's words, "the scope and complexity of the nation's racial problems" and "the inflexibility and hates of American whites."[54] Meanwhile, he developed significant personal relationships with blacks. For example, he later remembered going to Ted Poston's apartment on election night in 1944 "to drink to the mounting returns for FDR from both white and black areas." Drinking with a black colleague to celebrate black votes was a far cry from the political world of Josephus Daniels or even that of the Jonathan Daniels of 1936, for whom eating and drinking across race lines were "invested with a symbolical quality which even we so-called free moderns do not wholly escape."[55]

Whether or not Daniels "wholly escaped" the racism of his earlier years, his work in Washington was vital to his evolution as a racial liberal. He jumped at the chance to become Roosevelt's press secretary in March 1945, telling his agent that to do so was "like moving from the bleachers to the boxes" from a writer's point of view.[56] He would write a great deal about his observations of wartime Washington over the next three decades, even becoming the first to reveal Roosevelt's extramarital affair with Lucy Mercer when he published *The Time Between the Wars* in 1966. (In his own defense, Daniels argued in *Life* magazine that Roosevelt should not be "denied [his] human dimension" and was "the kind of man who . . . would have wanted nothing hidden from history. I do not feel, therefore, that from privileged position I have peeped and told.")[57]

Even if his next book was always in the back of his mind, Daniels was unquestionably and deeply loyal to Roosevelt. When the president died in April 1945, he was devastated. After a memorial service at the White House, David Lilienthal wrote in his diary that the "most broken person I talked to was Jonathan Daniels. Really looked very bad, red-eyed, evidently had about all he could stand."[58]

"Actually Lilienthal then had more to lose than I, though his grief was less personal," Daniels demurred in a 1975 memoir. "With his term of office coming to an end he feared that his great work and achievement at the TVA might be ended."[59] Instead, President Truman supported Lilienthal's

Jonathan and Lucy Cathcart Daniels with President Franklin Roosevelt
on March 24, 1945, when Roosevelt commissioned Daniels as press secretary.
Harris and Ewing photograph, courtesy of Lucy Daniels.

reappointment as director of the TVA and then made him head of the new
Atomic Energy Commission. The change of jobs was a sign that, regardless
of whether the New Deal had truly ended, as historians debate, the Cold
War had definitely begun.

Jonathan liked Harry Truman and would advise him, campaign for him,
and even write his official biography, *The Man of Independence* (1950). But he
did not see in Truman "the great prince which Roosevelt even in his lightest
moments was to those around him." Truman had Roosevelt's "intestinal
fortitude" without his accompanying grace; he was a man "fit to fill" Roosevelt's chair but not one who could keep Daniels away from home any longer.[60] After serving briefly as Truman's press secretary, he left Washington
in the middle of 1945 and returned to Raleigh, where he found Josephus, at
eighty-three, still going strong—"still robustly able to handle the editorial
policy" of the *News and Observer*.[61] Meanwhile, Jonathan's oldest daughter was
nearing twenty, his youngest was six, and his beloved mother, Addie, had
died just before Christmas in 1943.

By necessity if also by choice, Jonathan worked mostly at managerial
rather than editorial tasks for the *News and Observer* in the mid-1940s while

pouring his creative energies into other kinds of writing. He published numerous articles in national magazines and offered a chatty description of
wartime Washington in *Frontier on the Potomac* (1946). Then, in January 1948,
Josephus Daniels died after a brief illness, and Jonathan once again took
over as editor. He would continue to edit the *News and Observer* for almost
two decades, moving "slowly into retirement" only in the mid-1960s (after
which the born editor would help start a new paper, the Hilton Head, South
Carolina, *Island Packet*).[62]

As always, Daniels maintained multiple commitments in the final two
decades of his career, writing books and articles in addition to his editorials
and staying active in politics and even government service. From 1947 to
1952, he served on the United Nations Subcommission for the Prevention
of Discrimination and the Protection of Minorities. Its purpose was to define international principles of antidiscrimination and suggest resolutions
for pressing problems. But Daniels found the work frustrating because of
the extent to which the deepening Cold War made minority rights a propaganda issue between the United States and the Soviet Union, hindering the
group's ability to do anything more than endlessly debate. He felt he was
able to get more concrete results at home, working for Truman's successful
1948 campaign and helping persuade North Carolina governor W. Kerr
Scott to appoint Frank Porter Graham to a vacant Senate seat in 1949. Graham's losing battle to keep his seat in 1950 proved bitterly disappointing. The
"only possible way [his opponents] could defeat Frank," Daniels wrote to
Eleanor Roosevelt, "would be in a horrible 'nigger-communist' campaign,"
which turned out to be precisely the kind of race Graham's chief rival, Willis Smith, ran. With Daniels acting (in the words of Smith's supporters) as
Graham's "real, behind-the-scenes campaign manager" and "undisputed
political boss," the widely admired "Dr. Frank" lost a run-off election in the
1950 Democratic primary. The main reason, in Daniels's view, was "race
fears which had been violently stirred."[63]

Advocating change while trying to keep a lid on white southerners' fears
so they could not be stirred was Daniels's most important job in the post–
World War II years. Having come around himself on the need for federal
civil rights initiatives, he wrote carefully calibrated editorials encouraging
white readers to do the same. He endorsed Truman's comparatively bold
policies, which included the desegregation of the military and support for antilynching and anti–poll tax laws and a permanent FEPC. Though Truman,
like Roosevelt, was trapped in the southern cage of a hostile Congress and
failed to get much of his civil rights agenda passed, racial change nonetheless

accelerated in the late 1940s and 1950s. NAACP-sponsored cases resulted in Supreme Court decisions outlawing segregation in interstate transportation in 1946 and in education at the graduate and professional school level in 1950. The *Brown* decision of 1954 overturned the very principle of "separate but equal" and gave a tremendous boost to civil rights activists, even if it resulted in few integrated schools in the short term. The successful Montgomery bus boycott of 1955–56 and Martin Luther King's rise to prominence were even more important indicators that the most successful phase of the long civil rights movement had begun.

From his desk in Raleigh, Daniels found it easy to encourage readers of the *News and Observer* to obey the *Brown* decision and other federal laws, even if he fretted over boycotts and direct-action protests that he feared might bring a violent backlash along with the needed media attention and government support. Sensitive to the prejudices of his audience, Daniels never came out in advance of civil rights activists' evolving goals or even the current state of federal policy. But he did continuously call upon whites to live up to the letter of the law and their own best principles, and he also adapted more readily than most white Americans (again, not merely southerners) to the prospect of a fully integrated society. Even by the mid-1940s Daniels had come to understand that *racism*, not race, was the problem. At times, he had disavowed the very notion of race, as when he persuaded the United Nations subcommission on which he served to approve a plan "for spreading scientific information to demonstrate that no basic differences existed among races."[64]

Jonathan Daniels traveled a long way over the course of his seventy-nine years before his death in 1981. Even before he went to Washington in 1942, his journey around the South in 1937 contributed to his personal and intellectual growth. His account of his travels in *A Southerner Discovers the South* also helped many readers see the region and its race and class issues more clearly and honestly than such "extreme legends of the right and the left" as *Gone with the Wind* and *Tobacco Road*. Daniels achieved his primary goal of depicting a more complex and realistic South, whether or not he persuaded contemporary readers to support the New Deal–inspired initiatives that were trying to bring progress to his native land.

By the time Daniels published a new edition of *A Southerner Discovers the South* in 1970, much of the southern landscape, both actual and metaphorical, had changed. Yet the first paragraph of his new introduction sounded like the same old Jonathan. He opened with some rather sexist imagery, suggesting that "unlike a lady, a land may be more beautiful—certainly more worth loving and cherishing—as it ages." He also slipped in an archaic and offensive but, to his mind, hard-hitting term when he wrote that "'Niggertown' may be an unmentionable word today, but spreading city slums certainly deserve an ugly word expressive of indignation about the places if not the people captured in them."[65]

If Jonathan was, in personality, much the same observer, the scene he surveyed was markedly different. The South of 1970 was a much more urban and suburban, industrialized, technologically modern and forward-looking place than the South of 1937 had been. The newest thing of all was the possibility that "the main stream of America in the future will not be one upon which the South is finally permitted to sail but one which flows out of the South itself." Industries were rapidly departing the Northeast and Upper Midwest in favor of the southern and southwestern states that had only recently been nicknamed the Sunbelt. As Daniels put it, "Southern shores and hills are filled with those who have come from other areas to enjoy the South's climate and charm."

At the same time, the whole country was feeling the effects of the earlier migration of the South's poor, especially its poor blacks, many of whom were now struggling with anger and despair in northern and western ghettoes devoid of jobs. This "mobile poverty" was "giving national dramatization to problems which once seemed so much Southern and are at last disclosed as the shame of dreadful destitution in the whole of an opulent land." There were "still too many white columns in our minds and too many shantys in our yards," not only in the South but throughout the United States.[66]

Daniels hoped, as he always had, for something better, for a South that would "best serve the nation and itself" by leading the way in "a recommitment of the nation to a fair, good chance for every man. That was the American dream. That is the American main stream. It may seem a twisting river, but it could flow out of Alabama, through Harlem, back to the old loved—and the old despised—Southern land." Holding onto the dream would be difficult and depended at the very least on the survival of what Daniels called the "second Reconstruction," a term that, in his usage, encompassed both civil rights activism and late 1960s urban unrest. Ever mindful that there had been "that other Reconstruction which passed away in violent Southern distaste and mounting Northern disregard," he offered the caveat that "nothing is certain. Our slums may grow more crowded and more fetid. . . . Protests may be backlashed into the rat-infested tenements." The hope of the 1960s might prove "to be only a disagreeable interlude from

which the well-to-do emerge in comfort and the poor [are] again forgotten."
The task of achieving social justice would be difficult, "but we shall enter the
American main stream, or bring the nation back into it, only when we insist
upon solutions which will suffice for the chance, the decency, and the dignity of all men." Daniels concluded with a 1960s update of his 1938 vision of
"white man, black man, big man" emerging from the "warm dark" into day-
light together. "Only all together," he wrote, "shall any of us overcome."[67]

NOTES

Abbreviations

ACES   Alabama Cooperative Extension System Records, RG 71, Auburn University Archives and Manuscripts Department, Auburn

ADAH   Alabama Department of Archives and History, Montgomery

AFIC   Alabama Fuel and Iron Company Records, W. S. Hoole Special Collections Library, University of Alabama, Tuscaloosa

D-COHP   Jonathan Daniels, interview by Daniel Singal, March 22, 1972, Columbia Oral History Project, transcript in folders 2543–45, Jonathan Daniels Papers #3466, Southern Historical Collection, Wilson Library, University of North Carolina at Chapel Hill

DP   Jonathan Daniels Papers #3466, Southern Historical Collection, Wilson Library, University of North Carolina at Chapel Hill

D-SOHP   Jonathan Worth Daniels, interview by Charles W. Eagles, March 9–11, 1977, Southern Oral History Program Collection, transcript, Documenting the American South, University Library, University of North Carolina at Chapel Hill, http://docsouth.unc.edu/sohp /A-0313/menu.html (accessed February 21, 2016)

JDP   Josephus Daniels Papers, MSS17715, Manuscript Division, Library of Congress, Washington, D.C.

Journal   Jonathan Daniels, "Notes Made on Tour," typescript, folder 2089b, Jonathan Daniels Papers, #3466, Southern Historical Collection, Wilson Library, University of North Carolina, Chapel Hill

PFDOJ   Peonage Files of the U.S. Department of Justice, 1901–1945, microfilm edition (Bethesda, Md.: University Publications of America, 1989)

PISF-SF   Public Information Subject File—Surname File for "Dickson," SG002630, roll 166 (microfilm)

Scrapbook   *A Southerner Discovers the South* scrapbook, folder 2089c/SV-3466/1, Jonathan Daniels Papers, #3466, Southern Historical Collection, Wilson Library, University of North Carolina, Chapel Hill

SDS   Jonathan Daniels, *A Southerner Discovers the South* (New York: Macmillan, 1938)

SHC   Southern Historical Collection, Wilson Library, University of North Carolina at Chapel Hill

SOHP   Southern Oral History Program Collection

STFU   Southern Tenant Farmers Union Papers, microfilm edition (Glen Rock, N.J.: Microfilming Corporation of America, 1971)

T-ASU   Biographical sketch of Victor C. Turner Sr., John Garrick Hardy Collection, Alabama State University Archives, Montgomery

UGA   Hargrett Rare Book and Manuscript Library, University of Georgia, Athens

Introduction

1. *SDS*, 1, 8.

2. *SDS*, 9–10.

3. The 75,000 figure is for 1938; see Katznelson, *Fear Itself*, 54. On the growth of the Communist Party-USA "from twenty-six thousand in 1934 to eighty-five thousand in 1939," see Gilmore, *Defying Dixie*, 185. Because affiliation with the party was comparatively central to Communist identity, I have chosen to capitalize "Communist" throughout while capitalizing "Socialist" only when referring specifically to the Socialist Party of America.

4. Roosevelt expressed his hope for generational change to Socialist Party leader Norman Thomas; see Thomas to Howard Kester, May 8, 1935, reel 1, STFU. He also referred to a "new school of thought" among "younger men and women" in the South in a speech at the University of Georgia; see Roosevelt, "In These Past Six Years," 471. On his friendship with Josephus Daniels, see Kilpatrick, *Roosevelt and Daniels*.

5. Roosevelt, "United States Is Rising," 165, 167–68. On the significance of this speech, see Leuchtenburg, *White House Looks South*, 86; and Sullivan, *Days of Hope*, 62.

6. Leuchtenburg, *White House Looks South*, 87.

7. Many historians have discussed the discriminatory tailoring of New Deal legislation and Roosevelt's conflicts with conservative southern congressmen. For an especially valuable, recent study, see Katznelson, *Fear Itself*.

8. Moore, "Senator Josiah W. Bailey."

9. Roosevelt, letter to members of the Conference on Economic Conditions in the South, 42. The official publication date of *A Southerner Discovers the South* was July 12.

10. This sentence paraphrases Brueggemann, "Racial Considerations and Social Policy," 139.

11. For example, see Auerbach, "New Deal, Old Deal, or Raw Deal." More recently, the phrase "raw deal" has emerged in conservative critiques, as in Burton W. Folsom Jr., *New Deal or Raw Deal? How FDR's Economic Legacy Has Damaged America* (New York: Simon & Schuster, 2008).

12. Leuchtenburg, *White House Looks South*, 75.

13. For an interpretation of Roosevelt's goals, see Milkis, *President and the Parties*, which also discusses Stanley High's *Saturday Evening Post* article "Whose Party Is It?" (52).

14. Sugrue, *Sweet Land of Liberty*, 20.

15. For overviews of relevant scholarship, see Brueggemann, "Racial Considerations and Social Policy"; and Williams, "African Americans and the Politics of Race."

16. Alex Lichtenstein asserts that "blame the Cold War" is "an argument that by now has become familiar" in historians' efforts to explain why the promising World War II–era civil rights struggle "deliver[ed] such limited gains." He goes on to explore what might be called the "blame Myrdal" component of this argument: the claim that the enormous influence of Gunnar Myrdal's *American Dilemma* (1944) directed Americans' attention away from structural and economic understandings of racism toward "the more powerful—and politically palatable—idea that 'eliminating racial inequality was a matter of changing attitudes and beliefs.'" The *Brown* decision has been similarly criticized, and Lichtenstein is correct to see a "declension narrative" in much recent scholarship. Whether or not that sense of decline is a "weakness" is debatable. See Lichtenstein, "Other Civil Rights Movement," 355, 359.

17. Goluboff, *Lost Promise of Civil Rights*, 9, 12.

18. Kennedy, *Freedom from Fear*, 314; Zieger, *CIO*, 2. For a recent overview of labor history scholarship, see Taylor, "Organized Labor, Reds, and Radicals."

19. Denning, *Cultural Front*, 4, 5–6.

20. Ibid., 4, 8.

21. Sullivan, *Days of Hope*, 9, 6.

22. Gilmore, *Defying Dixie*, 4.

23. Hall, "Long Civil Rights Movement"; Jacquelyn Dowd Hall, "Longer, Broader, Deeper: Rethinking the Civil Rights Movement and the Resistance to It," N. Jack Stallworth Lecture, University of South Alabama, November 9, 2011, paper in author's possession.

24. Having conceived of this project as a way to explore the late-1930s origins of the long civil rights movement (LCRM), I initially shifted to the "long civil rights era" (LCRE) in hopes of making it clear that I do not think of Jonathan Daniels as a civil rights activist. He was a mostly sympathetic observer. Further reflection suggested the value of the LCRE concept to help frame *Discovering the South* as a book that examines opposition to racial change in the 1930s in addition to New Deal–era efforts to achieve it. Ultimately, I hope the LCRE idea can help readers see the value of the LCRM framework while allaying critics' concerns that it conflates earlier and later phases of the civil rights struggle and overstates the power of the left, particularly the Communist Party. Critiques that have influenced my thinking include Arnesen, "Reconsidering the 'Long Civil Rights Movement'"; Arnesen, "Civil Rights and the Cold War at Home"; Lawson, "Long Origins of the Short Civil Rights Movement"; Lichtenstein, "Other Civil Rights Movement"; and Cha-Jua and Lang, "'Long Movement' as Vampire." Although I came to the idea separately, I am grateful to Patricia Sullivan for pointing me to Nikil Pal Singh's use of "long civil rights era" in *Black Is a Country*, 6, 8, 52–53.

25. Ward, *Defending White Democracy*.

26. My discussion of "regionalist" liberalism draws on Carlton and Coclanis, "Another 'Great Migration.'"

27. On the "I've seen America" book as a subgenre of Depression-era documentary and Daniels's book as an example of it, see Stott, *Documentary Expression and Thirties America*, 251–52.

28. Gerald W. Johnson, "Here Is the Best Book on the Modern South," *New York Herald Tribune*, July 17, 1938, in Scrapbook.

29. Tindall, *Emergence of the New South*, 741.

30. Brown, "South on the Move," 19.

31. Leuchtenburg, untitled essay in *Books of Passage*, 112, 113. The other North Carolina editor I refer to was Wilbur J. Cash, whose *Mind of the South* (1941) has inspired far more commentary from historians than Daniels's book. This is unfortunate, in my view, because of the more nuanced understanding of the region that Daniels provides. On Cash's influence, see Cobb, "Does *Mind* No Longer Matter?"

32. On the "generation of 1900," see Pyron, "Gone with the Wind and the Southern Cultural Awakening." It is worth noting that many of the black intellectuals and artists of the Harlem Renaissance were also southerners, though most were slightly older than the white cohort Darden Asbury Pyron identifies.

33. On Josephus Daniels's prominence in North Carolina's politics of disfranchisement, see Gilmore, *Gender and Jim Crow*; Kirshenbaum, "'Vampire That Hovers over North Carolina'"; Campbell, "'One of the Fine Figures of American Journalism'"; and Justesen, "George Henry White." For a broader, biographical view, see Craig, *Josephus Daniels*.

34. Korstad, *Civil Rights Unionism*, 58.

35. "Progressivism—for Whites Only" is a chapter title in C. Vann Woodward's classic *Origins of the New South*.

36. *SDS*, 10.

37. I offer Douglas A. Blackmon's book title, *Slavery by Another Name*, as a convenient shorthand for readers unfamiliar with the term "debt peonage." However, I disagree with Blackmon's claim that scholars have neglected the topic. The foundational work is Daniel, *Shadow of Slavery*, and a short list of related titles includes Mancini, *One Dies, Get Another*; Lichtenstein, *Twice the Work of Free Labor*; and Oshinsky, *Worse than Slavery*.

38. Hartwell Davis to U.S. Attorney General, February 12, 1946, case file 50-2-6, reel 20, PFDOJ; *SDS*, 261.

39. *SDS*, 287.

40. Quoted in Sullivan, *Days of Hope*, 67.

41. *SDS*, 10.

42. Eagles, *Jonathan Daniels and Race Relations*, 99.

Chapter One

1. Harold Strauss to Jonathan Daniels, February 25, 1937, folder 151, DP. That February 26 was cloudy is based on the *Raleigh News and Observer*.

2. Jonathan Daniels to Josephus Daniels, [February 27, 1937], folder 151, DP.

3. Josephus Daniels to Jonathan Daniels, February 4, 1937, reel 18, JDP.

4. Strauss to Daniels, February 25, 1937.

5. D-COHP, 42–43. The "monkey bill" was Tennessee's Butler Act of 1925, the law that John T. Scopes violated by teaching evolution in a high school biology class.

6. On southern modernism as a rebellion against Victorian thought and culture, see Daniel Joseph Singal's classic *War Within*, including his discussion of identifying signs of modernism (8). On Mencken's influence on Daniels's peers in the southern press, see Kneebone, *Southern Liberal Journalists*, 23–24, 32–34.

7. Daniels, *Clash of Angels*, 13.

8. D-COHP, 55.

9. Worth Daniels to Jonathan Daniels, September 15, 1928, folder 5, DP.

10. Unsigned to Jonathan Daniels, June 27, 1929, folder 6, DP. The salutation to "Jona" (Daniels's childhood nickname) and internal evidence indicate that this letter was from one of Daniels's brothers.

11. Woodward, "Why the Southern Renaissance?," 224–25.

12. Daniels described his plan for the novel in his application for a Guggenheim fellowship, included among his 1929 correspondence in folder 6, DP.

13. For General Order 99, which banned alcohol in the Navy, see Craig, *Josephus Daniels*, 245. On the folk etymology of "cup of Joe," see David Mikkelson, "Cup of Joe," Snopes.com, February 5, 2009, http://www.snopes.com/language/eponyms/cupofjoe.asp (accessed February 21, 2016).

14. Gerald W. Johnson to Jonathan Daniels, March 27, 1930, folder 8, DP. "Cobweb blasphemy": D-COHP, 43. "Nice little part of your juvenilia": D-SOHP, 36.

15. Jonathan Daniels to Ann Preston Bridgers, March 28, 1928, folder 5, DP.

16. Quoted in Jonathan Daniels to Josephus and Addie Daniels, April 8, 1930, reel 18, JDP.

17. D-SOHP, 9.

18. Daniels, *End of Innocence*, 20.

19. Daniels, *Tar Heel Editor*, 242. On leaving St. Albans without graduating, see D-SOHP, 46.

20. D-SOHP, 54–55, 58.

21. D-SOHP, 62–63; D-COHP, 25.

22. D-SOHP, 58, 60.

23. D-SOHP, 65–66. On Robert Rufus Bridgers Sr. as a political enemy, see Daniels, *Tar Heel Editor*, 402.

24. Josephus Daniels to Jonathan Daniels, July 9, 1922, folder 3, DP.

25. D-SOHP, 71.

26. D-SOHP, 69–75.

27. Jonathan Daniels to Addie Daniels, June 13, 1926, reel 18, JDP. I infer that the birth was by caesarian section based on a reference to "the old incision" in an unsigned typed letter, first page missing, [1930], folder 9, DP.

28. This period is well documented in family letters, and Daniels also mentioned his work on his father's memoirs in D-SOHP, 75. On Adelaide Ann Worth Bagley's "pianistic feat," see Morrison, *Josephus Daniels*, 154. On the death of Worth Bagley, see Craig, *Josephus Daniels*, 177.

29. D-SOHP, 78–81.

30. On Bab's irregular menstruation, see unsigned typed letter [1930]. Uncertainty about the due date is also evident in Jonathan Daniels to Emily Bridgers, May 9, 1929, folder 7, Ann Preston Bridgers Papers, David M. Rubenstein Rare Book and Manuscript Library, Duke University, Durham, N.C..

31. Warner Wells, "Elizabeth Delia Dixon-Carroll" (from *Dictionary of North Carolina Biography* [University of North Carolina Press, 1986]), *NCPedia*, http://ncpedia.org/biography/dixon-carroll-elizabeth (accessed April 16, 2016). See also Rogers, "Dr. Delia Dixon-Carroll." Although Daniels and Bridgers family letters refer to Bab's doctor only as "Dr. Carroll" and with feminine pronouns, *Hill's Raleigh City Directory* (Richmond, Va.: Hill Directory Co., 1929) confirms that Elizabeth Delia Dixon-Carroll was the only female physician named Carroll living in Raleigh at the time.

32. Unsigned typed letter [1930]. I attribute this letter to Addie Daniels based on internal evidence, particularly the fact that its author took care of three-year-old Adelaide Ann during Bab's ordeal and was not one of "the Bridgers." In addition to attributing authorship, I have made two educated guesses about Bab's treatment. One is that the oil prescribed to induce labor was castor oil. The other is that the procedure in which the doctors "inserted bags in the mouth of the uterus," as the letter put it, involved fluid-filled bags and was what is commonly known as balloon dilation.

33. Unsigned typed letter [1930].

34. D-COHP, 43.

35. Josephus Daniels to Jonathan Daniels, December 24, 1929, folder 6, DP.

36. D-SOHP, 81.

37. Jonathan Daniels to Addie Daniels, January 5 and January 8, 1930, reel 18, JDP.

38. Josephus Daniels to Jonathan Daniels, April 26, 1930, folder 9, DP.

39. Cobb, *Away Down South*, 68. See also Gaston, *New South Creed*.

40. Guggenheim application, folder 6, DP.

41. Ibid.

42. D-COHP, 52.

43. D-COHP, 48. Drafts and notes for the unpublished novel can be found under the title "Eat, Mule, Eat the Azaleas" in folders 2188 and 2189, DP. Daniels also discussed his progress on the manuscript and his futile efforts to get it published in various letters to family members.

44. Handwritten diary entry, January 30, 1932, folder 2523, DP. Daniels does not appear to have kept diaries consistently, but there are a few scattered volumes among his papers.

45. Jonathan Daniels to Lucy Cathcart, [postmark March 19, 1932], folder 11, DP.

46. *The Philadelphia Story*, directed by George Cukor (1940; Burbank, CA: Turner Entertainment and Warner Home Video, 2000), DVD. I intend this allusion to have a somewhat negative connotation, although I have chosen not to research Daniels's personal life after his second marriage to the same extent as his earlier years. For a troubled account written by one of his daughters, see Daniels, *With a Woman's Voice*. Another perspective based on interviews with various Daniels family members can be found in Craig, *Josephus Daniels*, 394–96.

47. D-COHP, 54–55.

48. My discussion of the attitudes and activities of Josephus Daniels's generation of North Carolina Democrats owes much, including stylistically, to Gilmore, *Gender and Jim Crow*, esp. 65–67.

49. Korstad, *Civil Rights Unionism*, 50–51; Gilmore, *Gender and Jim Crow*, 78. On North Carolina's "fusion," see also Edmonds, *Negro and Fusion Politics*; and Kousser, *Shaping of Southern Politics*, esp. 183–95.

50. Editorial, *Raleigh News and Observer*, November 1, 1896, quoted in Gerber, *Limits of Liberalism*, 84–85. On Josephus Daniels's role in the white supremacy campaign, see esp. Gilmore, *Gender and Jim Crow*, 83–84, 88–89; Craig, *Josephus Daniels*, 178–89; and Campbell, "'One of the Fine Figures of American Journalism.'"

51. Daniels, *Editor in Politics*, 148.

52. "The Vampire That Hovers over North Carolina" and "Why the Whites Are United," cartoons, *Raleigh News and Observer*, September 27 and October 28, 1898. For digital versions of these and other cartoons, see "The 1898 Election in North Carolina," UNC Libraries, http://exhibits.lib.unc.edu/exhibits/show/1898/history (accessed February 21, 2016).

On the cartoons' impact, see Kirshenbaum, "'Vampire That Hovers over North Carolina.'"

53. There is extensive scholarship on lynching. One good starting point is Brundage, *Lynching in the New South*. Ida B. Wells's antilynching campaign has been detailed in a number of biographies and other scholarly works, including Schechter, *Ida B. Wells-Barnett and American Reform*; Giddings, *Ida: A Sword among Lions*; Feimster, *Southern Horrors*; and Bay, *To Tell the Truth Freely*.

54. Hall, *Revolt against Chivalry*, 151.

55. Whites, "Love, Hate, Rape, Lynching," 143–62; quotations from Felton's speech appear ibid., 149, 153. On Felton, see also Feimster, *Southern Horrors*.

56. Whites, "Love, Hate, Rape, Lynching," 149.

57. Gilmore, *Gender and Jim Crow*, 92. For the March 1898 meeting between Daniels, Simmons, and Aycock, see Gilmore, "Murder, Memory, and the Flight of the Incubus," 74.

58. Gilmore, "Murder, Memory, and the Flight of the Incubus," 75.

59. Unsigned editorial attributed to Alexander Manly, *Wilmington Daily Record*, August 18, 1898; full text at "1898 Election in North Carolina." On Manly's paternity, see Prather, "We Have Taken a City," 23–24, 40n23.

60. For Wells's editorial, see Royster, *Southern Horrors*, 52.

61. Cecelski and Tyson, "Introduction," 5.

62. Daniels, *Editor in Politics*, 308.

63. On White, whom Josephus Daniels helped drive from office, see Justesen, "George Henry White."

64. Daniels, *Editor in Politics*, 145.

65. Roosevelt, "United States Is Rising," 168.

66. Steven Hahn provides a fascinating exploration of the opportunities for and obstacles against political biracialism in the post-emancipation South in *Nation under Our Feet*. See also Dailey, *Before Jim Crow*.

67. Korstad, *Civil Rights Unionism*, 57.

68. Morrison, *Josephus Daniels*, 242.

69. Jonathan Daniels, "A Shocking Verdict," *Raleigh News and Observer*, April 10, 1933; Jonathan Daniels to Josephus Daniels, July 1, 1933, DP. See also Eagles, *Jonathan Daniels and Race Relations*, 3; and Craig, *Josephus Daniels*, 393. On the fanfare surrounding Josephus and Addie Daniels's departure, see Morrison, *Josephus Daniels*, 171.

70. There is a large body of scholarship on white liberals and radicals in the mid-twentieth-century South. A few majors works are Sosna, *In Search of the Silent South*; Hall, *Revolt against Chivalry*; Dunbar, *Against the Grain*; Eagles, *Jonathan Daniels and Race Relations*; Hobson, *Tell about the South*; Hobson, *But Now I See*; Kneebone, *Southern Liberal Journalists*; Egerton, *Speak Now against the Day*; Sullivan, *Days of Hope*; Kelley, *Hammer and Hoe*; and Gilmore, *Defying Dixie*.

71. Brundage, *Lynching in the New South*, 95; see also appendix A. Virginia and North Carolina first successfully prosecuted lynchers in 1898 and 1906, respectively, also in cases involving white victims (ibid., 95, 326n30).

72. Carlton and Coclanis, "Another 'Great Migration,'" 37–38.

73. Schulman, *From Cotton Belt to Sunbelt*, 41. On Odum, see O'Brien, *Idea of the American South*; and Singal, *War Within*.

74. Carlton and Coclanis, "Another 'Great Migration,'" 38.

75. On Dabney, see Kneebone, *Southern Liberal Journalists*.

76. Eagles, *Jonathan Daniels and Race Relations*, 11.

77. D-SOHP, 4. See also D-COHP, 5; *SDS*, 3–4.

78. Jonathan Daniels to Elizabeth Bridgers Daniels, September 2, 1926, folder 4, DP.

79. Ibid. *Flaming Youth* was a 1923 silent film based on a book of the same title by Samuel Hopkins Adams.

80. "Underdog-supporting": D-SOHP, 72.

81. On the Ericson affair, see Eagles, *Jonathan Daniels and Race Relations*, 45–51.

82. W. T. Couch to Jonathan Daniels, October 31, 1936, folder 130, DP.

83. Josephus Daniels to Jonathan Daniels, November 4, 1936, folder 131, DP. See also Eagles, *Jonathan Daniels and Race Relations*, 49.

84. Eagles, *Jonathan Daniels and Race Relations*, 49.

85. Jonathan Daniels to Oswald Garrison Villard, November 7, 1936, folder 132, DP.

86. Jonathan Daniels to W. T. Couch, November 2, 1936, folder 131, DP.

87. Charles W. Eagles suggests the 1937 trip was important to Daniels's evolution as a racial liberal but offers only a brief discussion of it in *Jonathan Daniels and Race Relations*, 51.

88. Jonathan Daniels to Josephus Daniels, April 19, 1937, folder 151, DP. On the lunch, see *SDS*, 2; and D-COHP, 75.

89. Lucy Cathcart Daniels to Josephus and Addie Daniels, April 12, 1937, reel 18, JDP.

90. Jonathan Daniels to Josephus Daniels, April 19, 1937.

91. Jonathan Daniels to Josephus and Addie Daniels, April 28, 1937, folder 151, DP.

92. Jonathan Daniels, "An American Editor Studies America's Problems," typescript, [July 1, 1940], folder 2469, DP.

Chapter Two

1. Quotations from *SDS*, 25–26. Daniels recorded his departure time and the other details noted here in Journal, 1. Although his papers include this travel diary in its original handwritten form, I have relied on a typed transcript with handwritten notes that Daniels presumably added as he was drafting *SDS*. I have silently corrected typographical errors and misspellings and have occasionally added punctuation for clarity.

Many passages of *SDS* replicate Daniels's journal almost verbatim. My preference has been to quote from the journal rather than the book as much as possible, though I typically provide the relevant *SDS* page numbers as well.

Because Daniels recorded only the names of towns and other landmarks, my references to specific roads are based on deduction. To trace his route from Raleigh to Knoxville, I compared his notes to a 1936 map of the North Carolina State Highway System in "State Highway System of North Carolina, 1936," *North Carolina Maps*, http://www2.lib.unc.edu/dc/ncmaps/interactive/MC_150_1936nb.html (accessed March 4, 2016).

2. On Daniels's editorials and their reception, see Hall et al., *Like a Family*, 334. Quotation is from Jonathan Daniels to Josephus Daniels, September 20, [1934], folder 17, DP.

3. *SDS*, 148.

4. Carlton and Coclanis, *Confronting Southern Poverty*, 54–55.

5. Daniels reviewed Odum's *Southern Regions* in "From Sectionalism to Regionalism." He mentions having read Raper's *Preface to Peasantry* in *SDS*, 140.

6. On "the catastrophic impact of the Great Depression and the disruptive effect of New Deal farm programs," see Bartley, "Southern Enclosure Movement," 439.

7. Journal, 4. Daniels explained that "every night I would get to the hotel and write that day, send it back to Lucy, who would type it up, and then when I got home I had these notes." See D-COHP, 97.

8. *SDS*, 32.

9. Journal, 4.

10. *SDS*, 27–33.

11. Journal, 4–5; *SDS*, 34–35.

12. Journal, 2.

13. Daniels, "Poor Whites"; Jonathan Daniels, "Strong Story of Forgotten Lives," *Raleigh News and Observer*, March 5, 1933.

14. *SDS*, 7.

15. Daniels is quoted in "True South Photos Sought," June 1938, clipping in Scrapbook.

16. *SDS*, 34, 35.

17. For Daniels's description of the store near Conestee, see Journal, 5. The letter was Harold Strauss to Jonathan Daniels, February 25, 1937, folder 151, DP.

18. Journal, 5–8; *SDS*, 35–41.

19. On May 7, Daniels noted an odometer reading of 22,675, from which I have subtracted his starting mileage of 22,246.2 to get the rounded figure of 429 miles. See Journal, 1, 8.

20. *SDS*, 9. On the plowman, see Journal, 9; *SDS*, 43.

21. *SDS*, 136.

22. Journal, 10. A "gyp": *SDS*, 44.

23. Journal, 10. Maher, *Nature's New Deal*, 110; Salmond, "Civilian Conservation Corps," 76.

24. On Civilian Conservation Corps work in Great Smoky Mountains National Park, see Maher, *Nature's New Deal*, 131–50.

25. Journal, 10; *SDS*, 45.

26. Journal, 14. On the Ethiopian Clowns, see Mohl, "Clowning Around"; and Lanctot, *Negro League Baseball*, 107–10, 138.

27. Quoted in Neuse, *David E. Lilienthal*, 67.

28. Quoted in Maher, *Nature's New Deal*, 187.

29. Roosevelt, "Growing Up by Plan," 483.

30. On the appeal of planning at the regional level, see Grant, *TVA and Black Americans*, xxvii.

31. Background on the Tennessee Valley is based on Grant, *TVA and Black Americans*, xxvii. Quotations from Bartley, "Southern Enclosure Movement," 442; Roosevelt, "Suggestion for Legislature," 122–23; and Russell B. Porter, "TVA's Domain: A Land of Individualists," *New York Times Magazine*, July 10, 1938, 93.

32. Maher, *Nature's New Deal*, 191.

33. Ibid., 194.

34. On the origins of the Tennessee Valley Authority, see Grant, *TVA and Black Americans*, 6–8.

35. Neuse, *David E. Lilienthal*, 69–70.

36. *SDS*, 48–49, 66. For Daniels's support for the Tennessee Valley Authority, see his "Three Men in a Valley," "Banner on a Yardstick," and "Diagram for Democracy." On Josephus Daniels's support for lower utility rates and his conflicts with Duke Power, see Morrison, *Josephus Daniels*, 146; and Durden, *Electrifying the Piedmont Carolinas*, 45, 49–51.

37. Journal, 18; see also *SDS*, 56–57.

38. *SDS*, 60.

39. *SDS*, 48. Daniels's reflection that Norris "may do more to make enemies for planned economy than all the Republican speeches and power company briefs in the world" appears in *SDS*, 57. He initially expressed the idea in a more personal form, writing Norris "has done more to make me the enemy of planned economy than all the Republican speeches in the world" (Journal, 18).

40. Journal, 18. I have edited this quotation, cutting the word "malignance" in favor of the words "imposition from above," which are handwritten in the typescript. See also *SDS*, 57.

41. Journal, 18. On the exclusion of blacks from Norris, see Grant, *TVA and Black Americans*, 37–38, 168n46.

42. *SDS*, 48.

43. Journal, 17–18; see also *SDS*, 66–67.

44. Grant, *TVA and Black Americans*, xxvi.

45. On "grassroots democracy," see Badger, *New Deal*, 176.

46. *SDS*, 64.

47. Neuse, *David E. Lilienthal*, 121.

48. *SDS*, 91–92; see also Journal, 21.

49. Woodward, *Origins of the New South*, 211. On job and wage discrimination, see Grant, *TVA and Black Americans*.

50. Journal, 32; see also *SDS*, 92, 152.

51. *SDS*, 92.

52. On the visceral and sensory characteristics of white southerners' racism, see Smith, *How Race Is Made*.

53. Francis Pickens Miller to Frank Porter Graham, December 21, 1938, copy in folder 236, DP.

54. Roosevelt, "Recommendations to the Congress to Curb Monopolies," 305.

55. My discussion of transformations in liberal ideology has been influenced by Rossinow, *Visions of Progress*, and Milkis, *President and the Parties*. See also Gerstle, "Protean Character of American Liberalism."

56. *SDS*, 1, 7, 8.

57. *SDS*, 64, 72.

58. Journal, 17. I added the parentheses for clarity. On the feud between Lilienthal and Morgan, see Neuse, *David E. Lilienthal*, esp. 93–101.

59. *SDS*, 67.

60. MacLean, *Behind the Mask of Chivalry*, 80.

61. On the Jeffersonian Democrats of 1936, see Ward, *Defending White Democracy*, 19–20. For an interesting look at twentieth-century politicians' appropriation of Jefferson's legacy, see Burstein, *Democracy's Muse*.

62. Quoted in Gerber, *Limits of Liberalism*, 19.

63. My emphasis on the importance of workers' and their allies' demands that federal standards be enforced is in keeping with Nancy MacLean's excellent analysis of how the Civil Rights Act of 1964 was implemented in *Freedom Is Not Enough*.

64. *SDS*, 67.

65. Journal, 21; *SDS*, 81–82.

66. Built in 1928, Lookout Mountain Hotel struggled through the Depression. The building was eventually purchased by Covenant College and is now Carter Hall; see "Carter Hall," Covenant College, http://www.covenant.edu/visit/campus/carter (accessed March 4, 2016).

67. John T. Kneebone uses the phrase "shouting match" and refers to the Tate-Amberson episode as "almost legendary" in *Southern Liberal Journalists*, 139.

68. Tindall, *Emergence of the New South*, 409. There is a substantial body of scholarship on the transformation of southern agriculture in the mid-twentieth century. For an overview, see Bartley, "Southern Enclosure Movement."

69. Daniels, "Democracy Is Bread," 489.

Chapter Three

1. Journal, 23.

2. *SDS*, 102.

3. *SDS*, 101.

4. *SDS*, 104, 106.

5. *SDS*, 106.

6. Quotations from Carter, *Scottsboro*, 8. My account of the Scottsboro case is based more or less equally on Carter's book and Goodman, *Stories of Scottsboro*.

7. Gilmore, *Defying Dixie*, 118–19. On the policy of self-determination for the Black Belt, see ibid., 61–66. For the NAACP's perspective, see Sullivan, *Lift Every Voice*, 145–51.

8. *Powell v. Alabama*, 287 U.S. 45 (1932).

9. Goodman, *Stories of Scottsboro*, 92. See also Carter, *Scottsboro*, 6.

10. My account of the fight is based on Goodman, *Stories of Scottsboro*, 3–5.

11. Ibid., 101 and 101–10 passim. See also Carter, *Scottsboro*, 181–83.

12. Goodman, *Stories of Scottsboro*, 125–27. See also Carter, *Scottsboro*, 204–13.

13. Goodman, *Stories of Scottsboro*, 127–28. See also Carter, *Scottsboro*, 213–14.

14. Goodman, *Stories of Scottsboro*, 132.

15. Quoted in Goodman, *Stories of Scottsboro*, 133.

16. Jonathan Daniels, "Southern Honor on Trial," *Raleigh News and Observer*, April 8, 1933.

17. Goodman, *Stories of Scottsboro*, 170.

18. Daniels, letter to the editor.

19. Jonathan Daniels, "A Shocking Verdict," *Raleigh News and Observer*, April 10, 1933. "Common tradition of justice": quoted in Goodman, *Stories of Scottsboro*, 104.

20. Quoted in Goodman, *Stories of Scottsboro*, 134–35.

21. Jonathan Daniels, "A Suggestion to the South," *Raleigh News and Observer*, April 11, 1933.

22. Acker, *Scottsboro and Its Legacy*, 204–5.

23. Daniels, letter to the editor.

24. For Daniels's use of the word "whores," see D-SOHP, 62.

25. Carter, *Scottsboro*, 13–14, 81–82. See also Goodman, *Stories of Scottsboro*, 126.

26. Goodman, *Stories of Scottsboro*, 42–43. See also Carter, *Scottsboro*, 82–83.

27. Goodman, *Stories of Scottsboro*, 196–97. See also Carter, *Scottsboro*, 232–33.

28. Goodman, *Stories of Scottsboro*, 145, 153. See also Carter, *Scottsboro*, 239–40.

29. Carter, *Scottsboro*, 243–44. See also Goodman, *Stories of Scottsboro*, 147–48.

30. *SDS*, 105–6.

31. Daniels, "Suggestion to the South."

32. Horton's statement is quoted in Goodman, *Stories of Scottsboro*, 180–81. For his later revelation, see Carter, *Scottsboro*, 214–15. In a footnote, Carter acknowledges that Lynch denied Horton's claim.

33. Jonathan Daniels, "A Wise Judge Points the Way," *Raleigh News and Observer*, June 23, 1933.

34. Jonathan Daniels, "Where the Stars Fell," *Raleigh News and Observer*, April 3, 1935.

35. Kneebone, *Southern Liberal Journalists*, 148, 199; Egerton, *Speak Now against the Day*, 48–49. For a more positive assessment of blacks' influence within the Commission on Interracial Cooperation, see Mazzari, *Southern Modernist*, 60.

36. Quoted in Sosna, *In Search of the Silent South*, 26.

37. Ibid., 32.

38. Sullivan, *Lift Every Voice*, 105–6.

39. Rable, "The South and the Politics of Antlynching Legislation," 203–4. See also Zangrando, *NAACP Crusade against Lynching*.

40. Sullivan, *Lift Every Voice*, 109.

41. Rable, "South and the Politics of Antilynching Legislation," 204–5.

42. Sullivan, *Lift Every Voice*, 194.

43. On the Neal case, see McGovern, *Anatomy of a Lynching*.

44. Rable, "South and the Politics of Antilynching Legislation," 208–9.

45. Ibid., 212.

46. Ibid., 209. On Roosevelt's reticence, see also Kennedy, *Freedom from Fear*, 210, 343.

47. Raper, *Tragedy of Lynching*, 1, 37. See also Mazzari, *Southern Modernist*, 88–89. Other helpful summaries of Raper's book and its significance include Hall, *Revolt against Chivalry*, 137–39; and Sosna, *In Search of the Silent South*, 32–33.

48. Mazzari, *Southern Modernist*, 89.

49. Jonathan Daniels, "The Tragedy of Lynching," *Raleigh News and Observer*, April 13, 1933; Mazzari, *Southern Modernist*, 97–101.

50. Daniels, "Tragedy of Lynching."

51. Sosna, *In Search of the Silent South*, 33; Mazzari, *Southern Modernist*, 95.

52. Hall, *Revolt against Chivalry*, 245.

53. Jonathan Daniels, "Arm the States," *Raleigh News and Observer*, December 26, 1933.

54. Rable, "South and the Politics of Antilynching Legislation," 207. Daniels emphasized the decline in lynching and praised local and state efforts to eradicate the practice in a number of *News and Observer* editorials, including "Kentucky's Lynch Law," May 19, 1933; "In Sympathy and Respect," November 21, 1934; and "Good Sign," December 29, 1934. I am indebted to Charles W. Eagles's *Jonathan Daniels and Race Relations* for guiding me to Daniels's editorials.

55. Jonathan Daniels, "R.S.V.P.," *Raleigh News and Observer*, October 28, 1934.

56. Hall, *Revolt against Chivalry*, 139.

57. Jonathan Daniels, "Need for Co-operation," *Raleigh News and Observer*, April 2, 1937.

58. Wood, *Lynching and Spectacle*, 197.

59. Jonathan Daniels, "Southern Scene," *Raleigh News and Observer*, April 15, 1937.

60. See Wise, *William Alexander Percy*. Daniels's meeting with Percy was unplanned. He arrived in Greenville and had trouble getting a hotel room until "this young newspaperman came up and introduced himself to me. His name was Hodding Carter. He got a hotel room for me, and then he took me around, and we spent the evening at Will Percy's house." D-COHP, 93.

61. Journal, 48, 53.

62. *SDS*, 179.

63. Journal, 52.

64. *SDS*, 180.

65. Jonathan Daniels, "Anti Lynching Bills," *Raleigh News and Observer*, June 15, 1937.

66. Jonathan Daniels, "A Red Whale," *Raleigh News and Observer*, January 11, 1938.

67. Goodman, *Stories of Scottsboro*, 257–58. Goodman's account differs from Carter, *Scottsboro*, 347–48, which indicates the juror thought Patterson was innocent of the rape.

68. Goodman, *Stories of Scottsboro*, 259–61; Carter, *Scottsboro*, 348–50.

69. Chalmers, *They Shall Be Free*, 57–58.

70. On Chappell, see *SDS*, 273–74, 276–77; and Journal, 94. Chappell's election as president of the Southern Newspaper Publishers Association is recorded in "Sees Class War in South," *New York Times*, May 20, 1936, 2.

71. Goodman, *Stories of Scottsboro*, 299. Goodman attributes Hall's change of heart to the death of his friend Thomas Knight.

72. Goodman, *Stories of Scottsboro*, 290.

73. Chalmers, *They Shall Be Free*, 82, 84.

74. On these negotiations, see Goodman, *Stories of Scottsboro*, 287–92.

75. Chalmers, *They Shall Be Free*, 102.

76. For the cause of Knight's death, I have relied on "Scottsboro Figure Dies," *Washington Post*, May 18, 1937, 4.

77. Acker, *Scottsboro and Its Legacy*, 206.

78. Ibid., 196–97.

79. Ibid., 198.

80. Gilmore, *Defying Dixie*, 109.

Chapter Four

1. Journal, 23–24; see also *SDS*, 106–10.

2. Beidler, "Yankee Interloper and Native Son," 29.

3. In fact, Harold Strauss mentioned Carmer's work as, not a "precise parallel," but "the closest I can come by way of illustration" to the book he proposed for Daniels to write; see Harold Strauss to Jonathan Daniels, February 25, 1937, folder 151, DP.

4. *SDS*, 10.

5. Stott, *Documentary Expression and Thirties America*, 251. I have relied on Stott's classic book for my broad outline of the documentary genre, as well as my characterization of the "I've seen America" book as a circumspect and politically centrist subgenre. However, I avoid Stott's label for this subgenre—"Documentary Reportage: 'Conservative'"—in order to avoid confusion with other uses of the word "conservative" in this chapter. I also find Stott's book a bit dismissive of what he calls "Documentary Reportage: Radical," including the works by Spivak and Rorty that I mentioned.

6. Quotations from *SDS*, 113, 9–10. I am indebted to Michael O'Brien's *Idea of the American South* for the recognition that Davidson had "the least modern mind" (xxiv) among the Agrarians and therefore would not appreciate the modernism of Daniels's documentary approach.

7. Davidson claimed not to have read *A Southerner Discovers the South* in "Class Approach to Southern Problems," 134. His review of Sherwood Anderson's *Puzzled America* is quoted in Stott, *Documentary Expression and Thirties America*, 246.

8. My use of "conservative" instead of "reactionary" or some other term reflects

my sense of how the Agrarians, and Davidson in particular, have generally been characterized in scholarship. Emily S. Bingham and Thomas A. Underwood note the variety of "conservative styles" among the Agrarians and provide a very helpful literature review in *Southern Agrarians and the New Deal*, 8–11. For another useful review essay, see Nicolaisen, "Southern Conservatism at Bay."

9. Malvasi, *Unregenerate South*, 204, 158. For Mark G. Malvasi's affinity for Davidson's views, see esp. 217. Peter Nicolaisen's "Southern Conservatism at Bay" emphasizes Malvasi's conservatism, while a discussion of his ties to neo-Confederate groups can be found in Hague, Beirich, and Sebesta, *Neo-Confederacy*, 72n67.

10. On agrarian movements of the late twentieth and twenty-first centuries, see Major, *Grounded Vision*; Major discusses the problematic legacy of the Nashville Agrarians only briefly at 7.

11. On the Agrarians' role in later culture wars and especially for reactions to historian Eugene Genovese's views, see Davis, "Southern Comfort"; and Kreyling, *Inventing Southern Literature*.

12. Donald Davidson, "The Trend in Literature," quoted in Malvasi, *Unregenerate South*, 190. Daniels described Davidson as "sensitive" and "soft-spoken" in Journal, 25; and *SDS*, 113.

13. *SDS*, 113. My description of the hotel is based on "Andrew Jackson Hotel," *Historic Nashville*, February 20, 2009, http://historicnashville.wordpress.com/2009/02/20/andrew-jackson-hotel/ (accessed March 5, 2016).

14. *SDS*, 112–13.

15. *SDS*, 113, 118. Daniels mentions taking taxis in Birmingham, though not in Nashville; see *SDS*, 273.

16. Journal, 25. The scandal that served as the basis for Warren's 1943 novel involved Senator Luke Lea, who was the publisher of the *Nashville Tennessean*. For a brief account including the impact of Lea's downfall on Davidson, who reviewed books for the *Tennessean*, see Winchell, *Where No Flag Flies*, 151.

17. Conkin, *Southern Agrarians*, 24. On the defensiveness of the Nashville Agrarians (and white southerners generally), see Maxwell, *Indicted South*.

18. Conkin, *Southern Agrarians*, 59.

19. Ibid., 46–47.

20. Ibid., 70–72.

21. Donald Davidson to H. C. Nixon, January 5, 1930, quoted in Bingham and Underwood, *Southern Agrarians and the New Deal*, 93n6. See also Shouse, *Hillbilly Realist*, 52.

22. A number of other authors have written more detailed explications of Agrarian thought than I am able to provide in this chapter. For an overview of works published before 2001, see Bingham and Underwood, *Southern Agrarians and the New Deal*, 8–17. For a more recent work of southern intellectual history with three chapters on the Agrarians, see Maxwell, *Indicted South*.

23. Twelve Southerners, *I'll Take My Stand*, xxiii–xxiv.

24. Davidson to Nixon, January 5, 1930.

25. Conkin, *Southern Agrarians*, 72.

26. For Davidson's account of who made the list for possible recruitment, see Davidson, "*I'll Take My Stand*: A History," 98. All were white men except for South

Carolina novelist Julia Peterkin. Some were known for liberal views, including Will Alexander and Julian Harris.

27. Malvasi, *Unregenerate South*, 215–16. My claim that the Agrarians have appealed most to audiences sensing a loss of cultural identity and political power draws on Kreyling, *Inventing Southern Literature*, esp. 167–82.

28. Davidson, "*I'll Take My Stand*: A History," 90.

29. Conkin, *Southern Agrarians*, 73–75.

30. Twelve Southerners, *I'll Take My Stand*, xx.

31. Davidson, "*I'll Take My Stand*: A History," 99.

32. Kneebone, *Southern Liberal Journalists*, 59.

33. Twelve Southerners, *I'll Take My Stand*, xxi.

34. Ibid., xxii–xxviii.

35. Ibid., xxviii–xxix.

36. Ibid., xxix–xxx.

37. Conkin, *Southern Agrarians*, 76.

38. Quoted in Davidson, "*I'll Take My Stand*: A History," 99–100. On Tate's proposed title, see Conkin, *Southern Agrarians*, 71.

39. On the critical response, see Conkin, *Southern Agrarians*, 86–87.

40. Jonathan Daniels to Donald Davidson, August 25, 1937, in Donald Grady Davidson Papers, Special Collections, Jean and Alexander Heard Library, Vanderbilt University. This and one other brief letter are the only correspondence from Daniels in Davidson's collection.

41. *SDS*, 114; D-COHP, 102.

42. *SDS*, 115; Donald Davidson, "A Mirror for Artists," in Twelve Southerners, *I'll Take My Stand*, 59.

43. O'Brien, *Idea of the American South*, 31.

44. On Odum, see O'Brien, *Idea of the American South*, 31–93. Other works that discuss this important figure include Tindall, *Emergence of the New South*; Sosna, *In Search of the Silent South*; Singal, *War Within*; Hobson, *Tell about the South*; and Gilmore, *Defying Dixie*.

45. Holladay, "Gods That Failed," 293. See also O'Brien, *Idea of the American South*, 54–55.

46. Southern Policy Conference, *Southern Policy*, 3; the twenty-seven delegates and two "invited guests" who attended the first meeting are listed at 2. The six delegates Daniels visited in 1937 were J. Charles Poe, Julian Harris, Donald Davidson, H. C. Nixon, Tarleton Collier, and A. Steve Nance. All but Nixon are named in *SDS*. Daniels's journal makes it clear that Nixon is the "young professor" mentioned in *SDS*, 244.

47. For Daniels's discussion of the Southern Policy Committee, see *SDS*, 82. On the organization, see Miller, *Man from the Valley*, esp. 79–81; Tindall, *Emergence of the New South*, 592–94; Kneebone, *Southern Liberal Journalists*, 133–52, 168; Shouse, *Hillbilly Realist*, 78–94, 104–5; Egerton, *Speak Now against the Day*, 175–77; Schulman, *From Cotton Belt to Sunbelt*, 40–43; and Carlton and Coclanis, *Confronting Southern Poverty*, 11–13.

48. Kneebone, *Southern Liberal Journalists*, 133, 148; Holladay, "Gods That Failed," 298.

49. Bingham and Underwood, *Southern Agrarians and the New Deal*, 7. On Mencken's article and Owsley's essay as a rebuttal, see Maxwell, *Indicted South*, 137–39.

50. Owsley, "Pillars of Agrarianism," 202, 210–11.

51. There is extensive scholarship on the origins of sharecropping and other post–Civil War developments in southern agriculture. For an interesting discussion of the historiography, see Marler, "Fables of the Reconstruction."

52. Tenancy figures and crop prices are from Wright, *Old South, New South*, 121, 226.

53. Schulman, *From Cotton Belt to Sunbelt*, 16–17. On the pig reduction program, see Culver and Hyde, *American Dreamer*, 124.

54. Quoted in Schulman, *From Cotton Belt to Sunbelt*, 31.

55. Owsley, "Pillars of Agrarianism," 211. For Southern Policy Committee delegates' reaction to Owsley's sectionalism, see Southern Policy Conference, *Southern Policy*, 19.

56. Southern Policy Conference, *Southern Policy*, 8–9.

57. Conkin, *Southern Agrarians*, 116; Conkin says Davidson and Owsley represented the Agrarians at the meeting, but Owsley's name does not appear on the list of delegates, while Waller's does. See Southern Policy Conference, *Southern Policy*, 2.

58. Southern Policy Conference, *Southern Policy*, 19.

59. Conkin, *Southern Agrarians*, 122–24.

60. Danforth Ross, "Memories of Allen Tate," quoted in Underwood, *Allen Tate*, 248–49.

61. My account of this debate is based primarily on Woodward, *Thinking Back*, 18–19. For the parting words attributed to Tate, see Roper, *C. Vann Woodward, Southerner*, 91–92, 325n20.

62. D-COHP, 102.

63. *SDS*, 118; Conkin, *Southern Agrarians*, 123.

64. *SDS*, 117.

65. O'Brien, *Idea of the American South*, 195.

66. Owsley, "Mr. Daniels Discovers the South," 665–66, 667, 668.

67. Journal, [111]; *SDS*, 12.

68. Owsley, "Mr. Daniels Discovers the South," 666–67, 670–72. For "the Mencken period," see D-SOHP, 58.

69. For Daniels's misattribution of the negative review to Broadus Mitchell, see D-COHP, 101.

70. Owsley, "Mr. Daniels Discovers the South," 670.

71. Conkin, *Southern Agrarians*, 127–32. In *The Indicted South*, Angie Maxwell argues that the New Criticism was more of an extension of Agrarian thought than is often acknowledged, asserting that "the New Critics, by championing white southern aesthetic values, stripped the American literary canon of any diversity or challenge to their southern perspective" (89). This view is compatible with my observations about the Agrarians' tendency to universalize and naturalize their specific and historically constructed form of southern identity. Nevertheless, because of my focus on Davidson, it makes more sense for me to emphasize Agrarianism's apparent demise rather than the continuities to be found in New Criticism.

72. On Davidson's political thought, see Malvasi, *Unregenerate South*; O'Brien, *Idea of the American South*, 202–9; and Winchell, *Where No Flag Flies*.

73. Conkin, *Southern Agrarians*, 99, 146.

74. Davidson, "That This Nation May Endure," 130–32.

75. Donald Davidson to John Donald Wade, March 3, 1934, quoted in Conkin, *Southern Agrarians*, 151. On Davidson's racial views, see especially his "Preface to Decision."

76. Winchell, *Where No Flag Flies*, 295.

77. Quoted in Conkin, *Southern Agrarians*, 160.

78. Winchell, *Where No Flag Flies*, 298–99.

79. Ibid., 338.

80. Woodward, *Burden of Southern History*, 6–7.

81. Ibid., 3, 8–9, 12.

82. Winchell, *Where No Flag Flies*, 352.

83. Woodward, *Burden of Southern History*, 3.

84. Winchell, *Where No Flag Flies*, 354–55.

85. Davidson, "Class Approach to Southern Problems," 134.

86. *SDS*, 114; Davidson, "Class Approach to Southern Problems," 134.

87. On this point, see Kreyling, *Inventing Southern Literature*, 167–82.

Chapter Five

1. Cohn, *God Shakes Creation*. On the hotel, see "History of The Peabody Memphis," http://www.peabodymemphis.com/history/ (accessed March 5, 2016). "Plight of the sharecroppper" is an allusion to Norman Thomas's 1934 *Plight of the Share-Cropper*.

2. Journal, 25. The hitchhiker told one of the more bizarre stories Daniels heard on his trip: he was on his way to Texas, where he hoped to get work in a hospital like the one in which he had recently convalesced after suffering a monkey attack while working on a primate ranch, apparently in North Carolina.

3. Journal, 25.

4. *SDS*, 120, 346.

5. *SDS*, 123. Daniels was quoting verbatim from his notes about his conversation with Butler; see Journal, 25. For his assessment of Norman Thomas, whom he did not meet during his travels, see *SDS*, 133.

6. Schulman, *From Cotton Belt to Sunbelt*, 20.

7. Manthorne, "View from the Cotton," 25.

8. Ibid., 24, 28–30. See also Ross, "'I Ain't Got No Home.'" On some members' "expectation that the union's main purpose was to support those in need and supplant the paternalism of the planters with a less exploitative model," see Fannin, *Labor's Promised Land*, 171–72.

9. Dunbar, *Against the Grain*, 19, 24–25.

10. Kester, *Revolt among the Sharecroppers*, 55–56.

11. Mitchell, *Mean Things*, 43.

12. H. L. Mitchell, "Early Days Southern Tenant Farmers Union," 1936, reel 58, STFU. See also Manthorne, "View from the Cotton," 26–27. On the Elaine massacre, see Whitaker, *On the Laps of Gods*; and Woodruff, *American Congo*, 82–109.

13. Mitchell, "Founding and Early History," 351–52. For an intriguing argument that Shaw was a composite character, see Manthorne, "View from the Cotton," 27, 43n9.

14. *SDS*, 133. Bayard Rustin's naming of the 1954–65 period as the "classical" phase of the civil rights movement has been widely cited in scholarship. See Rustin, "From Protest to Politics"; and Hall, "Long Civil Rights Movement," 1234.

15. Hall, "Long Civil Rights Movement," 1235.

16. Manthorne, "View from the Cotton," 23.

17. For the car, see Mitchell, *Mean Things*, 59.

18. Mitchell recounted this story in both "Founding and Early History," 352–54, and *Mean Things*, 59–61, and it also appears in Kester, *Revolt among the Sharecroppers*, 65. I chose the "Founding and Early History" version of McKinney's words for their somewhat more natural sound as dialogue; all other quotations from *Mean Things*.

19. Mitchell, *Mean Things*, 102–5. Donald Grubbs attributes the assassination attempt to Moskop's belief that Mitchell was embezzling; see *Cry from the Cotton*, 62. Anthony P. Dunbar describes it as a "lunatic" act in *Against the Grain*, 130.

20. Rolinson, *Grassroots Garveyism*, 186. On McKinney, see also Gellman and Roll, *Gospel of the Working Class*, xvi; and Mitchell, *Mean Things*, 39.

21. For McKinney's particular dislike of Moskop, see Dunbar, *Against the Grain*, 122–23; and Grubbs, *Cry from the Cotton*, 68.

22. On segregated locals and McKinney's efforts to gain whites' respect, see Grubbs, *Cry from the Cotton*, 66–68.

23. Mitchell, *Mean Things*, 63–64.

24. Grubbs, *Cry from the Cotton*, 71, 78–79. On the Rodgers case, see also Mitchell *Mean Things*, 65.

25. Mitchell, *Mean Things*, 65–66; Thomas Fauntleroy, "Anarchy Suit Stirs Arkansas," *New York Times*, January 27, 1935, E6.

26. Grubbs, *Cry from the Cotton*, 49–51.

27. Quoted in Kester, *Revolt among the Sharecroppers*, 29.

28. Quoted in Kennedy, *Freedom from Fear*, 212.

29. Ibid., 209.

30. Norman Thomas to Howard Kester, May 8, 1935, reel 1, STFU. The final quotation in the paragraph is as quoted in Kennedy, *Freedom from Fear*, 210.

31. Kester, *Revolt among the Sharecroppers*, 80–81.

32. *SDS*, 134.

33. Grubbs, *Cry from the Cotton*, 73; F. Raymond Daniell, "Arkansas Violence Laid to Landlords," *New York Times*, April 16, 1935, 18.

34. On black women serving as union secretaries, see Dunbar, *Against the Grain*, 109. On the STFU's overall race and gender composition, see Manthorne, "View from the Cotton," 45n29. Mitchell devoted a chapter to "Women of the STFU" in *Mean Things*, 123–36. Other discussions of women's roles and gender dynamics include Payne and Boyle, "Lady Was a Sharecropper"; Fannin, *Labor's Promised Land*, chap. 4; and Stone, "'They Were Her Daughters.'"

35. Mitchell, *Mean Things*, 124–28; Dunbar, *Against the Grain*, 109.

36. Mitchell dedicated *Mean Things* to black organizer and songwriter John L. Handcox and "the hundreds of other black, brown, and white sharecroppers and farm workers who laid their lives on the line," adding that it had been his "privilege to be their hired hand and spokesman" (v).

37. Woodruff, *American Congo*, 169–70; Grubbs, *Cry from the Cotton*, 85–86.

38. Thompson, "Strange Case of Paul D. Peacher."

39. Dunbar, *Against the Grain*, 114–15; Grubbs, *Cry from the Cotton*, 96–97.

40. Holley, *Uncle Sam's Farmers*, 96–97.

41. Executive order 7027, May 1, 1935, in Roosevelt, *Public Papers and Addresses*, 4:143–44.

42. Journal, 26.

43. Evelyn Smith Munro, interview by Mary Frederickson, April 17, 1976, interview G-0043, transcript, 3–4, SOHP; Evelyn Smith to H. L. Mitchell, October 21, 1935, STFU.

44. *SDS*, 123–24.

45. Journal, 27.

46. Ibid.

47. Quoted in Underwood, *Allen Tate*, 225–26.

48. Journal, 27, 81; *SDS*, 87. For Daniels's view of Tate as "an intellectual who has taken himself up into the top of the temple and doesn't give a God damn really what happens to the people in the street," see D-COHP, 102.

49. Underwood, *Allen Tate*, 226–27.

50. On Amberson, see *SDS*, 84–85; and Ferguson, "Race and the Remaking of the Rural South," 32–42.

51. Journal, 26–27.

52. Journal, 27–28.

53. Journal, 27. I have added a comma for clarity in one of the quotations in this paragraph. On the founding of the Dyess Colony, see Holley, *Uncle Sam's Farmers*, 28, 30–51.

54. Amberson, "Forty Acres and a Mule," 264–66.

55. "Bulletin from Southern Tenant Farmers' Union," "Questionaire [*sic*] on Rehabilitation," and "Southern Tenant Farmers' Union — Questionnaire to Numbers," [1935], reel 1, STFU. See also Ross, "'I Ain't Got No Home,'" 111–13.

56. Ferguson, "Race and the Remaking of the Rural South," 60, 72, 90.

57. *SDS*, 131; Journal, 26. On Delta Cooperative's first-year profit, see Ferguson, "Race and the Remaking of the Rural South," 116.

58. *SDS*, 136; Southern Tenant Farmers Union, *Disinherited Speak*, 3. Daniels mentioned that "Evelyn Smith began to pile pamphlets on us" in *SDS*, 124.

59. *SDS*, 142–43.

60. *SDS*, 146–48.

61. Journal, 32; *SDS*, 148.

62. *SDS*, 151.

63. *SDS*, 154–55; Journal, 34–35.

64. *SDS*, 154–55.

65. Journal, 33.

66. Journal, 34; see also *SDS*, 150–51.

67. Ferguson, "Race and the Remaking of the Rural South," 130, 122–23.

68. Quoted in ibid., 152–53.

69. Ibid., 244, 247.

70. *SDS*, 131.

71. Dunbar, *Against the Grain*, 164.

72. Quoted in ibid., 169.

73. Grubbs, *Cry from the Cotton*, 114.

74. Quoted in Dunbar, *Against the Grain*, 172–73.

75. On the National Negro Congress, see Gellman, *Death Blow to Jim Crow*.

76. Woodruff, *American Congo*, 187.

77. Ibid., 189; Grubbs, *Cry from the Cotton*, 187.

78. Mitchell, *Mean Things*, 128; Evelyn Smith Munro interview, SOHP.

79. Grubbs, *Cry from the Cotton*, 188–89; *SDS*, 130.

80. Holley, *Uncle Sam's Farmers*, 103.

81. Sullivan, *Days of Hope*, 126–27, 129.

82. *SDS*, 135.

83. On the shifting emphases and tactics of the post–World War II segregationist movement, see esp. Lassiter, *Silent Majority*; Crespino, *In Search of Another Country*; and Ward, *Defending White Democracy*. The idea of the "smart" segregationist (or "smart segs" vs. "dumb segs") goes back at least as far as a 1977 *New Yorker* essay by Calvin Trillin. See Hustwit, "Smart Segregationists," 318.

Chapter Six

1. Journal, 47. Daniels's blowout took place on May 19 between Little Rock and Greenville, Mississippi.

2. Journal, 32.

3. *SDS*, 135.

4. Journal, 39–40; *SDS*, 162–64.

5. Journal, 55, 64.

6. The newsreel was "King Cotton's Slaves," *March of Time* newsreel, vol. 2, episode 8 (HBO Film Archives, August 7, 1936), https://www.hboarchives.com/apps/searchlibrary/ctl/marchoftime (accessed March 6, 2016). The 6,000 figure comes from Thompson, "Strange Case of Paul D. Peacher," 430. For a partial transcript of the newsreel, see Mitchell, *Mean Things*, 109–11.

7. On the marches and how "the planters also took to the roads," see Mitchell, *Mean Things*, 94.

8. "Terror Fills Cotton Fields, Woman and Clergyman Are Beaten," *Sharecropper's Voice* 2 (July 1936), 3.

9. Quoted in Mitchell, *Mean Things*, 125. See also ibid, 94.

10. Grubbs, *Cry from the Cotton*, 91, 109–10; "Arkansans Sued over 3 Floggings" and "Denials of the Defendants," both in *New York Times*, August 30, 1936, 12. On Dulaney, see also Thompson, "Strange Case of Paul D. Peacher," 435.

11. Mitchell, *Mean Things*, 94–95.

12. Blagden, "Arkansas Flogging," 236–37.

13. Dunbar, *Against the Grain*, 128.

14. Mitchell, *Mean Things*, 95.

15. Other than the words "young and impetuous," all quotations in this paragraph

are from Willie Sue Blagden, "Statement to the Workers Defense League," May 20, 1938, typescript, reel 8, STFU. I explore Blagden's story in more detail, with emphasis on how she has been mischaracterized in STFU scholarship, in Ritterhouse, "Woman Flogged."

16. For more on Blagden's education and background, see Ritterhouse, "Woman Flogged," 105–6.

17. "Woman Flogged," *Literary Digest*, June 27, 1936, 29; "Arkansas: Chivalry Has Flown," *Washington Post*, June 21, 1936, B4.

18. *Earle Enterprise*, as quoted in "Arkansas Editor Upholds the Lash," *New York Times*, June 24, 1936, 19.

19. "Arkansas Chivalry," *Chicago Daily Tribune*, June 26, 1936, 14.

20. Grubbs, *Cry from the Cotton*, 113.

21. "King Cotton's Slaves." The line I quote is misquoted in Mitchell, *Mean Things*, 111. For a critique of the film's ideological content, see Ellis, "Screen."

22. Evelyn Smith Munro, interview by Mary Frederickson, April 17, 1976, interview G-0043, SOHP.

23. Mitchell, *Mean Things*, 95–96.

24. "Woman Beaten in Cotton Belt Will Go Back," *Washington Post*, July 14, 1936, 3.

25. Blagden, "Arkansas Flogging," 237.

26. "Turns Up Alive; Disproves Dixie Flogging Death," *Chicago Daily Tribune*, May 19, 1937, 15; "'Finding' of Weems Opens Controversy in Arkansas," *Boston Globe*, May 19, 1937, 7.

27. Mitchell, *Mean Things*, 43; Complaints at Law, U.S. District Court for the Jonesboro District of the Eastern Division of Arkansas, *J. M. Reese v. Boss Dulaney et al.* [1936], reel 3, STFU; Grubbs, *Cry from the Cotton*, 113; C. A. Stanfield to J. R. Butler, September 30, 1938, reel 9, STFU.

28. Press release on the death of Eliza Nolden, [annotated 1936; actually 1938], reel 3, STFU; "Funeral Notice," May 22, 1938, reel 8, STFU. For the fact that King's body was taken from the emergency room at St. Joseph's Hospital, where he died, to the John Gaston Hospital morgue, see Thomas Fox, "Gaping Wound Claims Life, Hospital's Aid Is Futile," *Memphis Commercial Appeal*, April 5, 1968.

29. "Dies as $15,000 Suit Waits Action," *Chicago Defender*, May 28, 1938, 6.

30. U.S. census for 1930, Cross County, Arkansas, Population schedule, District 12, Tyronza Township, p. 176, Ancestry.com (accessed April 22, 2016). According to "Funeral Notice," Nolden was born in Senatoba, Mississippi, and moved to Earle, Arkansas, in 1927. She was said to have given birth to thirteen children, of whom James and William were the only ones still living, though no explanation for the others' deaths was given, nor did the STFU source mention her status as a widow. There is also a discrepancy about her age: the census record puts Nolden's age at forty-three in 1930, making her almost a decade younger than the funeral notice indicates.

31. Journal, 29.

32. Journal, 30–31. On the scholarship, see Ritterhouse, "Woman Flogged."

33. *SDS*, 135–36.

34. *SDS*, 12.

35. *SDS*, 136.

36. Whayne, *New Plantation South*, 1–2.

37. Ibid., 191; Amberson, "Forty Acres and a Mule," 264.

38. Whayne, *New Plantation South*, 191–92.

39. F. Raymond Daniell, "Arkansas Violence Laid to Landlords," *New York Times*, April 16, 1935, 18.

40. F. Raymond Daniell, "Tenant Law Clash Roils Cotton Belt," *New York Times*, April 18, 1935, 24. On the Norcross suit, see Grubbs, *Cry from the Cotton*, 43–54 passim.

41. Quoted in Grubbs, *Cry from the Cotton*, 58.

42. Journal, 28.

43. F. Raymond Daniell, "'Run Off Farms,' Tenants Declare," *New York Times*, April 20, 1935, 5. For Carpenter's biography, see also Journal, 28–29; and *SDS*, 138. An obituary can be found in "C. T. Carpenter Dies in Auto Crash," *Chicago Defender*, October 13, 1945, 11.

44. *SDS*, 138.

45. Journal, 28–29.

46. *SDS*, 139.

47. Journal, 28–29.

48. *SDS*, 140.

Chapter Seven

1. *SDS*, 165.

2. *SDS*, 167.

3. Journal, 43.

4. Journal, 65–66; "naked subsidy": *SDS*, 169.

5. *SDS*, 205, 210. On the Balance Agriculture with Industry plan, see Cobb, *Selling of the South*, chap. 1.

6. *SDS*, 211.

7. *SDS*, 176.

8. *SDS*, 196, 199.

9. *SDS*, 203.

10. *SDS*, 217, 218, 222, 223.

11. *SDS*, 238, 342. "Lost Present" and "Ghost in Louisiana" are *SDS* chapter titles. Huey Long continues to fascinate historians; one classic study is Brinkley, *Voices of Protest*. The 7.5 million figure is based on Tindall, *Emergence of the New South*, 614–15.

12. *SDS*, 249. For the julep, see *SDS*, 239; and Journal, 79. For the interview with Nixon, see *SDS*, 244; and Journal, 80–82.

13. *SDS*, 9.

14. Journal, 90–92. I infer from biographical information on the Washington family that it was Washington's younger son, Ernest Davidson Washington, rather than his older son, Booker T. Washington Jr., who escorted Daniels. Daniels recorded the man's name as "C. E. Washington," presumably a mistake.

15. Journal, 92–93.

16. Ibid. For an excellent discussion of the work of black Extension agents in Alabama, see Whayne, "Black Farmers."

17. Journal, 93.

18. *SDS*, 148; Jonathan Daniels to W. T. Couch, November 2, 1936, folder 131, DP.

19. Jonathan Daniels to Walter White, October 27, 1941, folder 390, DP; Eagles, *Jonathan Daniels and Race Relations*, 76.

20. Victor C. Turner Sr. and Albert L. Turner, the university registrar, are the only Turners listed in "Positions at Tuskegee Institute." This fact, plus correlations between Victor Turner's biography and the information Daniels recorded, persuade me that my identification is accurate.

My main biographical source on Turner is T-ASU. I have also been able to glean information from job application forms, particularly "U.S.D.A. Appointment Request for 1928," ACES. Information on Turner's parents, including their eventual status as landowners, comes from U.S. census for 1880, Taliaferro County, Georgia, Population schedule, Militia District 606, p. 25; U.S. census for 1900, Taliaferro County, Georgia, Population schedule, Militia District 606, p. 61; and U.S. census for 1920, Taliaferro County, Georgia, Population schedule, Militia District 606, p. 112, Ancestry.com (accessed April 22, 2016). Jake Turner's father, Spencer Turner, can be traced in earlier census records as a slave of Sarah W. Adkinson of Taliaferro County, Georgia. See also Record for Spencer Turner, no. 4829, August 19, 1872, in *Registers of Signatures of Depositors in Branches of the Freedman's Savings and Trust Company, 1865–1874* (Washington, D.C.: National Archives and Records Administration), Ancestry.com (accessed April 22, 2016).

21. T-ASU; "U.S.D.A. Appointment Request for 1928." Turner is mentioned in Thompson, *History and Views of Colored Officers Training Camp*.

22. T-ASU; "U.S.D.A. Appointment Request for 1928."

23. Victor C. Turner Jr., telephone interview by the author, February 3, 2012, notes in author's possession. On black middle-class parenting in the Jim Crow era, see Ritterhouse, *Growing Up Jim Crow*.

24. T-ASU.

25. Turner, "Agricultural Program for Alabama"; "Along the Color Line," *Crisis* 40 (August 1931), 277. Turner's name was also listed among Cornell students graduating with Master of Science degrees in "Modern Critics Hit in Cornell Sermon," *New York Times*, June 15, 1931, 14.

26. Journal, 93; see also *SDS*, 256. On the meanings attributed to pronunciation of the word "Negro," see Boyle, *Desegregated Heart*, 108–9.

27. Journal, 93.

28. Journal, 93–94.

29. In *Outside Agitator*, 99 and 283n30, Charles W. Eagles identifies Robert S. Dickson as an especially brutal labor lord, explaining that, in the oral history interviews he conducted, "numerous Lowndes natives referred to Dickson's violent ways." He also cites Daniels's 1937 journal as a source on Dickson, along with Charles Denby's *Indignant Heart*, 19, for its stories of a violent planter named Bob Dixon. When originally published in 1952, Denby's book used pseudonyms and claimed to describe conditions in southeastern Tennessee. A subsequent edition with an introduction by William H. Harris makes it clear that Denby's real name was Matthew Ward and the setting for the Bob Dixon stories was Lowndes County, Alabama.

J. W. Dickson, often spelled "Dixon," and his brothers are mentioned in scholarship on peonage and Lowndes County, including Daniel, *Shadow of Slavery*, 59–60; Blackmon, *Slavery by Another Name*, 208–9; and Jeffries, *Bloody Lowndes*, 18–19, 242, 261n27.

30. The family relationship to David Dickson is mentioned in "Miss Doris Dickson to Wed Henry Plant, Jr.," *Greenville Advocate*, July 8, 1948, clipping in PISF-SF, ADAH; and "Dickson, Robert Stiles," 271.

31. John C. and Sarah Jane (Williamson) Dickson are identified in "Dickson, Robert Stiles," 271. Additional information is based on U.S. census records for 1860, 1870, and 1880 for Lowndes County, Alabama, specifically 1860 Population schedule (Northern Division, p. 42) and Slave schedule (Northern Division, p. 101); 1870 Population schedule (Beat 9, p. 19); and 1880 Population schedule (Letohatchie Beat, p. 39), Ancestry.com (accessed April 22, 2016). I infer that a minister and his wife and child who were listed under the Dickson household in 1860 were boarders. One element of uncertainty is whether the "J. G. Dickson," age 1, listed in 1860 is the same as the "John G. Dickson," listed in 1870 and 1880 with a birth date of 1863.

32. For background on Lowndes County and the quotation, see Eagles, *Outside Agitator*, 91–93.

33. Muster roll, Montgomery, Alabama, August 8, 1864, Alabama Civil War Service Database, ADAH, http://www.archives.alabama.gov/civilwar/ (accessed March 7, 2016).

34. Eagles, *Outside Agitator*, 94.

35. 1870 U.S. census, Lowndes County, Alabama, Population schedule, Beat 9, p. 19. Dickson's farms are valued at $400 and his farm implements and machinery at $200 in U.S. census for 1870, Lowndes County, Alabama, Agriculture schedule, Beat 9, p. 1, Ancestry.com (accessed April 22, 2016).

36. On cotton production, see Eagles, *Outside Agitator*, 94–95. Birth years for Edwin and Lewis Dickson are based on U.S. census for 1870, Lowndes County, Alabama, Population schedule, Beat 9, p. 19. Census records list varying birthdates for Robert Stiles Dickson, but 1873 is noted in "Dickson, Robert Stiles," 271.

37. "Dickson, Robert Stiles," 271–72. I infer that John C. Dickson died in the 1870s based on the statement that Robert Dickson was "left fatherless while still very young" (271) and the fact that Joe Dickson is listed as the head of a household that included his mother in 1880 U.S. census, Lowndes County, Alabama, Population schedule, Letohatchie Beat, p. 39, Ancestry.com (accessed April 22, 2016).

38. *SDS*, 135–36. On Dicksonia, also known as the Turner-Dickson House, see Lowndesboro Heritage Society, *Lowndesboro's Picturesque Legacies*. The house was included in the Historic American Buildings Survey in 1934; see "Turner-Dickson House, State Highway 97 (County Road 29), Lowndesboro, Lowndes County, AL," Library of Congress, http://www.loc.gov/pictures/item/al0326/ (accessed March 7, 2016).

39. "Robert S. Dickson," *Alabama Journal*, March 17, 1949, clipping in PISF-SF, ADAH. That Dickson's initial purchase included 400 acres is based on Lowndesboro Heritage Society, *Lowndesboro's Picturesque Legacies*. Eagles notes that tax assessments for Lowndes County for 1947 list him as the owner of more than 10,000 acres; see *Outside Agitator*, 283n30.

40. "Robert S. Dickson," *Alabama Journal*, March 17, 1949; "R.S. Dickson Dies; Lowndes Planter," *Montgomery Advertiser*, March 17, 1949; and "Robert S. Dickson," *Greenville Advocate*, March 24, 1949, clippings in PISF-SF, ADAH. On the fire, see Lowndesboro Heritage Society, *Lowndesboro's Picturesque Legacies* and "Dickson, Robert Stiles," 272.

41. Quoted in Daniel, *Shadow of Slavery*, 44; on the 1903 investigation, see ibid., 43–61.

42. Warren S. Reese Jr. to the Attorney General, report related to peonage cases, June 15, 1903, file 5280-03, reel 2, PFDOJ.

43. Ibid.

44. Ibid.

45. Daniel, *Shadow of Slavery*, 61.

46. Ibid., 60.

47. Davis, *Growing Up in Lowndesboro*, 33, 36.

48. Newspaper clippings about the engagements and a biographical questionnaire completed by Robert Dickson Jr. can be found in PISF-SF, ADAH.

49. See case file 50-2-6, reel 20, PFDOJ. I identify the "Mrs. Frank Gordon" who appears in these records as "Clyde Gordon" based on Davis, *Growing Up in Lowndesboro*, which includes a hand-drawn map showing the location of the Gordons' house and store. Frank J. and Clyde W. Gordon are listed in the 1940 U.S. census, Lowndes County, Alabama, Population schedule, Lowndesboro Township, p. 255, Ancestry. com (accessed April 22, 2016).

50. The death of J. W. Dickson was reported in the *Montgomery Advertiser*, April 30, 1929, clipping in PISF-SF. Joseph T. Dickson died in 1912, as recorded in *Alabama, Deaths and Burials Index, 1881–1974*, Ancestry.com (accessed April 22, 2016). Edwin Hooper Dickson died in 1907 and is buried in Oakview Cemetery in Lowndesboro. I have been unable to locate a death record or a grave for the fifth Dickson brother, John G.

51. For all quotations as well as the basis for my account of these events, see affidavits by Aaron "Champ" Smith, Mrs. Frank Gordon, and Julius Johnson, as well as a report by FBI agent Spencer Robb, February 26, 1946, in case file 50-2-6, reel 20, PFDOJ.

52. Ibid.

53. Harvey Lupton, office memorandum, January 14, 1946, case file 50-2-6, reel 20, PFDOJ.

54. Report by FBI agent Spencer Robb, April 3, 1946, in case file 50-2-6, reel 20, PFDOJ.

55. Hartwell Davis to U.S. Attorney General, February 12, 1946, case file 50-2-6, reel 20, PFDOJ.

56. Theron L. Caudle, Assistant U.S. Attorney General, to Edward Burns Parker, U.S. Attorney, March 8, 1946, case file 50-2-6, reel 20, PFDOJ; "Grand Jury Declines to Indict Landowner," *Alabama Journal*, March 20, 1946, clipping in PISF-SF, ADAH.

57. Jonathan Daniels to James Putnam, April 16, 1938, folder 177, DP. Daniels discussed his portrayal of Turner at some length in this letter and provided rewrites that Putnam had evidently requested.

58. *SDS*, 254–55.

59. T. M. Campbell to Jonathan Daniels, August 11, 1938, folder 201, DP.

60. *SDS*, 256.

61. *SDS*, 257.

62. *SDS*, 257–58.

63. Journal, 94.

64. *SDS*, 260.

65. *SDS*, 170.

66. *SDS*, 260.

67. *SDS*, 261.

68. Daniels to Putnam, April 16, 1938.

69. On the absence of an NAACP branch in Tuskegee, see Verney, "To Hope till Hope Create." For insight into intraracial tensions over politics and "respectability" in Alabama in this period, see Kelley, *Hammer and Hoe.*

70. *SDS*, 257–58; Journal, 93.

71. *SDS*, 273, 276. On the hotel, see "Thomas Jefferson Hotel," *Forgotten Southeast*, http://www.forgottensoutheast.com/locations/thomasjeffersonhotel/ (accessed March 7, 2016).

72. "Meet Mr. James E. Chappell," *Montgomery Advertiser*, January 17, 1936.

73. *SDS*, 273–74; Journal, 94. Daniels's word choice alluded to Birmingham native James Saxon Childers's *A Novel about a White Man and a Black Man in the Deep South* (1936).

74. Journal, 94.

75. Ibid.

76. Ellis, "Calhoun School." See also Lasch-Quinn, *Black Neighbors*, 82–100.

77. Hamilton, *Looking for Clark Gable*, 25. For Hamilton's father's views on the Calhoun School in 1937, see McClellan Van Der Veer, "Introduction to Living," *Birmingham Age-Herald*, January 19, 1937, 6.

78. *SDS*, 276–77.

79. Journal, 94–95.

80. Jonathan Daniels to James Putnam and Jonathan Daniels to Susan Frink, both July 11, 1938, in folder 188, DP.

81. Journal, 95. According to her son William Barclift, Chappell succumbed to social pressure, gave up teaching, and settled into a more conventional lifestyle for a white woman of her social class after her two summers at Calhoun. Interview by the author, February 23, 2011, notes in author's possession.

82. *SDS*, 274.

83. Kelley, *Hammer and Hoe*, 49.

84. Rosengarten, *All God's Dangers*, 306.

85. Kelley, *Hammer and Hoe*, 50.

86. Journal, 96.

87. Kelley, *Hammer and Hoe*, 50–51.

88. *SDS*, 275; see also Journal, 96.

89. *SDS*, 276.

Chapter Eight

1. Journal, 96, 94. On the elevators, see also *SDS*, 279.

2. Journal, 96–97; *SDS*, 279–80.

3. *SDS*, 282, 285.

4. *SDS*, 282, 284; see also Journal, 98.

5. *SDS*, 288; Journal, 98.

6. Daniels, "Democracy Is Bread," 483. On the 1930s as a new moment of hope for organized labor in Birmingham, see esp. Norrell, "Labor at the Ballot Box."

7. Journal, 98; *SDS*, 281–83. Biographical information on Pratt is based on Armes, *Story of Coal and Iron*, 174–76, 280–82; and Herbert J. "Jim." Lewis, "Daniel Pratt," *Encyclopedia of Alabama*, June 12, 2007, http://www.encyclopediaofalabama.org/face/Article.jsp?id=h-1184 (accessed March 8, 2016).

8. Biographical information is based primarily on Fuller, "Henry F. DeBardeleben." Quotation is from Marlene Hunt Rikard, "DeBardeleben, Henry Fairchild," *American National Biography Online*, February 2000, http://www.anb.org/articles/10/10-00389.html (accessed April 10, 2016).

9. Armes, *Story of Coal and Iron*, 239–40. See also Bailey, "Ethel Armes."

10. Armes, *Story of Coal and Iron*, 335; Woodward, *Origins of the New South*, 128–29. On the Percy connection, see Samway, "Union of the DeBardeleben and Percy Families."

11. Fuller, "Henry F. DeBardeleben," 15–16.

12. *SDS*, 284. On "Pittsburgh Plus," see Kelly, *Race, Class, and Power*, 33.

13. Anne Permaloff, "Black Belt–Big Mule Coalition," in *Encyclopedia of Alabama*, January 17, 2008, http://www.encyclopediaofalabama.org/article/h-1434 (accessed March 8, 2016).

14. Norrell, "Labor at the Ballot Box," 208.

15. Biographical information is based on obituaries such as "Charles F. DeBardeleben, One of Alabama's Leaders, Is Dead," *Birmingham News*, September 1, 1941, 1; and Samway, "Union of the DeBardeleben and Percy Families."

16. Cruikshank, *History of Birmingham*, 370; Carolyn Green Satterfield, "Country Club of Birmingham," *Encyclopedia of Alabama*, February 10, 2009, http://www.encyclopediaofalabama.org/article/h-2027 (accessed March 8, 2016).

17. Letwin, "Early Years," 18.

18. Ibid., 20.

19. Kelly, "Having It Their Way," 38.

20. Ibid., 52.

21. Ibid., 50–51.

22. "The Debardeleben [*sic*] Oasis—Unionism's Last Frontier," *Alabama: The News Magazine of the Deep South* 2 (March 29, 1937), 10; Marvin, *Alabama Fuel and Iron Company*, 11, 4.

23. Brian M. Kelly observes that "TCI, the DeBardeleben empire, and Pratt Consolidated were at least as notorious locally for the elaborate spying systems they maintained as they were for the material improvements they had introduced for their employees" ("Having It Their Way," 51).

24. DeBardeleben, Letter to the editor, 74.

25. Woodrum, *Everybody Was Black Down There*, 25.

26. Norrell, "Labor at the Ballot Box," 215.

27. *SDS*, 288.

28. *SDS*, 285.

29. Eskew, "But for Birmingham," 23; *SDS*, 284. On unemployment in Birmingham, see also Badger, *New Deal*, 22.

30. Eskew, "But for Birmingham," 26.

31. For example, see Charles F. DeBardeleben, Annual Report of President, 1934, to the Stockholders and Directors, Alabama Fuel and Iron Company, box 4643, folder 2, AFIC.

32. "Debardeleben [*sic*] Oasis," 9–10. The quotation is from a first-page editorial in the same issue of *Alabama* magazine. For Daniels's quotations from the magazine, see *SDS*, 286.

33. *SDS*, 285–86.

34. *SDS*, 281. For his claim that his door was always open, see "Debardeleben [*sic*] Oasis," 10.

35. Journal, 98. See also *SDS*, 282–87.

36. *SDS*, 285, 286.

37. *SDS*, 281, 287.

38. *SDS*, 280–81; Journal, 97.

39. Alexander, "Rising from the Ashes," 68.

40. National Industrial Recovery Act of 1933, Public Law 67, 73rd Cong., 1st sess. (June 16, 1933), 198.

41. *SDS*, 281; Journal, 97.

42. Taft, *Organizing Dixie*, 84.

43. Sullivan, *Days of Hope*, 44–45, 50.

44. Henry T. DeBardeleben was part of a committee that went to Washington to present coal operators' views; see Taft, *Organizing Dixie*, 83.

45. Alexander, "Rising from the Ashes," 72–73.

46. Quoted in Taft, *Organizing Dixie*, 85–86.

47. Ibid., 89–90.

48. All quotations from Taft, *Organizing Dixie*, 91–92.

49. DeBardeleben, Annual Report of President, 1934, 1, 2, 7.

50. Woodrum, *Everybody Was Black Down There*, 58.

51. Ibid., 59. See also "Miner Killed, Six Wounded in Strike Battle," *Chicago Daily Tribune*, October 29, 1935, 7.

52. Quoted in Taft, *Organizing Dixie*, 92.

53. Woodrum, *Everybody Was Black Down There*, 59.

54. Resolution, n.d., p. [3/98-1] in Minutes of Meeting of Board of Directors, box 4643, folder 2, AFIC. Internal evidence indicates the committee that issued this resolution was formed at a meeting on September 17, 1936.

55. Ibid., p. [3/105-1]. Internal evidence indicates the committee that issued this resolution was formed at a meeting on June 17, 1937.

56. Journal, 98; see also *SDS*, 284. As Philip Taft writes, "The union had established itself in four years, and by 1937 most coal miners in the state were organized";

however, Alabama Fuel and Iron was "the exception" (*Organizing Dixie*, 93, 94). On the local ramifications of Myron Taylor's recognition of the CIO, see Ingalls, "Anti-radical Violence in Birmingham," 543.

57. McWhorter, *Carry Me Home*, 54.

58. Ibid., 53, 595n53. See also Norrell, "Labor at the Ballot Box," 217–18. A list of some of Marvin's publications can be found on WorldCat Identities, http://www .worldcat.org/identities/np-marvin,%20fred%20richard$1868%201939 (accessed March 8, 2016).

59. "28 Organized Groups Linked to Fascist Plot," *Washington Post*, July 24, 1942, 4.

60. On Kamp, see McWhorter, *Carry Me Home*, esp. 54. See also "Votes to Cite Kamp," *New York Times*, October 9, 1944, 25; and "Kamp's Conviction Upheld," *New York Times*, December 14, 1948, 35.

61. McWhorter, *Carry Me Home*, 53.

62. Daniels, "Democracy Is Bread," 489.

63. *SDS*, 67.

64. Ward, *Defending White Democracy*, 11, in reference to the founders of the Southern States Industrial Council.

65. U.S. Senate, *Report of the Special Committee*, 34.

66. Testimony of Thorny Riddle and G. W. England, January 7, 1932, in U.S. Senate, Committee on Privileges and Elections, 1168–94 and 1211–16.

67. U.S. Senate, *Report of the Special Committee*, 34–35.

68. Feldman, *Irony of the Solid South*, 120. Diane McWhorter discusses some of DeBardeleben's descendants in *Carry Me Home*.

69. *SDS*, 282.

70. Roosevelt, "United States Is Rising," 168.

71. *SDS*, 287; "DeBardeleben Funeral Today," *Birmingham Post*, September 1, 1941.

72. DeBardeleben died on August 31, 1941, and was buried the next day. Obituaries include "Charles F. DeBardeleben"; and "Industrialist in District Passes in Long Illness," *Birmingham Age-Herald*, September 1, 1941, 1, 3. Although it is accurate to say that DeBardeleben himself never signed a union contract, Taft may have been mistaken when he said Alabama Fuel and Iron "withdrew from the industry rather than recognizing the union" (*Organizing Dixie*, 95). Company records in AFIC indicate that Alabama Fuel and Iron continued to operate until 1953.

73. Journal, 99; *SDS*, 287–89.

Chapter Nine

1. Journal, 100; *SDS* 291, 293. On the hotel, see "Atlanta Biltmore Hotel and Biltmore Apartments," National Park Service, http://www.nps.gov/nr/travel/atlanta/bil .htm (accessed March 8, 2016).

2. *SDS*, 291.

3. *SDS*, 292–93.

4. *SDS*, 293.

5. For an insightful gender analysis of the 1920s Klan, see MacLean, *Behind the Mask of Chivalry*. On the 1906 massacre, see Godshalk, *Veiled Visions*.

6. *SDS*, 338, 341–42.

7. *SDS*, 290–91.

8. For Daniels's reflections on Chappell, see *SDS*, 276–77.

9. Biographical information is based on Pyron, *Southern Daughter*. For Mitchell's breakup with Upshaw and purchase of a pistol, see ibid., 251.

10. For contemporaries' view of John Marsh as dull, see ibid., 238–39.

11. For the dictionary, see ibid., 206.

12. Clark, "Margaret Mitchell," 190. For another perceptive analysis, see Faust, "Clutching the Chains That Bind."

13. Journal, 102.

14. Mitchell, *Gone with the Wind*, 149–50.

15. Journal, 101, 103.

16. Pyron, *Southern Daughter*, 419.

17. On the Pulitzer Prize and *Gone with the Wind*'s sales, see ibid., 435.

18. Journal, 102–3. My physical description of Mitchell is based on Pyron, *Southern Daughter*, 153–54.

19. Journal, 102.

20. Quoted in Pyron, *Southern Daughter*, 140.

21. Margaret Mitchell to Gilbert Govan, July 8, 1936, in Harwell, *Margaret Mitchell's "Gone with the Wind" Letters*, 24.

22. Margaret Mitchell to Julian Harris, April 21, 1936, in ibid., 2. Anne Sarah Rubin affirms that "part of the power of *Gone with the Wind* lies in its self-conscious presentation as accurate history" ("Revisiting Classic Civil War Books," 94).

23. Margaret Mitchell to Norman Berg, quoted in Harwell, *Margaret Mitchell's "Gone with the Wind" Letters*, xxxiii.

24. Quoted in ibid., xxxiii.

25. Journal, 102.

26. For "so-called free moderns," see Jonathan Daniels to W. T. Couch, November 2, 1936, folder 131, DP.

27. Jonathan Daniels, untitled essay on *Tobacco Road* and *Gone with the Wind*, [1942?], folder 2469, DP.

28. Journal, 102–3.

29. Mitchell, *Gone with the Wind*, 668, 550.

30. Ibid. 719.

31. Ibid., 719, 408.

32. Pyron, *Southern Daughter*, 420.

33. Ibid., 57.

34. Margaret Mitchell to Henry Steele Commager, July 10, 1936, in Harwell, *Margaret Mitchell's "Gone with the Wind" Letters*, 37–38.

35. Margaret Mitchell to Julia Collier Harris, April 28, 1936, in ibid., 5–6.

36. Margaret Mitchell to Edwin Granberry, July 8, 1936, in ibid., 29.

37. Margaret Mitchell to Reverend Monsignor James Murphy, March 4, 1937, in ibid., 126.

38. Mitchell, *Gone with the Wind*, 937.

39. Daniels, untitled essay.

40. Daniels, "F. O. B. Dixie," 3–4.

41. Ibid. For a perspective on the book's reception that also addresses Mitchell's efforts at realism, see Adams, "'Painfully Southern.'"

42. Daniels, untitled essay.

43. Ibid. For his thoughts on the film version of *Gone with the Wind*, see Daniels, "Perspective on the Old South," 15.

44. Journal, 102–3. I added punctuation for clarity.

45. Darden Asbury Pyron notes that "Mitchell's defensiveness about her husband became notorious, especially after she achieved worldwide fame" (*Southern Daughter*, 239).

46. Quoted in ibid., 565.

47. Quoted in ibid., 569–70.

48. Margaret Mitchell to Clifford Dowdey, August 22, 1938, in Harwell, *Margaret Mitchell's "Gone with the Wind" Letters*, 221. For the paragraph Mitchell referred to, see *SDS*, 345.

49. Margaret Mitchell to Herschel Brickell, July 16, 1938, box 9, Margaret Mitchell Family Papers, UGA. For the review that identified Mitchell, see "Postscript to a Book Review," July 24, 1938, clipping in Scrapbook. Brickell seems to have recognized Mitchell by her voice and may have been alluding to this when he described Daniels as "keen-eyed—and eared" in his review; see "Books on Our Table," *New York Post*, July 12, 1938, clipping in Scrapbook. Apparently, Brickell asked Daniels for confirmation, but Daniels offered "no admissions"; see Jonathan Daniels to Herschel Brickell, July 11, 1938, folder 191, DP.

50. Margaret Mitchell to Herschel Brickell, July 16, 1938. See also Jonathan Daniels to Hunt Clement Jr., June 16, 1937, box 30, Margaret Mitchell Family Papers, UGA.

Chapter Ten

1. *SDS*, 300, 305.

2. Journal, 107–8.

3. *SDS*, 305, 343.

4. *SDS*, 334.

5. *SDS*, 333. Although it is unclear precisely when Daniels got back to Raleigh, he told his mother he expected to be there before June 15; see Jonathan Daniels to Addie Daniels, May 30, 1937, in JDP. That he was home by this time is also suggested by the fact that he published an editorial, "Anti Lynching Bills," in the *Raleigh News and Observer* on June 15, 1937.

6. One of Daniels's friends sent him a photograph of the house where he wrote the book. See Aycock Brown to Jonathan Daniels, October 1938, folder 223, DP. For the reader report, see James Putnam to Jonathan Daniels, August 25, 1937, folder 151, DP. Daniels's correspondence with Putnam and others in the later months of 1937 indicate the manuscript was complete by the end of the year.

7. Journal, 107–8.

8. *SDS*, 306–7.

9. *SDS*, 344, 339.

10. *SDS*, 343–44.

11. *SDS*, 344, 343.

12. *SDS*, 343.

13. *SDS*, 117.

14. *SDS*, 343. On the exodus from the South, see Gregory, *Southern Diaspora*, which provides statistics on the migrants by race and estimates that "by 1920, southerners living outside their home region numbered more than 2.7 million and in 1930 more than 4 million" (13).

15. *SDS*, 339–40, 344.

16. *SDS*, 339.

17. *SDS*, 344.

18. *SDS*, 344–45.

19. *SDS*, 346.

20. "Opportune Opus for Dixie," *Richmond Times-Dispatch*, July 19, 1938, clipping in Scrapbook.

21. Virginius Dabney, "Discovering the South," [*Richmond Times-Dispatch*], clipping in Scrapbook.

22. Davis, "Progress below the Potomac," 5.

23. Nixon, review of *SDS*, 541. Nixon differed from other academic reviewers who criticized Daniels's book as superficial. See Buck, review of *SDS*; and Craven, review of *SDS*.

24. Nixon, review of *SDS*, 541.

25. Brown, "South on the Move," 19.

26. Morrow, review of *SDS*.

27. Daniel, review of *SDS*, 106.

28. Gertrude Martin, "Read More—Learn More," *Chicago Defender*, March 25, 1939, 17.

29. Brawley, "Southerner's Travels at Home," 553.

30. Hall, "South Discovers a Discoverer," 13–15.

31. Giles, "Double Exploitation," 27–28.

32. Hall, "South Discovers a Discoverer," 15.

33. Owsley, "Mr. Daniels Discovers the South"; Allen Tate to Jonathan Daniels, October 13, 1938, folder 219, DP.

34. Jonathan Daniels to Allen Tate, October 15, 1938, folder 220, DP. I added the comma after "misinterpreted." This letter included a number of handwritten corrections and may have been a draft.

35. James Rorty to Jonathan Daniels, November 23, 1938, folder 229, DP.

36. Jonathan Daniels to James Rorty, January 2, 1939, folder 238, DP.

37. Margaret Mitchell to Herschel Brickell, July 16, 1938, box 9, Margaret Mitchell Family Papers, UGA.

38. Mary L. Gullette to Jonathan Daniels, December 1, 1938, folder 230, DP.

39. Frances Doak, "Comments Picked Up at Random on Jonathan Daniels' Book," typescript in Scrapbook.

40. Josephus Daniels to Jonathan Daniels, July 18, 1938, folder 191, DP.

41. Doak, "Comments Picked Up at Random."

42. Ralph McGill, "One Word More: In Our Town," *Atlanta Constitution*, October 28, 1938, 10.

43. Mollie Huston Lee to Jonathan Daniels, November 29, 1938, folder 229, DP.

44. Walter White to Jonathan Daniels, July 13, 1938, folder 189, DP.

45. James E. Shepard to Jonathan Daniels, July 23, 1938, folder 193, DP.

46. Wilhelmina Roberts to Jonathan Daniels, December 16, 1938, folder 235, DP.

47. *Our Time, Our Place: Photographs of the Black South by Richard Samuel Roberts*, teaching kit (Columbia Museum of Art Education Department, 2011), 10, http://www.colum biamuseum.org/sites/default/files/Forms/RobertsTeachingKit.pdf (accessed April 17, 2016).

48. Wilhelmina Roberts Wynn's career as a teacher and social worker is mentioned in Jack Curry, "This Devoted Fan Pursues a Higher Calling," *New York Times*, September 4, 2006, D8. See also Wynn, "Pieces of Days."

49. Roberts to Daniels, December 16, 1938.

50. Jonathan Daniels to Wilhelmina Roberts, December 20, 1938, folder 235, DP.

51. Wilhelmina Roberts to Jonathan Daniels, December 28, 1938, folder 236, DP.

52. Jim Putnam to Jonathan Daniels, September 10, 1938, folder 208, DP; "Candidates for the Best Seller List," *Publishers Weekly*, August 6, 1938, 365; "Best Sellers," *Publishers Weekly*, September 3, 1938, 768. See also "Best Sellers of the Week," *New York Times*, September 5, 1938, 13.

53. "Atlanta Readers Preferred Books on South in 1938," *Atlanta Constitution*, December 26, 1938, 2.

54. "Opportune Opus for Dixie."

55. Garrett, "Problem South"; "Our 'No. 1. Problem,'" *Boston Herald*, clipping in Scrapbook.

56. John Oren, "Down the Spillway," *Baltimore Sun*, August 9, 1938, 8.

57. Brawley, "Southerner's Travels at Home," 553.

58. Pate, review of *SDS*, 86–88.

59. Carlton and Coclanis, *Confronting Southern Poverty*, 18. On the *Times* reporter and the leak, see ibid., 19–20.

60. Patricia Sullivan identifies 1938 as "the end of the legislative phase of the New Deal," though "the struggle over its political consequences was just beginning" (*Days of Hope*, 6). For a similar emphasis on the 1937–38 period, see Brinkley, *End of Reform*. Conversely, in *Fear Itself*, Ira Katznelson argues for a longer New Deal that encompasses the Truman years, ending in 1952.

61. Carlton and Coclanis, *Confronting Southern Poverty*, 14–15.

62. Ibid., 47, 44.

63. Roosevelt, Letter to members of the Conference on Economic Conditions in the South, 42.

64. Carlton and Coclanis, "Another 'Great Migration,'" 47.

65. Jonathan Daniels to Lowell Mellett, July 11, 1938, folder 188, DP. Daniels's subsequent letter to Mellett is quoted in Sullivan, *Days of Hope*, 66–67. See also Lowell Mellett to Jonathan Daniels, August 26, 1938, folder 204, DP.

66. Mary Fraser to Jonathan Daniels, June 21, 1938, folder 185, DP.

67. Caldwell and Bourke-White, *You Have Seen Their Faces*, 48.

68. Cowley, review of *You Have Seen Their Faces*, 78.

69. Dickstein, *Dancing in the Dark*, 99.

70. "True South Photos Sought," June 1938, clipping in Scrapbook.

71. My account of the Daniels-Eisenstaedt itinerary is based on letters in DP and clippings in Scrapbook, plus some of the locations Eisenstaedt photographed are identifiable. For examples, see the Discovering the South website (www.discoveringthe south.org).

72. Jonathan Daniels to Mary Fraser, July 11, 1938, folder 188, DP.

73. Wilson Hicks to Jonathan Daniels, July 16, 1938, folder 190, DP.

74. Mary Fraser to Jonathan Daniels, September 2, 1938, folder 206, DP.

75. Jonathan Daniels to Mary Fraser, September 5, 1938, folder 207, DP.

76. Roosevelt, "President Discusses Political Principles," 465, 469–70.

77. For his private doubts, see Jonathan Daniels to Josephus Daniels, [September 1938?], reel 20, JDP. His relevant editorials include "The Basis of the Problem" and "No Change," *Raleigh News and Observer*, August 12 and 15, 1938.

78. Quoted in Kneebone, *Southern Liberal Journalists*, 166.

79. John Temple Graves, "South Is Critical of the NEC Report," *New York Times*, August 21, 1938.

80. Katznelson, *Fear Itself*, 142.

81. Dunn, *Roosevelt's Purge*, 176; "Statistics of the Congressional Election of November 8, 1938," *Election Statistics, 1920 to Present*, U.S. House of Representatives, http://history.house.gov/Institution/Election-Statistics/Election-Statistics/ (accessed March 9, 2016).

82. Margaret Mitchell to Norma and Herschel Brickell, September 4, 1938, in Harwell, *Margaret Mitchell's "Gone with the Wind" Letters*, 224.

83. Sullivan, *Days of Hope*, 66.

84. Graves, "South Is Critical."

85. John Temple Graves to Jonathan Daniels, August 4, 1938, folder 198, DP.

86. Eleanor Roosevelt, "My Day," August 28, 1938, clipping in Scrapbook; Frank Porter Graham to Francis Pickens Miller, February 19, 1939, quoted in Sullivan, *Days of Hope*, 67.

87. The Birmingham meeting of the Southern Conference for Human Welfare (SCHW) is discussed at length in Egerton, *Speak Now against the Day*, and in greater or lesser detail in a number of other works, including Krueger, *And Promises to Keep*; Reed, *Simple Decency and Common Sense*; Carlton and Coclanis, *Confronting Southern Poverty*; Sullivan, *Days of Hope*; and Gilmore, *Defying Dixie*.

88. "Report of the SCHW Resolutions Committee," reprinted in Carlton and Coclanis, *Confronting Southern Poverty*, 149–60; quotation at 150.

89. Egerton, *Speak Now against the Day*, 187.

90. Ibid., 186.

91. On the growth of the Communist Party in Birmingham and throughout Alabama in the 1930s, see Kelley, *Hammer and Hoe*, which also discusses the Communist Party response to the SCHW and notes Frank Porter Graham's half-dozen figure (see 185–89).

92. Lucy Randolph Mason to Frank Porter Graham, December 6, 1938, Frank Porter Graham Papers, SHC.

93. Both Arthur Raper and Virginia Durr are quoted in Sullivan, *Days of Hope*, 99.

94. Journal, 97. Daniels's actual phrase is a "liberal lawyer," but I infer that Graves was referring to the Gelders flogging, which happened about eight months, not a couple of years, before his conversation with Daniels. Gelders was not a lawyer, but he had been trying to aid a jailed Communist Party member when he was attacked. For a detailed account of the flogging and the impact that evidence of Tennessee Coal, Iron and Railroad Company involvement had on Birmingham journalists, see Ingalls, "Antiradical Violence in Birmingham."

95. "Flogging Probe by La Follette," *Raleigh News and Observer*, January 16, 1937. On Gelders's background and views, see Gilmore, *Defying Dixie*, 270–71; and Kelley, *Hammer and Hoe*, 128–30.

96. On the local significance of the La Follette hearing and U.S. Steel's recognition of the CIO, see Ingalls, "Antiradical Violence in Birmingham," 543.

97. Sullivan, *Days of Hope*, 98.

98. Kneebone, *Southern Liberal Journalists*, 168.

99. Virginia Durr to Jonathan Daniels, [August 1938], folder 205, DP.

100. Johnson, "More Southerners Discover the South"; Couch, "Southerners Inspect the South."

101. Virginia Foster Durr, interview by Sue Thrasher, October 16, 1975, interview G-0023-3, SOHP.

102. Jonathan Daniels to Virginia Durr, September 28, 1938, folder 215, DP.

103. Jonathan Daniels to Bernice Baumgarten, November 7, 1938, folder 225, DP.

104. For the suggestion that Jonathan write what became *A Southerner Discovers New England*, see Josephus Daniels to Jonathan Daniels, July 30, 1938, folder 196, DP. Eleanor Roosevelt expressed enthusiasm for the idea in Eleanor Roosevelt to Jonathan Daniels, September 24, 1938, folder 213, DP.

105. Egerton, *Speak Now against the Day*, 193–94.

106. Carlton and Coclanis, *Confronting Southern Poverty*, 150.

107. Jonathan Daniels, "An Unfortunate Beginning," *Raleigh News and Observer*, November 26, 1938.

108. Jonathan Daniels to H. C. Nixon, January 20, 1939, folder 241, DP.

109. Murray, *Song in a Weary Throat*, 115.

110. Dot Coble, "Daniels Has No Objection to Entrance of Graduate Negroes," *Daily Tar Heel*, January 20, 1939.

Conclusion

1. Jonathan Daniels, "An Unfortunate Beginning," *Raleigh News and Observer*, November 26, 1938; Lucy Randolph Mason to Frank Porter Graham, December 6, 1938, Frank Porter Graham Papers, SHC; Jonathan Daniels to R. H. Gregory Jr., March 16, 1938, folder 172, DP.

2. Virginia Durr to Jonathan Daniels, [August 1938], folder 205, DP. On Dabney's self-identification as a "conservative," see Kneebone, *Southern Liberal Journalists*, 213.

3. Quoted in Krueger, *And Promises to Keep*, 37.

4. Charles F. DeBardeleben to Frank Porter Graham, January 2, 1939; see also DeBardeleben to Graham, December 2, 1938, both in Frank Porter Graham Papers, SHC.

5. Egerton, *Speak Now against the Day*, 195; Kneebone, *Southern Liberal Journalists*, 171.

6. Quoted in Kneebone, *Southern Liberal Journalists*, 171–72.

7. Francis Pickens Miller to Frank Porter Graham, December 21, 1938, copy in folder 236, DP.

8. Jonathan Daniels to Howard Odum, December 20, 1938, folder 235, DP.

9. Egerton, *Speak Now against the Day*, 521.

10. Krueger, *And Promises to Keep*, 38.

11. Sosna, *In Search of the Silent South*, 98, 100.

12. Sullivan, *Days of Hope*, 115.

13. Ibid., 117–20; Sosna, *In Search of the Silent South*, 103.

14. Virginia Foster Durr, interview by Sue Thrasher, October 16, 1975, interview G-0023-3, SOHP.

15. Schulman, *From Cotton Belt to Sunbelt*, xii–xiii, 100.

16. There is a growing scholarship on the midcentury origins of modern southern conservatism, including Ward, *Defending White Democracy*; Finley, *Delaying the Dream*; Crespino, *Strom Thurmond's America*; and Feldman, *Irony of the Solid South*.

17. Wright, "New Deal and the Modernization of the South," 66, 69, 71–72.

18. Ibid., 72.

19. Katznelson, *Fear Itself*, 287, 281.

20. Ibid., 16.

21. Fields, "Slavery, Race and Ideology," 106.

22. Ickes, *Inside Struggle*, 115.

23. Sullivan, *Days of Hope*, 117.

24. Sokol, Review of Ward, *Defending White Democracy*, 366–67.

25. Gilmore, *Defying Dixie*, 4, 6.

26. Ibid., 301–2.

27. Rossinow, *Visions of Progress*, 7–8.

28. On changes in anthropologists' thinking, see Baker, *From Savage to Negro*. Zoe Burkholder also offers a helpful account in *Color in the Classroom*.

29. Badger, *New Deal*, 254.

30. Guy Johnson, quoted in Kneebone, *Southern Liberal Journalists*, 172.

31. Gilmore, *Defying Dixie*, 310–11.

32. Executive Order 8802, June 25, 1941, in *Public Papers and Addresses of Franklin D. Roosevelt*, 1941 vol., 234–35. For a recent account of the March on Washington Movement and its relationship to the 1963 March on Washington, see Jones, *March on Washington*.

33. On the Fair Employment Practices Committee, see Reed, *Seedtime for the Modern Civil Rights Movement*; and Schultze, "FEPC and the Legacy of the Labor-Based Civil Rights Movement."

34. Craig, *Josephus Daniels*, 411.

35. For Daniels's experience in the Office of Civilian Defense, see Eagles, *Jonathan Daniels and Race Relations*, 86–95. Quotation is from Milkis, *President and the Parties*, 127.

36. Eagles, *Jonathan Daniels and Race Relations*, 99.

37. Daniels, "Native at Large: Virginia Democracy."

38. Daniels, "Native at Large: Dictators and Poll Taxes."

39. Eagles, *Jonathan Daniels and Race Relations*, 60.

40. Ibid., 100–2.

41. Ibid., 102–3. This lesser known order was Executive Order 9346, May 27, 1943. See *Public Papers and Addresses of Franklin D. Roosevelt*, 1943 vol., 228–30.

42. Leuchtenburg, *White House Looks South*, 65.

43. Quoted in ibid., 56.

44. Ibid., 66.

45. Quoted in Eagles, *Jonathan Daniels and Race Relations*, 97.

46. Ibid., 104–5.

47. Ibid., 105.

48. Ibid., 106.

49. Ibid., 103, 108, and 103–20 passim; Daniels, *White House Witness*, 205.

50. Eagles, *Jonathan Daniels and Race Relations*, 110.

51. Journal, 93.

52. Eagles, *Jonathan Daniels and Race Relations*, 110–11.

53. A brief account of Turner's life after 1945 can be found in T-ASU. There is a program from his funeral service on June 29, 1964, in Obituary Programs of People Associated with Tuskegee University. His death was also reported in *Wisconsin Alumnus* 66 (November 1964), 37.

54. Eagles, *Jonathan Daniels and Race Relations*, 119.

55. Daniels, *White House Witness*, 247; Jonathan Daniels to W. T. Couch, November 2, 1936, folder 131, DP.

56. Daniels, *White House Witness*, 254.

57. Daniels, "F.D.R. Was Not as Careful as His Protectors," 47–48.

58. Quoted in Daniels, *White House Witness*, 286.

59. Ibid., 286.

60. Ibid., 287.

61. Eagles, *Jonathan Daniels and Race Relations*, 121.

62. Ibid., 232.

63. Ibid., 147, 150, 152. On Daniels's work for the United Nations, see ibid., 127–35.

64. Ibid., 132–33. For a detailed discussion of Daniels's editorial positions in relations to the civil rights movement of the 1950s and 1960s, see ibid., chaps. 6 and 7.

65. Jonathan Daniels, introduction to *Southerner Discovers the South*, rpt. ed., ix.

66. Ibid., xvi–xvii, xviii.

67. Ibid., xviii, xvii, xix.

BIBLIOGRAPHY

Manuscript and Microfilm Collections

Athens, Ga.
  Hargrett Rare Book and Manuscript Library, University of Georgia
      Margaret Mitchell Family Papers

Atlanta, Ga.
  Manuscript, Archives, and Rare Book Library, Emory University
      Julian LaRose Harris Papers
      Margaret Mitchell Collection

Auburn, Ala.
  Auburn University Archives and Manuscripts Department
      Alabama Cooperative Extension System Records, record group 71

Birmingham, Ala.
  Birmingham Public Library
      Birmingham Biography (vertical file)
      Charles A. Fell Memoirs (microfilm)
      John Temple Graves Papers
      Philip Taft Papers

Chapel Hill, N.C.
  Southern Historical Collection, Wilson Library, University of North Carolina at
          Chapel Hill
      William Ruthrauff Amberson Papers
      Jonathan Daniels Papers
      Frank Porter Graham Papers
      Southern Oral History Program Collection
          Southern Tenant Farmers Union Papers, microfilm edition (Glen Rock,
          N.J.: Microfilming Corporation of America, 1971)

College Park, Md.
  National Archives and Records Administration
      Peonage Files of the U.S. Department of Justice, 1901–45, microfilm edition
          (Bethesda, Md.: University Publications of America, 1989)

Durham, N.C.
  David M. Rubenstein Rare Book and Manuscript Library, Duke University
      Ann Preston Bridgers Papers

Montgomery, Ala.
    Alabama Department of Archives and History
            Alabama Civil War Service Database
            Annual Reports of the Principals, Calhoun Colored School
            Lawrence Auld Calhoun Colored School Photograph Collection
            Public Information Subject File—Surname File
    Alabama State University Archives
            John Garrick Hardy Collection

Tuscaloosa, Ala.
    W. S. Hoole Special Collections Library, University of Alabama
            Alabama Fuel and Iron Company Records

Tuskegee, Ala.
    Special Collections and Archives, Tuskegee University
            Obituary Programs of People Associated with Tuskegee University,
                1881–Present
            "Positions at Tuskegee Institute, Names and Tenure," comp. by Daniel T.
                Williams

Washington, D.C.
    Library of Congress
            Josephus Daniels Papers

                        Newspapers and Magazines

Alabama: The News Magazine of the Deep South
Atlanta Constitution
Baltimore Sun
Birmingham Age-Herald
Birmingham News
Birmingham Post
Boston Globe
Boston Herald
Chicago Daily Tribune
Chicago Defender
Crisis
Daily Tar Heel
Literary Digest
Montgomery Advertiser
New York Herald Tribune
New York Post
New York Times
Publishers Weekly
Raleigh News and Observer
Richmond Times-Dispatch

Sharecropper's Voice
Washington Post
Wisconsin Alumnus

Published Primary Sources

Amberson, William R. "Forty Acres and a Mule." *Nation*, March 6, 1937, 264–66.

Armes, Ethel. *The Story of Coal and Iron in Alabama*. 1910; Tuscaloosa: University of Alabama Press, 2011.

Blagden, Willie Sue. "Arkansas Flogging." *New Republic*, July 1, 1936, 236–37.

Brawley, Benjamin. "A Southerner's Travels at Home." *Journal of Negro Education* 7 (October 1938): 553–54.

Brown, Sterling A. "South on the Move." In *Sterling A. Brown's "A Negro Looks at the South,"* edited by John Edgar Tidwell and Mark A. Sanders, 19–22. New York: Oxford University Press, 2007.

Buck, Paul H. Review of *A Southerner Discovers the South*. *Mississippi Valley Historical Review* 25 (March 1939): 579–80.

Caldwell, Erskine, and Margaret Bourke-White. *You Have Seen Their Faces*. 1937; Athens: University of Georgia Press, 1995.

Cash, Wilbur J. *The Mind of the South*. New York: Knopf, 1941.

Chalmers, Allan K. *They Shall Be Free*. Garden City, N.Y.: Doubleday, 1951.

Chamberlain, John. "Swing around the South." *New Republic*, July 13, 1938, 284–85.

Cohn, David L. *God Shakes Creation*. New York: Harper, 1935.

Couch, W. T. "Southerners Inspect the South." *New Republic*, December 14, 1938, 168.

Cowley, Malcolm. Review of *You Have Seen Their Faces*. *New Republic*, November 24, 1937, 78.

Craven, Avery. Review of *A Southerner Discovers the South*. *American Journal of Sociology* 44 (March 1939): 774–75.

Cruikshank, George M. *A History of Birmingham and Its Environs*. Vol. 2. New York: Lewis, 1920.

Dabney, Virginius. *Liberalism in the South*. 1932; New York: AMS Press, 1970.

Daniel, A. Mercer. Review of *A Southerner Discovers the South*. *Journal of Negro History* 24 (January 1939): 104–6.

Daniels, Jonathan. "After Ten Years: A Southerner Takes Another Look at the South." *Nieman Reports* 2 (October 1948): 12–13.

———. "Anti-social Philanthropy." *New Republic*, August 8, 1934, 335–37.

———. "Banner on a Yardstick." *New Republic*, August 24, 1938, 67–69.

———. "Breakfast with a Democrat." *Saturday Review*, April 23, 1938, 6–8.

———. *Clash of Angels*. New York: Payson and Clarke, 1930.

———. "Democracy Is Bread." *Virginia Quarterly Review* 14 (Autumn 1938): 481–90.

———. "Diagram for Democracy." *New Republic*, August 31, 1938, 95–98.

———. "Discovering the South." *Southern Association Quarterly*, August 1939, 1–12.

———. *The End of Innocence*. New York: J. B. Lippincott, 1954.

———. "The Face of America." *Saturday Review of Literature* February 18, 1939, 3–4.

———. "Farm and Mill." *Saturday Review of Literature*, February 18, 1933, 437.

———. "F.D.R. Was Not as Careful as His Protectors." *Life*, September 22, 1966, 46–48.

———. "F. O. B. Dixie." *Saturday Review of Literature*, August 29, 1936, 3–4.

———. "From Sectionalism to Regionalism." *Saturday Review of Literature*, July 25, 1936, 12.

———. "Gold Avenue." *Virginia Quarterly Review* 14 (Spring 1938): 177–86.

———. Letter to the editor. *Nation*, January 17, 1934, 74.

———. "A Native at Large: Dictators and Poll Taxes." *Nation*, February 22, 1941, 213.

———. "A Native at Large: Virginia Democracy." *Nation*, July 26, 1941, 74.

———. "Perspective on the Old South." *Saturday Review of Literature*, April 13, 1940, 15.

———. "Poor Whites." *Saturday Review of Literature*, March 5, 1932, 568.

———. "The Rich Begin to Pay." *Forum*, September 1935, 139–43.

———. "Seeing the South." *Harper's Magazine*, November 1941, 598–606.

———. *A Southerner Discovers New England*. New York: Macmillan, 1940.

———. *A Southerner Discovers the South*. New York: Macmillan, 1938.

———. *A Southerner Discovers the South*. Rpt. ed. New York: Da Capo, 1970.

———. "Three Men in a Valley." *New Republic*, August 17, 1938, 34–37.

———. *White House Witness, 1942–1945*. Garden City, N.Y.: Doubleday, 1975.

Daniels, Josephus. *Editor in Politics*. Chapel Hill: University of North Carolina Press, 1941.

———. *Tar Heel Editor*. Chapel Hill: University of North Carolina Press, 1939.

Daniels, Lucy. *With a Woman's Voice: A Writer's Struggle for Emotional Freedom*. Lanham, Md.: Madison Books, 2001.

Davidson, Donald. "Class Approach to Southern Problems." *Southern Review* 5 (1939): 261–72. Repr. in *The Southern Agrarians and the New Deal: Essays after "I'll Take My Stand*," edited by Emily S. Bingham and Thomas A. Underwood, 132–46. Charlottesville: University Press of Virginia, 2001.

———. "*I'll Take My Stand*: A History." *American Review* 5 (1935): 301–21; Repr. in *The Southern Agrarians and the New Deal: Essays after "I'll Take My Stand*," edited by Emily S. Bingham and Thomas A. Underwood, 89–103. Charlottesville: University Press of Virginia, 2001.

———. "Preface to Decision." *Sewanee Review* 53 (Summer 1945): 394–412.

———. "That This Nation May Endure: The Need for Political Regionalism." In *Who Owns America? A New Declaration of Independence*, edited by Herbert Agar and Allen Tate, 113–34. New York: Houghton Mifflin, 1936.

Davis, Lambert. "Progress below the Potomac." *Saturday Review of Literature*, July 16, 1938, 5–6.

Davis, Olivia Martin. *Growing Up in Lowndesboro, 1926–1936*. With sketches by Janie Martin Roberts. Donated to the Alabama Department of Archives and History, 1998.

DeBardeleben, Charles F. Letter to the editor. *Manufacturer's Record* 82 (October 5, 1922): 74.

Denby, Charles (Matthew Ward). *The Indignant Heart: A Black Worker's Journal*. Detroit: Wayne State University Press, 1989.

Ellis, Peter. "The Screen: The 'March of Time' and the Sharecroppers." *New Masses*, August 18, 1936, 29.

Garrett, Garet. "The Problem South." *Saturday Evening Post* 211 (October 8, 1938): 23, 85–86, 88–91.

Giles, Barbara. "Double Exploitation." *New Masses*, August 9, 1938, 27–28.

Graves, John Temple. "The South Still Loves Roosevelt." *Nation*, July 1, 1939, 11–13.

Hall, Rob F. "The South Discovers a Discoverer." *New South* 1 (October 1938): 13–15.

Hamilton, Virginia Van Der Veer. *Looking for Clark Gable and Other 20th-Century Pursuits: Collected Writings*. Tuscaloosa: University of Alabama Press, 1996.

Ickes, Harold L. *The Inside Struggle, 1936–1939*. Vol. 2 of *The Secret Diary of Harold L. Ickes*. New York: Simon and Schuster, 1954.

Johnson, Charles S. "More Southerners Discover the South." *Crisis* 46 (January 1939): 14–15.

Kester, Howard. *Revolt among the Sharecroppers*. With an introduction by Alex Lichtenstein. Knoxville: University of Tennessee Press, 1997.

Leighton, George R. "Birmingham, Alabama: The City of Perpetual Promise." *Harper's*, August 1937, 225–42.

Marvin, Fred. *Alabama Fuel and Iron Company and Its People: A Story of a Visit to Happy Communities*. Birmingham, Ala.: [Birmingham Publishing Co.], 1939.

Miller, Francis Pickens. *Man from the Valley: Memoirs of a 20th-Century Virginian*. Chapel Hill: University of North Carolina Press, 1971.

Milton, George Fort. "Dixie, U.S.A." *Nation*, July 16, 1938, 70–71.

Mitchell, H. L. "The Founding and Early History of the Southern Tenant Farmers Union." *Arkansas Historical Quarterly* 32 (December 1973): 342–69.

———. *Mean Things Happening in This Land: The Life and Times of H. L. Mitchell, Co-founder of the Southern Tenant Farmers Union*. 1979; Norman: University of Oklahoma Press, 2008.

Mitchell, Margaret. *Gone with the Wind*. 60th anniv. ed. New York: Scribner, 1996.

Morrow, E. Frederic. Review of *A Southerner Discovers the South*. *Crisis* 45 (October 1939): 340.

Murray, Pauli. *Song in a Weary Throat*. New York: Harper Collins, 1987.

Nixon, H. C. Review of *A Southerner Discovers the South*. *Journal of Southern History* 4 (November 1938): 540–41.

Owsley, Frank L. "Mr. Daniels Discovers the South." *Southern Review* 4 (1938): 665–75.

———. "The Pillars of Agrarianism." *American Review* 4 (1935): 529–47. Repr. in *The Southern Agrarians and the New Deal: Essays after "I'll Take My Stand,"* edited by Emily S. Bingham and Thomas A. Underwood, 199–211. Charlottesville: University Press of Virginia, 2001.

Pate, James E. Review of *A Southerner Discovers the South*. *William and Mary Quarterly* 19 (January 1939): 86–88.

Raper, Arthur F. *The Tragedy of Lynching*. Chapel Hill: University of North Carolina Press, 1933.

Roosevelt, Franklin D. "Growing Up by Plan." *Survey*, February 1, 1932, 483–85.

———. "In These Past Six Years, the South Has Made Greater Economic and Social Progress Up the Scale Than at Any Other Period in Her Long History." Address at University of Georgia, Athens, August 11, 1938. In *The Public Papers and Addresses of Franklin D. Roosevelt*, 1938 vol., *The Continuing Struggle for Liberalism*, edited by Samuel I. Rosenman, 471–75. New York: Macmillan, 1941.

———. Letter to members of the Conference on Economic Conditions in the South, July 5, 1938. In *Confronting Southern Poverty in the Great Depression: The Report on Economic Conditions of the South with Related Documents*, edited by David L. Carlton and Peter A. Coclanis, 42–43. Boston: Bedford, 1996.

———. "The President Discusses Political Principles, Social Objectives, and Party Candidates with His Fellow-Georgians. Address at Barnesville, Georgia. August 11, 1938." In *The Public Papers and Addresses of Franklin D. Roosevelt*, 1938 vol., *The Continuing Struggle for Liberalism*, edited by Samuel I. Rosenman, 463–71. New York: Macmillan, 1941.

———. *The Public Papers and Addresses of Franklin D. Roosevelt*, 1941 vol., *The Call to Battle Stations*, edited by Samuel I. Rosenman. New York: Harper, 1950.

———. *The Public Papers and Addresses of Franklin D. Roosevelt*, 1943 vol., *The Tide Turns*, edited by Samuel I. Rosenman. New York: Harper, 1950.

———. *The Public Papers and Addresses of Franklin D. Roosevelt*, Vol. 4, *The Court Disapproves, 1935: with a special introduction and explanatory notes by President Roosevelt*. New York: Random House, 1938.

———. "Recommendations to the Congress to Curb Monopolies and the Concentration of Economic Power, April 29, 1938." In *The Public Papers and Addresses of Franklin D. Roosevelt*, 1938 vol., *The Continuing Struggle for Liberalism*, edited by Samuel I. Rosenman, 305–32. New York: Macmillan, 1941.

———. "A Suggestion for Legislature to Create the Tennessee Valley Authority, April 10, 1933." In *The Public Papers and Addresses of Franklin D. Roosevelt, with a Special Introduction and Explanatory Notes by President Roosevelt*, Vol. 2, *The Year of Crisis, 1933*, 122–29. New York: Random House, 1938.

———. "The United States Is Rising and Is Rebuilding on Sounder Lines." Address at Gainesville, Georgia, March 23, 1938. In *The Public Papers and Addresses of Franklin D. Roosevelt*, 1938 vol., *The Continuing Struggle for Liberalism*, edited by Samuel I. Rosenman, 164–69. New York: Macmillan, 1941.

Rosengarten, Theodore. *All God's Dangers: The Life of Nate Shaw*. New York: Vintage, 1974.

Royster, Jacqueline Jones, ed. *Southern Horrors and Other Writings: The Anti-Lynching Campaign of Ida B. Wells, 1892–1900*. Boston: Bedford/St. Martin's, 1997.

Rustin, Bayard. "From Protest to Politics: The Future of the Civil Rights Movement." *Commentary* 39 (February 1965): 25–31.

Sawyer, Roland. "Discovering Jonathan Daniels." *Christian Science Monitor*, August 3, 1940, 6.

Southern Policy Conference. *Southern Policy: Report of the Southern Policy Conference in Atlanta, April 25–28, 1935* [New Orleans: Southern Policy Committee, 1935].

Southern Tenant Farmers Union. *The Disinherited Speak: Letters from Sharecroppers*. New York: Workers Defense League, 1937.

Thomas, Norman. *The Plight of the Share-Cropper.* New York: League for Industrial Democracy, 1934.

Thompson, John L. *History and Views of Colored Officers Training Camp: For 1917 at Fort Des Moines, Iowa.* Des Moines, Iowa: Bystander, 1917.

Turner, Victor Caesar. "An Agricultural Program for Alabama." M.S. thesis, Cornell University, 1931.

Twelve Southerners. *I'll Take My Stand.* 1930; New York: Harper, 1962.

U.S. Senate. Report of the Special Committee to Investigate Presidential, Vice Presidential, and Senatorial Campaign Expenditures, 1940, 76th Cong., 3rd sess., 1941.

U.S. Senate, Committee on Privileges and Elections. [Senator from Alabama.] Vol. 4, Hearings on S.R. 467 and S.R. 485, 72nd Cong., 1st sess., 1932.

Wynn, Wilhelmina Roberts. "Pieces of Days." *Callaloo* 27 (Spring 1986): 391–403.

Secondary Sources

Acker, James R. *Scottsboro and Its Legacy: The Cases That Challenged American Legal and Social Justice.* Westport, Conn.: Praeger, 2008.

Adams, Amanda. "'Painfully Southern': *Gone with the Wind*, the Agrarians, and the Battle for the New South." *Southern Literary Journal* 40 (Fall 2007): 58–75.

Alexander, Peter. "Rising from the Ashes: Alabama Coal Miners, 1921–1941." In *It Is Union and Liberty: Alabama Coal Miners and the UMW*, edited by Edwin L. Brown and Colin J. Davis, 62–83. Tuscaloosa: University of Alabama Press, 1999.

Arnesen, Eric. "Civil Rights and the Cold War at Home: Postwar Activism, Anticommunism, and the Decline of the Left." *American Communist History*, 11 (April 2012): 5–44.

———. "Reconsidering the 'Long Civil Rights Movement.'" *Historically Speaking* 10 (April 2009): 31–34.

Auerbach, Jerold S. "New Deal, Old Deal, or Raw Deal: Some Thoughts on New Left Historiography." *Journal of Southern History* 35 (February 1969): 18–30.

———. "Southern Tenant Farmers: Socialist Critics of the New Deal." *Labor History* 7 (Winter 1966): 3–18.

Badger, Anthony J. *The New Deal: The Depression Years, 1933–1940.* Chicago: Ivan R. Dee, 1989.

Bailey, Hugh C. "Ethel Armes and *The Story of Coal and Iron in Alabama.*" *Alabama Review* 22 (July 1969): 188–99.

Baker, Bruce E. *What Reconstruction Meant: Historical Memory in the American South.* Charlottesville: University of Virginia Press, 2007.

Baker, Lee D. *From Savage to Negro: Anthropology and the Construction of Race, 1896–1954.* Berkeley: University of California Press, 1998.

Bartley, Numan V. "The Southern Enclosure Movement." *Georgia Historical Quarterly* 71 (Fall 1987): 438–50.

Bay, Mia. *To Tell the Truth Freely: The Life of Ida B. Wells.* New York: Hill and Wang, 2009.

Beidler, Philip. "Yankee Interloper and Native Son: Carl Carmer and Clarence Cason, Unlikely Twins of Alabama Exposé." *Southern Cultures* 9 (Spring 2003): 18–35.

Berrey, Stephen A. *The Jim Crow Routine: Everyday Performances of Race, Civil Rights, and Segregation in Mississippi.* Chapel Hill: University of North Carolina Press, 2015.

Bingham, Emily S., and Thomas A. Underwood, eds. *The Southern Agrarians and the New Deal: Essays after "I'll Take My Stand."* Charlottesville: University Press of Virginia, 2001.

Blackmon, Douglas A. *Slavery by Another Name: The Re-enslavement of Black Americans from the Civil War to World War II.* New York: Anchor Books, 2008.

Boyle, Sarah Patton. *The Desegregated Heart: A Virginian's Stand in Time of Transition.* Edited by Jennifer Ritterhouse. Charlottesville: University Press of Virginia, 2001.

Brinkley, Alan. *The End of Reform: New Deal Liberalism in Recession and War.* New York: Vintage, 1995.

———. *Voices of Protest: Huey Long, Father Coughlin, and the Great Depression.* New York: Vintage, 1983.

Brueggemann, John. "Racial Considerations and Social Policy in the 1930s." *Social Science History* 26 (Spring 2002): 139–77.

Brundage, W. Fitzhugh. *Lynching in the New South: Georgia and Virginia, 1880–1930.* Urbana: University of Illinois Press, 1993.

Burkholder, Zoe. *Color in the Classroom: How American Schools Taught Race, 1900–1954.* New York: Oxford University Press, 2011.

Burstein, Andrew. *Democracy's Muse: How Thomas Jefferson Became an FDR Liberal, a Reagan Republican, and a Tea Party Fanatic, All the While Being Dead.* Charlottesville: University of Virginia Press, 2015.

Cahn, Susan K. *Sexual Reckonings: Southern Girls in a Troubling Age.* Cambridge, Mass.: Harvard University Press, 2007.

Campbell, W. Joseph. "'One of the Fine Figures of American Journalism': A Closer Look at Josephus Daniels of the *Raleigh News and Observer*." *American Journalism* 16 (October 1999): 37–55.

Carlton, David L., and Peter A. Coclanis. "Another 'Great Migration': From Region to Race in Southern Liberalism, 1938–1945." *Southern Cultures* 3 (Winter 1997): 37–62.

———, eds. *Confronting Southern Poverty in the Great Depression: "The Report on Economic Conditions in the South" with Related Documents.* Boston: Bedford/St. Martin's, 1996.

Carter, Dan T. *Scottsboro: A Tragedy of the American South.* Rev. ed. Baton Rouge: Louisiana State University Press, 2007.

Cecelski, David S., and Timothy B. Tyson. "Introduction." In *Democracy Betrayed: The Wilmington Race Riot of 1898 and Its Legacy*, edited by David S. Cecelski and Timothy B. Tyson, 3–13. Chapel Hill: University of North Carolina Press, 1998.

Cha-Jua, Sundiata Keita, and Clarence Lang. "The 'Long Movement' as Vampire: Temporal and Spatial Fallacies in Recent Black Freedom Studies." *Journal of African American History* 92 (Spring 2007): 265–88.

Clark, Kathleen. "Margaret Mitchell, 1900–1949: 'What Living in the South Means.'" In *Georgia Women: Their Lives and Times*, edited by Kathleen Clark and Anne Short Chirhart, 2:190–211. Athens: University of Georgia Press, 2013.

Cobb, James C. *Away Down South: A History of Southern Identity*. New York: Oxford University Press, 2005.

———. "Does *Mind* No Longer Matter? The South, the Nation, and *The Mind of the South*, 1941–1991." *Journal of Southern History* 57 (November 1991): 681–718.

———. *The Selling of the South: The Southern Crusade for Industrial Development, 1936–1980*. Baton Rouge: Louisiana State University Press, 1982.

———. *The South and America since World War II*. New York: Oxford University Press, 2012.

Cohen, Lizabeth. *Making a New Deal: Industrial Workers in Chicago, 1919–1939*. 2nd ed. New York: Cambridge University Press, 2008.

Conkin, Paul K. *The Southern Agrarians*. Knoxville: University of Tennessee Press, 1988.

Cox, Karen L. *Dreaming of Dixie: How the South Was Created in American Popular Culture*. Chapel Hill: University of North Carolina Press, 2011.

Craig, Lee A. *Josephus Daniels: His Life and Times*. Chapel Hill: University of North Carolina Press, 2013.

Crespino, Joseph. *In Search of Another Country: Mississippi and the Conservative Counterrevolution*. Princeton, N.J.: Princeton University Press, 2007.

———. *Strom Thurmond's America*. New York: Hill and Wang, 2012.

Culver, John C., and John Hyde. *American Dreamer: The Life and Times of Henry A. Wallace*. New York: Norton, 2000.

Dailey, Jane. *Before Jim Crow: The Politics of Race in Postemancipation Virginia*. Chapel Hill: University of North Carolina Press, 2000.

Daniel, Pete. *The Shadow of Slavery: Peonage in the South, 1901–1969*. Urbana: University of Illinois Press, 1972.

Davis, David Brion. "Southern Comfort." *New York Review of Books* 42 (October 5, 1995): 43–46.

Denning, Michael. *The Cultural Front: The Laboring of American Culture in the Twentieth Century*. New York: Verso, 1997.

"Dickson, Robert Stiles." In *Encyclopedia of American Biography*, n.s., edited by Winfield Scott Downs, 23:271–72. New York: American Historical Company, 1952.

Dickstein, Morris. *Dancing in the Dark: A Cultural History of the Great Depression*. New York: Norton, 2010.

Duck, Leigh Anne. *The Nation's Region: Southern Modernism, Segregation, and U.S. Nationalism*. Athens: University of Georgia Press, 2006.

Dunbar, Anthony P. *Against the Grain: Southern Radicals and Prophets, 1929–1959*. Charlottesville: University Press of Virginia, 1981.

Dunn, Susan. *Roosevelt's Purge: How FDR Fought to Change the Democratic Party*. Cambridge, Mass.: Harvard University Press, 2010.

Durden, Robert F. *Electrifying the Piedmont Carolinas: The Duke Power Company, 1904–1997*. Durham, N.C.: Carolina Academic Press, 2008.

Dykeman, Wilma, and James Stokely. *Seeds of Southern Change: The Life of Will Alexander*. Chicago: University of Chicago, 1962.

Eagles, Charles W. *Jonathan Daniels and Race Relations: The Evolution of a Southern Liberal*. Knoxville: University of Tennessee Press, 1982.

————. *Outside Agitator: Jon Daniels and the Civil Rights Movement in Alabama*. Chapel Hill: University of North Carolina Press, 1993.

Edmonds, Helen G. *The Negro and Fusion Politics in North Carolina, 1894–1901*. Chapel Hill: University of North Carolina Press, 1951.

Edwards, Laura. "Southern History as U.S. History." *Journal of Southern History* 75 (August 2009): 533–64.

Egerton, John. *Speak Now against the Day: The Generation before the Civil Rights Movement in the South*. New York: Knopf, 1994.

Ellis, R. H. "The Calhoun School, Miss Charlotte Thorn's 'Lighthouse on the Hill' in Lowndes County, Alabama." *Alabama Review* 37 (July 1984): 183–201.

Eskew, Glenn T. "But for Birmingham: The Local and National Movements in the Civil Rights Struggle." Ph.D. diss., University of Georgia, 1993.

————. *But for Birmingham: The Local and National Movements in the Civil Rights Struggle*. Chapel Hill: University of North Carolina Press, 1997.

Fannin, Mark. *Labor's Promised Land: Radical Visions of Gender, Race, and Religion in the South*. Knoxville: University of Tennessee Press, 2003.

Faust, Drew Gilpin. "Clutching the Chains That Bind: Margaret Mitchell and *Gone with the Wind*." *Southern Cultures* 5 (1999): 5–20.

Feimster, Crystal. *Southern Horrors: Women and the Politics of Rape and Lynching*. Cambridge, Mass.: Harvard University Press, 2009.

Feldman, Glenn. *The Irony of the Solid South: Democrats, Republicans, and Race, 1865–1944*. Tuscaloosa: University of Alabama Press, 2013.

Ferguson, Robert Hunt. "Race and the Remaking of the Rural South: Delta Cooperative Farm and Providence Farm in Jim Crow-Era Mississippi." Ph.D. diss., University of North Carolina at Chapel Hill, 2012.

Fields, Barbara Jeanne. "Slavery, Race and Ideology in the United States of America." *New Left Review* (May/June 1990): 95–118.

Finley, Keith M. *Delaying the Dream: Southern Senators and the Fight Against Civil Rights, 1938–1965*. Baton Rouge: Louisiana State University Press, 2008.

Fleischhauer, Carl, and Beverly W. Brannan. *Documenting America, 1935–1943*. Berkeley: University of California Press, 1988.

Fraser, Steve, and Gary Gerstle, eds. *The Rise and Fall of the New Deal Order, 1930–1980*. Princeton, N.J.: Princeton University Press, 1989.

Fuller, Justin. "Henry F. DeBardeleben, Industrialist of the New South." *Alabama Review* 39 (January 1986): 3–18.

Gaston, Paul M. *The New South Creed: A Study in Southern Myth-Making*. New York: Knopf, 1970.

Gellman, Eric S. *Death Blow to Jim Crow: The National Negro Congress and the Rise of Militant Civil Rights*. Chapel Hill: University of North Carolina Press, 2012.

Gellman, Eric S., and Jarod Roll. *The Gospel of the Working Class: Labor's Southern Prophets in New Deal America*. Chicago: University of Illinois Press, 2011.

Gerber, Larry G. *Limits of Liberalism: Josephus Daniels, Henry Stimson, Bernard Baruch, Donald Richberg, Felix Frankfurter, and the Development of the Modern American Political Economy*. New York: New York University Press, 1983.

Gerstle, Gary. "The Protean Character of American Liberalism." *American Historical Review* 99 (October 1994), 1043–74.

Giddings, Paula J. *Ida: A Sword among Lions: Ida B. Wells and the Campaign against Lynching.* New York: Amistad, 2008.

Gilmore, Elizabeth Glenda. *Defying Dixie: The Radical Roots of Civil Rights, 1919–1950.* New York: Norton, 2008.

———. *Gender and Jim Crow: Women and the Politics of White Supremacy in North Carolina, 1896–1920.* Chapel Hill: University of North Carolina Press, 1996.

———. "Murder, Memory, and the Flight of the Incubus." In *Democracy Betrayed: The Wilmington Race Riot of 1898 and Its Legacy,* edited by David S. Cecelski and Timothy B. Tyson, 73–93. Chapel Hill: University of North Carolina Press, 1998.

Godshalk, David Fort. *Veiled Visions: The 1906 Atlanta Race Riot and the Reshaping of American Race Relations.* Chapel Hill: University of North Carolina Press, 2005.

Goluboff, Risa L. *The Lost Promise of Civil Rights.* Cambridge. Mass.: Harvard University Press, 2007.

Goodman, Barak. *Scottsboro: An American Tragedy.* DVD. 2001; PBS Home Video, 2005.

Goodman, James. *Stories of Scottsboro.* New York: Vintage, 1994.

Gordon, Linda. *Dorothea Lange: A Life beyond Limits.* New York: Norton, 2009.

Grant, Nancy L. *TVA and Black Americans: Planning for the Status Quo.* Philadelphia: Temple University Press, 1990.

Gregory, James N. *The Southern Diaspora: How the Great Migrations of Black and White Southerners Transformed America.* Chapel Hill: University of North Carolina Press, 2005.

Grubbs, Donald. *Cry from the Cotton: The Southern Tenant Farmers' Union and the New Deal.* 1971; Fayetteville: University of Arkansas Press, 2000.

Hague, Euan, Heidi Beirich, and Edward H. Sebesta, eds. *Neo-Confederacy: A Critical Introduction.* Austin: University of Texas Press, 2008.

Hahn, Steven. *A Nation under Our Feet: Black Political Struggles in the Rural South from Slavery to the Great Migration.* Cambridge, Mass.: Harvard University Press, 2003.

Hall, Jacquelyn Dowd. "The Long Civil Rights Movement and the Political Uses of the Past." *Journal of American History* 91 (March 2005): 1233–63.

———. *Revolt against Chivalry: Jessie Daniel Ames and the Women's Campaign Against Lynching.* Rev. ed. New York: Columbia University Press, 1993.

Hall, Jacquelyn Dowd, James Leloudis, Robert Korstad, Mary Murphy, Lu Ann Jones, and Christopher B. Daly. *Like a Family: The Making of a Southern Cotton Mill World.* New York: Norton, 1987.

Harwell, Richard, ed. *Margaret Mitchell's "Gone with the Wind" Letters.* New York: Macmillan, 1976.

Hobson, Fred. *But Now I See: The White Southern Racial Conversion Narrative.* Baton Rouge: Louisiana State University Press, 1999.

———. *Tell about the South: The Southern Rage to Explain.* Baton Rouge: Louisiana State University Press, 1983.

Holladay, Bob. "The Gods That Failed: Agrarianism, Regionalism, and the Nashville-Chapel Hill Highway." *Tennessee Historical Quarterly* 64 (December 2005): 284–307.

Holley, Donald. *Uncle Sam's Farmers: The New Deal Communities in the Lower Mississippi Valley.* Urbana: University of Illinois Press, 1975.

Hustwit, William P. "Smart Segregationists: Southern Senators and Racial Politics from the 1930s to the 1960s." *Reviews in American History* 41 (June 2013): 318–24.

Ingalls, Robert P. "Antiradical Violence in Birmingham during the 1930s." *Journal of Southern History* 47 (November 1981): 521–44.

Jeffries, Hasan Kwame. *Bloody Lowndes: Civil Rights and Black Power in Alabama's Black Belt*. New York: New York University Press, 2009.

Jones, William P. *The March on Washington: Jobs, Freedom, and the Forgotten History of Civil Rights*. New York: Norton, 2013.

Justesen, Benjamin R., II. "George Henry White, Josephus Daniels, and the Showdown over North Carolina Disfranchisement, 1900." *North Carolina Historical Review* 77 (January 2000): 1–33.

Katznelson, Ira. *Fear Itself: The New Deal and the Origins of Our Time*. New York: Liveright, 2013.

Kelley, Robin D. G. *Hammer and Hoe: Alabama Communists during the Great Depression*. Chapel Hill: University of North Carolina Press, 1990.

Kelly, Brian M. "Having It Their Way: Alabama Coal Operators and the Search for Docile Labor, 1908–1921." In *It Is Union and Liberty: Alabama Coal Miners and the UMW*, edited by Edwin L. Brown and Colin J. Davis, 38–61. Tuscaloosa: University of Alabama Press, 1999.

———. *Race, Class, and Power in the Alabama Coalfields, 1908–1921*. Urbana: University of Illinois Press, 2001.

Kennedy, David M. *Freedom from Fear: The American People in Depression and War, 1929–1945*. New York: Oxford University Press, 1999.

Kilpatrick, Carroll, ed. *Roosevelt and Daniels: A Friendship in Politics*. Chapel Hill: University of North Carolina Press, 1952.

Kirshenbaum, Andrea Meryl. "'The Vampire That Hovers over North Carolina': Gender, White Supremacy, and the Wilmington Race Riot of 1898." *Southern Cultures* 4 (Fall 1998): 6–30.

Kneebone, John T. *Southern Liberal Journalists and the Issue of Race, 1920–1944*. Chapel Hill: University of North Carolina Press, 1985.

Korstad, Robert Rodgers. *Civil Rights Unionism: Tobacco Workers and the Struggle for Democracy in the Mid-Twentieth-Century South*. Chapel Hill: University of North Carolina Press, 2003.

Korstad, Robert, and Nelson Lichtenstein. "Opportunities Found and Lost: Labor, Radicals, and the Early Civil Rights Movement." *Journal of American History* 75 (December 1988): 786–811.

Kousser, J. Morgan. *The Shaping of Southern Politics and the Establishment of the One-Party South, 1880–1910*. New Haven, Conn.: Yale University Press, 1974.

Kreyling, Michael. *Inventing Southern Literature*. Jackson: University Press of Mississippi, 1998.

Krueger, Thomas A. *And Promises to Keep: The Southern Conference for Human Welfare, 1938–1948*. Nashville, Tenn.: Vanderbilt University Press, 1967.

Lanctot, Neil. *Negro League Baseball: The Rise and Ruin of a Black Institution*. Philadelphia: University of Pennsylvania Press, 2004.

Lasch-Quinn, Elizabeth. *Black Neighbors: Race and the Limits of Reform in the American*

Settlement House Movement, 1890–1945. Chapel Hill: University of North Carolina Press, 1993.

Lassiter, Matthew D. *Silent Majority: Suburban Politics in the Sunbelt South.* Princeton, N.J.: Princeton University Press, 2006.

Lassiter, Matthew D., and Joseph Crespino, eds. *The Myth of Southern Exceptionalism.* New York: Oxford University Press, 2010.

Lawson, Steven F. "Long Origins of the Short Civil Rights Movement, 1954–1968." In *Freedom Rights: New Perspectives on the Civil Rights Movement,* edited by Danielle L. McGuire and John Dittmer, 9–37. Lexington: University Press of Kentucky, 2011.

Letwin, Daniel. "The Early Years: Alabama Miners Organize, 1878–1908." In *It Is Union and Liberty: Alabama Coal Miners and the UMW,* edited by Edwin L. Brown and Colin J. Davis, 11–37. Tuscaloosa: University of Alabama Press, 1999.

Leuchtenburg, William E. *Franklin D. Roosevelt and the New Deal, 1932–1940.* New York: Harper, 1963.

———. Untitled essay in *Books of Passage: 27 North Carolina Writers on the Books That Changed Their Lives,* edited by David Perkins, 110–15. Asheboro, N.C.: Down Home Press, 1993.

———. *The White House Looks South: Franklin D. Roosevelt, Harry S. Truman, Lyndon B. Johnson.* Baton Rouge: Louisiana State University Press, 2005.

Lichtenstein, Alex. "The Other Civil Rights Movement and the Problem of Southern Exceptionalism." *Journal of the Historical Society* 11 (September 2011): 351–76.

———. "Proletarians or Peasants? Sharecroppers and the Politics of Protest in the Rural South, 1880–1940." *Plantation Society in the Americas* 5 (Fall 1998): 297–331.

———. *Twice the Work of Free Labor: The Political Economy of Convict Labor in the New South.* New York: Verso, 1996.

Link, William A. *The Paradox of Southern Progressivism, 1880–1930.* Chapel Hill: University of North Carolina Press, 1992.

Lipsitz, George. "The Possessive Investment in Whiteness: Racialized Social Democracy and the 'White' Problem in American Studies." *American Quarterly* 47 (September 1995): 369–87.

Lowndesboro's Picturesque Legacies. Lowndesboro, Ala.: Lowndesboro Heritage Society, 1979.

MacLean, Nancy. *Behind the Mask of Chivalry: The Making of the Second Ku Klux Klan.* New York: Oxford University Press, 1994.

———. *Freedom Is Not Enough: The Opening of the American Workplace.* Cambridge. Mass.: Russell Sage Foundation/Harvard University Press, 2008.

———. "Neo-Confederacy versus the New Right: The Regional Utopia of the Modern American Right." In *The Myth of Southern Exceptionalism,* edited by Matthew D. Lassiter and Joseph Crespino, 308–29. New York: Oxford University Press, 2010.

Maher, Neil M. *Nature's New Deal: The Civilian Conservation Corps and the Roots of the American Environmental Movement.* New York: Oxford University Press, 2008.

Major, William H. *Grounded Vision: New Agrarianism and the Academy.* Tuscaloosa: University of Alabama Press, 2011.

Malvasi, Mark G. *The Unregenerate South: The Agrarian Thought of John Crowe Ransom, Allen Tate, and Donald Davidson.* Baton Rouge: University of Louisiana Press, 1997.

Mancini, Matthew. *One Dies, Get Another: Convict Leasing in the American South, 1866–1928.* Columbia: University of South Carolina Press, 1996.

Manthorne, Jason. "A View from the Cotton: Reconsidering the Southern Tenant Farmers' Union." *Agricultural History* 84 (Winter 2010): 20–45.

Marler, Scott P. "Fables of the Reconstruction, Reconstruction of the Fables." *Journal of the Historical Society* 4 (Winter 2004): 113–37.

Matthews, John Michael. "Virginius Dabney, John Temple Graves, and What Happened to Southern Liberalism." *Mississippi Quarterly* 45 (Fall 1992): 405–20.

Maxwell, Angie. *The Indicted South: Public Criticism, Southern Inferiority, and the Politics of Whiteness.* Chapel Hill: University of North Carolina Press, 2014.

Mayberry, B. D. *The Role of Tuskegee University in the Origin, Growth and Development of the Negro Cooperative Extension System, 1881–1990.* Tuskegee, Ala.: Tuskegee University Cooperative Extension Program, 1989.

Mazzari, Louis. *Southern Modernist: Arthur Raper from the New Deal to the Cold War.* Baton Rouge: Louisiana State University Press, 2006.

McGovern, James R. *Anatomy of a Lynching: The Killing of Claude Neal.* Baton Rouge: Louisiana State University Press, 1982.

McWhorter, Diane. *Carry Me Home: Birmingham, Alabama, the Climactic Battle of the Civil Rights Revolution.* New York: Simon and Schuster, 2001.

Milkis, Sidney M. *The President and the Parties: The Transformation of the American Party System since the New Deal.* New York: Oxford University Press, 1993.

Miller, Dan B. *Erskine Caldwell: The Journey from Tobacco Road.* New York: Knopf, 1995.

Mixon, Wayne. *The People's Writer: Erskine Caldwell and the South.* Charlottesville: University Press of Virginia, 1995.

Mohl, Raymond A. "Clowning Around: The Miami Ethiopian Clowns and Cultural Conflict in Black Baseball." *Tequesta* 62 (2002): 40–67.

Moore, John Robert. "Senator Josiah W. Bailey and the 'Conservative Manifesto' of 1937." *Journal of Southern History* 31 (February 1965): 21–39.

Morrison, Joseph L. *Josephus Daniels Says . . . : An Editor's Political Odyssey from Bryan to Wilson and F.D.R., 1894–1913.* Chapel Hill: University of North Carolina Press, 1962.

———. *Josephus Daniels: The Small-d Democrat.* Chapel Hill: University of North Carolina Press, 1966.

Myrdal, Gunnar. *An American Dilemma: The Negro Problem and Modern Democracy.* New York: Harper, 1944.

Neuse, Steven M. *David E. Lilienthal: The Journey of an American Liberal.* Knoxville: University of Tennessee Press, 1996.

Nicolaisen, Peter. "Southern Conservatism at Bay: A Review Essay." *Southern Quarterly* 40 (Spring 2002): 163–71.

Norrell, Robert J. "Labor at the Ballot Box: Alabama Politics from the New Deal to the Dixiecrat Movement." *Journal of Southern History* 77 (May 1991): 201–34.

O'Brien, Michael. *The Idea of the American South, 1920–1941.* Baltimore: Johns Hopkins University Press, 1979.

Oshinsky, David. *Worse than Slavery: Parchman Farm and the Ordeal of Jim Crow Justice.* New York: Free Press, 1997.

Ownby, Ted. *American Dreams in Mississippi: Consumers, Poverty, and Culture, 1830–1998.* Chapel Hill: University of North Carolina Press, 1999.

Patton, Randall. "Lillian Smith and the Transformation of American Liberalism, 1945–1950." *Georgia Historical Quarterly* 76 (Summer 1992): 373–92.

Payne, Elizabeth Anne, and Louise Boyle. "The Lady Was a Sharecropper: Myrtle Lawrence and the Southern Tenant Farmers' Union." *Southern Cultures* 4 (1998): 5–27.

Perman, Michael. *Struggle for Mastery: Disfranchisement in the South, 1888–1908.* Chapel Hill: University of North Carolina, 2001.

Prather, H. Leon, Sr. "We Have Taken a City: A Centennial Essay." In *Democracy Betrayed: The Wilmington Race Riot of 1898 and Its Legacy,* edited by David S. Cecelski and Timothy B. Tyson, 15–41. Chapel Hill: University of North Carolina Press, 1998.

Puckett, John Rogers. *Five Photo-Textual Documentaries from the Great Depression.* Ann Arbor, Mich.: UMI Research Press, 1984.

Pyron, Darden Asbury. "Gone with the Wind and the Southern Cultural Awakening." *Virginia Quarterly Review* 62 (Autumn 1986): 565–87.

———. *Southern Daughter: The Life of Margaret Mitchell.* New York: HarperCollins, 1991.

Rable, George C. "The South and the Politics of Antilynching Legislation, 1920–1940." *Journal of Southern History* 51 (May 1985): 201–20.

Reed, Linda. *Simple Decency and Common Sense: The Southern Conference Movement, 1938–1963.* Bloomington: Indiana University Press, 1991.

Reed, Merl E. *Seedtime for the Modern Civil Rights Movement: The President's Committee on Fair Employment Practice, 1941–1946.* Baton Rouge: Louisiana State University Press, 1991.

Ring, Natalie J. *The Problem South: Region, Empire, and the New Liberal State, 1880–1930.* Athens: University of Georgia Press, 2012.

Ritterhouse, Jennifer. "Dixie Destinations: Rereading Jonathan Daniels's *A Southerner Discovers the South." Southern Spaces: An Interdisciplinary Journal about Regions, Places, and Cultures of the American South and Their Global Connections* (May 2010), www.southernspaces.org.

———. *Growing Up Jim Crow: How Black and White Southern Children Learned Race.* Chapel Hill: University of North Carolina Press, 2006.

———. "Woman Flogged: Willie Sue Blagden, the Southern Tenant Farmers Union, and How an Impulse for Story Led to a Historiographical Corrective." *Rethinking History: The Journal of Theory and Practice* 18 (January 2014): 97–121.

Rogers, Lou. "Dr. Delia Dixon-Carroll: A Woman Whose Dreams Came True." *We the People of North Carolina* 1 (December 1943): 12–13.

Rolinson, Mary G. *Grassroots Garveyism: The Universal Negro Improvement Association in the Rural South, 1920–1927.* Chapel Hill: University of North Carolina Press, 2007.

Roper, John Herbert. *C. Vann Woodward, Southerner.* Athens: University of Georgia Press, 1987.

Ross, James D., Jr. "'I Ain't Got No Home in This World': The Rise and Fall of the

Southern Tenant Farmers' Union in Arkansas." Ph.D. diss., Auburn University, 2004.

Rossinow, Doug. *Visions of Progress: The Left-Liberal Tradition in America*. Philadelphia: University of Pennsylvania, 2008.

Rubin, Anne Sarah. "Revisiting Classic Civil War Books: Why *Gone with the Wind* Still Matters; or Why I Still Love *Gone with the Wind*." *Civil War History* 59 (March 2013), 93–98.

Salmond, John A. "The Civilian Conservation Corps and the Negro." *Journal of American History* 52 (June 1965): 75–88.

———. *Miss Lucy of the CIO: The Life and Times of Lucy Randolph Mason, 1882–1959*. Athens: University of Georgia Press, 1988.

Samway, Patrick. "The Union of the DeBardeleben and Percy Families." *Mississippi Quarterly* 51 (Winter 1997/98): 15–32.

Schechter, Patricia A. *Ida B. Wells-Barnett and American Reform, 1880–1930*. Chapel Hill: University of North Carolina Press, 2001.

Schulman, Bruce J. *From Cotton Belt to Sunbelt: Federal Policy, Economic Development, and the Transformation of the South, 1938–1980*. Durham, N.C.: Duke University Press, 1994.

Schultz, Kevin M. "The FEPC and the Legacy of the Labor-Based Civil Rights Movement of the 1940s." *Labor History* 49 (February 2008), 71–92.

Schwarz, Jordan A. *The New Dealers: Power Politics in the Age of Roosevelt*. New York: Knopf, 1993.

Shapiro, Edward S. "Donald Davidson and the Tennessee Valley Authority: The Response of a Southern Conservative." *Tennessee Historical Quarterly* 33 (December 1974), 436–51.

Shouse, Sarah Newman. *Hillbilly Realist: Herman Clarence Nixon of Possum Trot*. Tuscaloosa: University of Alabama Press, 1986.

Singal, Daniel Joseph. *The War Within: From Victorian to Modernist Thought in the South, 1919–1945*. Chapel Hill: University of North Carolina Press, 1982.

Singh, Nikhil Pal. *Black Is a Country: Race and the Unfinished Struggle for Democracy*. Cambridge, Mass.: Harvard University Press, 2004.

Smith, Mark M. *How Race Is Made: Slavery, Segregation, and the Senses*. Chapel Hill: University of North Carolina Press, 2006.

Sokol, Jason. Review of Ward, *Defending White Democracy*. *Social History* 37 (August 2012): 366–67.

Sosna, Morton. *In Search of the Silent South: Southern Liberals and the Race Question*. New York: Columbia University Press, 1977.

Staub, Michael E. *Voices of Persuasion: Politics of Representation in 1930s America*. New York: Cambridge University Press, 1994.

Stone, Jayme Millsap. "'They Were Her Daughters': Women and Grassroots Organizing for Social Justice in the Arkansas Delta, 1870–1970." Ph.D. diss., University of Memphis, 2010.

Stott, William. *Documentary Expression and Thirties America*. 1973; Chicago: University of Chicago Press, 1986.

Sugrue, Thomas. *Sweet Land of Liberty: The Forgotten Struggle for Civil Rights in the North*. New York: Random House, 2008.

Sullivan, Patricia. *Days of Hope: Race and Democracy in the New Deal Era*. Chapel Hill: University of North Carolina Press, 1996.

———. *Lift Every Voice: The NAACP and the Making of the Civil Rights Movement*. New York: New Press, 2009.

Taft, Philip. *Organizing Dixie: Alabama Workers in the Industrial Era*. Edited by Gary M. Fink. Tuscaloosa: University of Alabama Press, 1981.

Taylor, Gregory S. "Organized Labor, Reds, and Radicals of the 1930s." In *The New Deal and the Great Depression*, edited by Aaron D. Purcell, 145–65. Kent, Ohio: Kent State University Press, 2014.

Thompson, Robert F., III. "The Strange Case of Paul D. Peacher, Twentieth-Century Slaveholder." *Arkansas Historical Quarterly* 52 (Winter 1993): 426–51.

Tindall, George Brown. *The Emergence of the New South, 1913–1945*. Baton Rouge: Louisiana State University Press, 1967.

Underwood, Thomas A. *Allen Tate: Orphan of the South*. Princeton, N.J.: Princeton University Press, 2000.

Verney, Kevern. "To Hope till Hope Create: The NAACP in Alabama, 1913–1945." In *Long Is the Way and Hard: One Hundred Years of the NAACP*, edited by Kevern Verney and Lee Sartain, 105–20. Fayetteville: University of Arkansas Press, 2009.

Ward, Jason Morgan. *Defending White Democracy: The Making of a Segregationist Movement and the Remaking of Racial Politics, 1936–1965*. Chapel Hill: University of North Carolina Press, 2011.

Whayne, Jeannie M. "Black Farmers and the Agricultural Cooperative Extension Service: The Alabama Experience, 1945–1965." *Agricultural History* 72 (Summer 1998): 523–51.

———. *A New Plantation South: Land, Labor, and Federal Favor in Twentieth-Century Arkansas*. Charlottesville: University Press of Virginia, 1996.

Whitaker, Robert. *On the Laps of Gods: The Red Summer of 1919 and the Struggle for Justice That Remade a Nation*. New York: Three Rivers Press, 2008.

Whites, LeeAnn. "Love, Hate, Rape, Lynching: Rebecca Latimer Felton and the Gender Politics of Racial Violence." In *Democracy Betrayed: The Wilmington Race Riot of 1898 and Its Legacy*, edited by David S. Cecelski and Timothy B. Tyson, 143–62. Chapel Hill: University of North Carolina Press, 1998.

Williams, Gloria-Yvonne. "African Americans and the Politics of Race during the New Deal." In *The New Deal and the Great Depression*, edited by Aaron D. Purcell, 131–44. Kent, Ohio: Kent State University Press, 2014.

Winchell, Mark Royden. *Where No Flag Flies: Donald Davidson and the Southern Resistance*. Columbia: University of Missouri Press, 2000.

Wise, Benjamin E. *William Alexander Percy: The Curious Life of a Mississippi Planter and Sexual Freethinker*. Chapel Hill: University of North Carolina Press, 2012.

Wood, Amy Louise. *Lynching and Spectacle: Witnessing Racial Violence in America, 1890–1940*. Chapel Hill: University of North Carolina Press, 2009.

Woodruff, Nan Elizabeth. *American Congo: The African American Freedom Struggle in the Delta*. Cambridge, Mass.: Harvard University Press, 2003.

Woodrum, Robert H. *Everybody Was Black Down There: Race and Industrial Change in the Alabama Coalfields*. Athens: University of Georgia Press, 2007.

Woodward, C. Vann. *The Burden of Southern History*. Baton Rouge: Louisiana State University Press, 1968.

———. *Origins of the New South, 1877–1913*. 1951; Baton Rouge: Louisiana State University Press, 1993.

———. *The Strange Career of Jim Crow*. Commemorative ed. with Afterword by William S. McFeely. New York: Oxford University Press, 2002.

———. *Thinking Back: The Perils of Writing History*. Baton Rouge: Louisiana State University Press, 1986.

———. "Why the Southern Renaissance?" *Virginia Quarterly Review* 51 (Spring 1975): 222–39.

Wright, Gavin. "The New Deal and the Modernization of the South." *Federal History* (January 2010): 58–73.

———. *Old South, New South: Revolutions in the Southern Economy since the Civil War*. New York: Basic Books, 1986.

Zangrando, Robert L. *The NAACP Crusade against Lynching, 1909–1950*. Philadelphia: Temple University Press, 1980.

Zieger, Robert H. *The CIO, 1933–1955*. Chapel Hill: University of North Carolina Press, 1995.

INDEX

Page numbers in italics refer to illustrations and illustration captions.

Abbott, George, 27
Against the Grain (Dunbar), 8
Agar, James, 118
Agee, James, 12
Agrarians, 11, 18, 69, 102, 104, 105–14, 117–27
Agricultural Adjustment Act (1933), 3, 69, 116, 130, 133, 183, 193
Agricultural Adjustment Administration (AAA), 116, 133, 138–39, 143, 172, 173, 257
Alabama Fuel and Iron Company, 207–10, 215–17, 219–20, 271
Alabama Power, 59
Alabama Scottsboro Fair Trial Committee, 95, 96, 97, 99, 197
Alexander, Will, 83–84, 113, 158
Alice Furnace Company, 206
Allen, Isabelle, 73
Allen, James, 73
Allen, John, 134
All God's Dangers (Rosengarten), 200
Alpha Tau Omega, 79
Amberson, William R., 129, 131, 143, 150, 172; Tate vs., 69, 119, 144–45, 250, 251, 250, 251–52; background of, 146; agricultural policy viewed by, 147–48, 158; Delta Cooperative and, 148–49, 152, 153, 157
America Faces the Barricades (Spivak), 100
American Civil Liberties Union, 94, 138
American Dilemma, An (Myrdal), 264
American Federation of Labor (AFL), 7, 274

American Federation of Teachers, 264
Ames, Jessica Daniel, 88–89
Anderson, Sherwood, 101
Association of Southern Women for the Prevention of Lynching, 36, 88
Aswell, Edward, 48
At Heaven's Gate (Warren), 104
Atlanta Constitution, 36, 256
Atomic Energy Commission, 289
Attack on Leviathan, The (Davidson), 119
Aycock, Charles B., 37

Badger, Anthony J., 281
Bagley, William Henry, 26
Bagley, Worth, 26
Bailey, Carl Edward, 175, 258
Bailey, Josiah W., 3, 85–86, 87
Baldwin, C. B. "Beanie," 158
Bankhead-Jones Farm Tenant Act (1937), 117, 143, 158
Barham, L. L., 162
Barnett, Claude, 287
Baseball, 57
Bassett, John Spencer, 46
Bates, Ruby, 76–77, 78, 79, 80, 81, 82, 98, 167
Baxley, William, 97
Bentley, Milo, 201
Berg, Norman, 230, 231
Bethune, Mary McLeod, 264, 274, 285
Biddle, Francis, 286
Birth of a Nation (film), 28
Black, Hugo, 86, 263
Blackmon, Douglas A., 298n37
Blagden, Willie Sue, 161, 162–69, 174, 196, 280
Boas, Franz, 165

Book-of-the-Month Club, 228

Bourke-White, Margaret, 12, 101, 259–61

Bradford, Mary Rose, 160–61

Bradford, Roark, 91–92, 160

Brawley, Benjamin, 249, 250, 253, 255, 256

Brickell, Herschel, 239–40

Bridgers, Annie Cain, 25

Bridgers, Ann Preston, 26–27

Bridgers, Elizabeth "Bab" (wife of Jonathan Daniels), 25, 27, 28–29, 45

Bridgers, Emily, 26–27

Bridgers, Robert Rufus, 25

Bridgers, Robert Rufus, Jr., 25

Bridges, R. R., 76, 82

Brotherhood of Sleeping Car Porters, 281

Broun, Heywood, 23

Brown, John, 22, 177–78

Brown, Kay, 228–29

Brown, Sterling A., 13, 248, 253

Brown v. Board of Education (1954), 6, 123, 124, 268, 279, 281, 291

Bryan, Jack, 169

Bryan, William Jennings, 14, 34

Buell, Raymond Leslie, 112–13

Burke, Donald, 273

Butler, J. R., 129, 130, 137, 143–44, 154, 155, 156, 157

Byrd, Harry F., 273

Byrnes, James F., 86

Caldwell, Erskine, 12, 53–54, 55, 71, 101, 130, 243–44, 256, 259–61

Calhoun, John C., 123

Calhoun Colored School, 197–200

Callahan, William, 82, 94, 96

Camp, Lawrence, 261

Campbell, Thomas Monroe, 192

Candler, Asa Briggs, 222

Carlton, David L., 42, 43, 259

Carmer, Carl, 100

Carmichael, Albert A., 96

Carolina Playmakers, 24

Carpenter, C. T., 139, 172–74

Carr, Elias, 34

Carroll, Elizabeth Delia Dixon, 27–28

Carter, Dan, 82

Carter, Hodding, 307n60

Carter, Lester, 76

Carver, George Washington, 131, 179

Cathcart, Lucy (wife), 32, 33, 47, 48, 52, 267

Cathcart, Noble, 27, 32

Chalmers, Allan Knight, 94–95, 96, 97

Chapel Hill Regionalists. *See* Regionalists

Chappell, James E., 94, 95, 97, 196–97, 199–200

Chappell, Mary, 197, 198–200, 225, 240

Chase, Harry Woodburn, 24

Chattanooga News, 95, 262, 272

Chavez, Cesar, 157

Cherry, Earl, 162

Chicago Defender, 168

Chicago Tribune, 166–67, 168

Chickamauga Dam, 62, 63, 68

Child labor, 40, 257

"Chivalry," 18, 36, 161, 165–66, 167

Chivers, Walter R., 88

Civilian Conservation Corps (CCC), 56, 58

Civil Rights Act (1964), 68

Civil War, 4, 176, 230–32

Clansman, The (Dixon), 28

Clark, Kathleen, 226

Clash of Angels (Daniels), 21–22, 23, 26–27, 29–30, 47

Clement, Hunt, 239–40

Cobb, James C., 31

Cobb, Ned, 200–201

Coca-Cola, 222

Coclanis, Peter A., 42, 43, 259

Cohn, David L., 91–92, 128

Coleman, C. C., 191

Coleman, Ronald, 229

Commager, Henry Steele, 233

Commission on Interracial Cooperation (CIC), 42, 69, 83–84, 88, 113, 158

Commonwealth and Southern (C&S; holding company), 59

Communist International (Comintern), 7

Communist Party, 7, 45, 129, 146, 156, 165, 201, 231, 247, 264, 265; Daniels's mistrust of, 2, 70, 98, 183; influence of, 8, 9, 64, 195; Scottsboro case and, 17, 71, 73, 74, 75, 77, 85, 98, 159, 200, 264, 279–80; racial equality stressed by, 42, 279, 281; Agrarian opposition to, 113–14, 144–45; UCAPAWA leadership linked to, 154–55; in Alabama, 194, 200; left coalition suspicious of, 270, 272–73, 280

Congress of Industrial Organizations (CIO), 154, 203, *214*, 218, 258, 264, 265; militancy of, 7, 143; racial inclusivity of, 7, 18–19, 156; breakup of, 9; poll taxes opposed by, 274

Conkin, Paul, 109

Connor, Theophilus Eugene "Bull," 267, 271, 272

Constitutional Educational League, 218, 219

Cooperative farming, 64, 69, 117–18, 127, 131, 144, 146–47; Delta Cooperative Farm, 63, 129, 148–49, 150–53, 157, 169

Corrupt Practices Act, 219

Cosmos Club, 143

Costigan, Edward P., 85–87

Cotton, 51, 114–16, 142

Couch, W. T., 45, 46, 47, 51, 118, 180, 264

Cowley, Malcolm, 260

Dabney, Virginius, 43, 118, 248, 271, 272, 273, 284

Daily Record (Wilmington), 37–38

Daily Worker, 238

Dams, 58–61, 62, *63*

Daniel, A. Mercer, 249

Daniel, Pete, 189

Daniell, F. Raymond, 172–73

Daniels, Adelaide Ann (daughter; later Elizabeth Daniels), 26, *27*, 30, 32, 33, 45, 289

Daniels, Adelaide Worth Bagley "Addie" (mother), *22*, 26, 28–29, 41, 44, 67, 77, 252, 289

Daniels, Elizabeth (daughter; originally Adelaide Ann Daniels), 26, *27*, 30, 32, 33, 45, 289

Daniels, Elizabeth Bridgers (wife), 25, *27*, 28–29, 45

Daniels, Frank (brother), *22*

Daniels, Jonathan Worth, *22*, *27*; democratic purpose of, 1–2; Communists mistrusted by, 2, 70, 98, 183; liberal evolution of, 4, 15, 17, 19, 47, 65, 87, 88–90, 286, 288; documentary impulse of, 11–13, 16, 100, 193; conflicts facing, 13–14; charisma of, 16; as presidential adviser, 19, 283; literary ambitions of, 20–23, 47–48; father's differences with, 23; drinking habits of, 23, 24–25; precocity of, 23–24; as sportswriter, 25–26; as Washington correspondent, 26, 44; Guggenheim fellowship awarded to, 31–32; Scottsboro case viewed by, 40–41, 71–72, 76–79, 81, 82–83; editorials by, 40–41, 87–88, 90; as regionalist, 43–44, 47, 245; Klansmen viewed by, 45; women judged by, 45, 54–55, 144, 243; segregation accepted by, 46–47, 62, 245, 267–68; itinerary planned by, 48–49; white working class viewed by, 50, 52–53, 67–68; agricultural poverty viewed by, 51, 117, 154, 169; TVA projects visited by, 57, 59–60; blackness feared by, 63–64; lynching decried by, 70, 223; antilynching law opposed by, 72, 87, 90, 93, 283; as modernist, 102; Agrarians distinguished from, 106; Agrarians viewed by, 110–11; as SPC member, 112; planters' power viewed by, 158–59; anti-Semitic tendencies of, 160–61; informants' identities obscured by, 192–93; Charles DeBardeleben viewed by, 220–21; Atlanta viewed by, 223–25, 240, 242; Margaret Mitchell viewed by, 231–32, 236, 237–38, 240–41; plantation myth disdained by, 235–40; critical responses to, 247–55; commercial success of, 256–57; anti–poll tax law opposed by, 283–84

Daniels, Josephus (father), 2, 14, 20, 22, 23, 25, 44, 106, 242, 252, 267, 289; autobiography of, 26; son's novel disapproved of by, 29–30; as ambassador to Mexico, 33, 41, 77; racist policies espoused by, 33–35, 37, 39–40, 44–45; democratic philosophy of, 43; rural poverty witnessed by, 51; as Jeffersonian, 67; death of, 290

Daniels, Josephus, Jr. (brother), 22

Daniels, Lucy Cathcart (wife), 32, 33, 47, 48, 52, 267

Daniels, Mary Cleves (daughter), 267, 289

Daniels, Worth (brother), 21–22, 24, 30

Davidson, Donald, 18, 57, 69, 101–8, 110–14, 117, 119–22, 127, 143, 204; centralized government opposed by, 122–24; declining years of, 124–25, 126; anti-integration fight abandoned by, 126

Davis, Hartwell, 191

Davis, John P., 273

Davis, Lambert, 247–48

Days of Hope (Sullivan), 9

DeBardeleben, Charles Fairchild, Sr., 18–19, 204, 207

DeBardeleben, Charles F., Jr., 207–11, 212, 215–21, 223, 271–72, 278

DeBardeleben, Ellen Pratt, 206, 207

DeBardeleben, Henry Fairchild, 205–8

DeBardeleben, Henry T., 215–16

DeBardeleben, Margaret Prince, 207

DeBardeleben, Prince, 207

DeBardeleben Coal and Iron Company, 206, 215, 216

Deforestation, 58

Defying Dixie (Gilmore), 9

Delta Cooperative Farm, 63, 129, 148–49, 150–53, 157, 169

Delta Kappa Epsilon, 24

Denning, Michael, 7–8

Dibble, Eugene, 201

Dickson, David, 184

Dickson, Edwin, 185–86

Dickson, John G., 18, 184, 185–86

Dickson, John Calhoun, 184–85

Dickson (Dixon), John W. ("J.W."), 184, 185–86, 188–89, 191

Dickson, Joseph T., 184, 185–86

Dickson, Lewis, 185

Dickson, Robert Stiles ("Bob"), 18, 184–93, 195, 196, 197, 204

Dickson, Robert Stiles, Jr. 189

Dickson, Sarah, 184–85

Dickstein, Morris, 260

Diehl, Charles Edward, 145–46

Dies, Martin, 64, 271

Dillingham, Mabel, 198

Disinherited Speak, The, 149

Dixon, Thomas, Jr., 28

Doak, Frances, 253

Doll's House, A (Ibsen), 199

Dowdey, Clifford, 238, 239

Du Bois, W. E. B., 83, 280

Duke Power, 59

Dulaney, John "Boss," 162–63, 167

Dunbar, Anthony P., 8

Durr, Virginia, 265, 266–67, 269, 270, 274, 275

Dust Bowl, 114

Dyer, Leonidas C., 84

Dyess, William, 147

Dyess Colony, 147, 149–50, 180

Eagles, Charles W., 8, 43, 180, 185, 285, 286–87

Earle Enterprise (newspaper), 165–66

East, Alex, 172

East, Clay, 133–34, 137, 172

East, Maxine, 142, 189

Eddy, Sherwood, 148, 151–52
Edmundson, Charles F., 200, 201
Egerton, John, 9, 263–64, 272
Eighteenth Amendment, 84
Eisenstaedt, Alfred, 12, *244*, 259–61
Elaine Massacre (1919), 132, 134
Electrification, 59, 66
Ericson, Eston Everett, 45–46, 47
Ervin, Joseph, 24
Ervin, Sam, 24
Eskew, Glenn T., 211
Evans, Walker, 12

Fair Employment Practices Committee
     (FEPC), 68, 282–83, 284–85, 286,
     290
Fair Labor Standards Act, 257
Farley, James, 3
Farm Security Administration (FSA),
     158
Faulkner, William, 13, 22, 32, 91
Federal Emergency Relief Administra-
     tion, 116
Fellowship of Reconciliation, 132
Fellowship of Southern Churchmen,
     157
Felton, Rebecca Latimer, 36–37
Ferguson, Robert Hunt, 152–53
Fertilizer, 58, 241
Fields, Barbara Jeanne, 278
Fies, Milton, 215
Fifteenth Amendment, 14, 39
Fitzgerald, F. Scott, 24
Fletcher, John Gould, 77–78, 124
Flood control, 58–59
Folse, L. J., 176
Fool's Gold (Marvin), 218
Ford, Henry, 59, 108
Ford, James W., 45–46
Foreign Policy Association, 112–13
Foreman, Clark, 257–58
Fortune, 30, 32
Fosdick, Harry Emerson, 80
Fourteenth Amendment, 14, 82
Frank, Jerome, 138–39, 173, 257, 258

Franklin, Sam, 148, 150–53
Fraser, Mary, 259, 261
Freeman, Dillard, 188, 189
Frontier on the Potomac (Daniels), 290
Fugitive (literary magazine), 104
Fusion movement, 34

Gaines, Lloyd, 281
Gaines v. Canada (1938), 268, 281, 282
Garvey, Marcus, 136
Gaston, Paul M., 31
Gavagan, Joseph A., 90, 93
Gelders, Joseph, 265–66
General Textile Strike (1934), 50
George, Walter F., 86, 238, 261, 262
Georgia Power, 59
Geyer, Lee, 274
GI Bill, 276
Giles, Barbara, 249, 251
Gilley, Orville, 75, 76
Gilmore, Glenda Elizabeth, 9, 74, 98,
     280
God's Little Acre (Caldwell), 54
Goluboff, Risa L., 6–7
Gone with the Wind (Mitchell), 225, 227,
     228–39, 256, 278, 291
Goodman, James, 77
Gordon, Caroline, 145–46, 251
Gordon, Clyde, 189–90
Gordon, Frank, 189–90
Grady, Henry W., 31
Graham, Frank Porter, 258, 263, 264,
     270, 271, 272–73, 283, 290
Grandfather clauses, 39
Grassroots democracy, 61–62, 68, 70
Graves, Bibb, 178, 207
Graves, John Temple, 200, 262–63, 264,
     265
Great Depression, 12, 13, 51, 64, 171
Great Migration, 5, 84, 245
Great Smoky Mountains National Park,
     55, 56
Green, Paul, 24, 111
Grubbs, Donald, 166
Gullette, Mary L., 252

Hall, Grover C., 94, 95–96, 97
Hall, Jacquelyn Dowd, 10, 11, 36, 135, 275
Hall, Rob F., 249–51, 264, 268
Hamilton, Virginia Van Der Deer, 198
Hampton Institute, 197–98
Handcox, John L., 313n36
Hard-Boiled Virgin, The (Newman), 229
Harding, Warren G., 84
Harlem Renaissance, 83
Harper & Brothers (book publisher), 48
Harper's, 238
Harris, Julia Collier, 234
Harris, Julian, 230
Hayes, Helen, 27
Henderson, Donald, 154
Hepburn, Katharine, 32
Herring, Harriet, 112
Hicks, Granville, 108
Hicks, Wilson, 261
Hill, Lister, 273
Hine, Lewis, *63*
Hiss, Alger, 139
Hitler, Adolf, 70
Hobbes, Thomas, 122
Hoover, Wesley, 44
Hopkins, Harry, 116
Horton, James E., 78–79, 80, 81–82, 97
House Un-American Activities Committee, 64, 238, 271
Howard, Alice, 131
Human Geography of the South (Vance), 42
Hydroelectricity, 57, 59, 215

Ibsen, Henrik, 199
Ickes, Harold L., 278–79, 285, 286
I'll Take My Stand, 101, 104–11, 112, 113, 117, 120
Industrial Social Security in the South, 119
Inman, John, 206
International Labor Defense (ILD), 73, 75, 81, 85, 94, 98
International Ladies' Garment Workers' Union (ILGWU), 157

Jackson, Gardner, 143
Jackson, Juanita, *74*
Jackson, Thomas "Stonewall," 31
James, Clifford, 200–201
Jefferson, Thomas, 67, 102, 106
Jennett, Norman E., 34–35, 37
Johnson, Charles S., 43, 264, 267
Johnson, Gerald, 263
Johnson, James Weldon, 85
Johnson, Julius, 190–91
Jonathan Daniels and Race Relations (Eagles), 8
Jones, John, 216
Jones, Thomas Goode, 187, 189

Kamp, Joseph P., 218–19
Katznelson, Ira, 262, 277
Kelley, Robin D. G., 200, 201
Kellum, Laura, *74*
Kelly, Brian, 208
Kester, Howard, 139, 141, 143, 162, 264; religious background of, 131, 157; STFU founding recounted by, 132, 133–34, 135; as socialist, 132, 137; UCAPAWA mistrusted by, 155, 156
King, Martin Luther, Jr., 126, 134–35, 168, 282, 291
Kneebone, John T., 8, 266, 272
Knight, Thomas E., Kr., 82, 94, 96
Korstad, Robert, 14, 40
Ku Klux Klan, 13, 44–45, 67, 70, 108

La Follette, Robert M., Jr., 143, 265
Landis, James M., 283
Landon, Alf, 67, 219, 220
Land reform, 11, 121, 127
Lang, Fritz, 109
Lange, Dorothea, 12, *115, 133, 151*
Lanterns on the Levee (Percy), 91
Lea, Luke, 309n16
League for Industrial Democracy, 94
League of Women Voters, 274
Lee, Robert E., 31, 169, 174, 260
Leibowitz, Samuel, 75–82, 92, 95, 96, 97

Leigh, Effie, 160
Leigh, Gilbert, 160
Le May, Ernest D., 203, 265, *266*
Lend-Lease Act (1941), 277
Let Us Now Praise Famous Men (Agee and Evans), 12
Leuchtenberg, William E., 13, 285
Leviathan (Hobbes), 122
Lewis, John L., 143, 203, 204, 213
Lewis, Nell Battle, 26
Lichtenstein, Alex, 297n16
Life, 259
Lilienthal, David E., 59, 61–62, 65–67, 68, 175, 176, 219, 250, 288–89
Literacy tests, 39
Long, Huey, 177–78
"Long Civil Rights Movement" (Hall), 10
Look Homeward, Angel (Wolfe), 20, 22
Louisville Courier-Journal, 118
Louisville Times, 25
Loveman, Amy, 27, 47
Luce, Henry, 30
Lumpkin, Katharine Du Pre, 238
Lynch, Marvin, 82
Lynching, 13, 35–38, 41, 70, 71, 72, 83–93, 95, 99, 132, 159

MacLean, Nancy, 67
Macmillan (book publisher), 47–48, 228, 231, 238, 243, 256
Maher, Neil M., 56
Mangus, Percy, 162
Manly, Alexander, 37–38
Mann Act, 76
Man of Independence, The (Daniels), 289
Manthorne, Jason, 131, 135
March of Time (newsreel), 161, 166
Marsh, John, 225–26, 228, 237
Martin, Gertrude, 249
Marvin, Fred Richard, 210, 218, 219
Marx, Karl, 106
Mason, Lucy Randolph, 258–59, 264–65, 266, 270
Maverick, Maury, 274

Maxwell, Angie, 311n71
Mays, Benjamin, 264
McDaniels, Robert "Bootjack," 90–91
McGill, Ralph, 253, 256
McKinney, Edward Britt, 135, 136–38, 141, 155–56
McWhorter, Diane, 219
Mechanization, 51, 142, 147
Mellett, Lowell, 258, 259
Mencken, H. L., 21, 24, 104, 113, 120
Mercer, Lucy, 288
Meredith College, 28
Methodist Federation for Social Service, 94
Metropolis (Lang), 109
Meyers, Mary Connor, 138–39, 173
Miller, Balfour, Mrs., 177
Miller, Francis Pickens, 113, 264, 273
Milton, George Fort, 95, 108, 262, 264, 272, 284
Mississippi Power, 59
Mitch, William, 18–19, 203, 213–17, 264, 274
Mitchell, Eugene, 225
Mitchell, Harry Leland "Mitch," 132–36, 137, 142, 146, 258–59, 264; union merger doubted by, 154, 155; Marked Tree incident and, 162, 163, 165, 166–67
Mitchell, Margaret, 10, 19, 225–40, 252, 262
Mitchell, May Belle Stephens, 225
Mitchell, Stephens, 226
Montgomery, Olen, 73, 75, 96, 97
Montgomery Advertiser, 95
Montgomery bus boycott, 291
Moore, Dayton, 128, 144, 154
Morgan, Arthur E., 66
Morgan, J. P., 206
Morrow, E. Frederic, 248–49
Moskop, Walter, 135, 136, 137
Murray (Lowndes County resident), 183–84, 194, 195, 197
Murray, Pauli, 268–69
Murray, Philip, 274

Mussolini, Benito, 70
Myrdal, Gunnar, 264, 297n16

Nash, Ogden, 25
Nash, Philleo, 287
Nashville Agrarians. *See* Agrarians
Nashville Tennessean, 110
Nation, 46, 77, 145, 238, 251, 283
National Association for the Advance-
    ment of Colored People (NAACP),
    6–7, 15, 17, 41, 83, 180, 182, 196, 281;
    Communists vs., 73; Scottsboro case
    and, 73–74, 75, 94, 97; antilynching
    campaign by, 84–85, 132, 159; STFU
    befriended by, 138; wage discrim-
    ination opposed by, 215; poll taxes
    opposed by, 274; founding of, 279;
    postwar civil rights litigation by, 291
National Committee for the Defense of
    Political Prisoners, 265
National Committee to Abolish the
    Poll Tax, 274
National Emergency Council (NEC),
    256–58, 261, 262, 266
National Farmers Union, 274
National Farm Labor Union, 157
National Industrial Recovery Act
    (NIRA; 1933), 3, 210, 213, 214
National Labor Relations Board, 218
National Negro Congress, 156, 273, 274,
    279, 281
National Recovery Administration
    (NRA), 214–17
National Urban League, 215, 279
National Youth Administration, 157,
    264
Neal, Claude, 85, 89–90
Negro Cooperative Extension System,
    180, 195
Neuse, Steven M., 62
New Deal, 2, 7–10, 12, 20, 41, 85, 119,
    130, 131, 175, 245, 253, 256, 258, 269,
    276, 291; political changes wrought
    by, 3, 5, 6, 15, 17, 123, 171, 220, 271,
    275; southern opposition to, 3, 6, 67,
    102, 122, 204, 215, 219, 238, 257, 277;
    racial limitations of, 5, 40, 219, 275,
    281; agricultural policies of, 11, 69,
    114, 136, 146–47, 157; TVA established
    by, 17, 51, 57–63, 66, 99, 123, 144, 215,
    237, 247; states' rights vs., 41, 83, 85;
    CCC established by, 56; "grassroots
    democracy" stressed by, 61, 70; south-
    ern politicians threatened by, 87;
    communist support for, 98; antipov-
    erty programs of, 116; public support
    for, 117, 121–22, 271, 273; unions em-
    powered by, 210–11; efforts to expand,
    242, 246, 257; southern disfranchise-
    ment and, 252
New Federalism, 123
Newman, Frances, 229, 231
New Masses, 249
New Republic, 163, 167, 238
New Right, 10, 126
News and Observer (Raleigh). See *Raleigh
    News and Observer*
New York Times, 168, 256, 257
Nixon, Herman Clarence, 105, 106,
    108, 145, 178, 248, 264; cooperatives
    backed by, 117, 127; Daniels refuted
    by, 268
Nolden, Eliza, 162, 163, 167, 168–69
Nolden, James, 168
Nolden, William, 168
Norcross, Hiram, 133, 171–73
Norrell, Robert J., 207
Norris, Clarence, 73, 75, 82, 96, 97, 98
Norris, George, 59
Norris Dam, 59–61, *63*
Norris v. Alabama (1935), 82, 85, 94, 98
Nullification, 123
Nunnally, Alvin, 134, 135

O'Brien, Michael, 111
Odum, Howard W., *44*, 88, 117, 118, 174,
    273; as Regionalist, 42, 58; *Southern
    Regions of the United States*, 51, 111–12,
    241, 246, 263
Office of War Information (OWI), 287

Our Government and Its Enemies (Marvin), 218

Owsley, Frank, 113–14, 117, 118, 120–24, 126, 158, 251

Panic of 1873, 205

Petterson, Frederick D., 264, 287

Patterson, Haywood, 73, 74–75, 76, 78, 81–82, 94, 95, 96, 97

Peacher, Paul, 142, 189

Pepper, Claude, 273, 274

Percy, LeRoy, 260

Percy, Walker (lawyer), 206, 207

Percy, Walker (novelist), 91

Percy, William Alexander, 10, 91, 176, 211

Perkins, Frances, 216

Philadelphia Story, The (Barry), 32

Platt, David, 238

Plessy v. Ferguson (1896), 279

Poe, Joe, 71, 81, 221

Pollock, Syd, 57

Poll taxes, 14, 39, 262, 265, 273–75, 279, 283–84, 290

Popular Front, 9, 71, 155–56; composition of, 7, 94; leftward push by, 8, 43–44, 98, 129, 280; traditional liberals vs., 43, 64, 154, 165, 166

Populists, 33–34, 37, 87, 131

Porter, Garland Burns, 222, 223

Poston, Ted, 287, 288

Powell, Ozie, 73, 75, 94, 96, 97

Powell v. Alabama (1932), 74, 98

Pratt, Daniel, 205

Pratt, Ellen, 206, 207

Pratt, Esther, 205

Pratt, Mary, 206

Pratt Coal and Coke, 206

Preface to Peasantry (Raper), 51

President's Committee on Farm Tenancy, 157–58, 196

Price, Victoria, 76, 78, 79, 80, 81, 82, 97–98, 167

Prince, Margaret, 207

Progressive Era, 14, 33, 57

Progressive Farmers and Household Union of America, 134

Prohibition, 23, 45, 84

Public Works Administration, 257

Putnam, James, 47

Puzzled America (Anderson), 101

Pyron, Darden Asbury, 233, 326n45

Racial capitalism, 14, 17, 18, 20, 39, 40, 204, 207, 271, 282

Raleigh News and Observer, 21, 25–26, 33, 44, 283, 289–91; white supremacy backed by, 34, 37, 39, 45–46; Scottsboro case and, 40–41, 72, 81; Daniels's editorials in, 40–41, 87–88, 90

Randolph, A. Philip. 274, 281–82

Rankin, John E., 276

Ransom, John Crowe, 104–5, 108–9, 113, 121–22, 123, 124

Raper, Arthur F., 19, 41, 51, 87–90, 112, 264, 265

Reams, Joe, 68

Reconstruction, 33, 39, 230–32

"Redeemers," 33

Red Mountain Iron and Coal Company, 205

Red scare, 218, 271

Reese, J. M., 162, 163, 167, 168, 169

Reese, Warren S., Jr., 186–89

Regionalists, 107, 119, 122, 125, 259; economic emphasis of, 17, 42, 119; social science approach of, 42–43, 44, 58, 119, 174; influence of, 112; modernity accepted by, 117; racial issues sidestepped by, 245, 270

Republic Steel, 211

Resettlement Administration (RA), 143, 147, 150, 157–58

Revolt among the Sharecroppers (Kester), 131, 132, 141

Richards, Ernest, 162

Richardson, L. C., 215

Richmond Times-Dispatch, 43, 118, 247

Roberson, Willie, 73, 75, 96, 97

Roberts, Richard Samuel, 254–55

Roberts, Wilhelmina, 254–55, 269

Robinson, Joseph, 139

Rockefeller Foundation, 137–38, 198

Rodgers, Ward, 137–38, 145

Rolinson, Mary G., 137

Roosevelt, Eleanor, 4, 263, 266, 267, 274, 281, 283, 285, 290

Roosevelt, Franklin Delano, 4, 19, 54, 85; Daniels's support for, 2, 47; southern backwardness denounced by, 2, 14, 39, 220; southern generational change awaited by, 2, 66, 141, 175, 275; southern opposition to, 2–3, 6, 66, 123–24, 177, 204, 220, 238; court-packing plan of, 3, 257; southern conservatives circumvented by, 6, 257; election of, 33; second inaugural address of, 51; social planning favored by, 57; TVA unveiled by, 58–59; fascism denounced by, 64–65; public support for, 87, 253; pragmatism of, 93, 101; agricultural policies of, 116, 139, 141, 143, 157, 166, 196; reelection of, 118, 220, 237; purge of southern conservatives attempted by, 238, 261–62, 277; New Deal expansion sought by, 242, 257, 273; southern economy viewed by, 256–58; "Black Cabinet" of, 264, 281; voting rights backed by, 266, 273; defense policies of, 275, 277; antidiscrimination policies of, 281–88; Truman contrasted with, 289

Rorty, James, 100, 145–46, 251–52

Rorty, Richard, 145

Rosengarten, Theodore, 200

Rossinow, Doug, 280

Rothstein, Arthur, *209, 214*

Royster, Hubert, 27

Royster, Virginia, 27

Rural Electrification Administration, 283

Russell, Daniel, 34

Rustin, Bayard, 313n14

Sampson Democrat, 34

Sanderson, John A., 191

Sanderson, Lamar, 191

Sartoris (Faulkner), 22

Saturday Review of Literature, 27, 32, 47, 65, 227, 238

Schulman, Bruce J., 42–43, 275–76

Scopes trial, 104

Scott, W. Kerr, 290

Scottsboro Boys, 71–99, 106, 124, 167, 197, 271; Communist Party and, 17, 71, 73, 74, 75, 77, 85, 98, 159, 200, 264, 279–80; Daniels's view of, 40–41, 71–72, 76–79, 81, 82–83; NAACP and, 73–74, 75, 94, 97; *Raleigh News and Observer* and, 40–41, 72, 81

Scottsboro Defense Committee (SDC), 94, 96, 97, 197

"Search for Southern Identity, The" (Woodward), 125, 126

Second Reconstruction, 5, 15, 17, 19, 282

Selznick, David O., 228–29

Servicemen's Readjustment Act (1944), 276

Shahn, Ben, *170*

Share Cropper's Union (SCU), 200–201

Shaw, "Ike," 134

Shepard, James E., 254

Shepherd, Charles, 217

Sherman, William Tecumseh, 60

Simmons, Furnifold McLendel, 37

Slavery, 4, 114, 185

Smethurst, Frank, 46

Smith, Aaron "Champ," 189–91

Smith, C. H., 134

Smith, Ellison D. "Cotton Ed," 86, 139, 261, 262

Smith, Evelyn, 141–42, 144, 149, 157, 162, 166, 189

Smith, Lillian, 238

Smith, Willis, 290

Smith v. Allwright (1944), 281

Social Forces (journal), 111

Socialist Party of America, 7, 94, 95, 129, 132, 137, 146, 157
Social Security Act (1935), 3, 5, 122, 210
Soil Conservation Service, 58
Soil erosion, 58, 258
Sokol, Jason, 279
So Red the Rose (Young), 54
Sosna, Morton, 273–74
Sound and the Fury, The (Faulkner), 22
Southern Commission on the Study of Lynching, 88, 95
Southern Conference for Human Welfare (SCHW), 263, 264–65, 267–75, 279, 283
Southerner Discovers New England, A (Daniels), 267, 283
Southern Liberal Journalists and the Issue of Race (Kneebone), 8
Southern Newspaper Publishers Association, 95, 194
Southern Policy Committee (SPC), 68, 119, 158, 178, 257–58, 264; founding of, 69, 112, 113, 273; Tate vs. Amberson at meeting of, 69, 144–45, 250; Agrarians and Regionalists brought together in, 112; farm bill backed by, 117, 143
Southern Railway, 71
Southern Regions of the United States (Odum), 51, 111–12, 241, 246, 263
Southern Renaissance, 21, 22, 31, 235
Southern Tenant Farmers Union (STFU), 48, 127, 128–38, 142–45, 158–59, 189, 193, 264, 265, 280; socialist leadership of, 10, 18, 69, 129, 132, 136–37, 142, 148; strikes by, 129, 142, 161–62; racial politics within, 130–31, 135, 141, 152; founding of, 132, 133–34, 135, 171, 172; publicity by, 143, 146; UCAPAWA affiliation with, 154–56; decline of, 157; Blagden's split with, 164, 165, 166; sharecropper evictions challenged by, 172–73
Soviet Union, 8, 61, 280, 281, 290

Speak Now Against the Day (Egerton), 9
Spivak, John L., 100
Stars Fell on Alabama (Carmer), 100
States' rights, 65, 85, 86, 87
Steinbeck, John, 12, 101
Stephens, May Belle, 225
Stevens, George, 47
Stott, William, 101
Strauss, Harold, 20, 21, 47, 54
Sugrue, Thomas, 6
Sullivan, Patricia, 9, 158, 262, 274
Sumners, Hatton W., 274, 328n60

Taft, Philip, 323–24n56, 324n72
Taggart, Ernest W., 74
Talmadge, Eugene, 238, 262, 278
Tar Heels (Daniels), 283
Tariffs, 121, 122, 247
Tate, Allen, 13, 104–10, 118, 121–24, 146, 272; Amberson vs., 69, 119, 144–45, 250, 251, 250, 251–52; Daniels confronted by, 251
Tate, Merze, 254
Taylor, Alva, 131
Taylor, Myron, 218, 265
Tennessee Coal, Iron and Railroad Company (TCI), 203, 206, 207, 211, 265
Tennessee Electric Power Company, 59
Tennessee Federation for Constitutional Government, 124, 126
Tennessee Valley Authority (TVA), 57, 65, 70, 99, 144, 215, 237, 245, 246, 247, 250, 288–89; racial inequities of, 17, 60–63, 123, 275, 276; transformations wrought by, 51–52, 58–59; cheap power provided by, 59–60, 66, 215; opposition to, 60, 99, 237; Daniels as liaison to, 283
Textile industry, 40, 50–52
Thirteenth Amendment, 18
Thomas, Norman, 94, 95, 129–30, 133, 139, 141, 143, 166
Thomas, Virgil, 217

Thorn, Charlotte, 198
Time between the Wars, The (Daniels), 288
Tindall, George Brown, 12
Tobacco, 40, 114–16
Tobacco Road (Caldwell), 53–54, 130, 236–37, 256, 291
Townes, Roosevelt, 90–91
Tragedy of Lynching, The (Raper), 41, 87, 88, 264
Truman, Harry, 93, 277, 285, 289, 289, 290
Tugwell, Rexford, 57, 143, 158
Turner, Jake, 181
Turner, Katie, 191
Turner, Mariah, 181
Turner, Victor, Jr., 181–82
Turner, Victor Caesar, Sr., 180–83, 191–96, 197, 200, 201, 243, 287–88
Tuskegee Institute, 10, 55, 178, 179, 181, 195–96
Twenty-Fourth Amendment, 275

United Cannery, Agricultural, Packing, and Allied Workers of America (UCAPAWA), 154–56
United Mine Workers of America (UMW), 203, 208, 209, 213–18, 264
United Nations Subcommission for the Prevention of Discrimination and the Protection of Minorities, 290, 291
U.S. Department of Agriculture, 136, 138, 157–58, 173, 174, 180, 283, 288
U.S. Steel, 203, 206, 218
Universal Negro Improvement Association, 136–37
University of Georgia, 36
University of North Carolina, 24, 79, 111, 245, 258, 268–69
University of North Carolina Press, 45, 51, 118, 264
Upshaw, Berien, 225

Vachon, John, *140*
Valentino, Rudolph, 230
Vance, Rupert B., 42, 112, 117, 118, 174

Vanderbilt University, 103, 104, 105, 118, 121, 124, 126, 131
Villard, Oswald Garrison, 46
Vote CIO and Get a Soviet America (Kamp), 218–19
Voting rights, 14, 39, 262, 265, 266, 273–75, 279, 283–84, 290
Voting Rights Act (1965), 275

Waddell, Alfred Moore, 38
Wade, John Donald, 123–24
Wagner, Robert F., 85–87
Wallace, George, 97
Wallace, Henry A., 9, 136, 138, 139, 173
Waller, James, 117
Wann, M. L., 73
Ward, Jason Morgan, 11, 219
Warren, Robert Penn, 13, 22, 32, 104, 105, 107, 121, 124
Washington, Booker T., 46, 107, 178, 179, 196, 197–98
Washington, Ernest Davidson, 179
Wasted Land, The (Johnson), 263
Watauga Club, 33
Weaver, Robert, 285
Webb, N. W., 135
Weems, Charlie, 73, 75, 96, 97
Weems, Frank, 162, 163, 167, 169
Wells, George, 149
Wells, Ida B., 35, 38
Western Federation of Miners, 218
Whayne, Jeannie M., 171
Where Life Is Better (Rorty), 100
White, George Henry, 39
White, Hugh L., 176
White, Walter, 85, 180, 254, 255, 285
Who Owns America?, 118, 123
Williams, Burt, 134
Williams, Claude, 155, 162–64, 196
Williams, Eugene, 73, 74, 75, 96, 97
Willkie, Wendell, 219, 220
Wilmington Messenger, 37, 38
Wilson, Woodrow, 2
Wilson Dam, 59
Winchell, Mark, 124

Wolcott, Marion Post, *140*
Wolfe, Thomas, 13, 20, 22, 24, 32
Woman's Christian Temperance Union, 36
Women's Trade Union League, 264
Woodruff, Nan Elizabeth, 156
Woodward, C. Vann, 22, 62, 118–19, 125–26, 206, 264
Woofter, T. J., Jr., 84, 88
Workers Defense League, 157
Wright, Andy, 73, 74, 75, 96, 97
Wright, Gavin, 276

Wright, Roy, 73, 74, 75, 96, 97
Wright, Wade, 77

You Have Seen Their Faces (Caldwell and Bourke-White), 12, 101, 260, 261
Young, Stark, 54
Young Men's Christian Association (YMCA), 69, 131, 274
Young Women's Christian Association (YWCA), 69